T H E

CHINA VENTURE

America's Corporate Encounter with the People's Republic of China

THE
CHINA VENTURE

America's Corporate Encounter
with the People's Republic of China

Christopher Engholm

Scott, Foresman and Company
Glenview, Illinois   **London**

Photographs by Christopher Engholm.

The author is grateful to the publishers and authors who have generously given permission to redraw and adapt illustrations and data from copyrighted works on the following pages:

p. 7, 11, 13, 15, 20, 23, 203, 208, 234, 235, 303, 361   Redrawn and adapted by permission of China Statistical Information & Consultancy Service Centre.

p. 71, 89, 273   Redrawn and adapted by permission of South China Morning Post Publishers Limited, Hong Kong.

p. 26 and 277   Data in table (p. 26) and figure (p. 277) courtesy of *Intertrade* magazine.

p. 132   Reprinted by permission of the author.

p. 253   Redrawn by permission of the authors.

p. 259   Reprinted from "Cultural Assumptions and Productivity: The United States and China," by Edwin C. Nevis in *Sloan Management Review*, Spring 1983, by permission of the publisher. Copyright © 1989 by the Sloan Management Review Association. All rights reserved.

p. 383-385   Reprinted by permission of the U.S.-China Business Council.

p. 393-395   Reprinted by permission of the author.

p. 222-223   Redrawn by permission of the author.

ISBN 0-673-18656-3

Jacket cover: Like a looking glass into China's future, the imposing facade of the Great Wall Hotel, the first Sino-foreign joint venture, rises above a traditional Chinese moondoor in Beijing.

Library of Congress Cataloging-in-Publication Data

Engholm, Christopher.
   The China venture : America's corporate encounter with the
People's Republic of China / Christopher Engholm.
      p.   cm.
   Bibliography: p.
   Includes index.
   ISBN 0-673-18656-3
   1. United States—Foreign economic relations—China.   2. China-
Foreign economic relations—United States.   I. Title.
HF1456.5.C6E53   1989   88-11377
658.8′48—dc 19   CIP
                                                                               Rev.

1 2 3 4 5 6 RRC 94 93 92 91 90 89

*For
Grand Jim*

Acknowledgments

The author would like to thank the numerous people who have contributed their time and knowledge to make this book a reality. Writing a book such as this, as I reluctantly discovered, is a monumental task, and it would not have been possible without much patience and perseverance on the part of all the persons who responded to questions, assisted in the research, and remained at my side during the hard times.

I am particularly indebted to Dr. Denis Fred Simon of Tufts University, who worked in close collaboration with me on this project and whose influence on my thinking about China is felt on the book's every page. Many of his superb papers were extremely helpful and I recommend them highly to the business person bound for China. Of course, any errors or omissions in the text remain my own.

The scope of this book is wide; indeed, I could hardly claim distinguished expertise on all of the areas that it covers. I am, therefore, deeply grateful to the numerous authors in many academic disciplines who have granted their permission to cite themes contained in their recently published, and unpublished papers. They include, in random order: Charles S. Mayer, Hui Fang Lim, L. Huan-ming Ling, Barbara Krug, Wang Zheng-xian, John A. Reeder, Alex J. Easson, Chen Zhe, Benny Rigaux-Bricmont, Audrey Heung-heung Chan, Mun Kin-chok, Eugen Jehle, Peter J. Buckley, Duo Qin, Jing Shen, John Frankenstein, Sally Stewart, Yeung Yun Choi, Edward E. Williams, Thomas A. Kindel, Barry Kellman, Otto Schnepp, Arrind Bhambri, Mary Ann Von Glinow, John S. Henley, Nyaw Mee-kau, Martin Lockett, Nigel Campbell, Richard H. Holten, John Child, Ray G. Hunt, Jing Lun Han, and William A. Fischer.

My gratitude also extends to: Fred Laughter of Hannon & Associates for assisting in the revision of the manuscript; Jeff Lachina for his tireless efforts editing the final manuscript; Richard Carter for networking the people that got the project under way; James Wen for his help and insight into China's business culture; Chuck Wein for advice on the broad themes of the book; Tom and Nancy Woolsey, and Barney and Yvonne Engholm for their support; Pete Silbering for his guidance on getting the book completed; Jack Lewis and Dean Cummins of IBEAR at the University of Southern California for offering space at their China Program; William A. Fischer for reviewing the book at an early stage; Joshua Muldavin of JCI, Inc. for arranging access to restricted areas of China; Al Kern and Dave Stryder for supplying word processing equipment; economist Leslie Lipper for her assistance as a friend and interpreter in China; Jeanie McClaren for word processing at the Sloan School of Management at M.I.T; author David Dobrin for his informed advice and enthusiastic support; Helen Bloomfield of Word Perfect Secretarial Service for word processing from dictation tapes; Elizabeth Wehmeyer for disseminating and processing corporate questionnaires and lending moral support; William Gladstone and Amy Davis for their patience; the *California Management Review*; and all of the American company executives, diplomats, lawyers, and managers interviewed in the United States, Hong Kong, and China who shall remain anonymous.

I especially want to thank my friends in the People's Republic, who in their quest to transform their country into a more economically prosperous and technologically advanced nation have instilled in me deep admiration and respect for the Chinese people as a whole.

Contents

Introduction

Napoleon once remarked, "When China awakes, the world will shake." The process has already begun. Corporate executives, scholars, and policymakers from around the world have started to take note of China's awakening not under the revolutionary leadership of Chairman Mao, as had always been thought, but rather under the tutelage of Deng Xiaoping, who accepted the monumental task of modernizing the People's Republic of China and bringing the Chinese nation into the twenty-first century on its own terms.

China's efforts to become a more active participant in both regional and global economic affairs have been heralded as major events of the latter twentieth century. The more visible role sought by the Chinese in international business affairs is particularly noteworthy in view of its almost continuous isolation from the mainstream of the global economy during the last three decades.

China's immense population, its vast reserves of untapped natural resources, and its rapidly expanding industrial and technological bases are coming together to form a growing presence in the world economy. The People's Republic has the potential to be a key player in shaping the dynamics of both regional and global competition well into the twenty-first century.

CHINA'S OPEN DOOR: THE CHALLENGE TO AMERICAN BUSINESS

China's open door to trade, foreign investment, and imported technology constitutes the primary vehicle through which the nation will make its presence felt in the world economy. The leaders of the People's Republic believe that through increased exposure to modern management methods, technical expertise, and the dynamics of foreign markets, Chinese enterprises will become more productive and efficient. If China's modernization program is indeed successful, its enterprises should be able to offer a more competitive assortment of products in key overseas markets such as the United States, Western Europe, and Japan, in addition to better serving the growing domestic market within China. While there are obvious political and military ramifications of China's modernization and its renewed relationship with the outside world, there is also little doubt that the emergence of the People's Republic is critically important for international business.

The scope of China's emergence is potentially as vast as its geographic dimensions. China has steadily become an important exporter of such products as textiles, natural resources, and consumer goods, while importing a wide range of technologies and specialized equipment. As a result of their expanding unilateral trade, the Chinese are faced with a serious concern over foreign exchange spending, and likewise are uneasy about building up a large foreign debt. Therefore, like the Koreans and Japanese before them, they are committed to utilizing exports to generate revenue. As Chinese leaders reiterate: the more they sell, the more they can buy from the West. This seemingly simple axiom is in reality the underlying dynamic that promises to propel the Chinese economy into the future. Although the obstacles to the success of this strategy are obvious—increased international protectionism, for example—China remains undaunted.

There are major changes under way in China that have already altered in a new and fundamental way previous methods of economic, financial, and technology management problem solving. Under Deng Xiaoping and his successor, Zhao Ziyang, a massive program of administrative and economic reform has been launched. One of the defining characteristics of this movement is its attempt to provide more fertile ground for foreign investors and technology suppliers to set up shop and become part of China's modernization effort. China's leaders have even gone so far as to allow foreigners to hold managerial positions in domestic enterprises as a means of inculcating Chinese workers and managers with new values. An entire legal infrastructure has been created just to facilitate the arrival and start-up of foreign corporations. All of this indicates that the Chinese are indeed serious about joining the world economy and have taken radical steps to ensure that their country will be an attractive site for foreign investment, production, sourcing, and cooperative R&D.

China has the world's largest untapped reservoir of inexpensive labor. The importance of China's labor force is not just in its sheer size, but in its quality, which is improving steadily as a result of the training and educational reforms being introduced throughout the country. As wage rates rise significantly in places such as South Korea, Singapore, and Taiwan, the People's Republic remains one of the few countries where labor-intensive production activities can be carried out on a competitive basis. This is not to suggest that all labor in China is cheap. Early in the period of the open-door policy, Chinese political concerns about fairness and equity prompted the government to insist on wage-rate parity with the West, which prevented many ventures from materializing because China's demands were unrealistic and impractical. However, major aspects of this policy have been reconsidered and reversed, especially as it applies to the special economic zones along China's southern coast. These changes have created new opportunities for workers to increase their material benefits by working harder and being more productive, the potential impact of which cannot be ignored.

Over the next decade, China will influence the world economy as an importer of capital goods and technology, as an exporter of light industrial and consumer products, as an export-oriented manufacturing center, and as a source of raw materials such as energy and natural resources. Based on these predictions it is clear that China should not be viewed as merely a source of cheap unskilled labor waiting to be exploited by multinational firms. In addition, the high cost of rapid technological change has forced U.S. firms to search for higher value-added offshore manufacturing, and even to return to onshore manufacturing in the United States. This competition for manufacturing sites, combined with market-related changes within China regarding the cost of labor, suggests that unless better trained and managed China's huge work force may eventually become more of a liability than an asset. The same thing, however, cannot be said about China's contingent of scientific and engineering specialists, which may become an important target for foreign firms in much the same way that these firms view technical workers in Taiwan, Singapore, and South Korea.

Over the past ten years, major changes have occurred in China as a result of Deng Xiaoping's economic reforms and open-door policy. China's economy has sustained high industrial growth rates, emerging "pockets of excellence," especially in electronics and textiles, and appreciable progress in quality control and production standards. This changing economic landscape has signaled many U.S. companies that China has the potential to leap suddenly onto the world export stage, much as Japan did in the late 1960s and Singapore and Taiwan in the 1970s. After losing their competitive edge to these emerging nations throughout the 1980s, many American manufacturers remain apprehensive about assisting China's emergence. Despite their apprehensions, they realize that failing to play a role in China's overall economic modernization could spell trouble in the future if current difficulties such as bureaucratic red tape and low productivity disappear. Only by working with China today can American firms hope to position themselves strategically to reap competitive benefits in the future.

The opening of the China market is also part of a grander phenomenon in Asia that I call "the Pacific Halcyon." Unfortunately, Americans, especially workers and managers in smokestack industries, textiles, and computer electronics, view the rise of the Asian economies as more of a threat to the American Dream and the U.S. economy than a triumph for market-oriented democracy in the region. They point to the fact that U.S. trade with Asia accounts for roughly half of America's current trade deficit ($136 billion in 1988). America's trade with China, however, has remained in much closer balance. China, a new player in the Pacific region, may turn out to be a more equitable trading partner for the U.S. than other Asian nations.

The overvalued dollar during the first half of the 1980s was certainly a factor in the noncompetitiveness of U.S. products in China and Asia in general. However, one cannot ignore the fact that the U.S. market has been open to Asian nations on a virtually nondiscriminatory basis while the openness of Asian nations to American marketers ranges from a state of opening gradually to one that is completely closed. Indeed, many U.S. firms have been thwarted in East Asian markets—China included—by what John LaFalce, chairman of the Committee on Small Business, has termed "Byzantine regulations and bewildering bureaucracies."[1] Given the difficulties experienced by U.S. businesses in East Asia before China's open-door policy, the China market now represents a promising opportunity for many companies to regain market share vis-à-vis their Asian competitors.

In many respects, the high hopes are warranted. China views the United States as a major source of technology, equipment, and capital to support its overall modernization effort. For better or worse, the Chinese like dealing with Americans. They also crave American technology, though some say this penchant is a reflection of their uneasiness about dealing with Japan and their concerns about the quality of Western European technology. The Chinese have not stopped purchasing products and goods from these latter two sources, however, and they have sought out products from the Soviet Union and Eastern Europe as well. Yet they prefer to buy American. In some respects, this is an amusing fact in a region where the United States has lost some of its competitive advantage. Nonetheless, it opens up a number of exceptional possibilities for the U.S. business community. Clearly, it is in the best interest of American business to become involved in the China market.

If there were one primary factor responsible for the writing of this book, it is the author's perception that somehow American businesses have not been able to take advantage of this seemingly spectacular opportunity. It is clear from the trade and technology transfer statistics, and from the number of success stories of foreign firms entering the China market, that U.S. firms have not been at the forefront of Chinese trade. Of course, there have been exceptions. But acknowledging these exceptional cases does not undo the reality that American industry has not been as successful in China as might have been expected.

Admittedly, there have been many Chinese problems that have prevented effective business relationships from being cemented. The inefficiency of the Chinese bureaucracy, the imprecise nature of investment regulations, and the cost of doing business in China have all been inhibitors. Though many would place all responsibility for the delay in the expansion of the China market on Chinese shoulders, it is the foreign business community, particularly in the United States, that must take responsibility for having failed to prepare adequately before addressing the China market. Many firms may take exception to this assertion. Nonetheless, this book will attempt to show that much more can be accomplished with the right information, the right strategy, and the right perspective.

China has already emerged as the next proving ground for competition between the United States and Japan, and to some observers the Japanese have already gained an edge on the Americans. It is not uncommon to hear in discussions on this subject that the Japanese are everywhere in the People's Republic. Representatives of Japanese trading companies and manufacturing firms can be found all over China, in small cities and outlying areas, while the Americans prefer to stay in the big cities, where they are more likely to find Western comforts. As a result, Japanese industry has been able to penetrate deep into the fabric of the Chinese economy. One of the reasons for the extent of its presence in China is that Japan, unlike the United States, sees China's modernization as an integral part of its own economic development. Japanese firms have shown themselves to be shrewd and capable of effectively diagnosing a foreign market and positioning themselves to respond to the requirements of that market in any way possible.

By contrast, the experience of American firms in China has been marked by the generic weaknesses of U.S. companies in conducting business overseas and by the structural limitations of the American system, particularly the role of the government in promoting American commercial interests abroad. Even some U.S. commercial officers admit that U.S. government trade promotion has been underfunded and overpoliticized. As one corporate source remarked during an interview, U.S. commercial officers "just don't get us the right information, at the right time, in the right way." Often, U.S. export controls on the sale of technology to China have been disabling to U.S. business. Moreover, any information procured by government analysts is treated as part of the public domain, and, thus, is helpful to both domestic firms as well as their competitors abroad. The export funding sponsored by the U.S. government to promote American exports in developing countries has still not hit its target. This is largely the result of the budget cuts that took place under the Reagan Administration and because the vast majority of U.S. companies are simply not interested in selling overseas. Until 1986, corporate America had been a reluctant exporter; only 250 of the nation's corporations accounted for nearly 80 percent of the dollar volume of American exports. The Department of Commerce has estimated that 20,000 to 30,000 small U.S. firms possess unrealized export potential. Closed markets and insufficient government assistance are culpable in part, but so is corporate America's lack of initiative and its inability to gain market share beyond the borders of the U.S. domestic market.

Many U.S. firms do not have the time, energy, or resources—human or financial—to invest in overseas marketing, obtain import licenses and approvals, or adapt their products to the preferences and tastes of overseas customers. (Of course, they do have the resources to do all these things for their home market.) Some companies fear that developing countries like China will copy their products if they export them; yet, they fail to see how easy it is for Chinese, Japanese, and Koreans to purchase their products in the United States and ship them home to be reverse engineered, as American companies often do. A great many U.S. firms simply have little interest in a global presence since their home market sales meet the limits of their capacity. This seems plausible when one considers that the entire world market is only four times the size of the U.S. domestic market. However, by failing to meet their competition in overseas markets, U.S. firms often get broadsided in their own backyard when foreign competitors, bolstered by an overseas market share, enter the U.S. market. Finally, there is no doubt that many corporate executives, many of whom fought the Chinese, Japanese, and Koreans in World War II and the Korean War, are quite simply too narrow-minded, even ethnocentric, to make a concerted effort to conduct business with Asian nations. One consultant that the author spoke to remarked, "many American executives perceive the Asia/Pacific region more like an island outpost in an episode of *Victory at Sea* than the most important burgeoning market in their lifetimes." This may not be fair, but the problem of attitude toward doing business in China is prevalent. Unfortunately, many U.S. executives still think of the People's Republic as an "evil Communist empire."

As American firms enter the global frontier of business, it is vital that they face their shortcomings in international marketing, manufacturing, and acquiring new technology, and issue a response that will regain their superior position in the global business community. Current U.S. policies such as lowering the value of the dollar and the Export Now campaign, which is a government-funded program aimed at enhancing U.S. exports through market information gathering, trade exhibitions, and export funding, may place corporations in a more advantageous position in the People's Republic, as well as in East Asia. Certainly the lowered dollar has given new impetus to American exporters. But without a concerted effort to make the required long-term investment in places such as China—through specialized products, marketing analysis, and distribution networks--the gains in market share that result from the weaker dollar will evaporate.

China represents one of the last commercial frontiers for U.S. industry. Failing to make sufficient inroads into this market could mean substantial, long-term damage to American competitiveness abroad. This prediction may seem rather alarmist. After all, China has a long way to go before it becomes an economic superpower. One thing is certain, though, China will modernize with or without U.S. participation. Some U.S. firms have chosen to disregard the potential of the China market, believing they can somehow thwart China's active partic-

ipation in world trade by only paying lip service to China's modernization imperative. Nothing could be further from reality. By participating
in the modernization of China, we are actually recognizing that we live
in a highly competitive *global* economy dominated by *global* industries. The United States is just one player, albeit a key one, in this global
economy. As a key player, the United States has an opportunity to shape
the broad parameters of China's modernization by becoming party to
one of the largest socioeconomic experiments in the history of man-
kind. Whether this country will rise to the challenge is difficult to predict. The hope is that this book will contribute to the process by which
corporate strategy for the China market is conceived in boardrooms
throughout the United States. This book offers prescriptions for managing a business venture in an environment that changes rapidly—and
dynamically—but where rigid traditions and socialist organization ensure that many things remain the same.

The book's eight chapters address the following fundamental
questions:

Chapter 1: What are the opportunities of the China market, and how
can U.S. firms seize these opportunities?

Chapter 2: What is China's investment climate like, and what has been
the experience of foreign firms that have invested there?

Chapter 3: How can foreign firms best forge partnerships in the People's Republic and appropriately structure their China ventures?

Chapter 4: How does China's business bureaucracy link up with and
cooperate with foreign firms? What types of Sino-foreign projects exist
and how are they approved?

Chapter 5: How is the Chinese enterprise managed? What constraints
on productivity faced by them can the foreign venture partner expect to
face in managing a China venture?

Chapter 6: How can the Chinese and foreigners succeed in manufacturing and marketing products in a comanaged venture in China?

Chapter 7: What are China's indigenous technological capabilities?
How can foreign firms utilize Chinese R&D and leverage their technology for market access and long-term advantage?

Chapter 8: Are there formulas for business success in China based on the success and failure of foreign firms doing business there? Can corporate America improve its position by learning from its rivals?

    The author of this book is a journalist and a business person. Hence, the book reflects a concern with both international corporate strategy as well as the experiences of U.S. firms grappling with the practical requisites of doing business in China. Data for the book were gathered through a number of avenues, including four research trips to China between 1986 and 1988. The author visited and photographed U.S.-China joint ventures, spoke with their managers, and held numerous conversations with Chinese officials regarding foreign investment, technology transfer, and economic modernization. Additional interviews were conducted with U.S. representatives of the Foreign Commercial Service in the People's Republic and Hong Kong and with American government officials in Washington, D.C. Three separate questionnaires were distributed and returned by thirty-nine U.S. corporations and twenty-two executives involved in China business. They serve to survey (1) the activities of U.S. companies involved in joint ventures in China, (2) the level of preparation of expatriates bound for duty in China, and (3) the experience of U.S. firms in marketing and advertising in the People's Republic. (The last questionnaire can be found in the appendix.) Much of the information and analysis in this book is the product of continuing discussions with numerous American companies regarding their business experiences in China. Most of the interviews were conducted in confidence because of concerns about possible adverse Chinese reactions to some of the frank comments that were made. Finally, the book reflects a careful reading of the American and Chinese press and scholarly literature regarding the China market and foreign investment in the People's Republic of China.

    The ultimate purpose of this book is to encourage the reader to think about China in new and different ways, to go beyond the stereotypes that come out of the many seminars about doing business in China that have sprung up throughout the country since 1980. A new approach to China is warranted, one that seeks to tie together business endeavors in Asian countries into a comprehensive "Asia strategy" that includes China as an important element. In this book, you will see some of the images of China confirmed, some recast, and others simply debunked. The hope is that U.S. business people will walk away from this experience not only better equipped to do business in China, but better equipped to do business internationally. If this book does nothing else but help promote greater understanding and alleviate misperceptions between American and Chinese business partners, then it will have succeeded in its intention.

CHINA VENTURE LEXICON

Foreign Investment.   In this book, the term *foreign investment* refers to investment by foreign firms in equity-based ventures such as joint ventures and wholly foreign-owned subsidiaries, in addition to joint business arrangements including joint development of resources, compensation trade, and cooperative ventures. Processing and assembling arrangements, on the other hand, are treated as service contract arrangements between Chinese and foreign entities rather than foreign investment.

Foreign-Investment Enterprise.   A *foreign-investment enterprise* (FIE) denotes any business entity in China in which a foreign company controls some, or all, of the equity. In this book, an FIE can be an equity joint venture, wholly foreign-owned venture, cooperative venture, or a compensation trade arrangement, but not an agreement for joint development of resources or processing and assembling.

Equity Joint Venture (*hezi jingying*).   A *limited partnership* company that is jointly owned and operated by foreign firm(s) and Chinese entities. Partners share risks and profits according to their equity position; that is, liability is limited to the capital each partner invests. The venture is led by a board of directors.

Cooperative Venture (*hezuo jingying*).   Often called a contractual joint venture (*qiyeshi heying*), this business arrangement usually involves foreign firm(s) and a Chinese entity cooperating in the manufacturing of a product or a service operation. In most cases, the Chinese side provides the land, building, and work force, while the foreign firm supplies the technical know-how, hard cash, and equipment. Output is usually shared, but it is not divided up according to an equity-based formula. Rather, it is shared according to the terms of a negotiated contract.

Wholly Foreign-owned Venture (*duzi jingying*).   In essence, this venture is a wholly owned subsidiary wherein a foreign entity uses its own capital and technology to establish an enterprise in the People's Republic. The firm controls all of the venture's equity and its output, assuming all risks and rewards. To some extent, this business form allows the foreign firm to manage its production independent of any overseeing Chinese organization.

Joint Development (*hezuo kaifa*).   Agreements concerning the joint development and exploitation of China's resources are entered into by foreign and Chinese entities under guidelines spelled out in special Chinese laws and regulations. Usually involving two stages, the foreign firm typically assumes the initial costs and risks of exploration and/or development of oil or mineral resources; later, the risk and cost of resource exploitation is shared by all partners. Though all parties share in the distribution of output according to the terms of their contract, the Chinese have also utilized joint development arrangements to acquire foreign technology, equipment, and expertise, which they pay for with discovered resources.

Compensation Trade (*buchang maoyi*). Under this agreement, the Chinese side acquires technology and equipment from a foreign firm on credit, and pays back the principal and interest with goods produced using the technology and equipment and/or labor ("direct compensation"). In some cases, payment is made with products from a third source within China ("counter purchase"). The foreign firm then markets the goods outside China.

Processing and Assembling (*lailiao jiagong, laijian zhuangbei*). These two business arrangements are merely labor contracts in which the foreign company delivers raw materials and/or components to the Chinese factory to be assembled or manufactured into finished goods. Often, the foreign firm supplies processing equipment that is purchased later by the Chinese side with production output. All goods produced are controlled by the foreign firm, which simply pays a fee to the Chinese enterprise for work completed.

CHINESE CURRENCY EXCHANGE RATE

US$1 = 3.72 Rmb (yuan)
(1989)

LIST OF ABBREVIATIONS

CAAC	Civil Aviation Administration of China
CATIC	China National Aeronautic-Technology Import and Export Control
CCIC	China Commodity Inspection Corporation
CCP	Chinese Communist Party
CCPIT	China Council for the Protection of International Trade
CEMA	China Enterprise Management Association
CITIC	China International Trust and Investment Corporation
CNAIC	China National Automotive Industry Corporation
CNOOC	China National Offshore Oil Corporation
COCOM	Coordinating Committee for Multinational Export Control
EEC	European Economic Community
ETDZ	Economic and Technical Development Zone
FEC	Foreign Exchange Certificate
FESCO	Foreign Enterprises Service Corporation
FIE	Foreign-Investment Enterprise
FTC	Foreign Trade Corporation
ITC	Internal Trading Certificates
JCAET	Japan-China Association for Economy and Trade
MACHIMPEX	China National Machinery Import and Export Corporation
MEI	Ministry of Electronics Industry
MOFERT	Ministry of Foreign Economic Relations and Trade
MOPI	Ministry of Petroleum Industry
NCUSCT	National Council for U.S.-China Trade
NICs	Newly Industrialized Countries
OPIC	Overseas Private Investment Corporation
OTA	Office of Technology Assessment
PLA	People's Liberation Army
Rmb	Renminbi (People's currency)
SEZ	Special Economic Zone
SITIC	Shanghai International Trade and Investment Corporation
TECHIMPORT	China National Technical Import Corporation

The China Market: Myth or Reality?

The Chinese seem to believe that a foreigner is born every minute.

A Beijing bureau chief of an American magazine

You don't sell to the Chinese—they buy. They know what they want, and they do tell you when you're trying to sell them something they don't want. But it's subtle—you've got to listen well.

Bob Yeager, Vice President
Rockwell International Overseas Corp.
(quoted in *Chinese Business Review*)

Beijing has been exploited by a parade of business suitors willing to indulge any local whim to romance local hosts to offer only the vague promise of further intimacies. At the same time, many foreign companies have waltzed into China, giddy about the prospects and ignorant of reality. The Chinese have a phrase for the resulting misperceptions: Tong chung yi meng—Same bed, different dreams.

James Sterba
Asian Wall Street Journal

In 1784, ten years after the Boston Tea Party, the United States became a participant in the Old China Trade when the *Empress of China* sailed into Canton harbor carrying furs, porcelain, and bundles of ginseng, the restorative herb grown in New England. Another American ship, the *Harriet*, had been sent to China one year before, but was intercepted at the Cape of Good Hope by British traders aghast that America was devising ways to compete with them in the Orient. The captain of the *Harriet* forsook his place in history and sold his China-bound cargo of ginseng to the Britishers at a sizable profit.[1] Thus began America's trade relationship with the oldest civilization on earth.

From the outset, China trade fed the imagination of early American entrepreneurs with its exotic handicrafts, textiles, teas, and vast market potential. Profit was not the only attraction of the China market; Americans were also drawn by the romantic exoticism and ineffable mystique of the country. And there was the distinctly American pioneering spirit of the time, the notion of seeking out distant lands and building up a legacy of commercial success.

Unfortunately, China's ancient and uncanny will to be economically self-reliant cut short America's pecuniary fantasy of market share in the Orient. Chinese merchants were simply more interested in trading among themselves than with "barbarians from across the great waters." The Chinese habitually neglected foreign merchants; hence, Sino-American trade never amounted to more than 4 percent of America's total trade. This was better than the British could claim, however, at least until they initiated the trading of opium to China and waged two wars to ensure its continuation.[2]

By 1900, the mythical China market had become synonymous with unfulfilled expectations. Yet, the image of China's vast market had been firmly implanted in the hearts and minds of America's new industrialists. James B. Duke (1865–1925), the American tobacco tycoon, learned of the invention of the cigarette machine in 1881 and said, "Bring me an atlas." He found China to have a population of 430 million and, pointing to the odd-shaped country, declared, "That is where we are going to sell cigarettes." By 1916, Duke's company held the lion's share of the cigarette market in China, selling $20.75 million* worth of cigarettes in that year alone. Under his aegis, the Shanghai branch of the British-American Tobacco Company—one of the first multinational corporations to enter China—made large-scale investments there, transferring cigarette processing technology and managerial techniques, setting up a wide distribution network, and training Chinese labor.[3] Thus began America's corporate encounter with China.

Throughout the first half of the twentieth century, China was considered a relatively important export market until the United States placed a trade embargo on China during the Korean War (1950). All Sino-American trade had ceased until Richard Nixon reopened relations with China in 1972 by signing the Shanghai Communiqué with China's premier, Zhou Enlai. In that year, the first sale of U.S. grain was made to China and U.S. firms were included for the first time in the Canton Trade Fair, then the only conduit for product promotion in the People's Republic. Between 1973 and 1979, business linkage between

---

*All amounts are given in U.S. dollars unless otherwise noted.

Washington and Beijing was initiated via office representation. During this time, large U.S. companies such as M.W. Kellogg, Coca-Cola, and Arco signed contract deals with China in the fields of ammonia manufacturing, soft-drink distributing, and offshore seismic surveying, respectively. Economic contacts between China and the United States grew only slightly during the 1970s. But in 1979, China abruptly opened its doors to foreign companies in an effort to obtain foreign technology and direct investment, and economic intercourse between the two countries began to achieve momentum. The first Sino-U.S. joint venture was signed in 1979 between the ES Pacific Development Corporation and China International Travel Service to construct and manage the Great Wall Hotel in Beijing; in 1982, Foxboro and Shanghai Instrument Industrial Company signed the first Sino-U.S. manufacturing joint venture agreement; in 1984, 3M company formed the first wholly foreign-owned subsidiary in the People's Republic. In 1980, the U.S. granted China most-favored nation status; in 1983, U.S. export controls regarding China were relaxed.[4] Today, it is commonplace to find Chinese trade promoters traveling the United States and the rest of the industrialized world pronouncing the great economic and investment opportunities in the China market. In new China, one could conceivably drive an AMC/Chrysler Cherokee Jeep up to the Great Wall, buy a bottle of Coke, unpack a carry-out box of Kentucky Fried Chicken, and watch a train pulled by a locomotive manufactured in the U.S. by General Electric snake through the valley below. It appears that America's once-inflated notion of China trade has become partially realized.

U.S.-CHINA TRADE COMES OF AGE

The East Asian market has steadily grown in importance to the U.S. economy over the last decade. Of America's twenty largest overseas customers, eight are in the Pacific region. Exports to the Far East have grown 1,200 percent since 1960, which constitutes a larger percentage of export growth in a shorter time than in any other area of the world.[5] As its role in the Asian market expands, China will become an important site for export-oriented manufacturing and as a domestic market for products made in Asia. China's expansion should also provide an important market for foreign technology, licensing, software, management consulting, technical services, and tourism.

The inauguration of China's opening and the lure of the market have given rise to two general attitudes among U.S. corporations. The first harks back to the old philosophy of China being the last and largest untapped market in the world, a notion epitomized in the 1840s when Great Britain promulgated the idea of lengthening the coats of every Chinese by one inch and thus saving the British textile industry from imminent collapse. Unfortunately, there were no wool coats in China at the time. Another pursuer of the untapped China market was John D. Rockefeller, who at one time anticipated selling substantial quantities of oil to China to fuel the lamps and homes of its huge populace. Today, this attitude is found in marketing executives who dream of exponential sales growth—ten trillion razor blades a year, five billion cans of cola a week, millions of telephones a year, or thousands of automobiles a month.

The other prevailing view of China's potential market is connected with broader corporate global strategies. As part of their regional or product-based strategies, many companies consider establishing an office and/or subsidiary in China as an opportunity to become acquainted with China's emerging economic and technological capabilities. In this way, a corporation can develop sales through its market presence, and simultaneously network inside China with an eye to linking up with the firm's other operations in the Asia/Pacific region. By looking at China with this somewhat more comprehensive and long-term view, companies are better able to gauge China's potential and appraise its investment climate while leveraging their Chinese contacts to enhance their global competitive position.

Spurred into action by the pronounced immediacy that the Chinese attach to their open-door policies, U.S. corporations are entering China in large numbers. They have made direct investments in more than 400 joint ventures worth over $2 billion in pledged American investment, by Chinese estimates. As part of their global strategy, the U.S. partners in China ventures have accepted comparatively strict operating requirements in order to gain a foothold in China. In contrast to the strategies that many of these American firms have pursued in Taiwan, Japan, and South Korea (that is, export-oriented manufacturing), they have licensed newer technology, trained more managers and workers, and set up factories in China with the overriding goal of selling to the Chinese domestic market.

To a certain extent, both of these attitudes reflect corporate America's belief that one billion Chinese customers are eagerly waiting to buy American consumer and industrial goods. Although many U.S.

corporations have gone into China confident in their ability to penetrate the bureaucracy and achieve their business objectives, as they have in other Asian countries, they have encountered a very different commercial reality.

Foreign corporations, realizing that China is steadily emerging as an important new player in the world export market, also see the Chinese as major buyers of foreign equipment and expertise to fuel this effort. China's total foreign trade reached almost $83 billion in 1987, and projections are that China's overall trade will surpass that amount for the remainder of the 1980s. Indeed, China buys over $3 billion worth of U.S. goods each year and maintains a foreign reserve balance of over $10 billion (1987). Many American companies believe they are well positioned to offer China the much-needed technology and expertise its economic modernization will require.

In effect, U.S. industries have approached the Chinese market with the belief that China will perceive American technology as the most advanced in the world. At the same time, however, they are aware that China does not intend to depend on one source or one country to meet all of its modernization needs. Though price is an important criterion in Chinese commercial decisions, China has been known to deal with so-called noncompetitive firms to avoid excessive dependence on one or two technology suppliers. This tendency, along with what Americans have been told (by the Chinese themselves) of Beijing's unwillingness to get too close to Japan, has attracted many U.S. firms that see potential niches in the Chinese market open to them.

The U.S.-China Trade Partnership

After the fall of the Gang of Four in 1976 and diplomatic recognition of China by the U.S. in 1979, trade between the U.S. and China began to take off. Between the years 1973 and 1987, the total volume of U.S.-China trade grew more than tenfold, from $805 million to over $10 billion. In 1979, and again in 1980, two-way trade between the U.S. and China doubled. Trading peaked in 1985 when the U.S. exported $3.85 billion worth of goods to China. (This figure dropped in 1986 to $3.11 billion and rose again to $3.49 billion in 1987.) Agricultural product traditionally accounted for more than half of U.S. exports to China, but this is changing. For example, U.S. exports of grain, cotton, and other agricultural products to China amounted to 70 percent of U.S. total sales there in 1978; in 1979, the figure had dropped to 58 percent; and in 1983, it stood at 25 percent.[6]

As total trade between the two countries has increased, the U.S. has been hard pressed to export to China as much as it imports. Currently, the U.S. is experiencing a relatively small trade deficit (roughly $2 billion) with the People's Republic as the Chinese expand their efforts to bolster and diversify their exports to offset the effects of the collapse of the crude oil market in 1986.

Market Share.   The Japanese traditionally have maintained the largest proportion of the China market—about 35 percent in the 1980s—but this figure has dropped as a result of both the appreciation of the yen against the dollar and China's unwillingness to tolerate increasing trade deficits with Japan. Hong Kong now surpasses Japan as the country's leading trading partner, claiming 27 percent of China's foreign trade. Japan holds second place with 20 percent; and the U.S. is third, with 9.5 percent. Competition for market share in China has sharpened as the perception of the market changes from one at the periphery of the world economy to one closer to the center. American business has not ignored this fact. In part due to the declining dollar, but more importantly, due to increased initiative on the part of corporate America to introduce products to the Chinese, the U.S. share of the market increased from 7.8 percent in 1986 to 8.8 percent in 1987; or in dollar amounts, from $3.1 to $3.5 billion. Even more encouraging has been the U.S. performance in 1988. Imports increased at a rate of over $100 million per month through March, while the Department of Commerce estimates U.S. imports to China will rise above $5 billion in 1989, increasing the U.S. market share to 10 or 11 percent.

Hong Kong's role as a trading partner, as well as an entrepôt trade conduit for U.S., South Korean, and Taiwanese goods entering China, has propelled its market share in China from 11.2 percent in 1985 to 19.7 percent in 1987. By official accounts, U.S. companies trade about $500 million worth of goods to the People's Republic via Hong Kong each year. (If interviews by the author with Hong Kong traders are any indication, this figure is likely to be much higher.)

In terms of specific China market sectors, the U.S. position as a leading vendor of technology and primary products is holding ground against intensifying competition from Japan, Europe, and other Asian countries. The U.S. market shares of scientific equipment (35 percent), telecommunications (5 percent), power generating equipment (22

China's Balance of Payments, Foreign Investment, and U.S.-China Trade
(In millions of U.S. dollars unless noted[1])

	1985	1986
Balance of Payments		
Chinese exports (FOB)[2]	26,500	39,500
Chinese imports (CIF)	40,200	43,200
Trade balance	−13,700	2,000
Current account balance	− 9,000	100[5]
Foreign exchange reserves (year end)	11,900	16,000
Foreign Investment		
Total (cumulative, approved)[3]	16,200	19,100
U.S. share (cumulative, approved)[3]	2,100	2,700
U.S. share (%)	12.9	14.1
U.S.-China Trade[4]		
U.S. exports to China (FAS)	3,852	3,110
U.S. imports from China (CIF)	4,224	5,240
Trade balance (U.S.)	− 372	− 2,130
U.S. share of Chinese exports (%)	15.9	8.24
U.S. share of Chinese imports (%)	9.6	7.2

NOTES: 1. U.S. dollar values are based on average exchange rates for the years given.
2. Chinese total trade data is based on official Chinese Customs data.
3. Data are based on official Chinese sources.
4. U.S.-China bilateral trade is based on U.S. government data.
5. Estimate by the Economic Intelligence Unit.

SOURCES: *Statistical Yearbook of China, 1986,* 1987 SSB Statistical Communiqué on 1986 Economic Performance, IMF International Financial Statistics, U.S. government trade data.

percent), and transport machinery (18 percent) have remained steady since 1983. In computer sales, the U.S. share has increased from 40 percent in 1983 to 50 percent in 1987.[7]

CHINA'S FIVE-PART MARKET

A company that intends to enter China and prosper there must have a broad, sector-specific knowledge of the opportunities the China market offers. Obviously, to cover the entire market in detail would require another volume,[8] but the following overview should acquaint the reader with what are perceived as the five segments of China's nonagricultural market, which are as follows:

1. Capital Goods
2. Foreign Technology
3. Consumer Goods/Health Products
4. Service Industries
5. Tourist Ventures

Within each segment of the China market, one will find three types of recognizable market scenarios: (1) existing markets, in which customer needs are being served; (2) latent markets, in which customer needs are present but not being adequately served; and (3) incipient markets, in which customer needs have not emerged.[9] As a developing international market, China tends to exhibit qualities of the latter two types.

In appraising the China market, a firm should begin by recognizing a few broad trends in China's recent buying patterns. First, the country's growing self-sufficiency in the food sector has been accompanied by a shift away from the importing of primary goods, including food and live animals, to importing manufactured goods. Imports of food and live animals declined steadily from $3.11 billion in 1983 to only $1.54 billion in 1985. Second, China's annual imports ($43.2 billion in 1987), originate from many more supplying countries than in the past. For example, Italy and France can now claim almost $1 billion each per year. In 1988, Japanese firms managed to actually enlarge their China-bound volume at a scorching rate of over $150 million per month, even though their overall market share has dropped. Third, the market has rapidly divided into a multitude of small, but expanding markets for high-technology manufactured products.

As China's industrial needs diversify, marketers sell more specialized products lines. Often these products make up only one element in a complex set of equipment. For example, astounding import growth in machinery and transport equipment (from $4.0 billion in 1983 up to $16.5 billion in 1985) no longer reflects purchases of turnkey plants and cargo vessels, as in the past. During the same period, imports of electrical machinery within this sector have improved from only $231 million in 1983 to a sizable $1.33 billion in 1985; office machinery imports increased from $270 million to $1.02 billion in the same period. Given that the dollar will probably continue on its downward slide against the yen, U.S. companies should be able to significantly increase their sales to China in these emerging market niches by 1990. The trad-

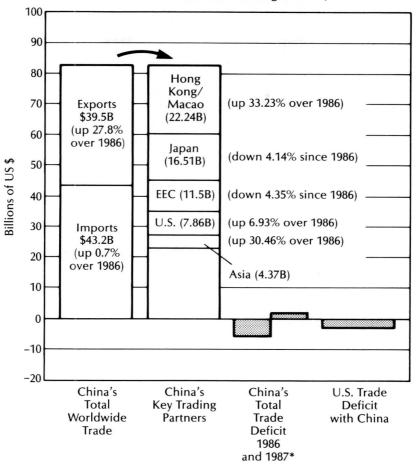

China's Trade Volume and Trading Partners, 1987

Billions of US $

China's Total Worldwide Trade
- Exports $39.5B (up 27.8% over 1986)
- Imports $43.2B (up 0.7% over 1986)

China's Key Trading Partners
- Hong Kong/Macao (22.24B) (up 33.23% over 1986)
- Japan (16.51B) (down 4.14% since 1986)
- EEC (11.5B) (down 4.35% since 1986)
- U.S. (7.86B) (up 6.93% over 1986)
- (up 30.46% over 1986)
- Asia (4.37B)

China's Total Trade Deficit 1986 and 1987*

U.S. Trade Deficit with China

- China is America's 16th largest trading partner.
- America is China's 3rd largest trading partner.
- U.S. exports to China equaled $3.49 billion in 1987, up 9 percent over 1986.
- Since 1986, China has increased exports, reduced imports, and turned away from Japan toward America in order to take advantage of the weakening dollar.

SOURCES: Department of Commerce, *China Trade Report*. *Beijing Review, February 1-7, 1988, 22.

ing partners that stay in closest touch with the segmentation of China's market will become the leading benefactors of China's opening.

Having touched upon the emerging elements of China's marketplace, one should remember that the infrastructural and raw material demands of the market will remain lasting areas of opportunity. This is because the speed at which Chinese industry is growing (17 percent annually in 1987) far outstrips its capacity to produce essential raw materials such as iron and steel, nonferrous metals, chemicals, cement, and lumber, to feed such expansion. In 1987, coal production was up only 2.9 percent; port capacity was up only 3.3 percent; and oil production was up only 2.6 percent. These low growth rates of raw material production cannot sustain an economy producing (and transporting) 17 percent more industrial output each year. Selected priority projects aimed at expanding infrastructure and the production of raw materials will become critical by 1990. Foreign assistance will be sought in chemical processing, including the licensing of foreign chemical manufacturing processes and the acquisition of whole plants to produce resins, emulsions, and road construction materials, among others.

Traditional raw material markets include: $2.5 billion per year for crude materials excluding fuels; $7.1 billion per year for iron and steel; and $4.5 billion per year for chemical products. Smaller infrastructural markets have also emerged alongside the traditional sectors: $1.3 billion per year for power machinery; $2.5 billion per year for telecommunications; $3.1 billion per year for land vehicles; and $2 billion per year for specialized industrial machinery.

China as a Market for Capital Goods

Chinese officials have announced plans to increase investments in energy, transportation, telecommunications, and the exploitation of natural resources. Foreign suppliers of advanced capital goods in these priority areas should find desirable prospects.

Electric Power. China's electricity shortage runs at about 50 billion kilowatt hours per year,[10] idling 20 percent of the country's production capacity. The country depends on oil and coal for 90 percent of its energy consumption. Recognizing the need for additional energy sources and a more balanced use of them, China's Seventh Five-Year Plan outlines plans for petroleum energy to be increased to 20 percent

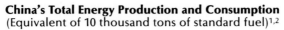

China's Total Energy Production and Consumption
(Equivalent of 10 thousand tons of standard fuel)[1,2]

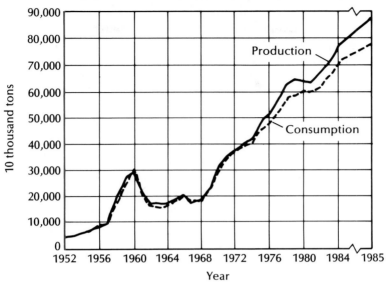

Consuming nearly all of the energy that it can produce, China also refines its coal, petroleum, hydropower, and natural gas energy resources in roughly the same proportions that it uses them. For example, coal accounts for approximately 75% of both production and consumption of China's energy. Petroleum equals 18%, hydropower 5%, and natural gas 2%. These proportions have remained virtually the same for the past decade.

Notes: 1. Fuels include coal, crude oil, natural gas, and hydropower; and exclude bio-energy, solar, geothermal, and nuclear energy.

2. All fuels are converted into standard fuel with thermal equivalent of 7,000 kilocalories per kilogram.

Source: *Statistical Yearbook of China, 1986*, State Statistical Bureau, People's Republic of China.

of total energy consumed and coal reduced to 70 percent (from its current level of 80 percent). Nonetheless, the country continues to approve coal, nuclear, hydroelectric, and steam-power energy projects. The energy sector presently receives a hefty 24 percent of China's total capital outlay.

Growth in the coal sector is restrained only by a lack of foreign exchange and insufficient transportation services to facilitate the movement of coal to the ports. Thus, construction of new rail lines has become critical. Thermal stations will be constructed near ports and load centers to protect the coal from freezing during transit and to enhance its exportability.

Foreign participation in this sector will be significant in open strip-mine development and the construction of coal-fired power stations, especially in project management services, engineering, and specialized equipment sales. Coal-related projects will include slurry pipelines, downstream coal utilization projects involving coal gasification, coal liquefaction, and coal chemical technology. Occidental Petroleum, under the leadership of probably the most bullish China hand, Armand Hammer, has signed joint venture coal development agreements with China, including a $750 million mine in the northern province of Shanxi and two cooperative contracts for projects in Henan involving a coal preparation plant and a licensing agreement for use of Occidental's phosphoric acid production technology.[11]

China's hydroelectric power needs are enormous as well, but have received adequate attention from foreign firms, mainly large Japanese general trading companies (called *soga sosha*) such as C. Itoh and Co. Japan's soga sosha companies specialize in drawing together large teams of subcontractors, financial institutions, and technical services, in addition to supplying the necessary project coordination to get a power plant built for the lowest cash cost to the Chinese. The massive Three Gorges hydroelectric project, located on the Changjiang (Yangtze) River in Hubei, has pitted Japanese, American, and European firms against each other in a battle for engineering and construction contracts. The project has been under consideration since the early 1980s, for which a number of studies have been completed that address the technical, environmental, and financial feasibility of the project.

In terms of nuclear power facilities, for which the United States possesses the world's most advanced technology, U.S. firms have been left out because of delays in approving technology transfer by the U.S. government, which cites China's lack of nuclear waste disposal legislation as its main point of concern.

Transportation.   The volume of passenger traffic in China doubles every four to five years. This means that infrastructural improvements in highways, railways, and airport facilities will expand commensurately, boosting sales of trucks, diesel engines for locomotives, railway technology, airplanes, and airport equipment. American Motors Corporation, Volkswagen, and numerous Japanese automakers

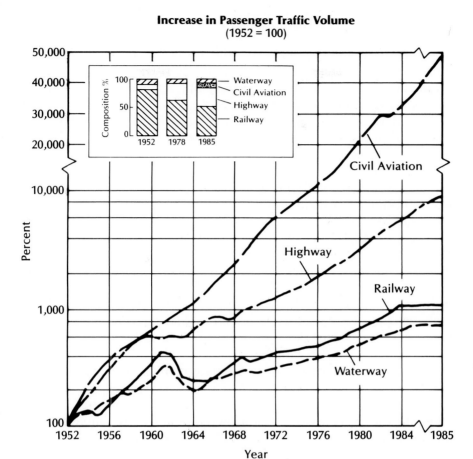

Increase in Passenger Traffic Volume
(1952 = 100)

All segments of China's transportation sector have experienced significant growth in numbers of passengers since 1952. Growth in highway use has outstripped that in railway use as a proportion of total transport, while use of air transport has skyrocketed. The volume of air travelers climbed 350% between 1978 and 1985, aided by rising numbers of tourists and eased restrictions on travel by Chinese citizens.

SOURCE: *Statistical Yearbook of China, 1986,* State Statistical Bureau, People's Republic of China.

have penetrated the market via joint manufacturing ventures, while the Japanese have far outperformed all other suppliers in direct sales of autos, trucks, motorcycles, and heavy vehicles. General Electric's multimillion dollar sale of 400 locomotive engines in the mid-1980s (which included local sourcing of several engine parts), is the most famous U.S. sale to China's transportation sector. The road vehicle sector seems fertile ground for technology licensing since China envisions increased self-reliance in that field. Recent deals include a heavy-truck production factory, an engine-making plant, loans for railway expansion, and direct sales of microbuses.

For U.S. companies, however, China's civil aviation market may be the most promising high-technology market, both in terms of U.S. competitiveness in the field and the potential for lucrative cash sales. The Civil Aviation Administration of China (CAAC), which maintains overall responsibility for the sector, has purchased over $1 billion worth of American-made aviation equipment, including Boeing 747s and Sikorsky helicopters.

Because China's civil aviation system has been restructured, the 1990s should witness the rise of independent regional airline carriers, managed autonomously under the administrative auspices of CAAC. It will become more important for foreign suppliers to forge direct links with upstart carriers as this occurs. Purchases will include small aircraft designed for business commuter flights, cargo aircraft, maintenance equipment, navigational equipment, and helicopters.

Telecommunications.　China continues to emphasize the upgrading of its telephone system and telephone services, and for good reason. The country's phone density stands at one phone per 333 persons, the lowest in the world. Rural telephone service in China features manual switchboards and open wires for long-distance calling. American Telephone and Telegraph recently installed twenty subscriber loop-carrier systems, and Ericsson Radio Systems of Sweden sold a cellular mobile telephone system to Shanghai. More impressive, U.S.-based Cortel has supplied fifty earth stations to China and has licensed its technology for satellite-based products. Those firms willing to transfer technology and offer concessionary financing in this sector are being given preferential treatment. Competition among the industrialized countries—United States, European nations, and Japan—depresses telecommunications equipment selling prices. Other related telecommunication areas include satellite receiving stations, direct-broadcast satellite systems, ship communication equipment, VHF-UHF equipment, portable airborne receivers, and defense-related telecommunication equipment.[12]

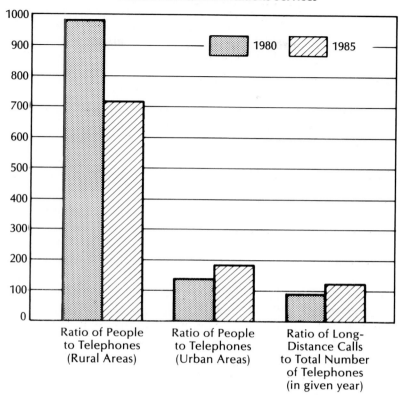

China's Telecommunications Services

- China had 3.12 million phones on-line in 1985, up from 2.14 million in 1980.
- Phone density is worsening in urban areas and improving in rural areas.
- The need for long-distance switching equipment intensified 24 percent from 1980 to 1985.

Source: *Statistical Yearbook of China, 1986*, State Statistical Bureau, People's Republic of China.

China as a Market for Foreign Technology

China has targeted world markets for its export goods through a program which develops export manufacturing based on imported technology, equipment, and managerial expertise. This program will provide for the technological renovation of many of China's 400,000 industrial factories, the value of each project ranging between $500,000 and $2 million. Import decision makers place high priority on acquiring the most advanced technology available in order to ensure product exportability and prevent rapid obsolescence. American firms offer this technology. Areas of emphasis include computers, electronics, food processing, and other projects likely to promote exports, reduce energy consumption, and lessen China's dependency on imports. Recently, transportation and communications have been added to the list. Trade organizations periodically release exhaustive lists of projects for which foreign participation is sought. (A list of current technological priorities appears in Chapter 7 on page 317.)

Computers. China has acquired a wide range of computer equipment over the last several years, much of it purchased from U.S. firms, and they will continue to purchase mainframes, peripherals, software, and semiconductors. The importation of microcomputers from foreign countries has been restricted through tariff barriers erected in 1985. As a result, there will continue to be a high dependence on foreign manufacturing joint ventures to initiate domestic computer production.

Electronics. Since China lacks sufficient production facilities to produce large-scale integrated circuits to meet the demands of its fledgling computer industry, the field of microelectronics may offer the greatest opportunities. Some of the most conspicuous items on China's import list are electrical home appliances such as radios, calculators, refrigerators, and audiocassette players. Foreign firms offering to license processing technologies in the electronic sector will find eager customers. Areas worth investigating include the following:

1. *Semiconductors and integrated circuits.* China needs the full range of equipment to produce semiconductors and integrated circuits. Also, equipment is needed to process the raw materials, such as silicon, that make up finished electronics products.
2. *Capacitors and resistors.* China is currently importing numerous specialized products in this field. Opportunities exist for sales and equipment to produce capacitors and resistors as well as technological know-how relating to advanced components.
3. *Printed circuit boards.* Opportunities exist in printing and etching equipment.

4. Other areas of opportunity include switches and relays, wire products, boxing products, packaging, and assembling processes.[13]

Food Processing. Widespread agrarian reform in China has increased average per capita caloric intake, while privatized agricultural enterprises have put a wider variety of food on the Chinese table. Demand for more and varied types of food increases every year, especially the desire for beef products.[14] In 1985, China spent over $150 million on food processing technology and equipment to produce food for its growing population as well as for export markets.

American participation has maintained a steady pace in China's food and food processing markets, starting with grain sales in the late 1970s and now including livestock, food processing equipment, and packaging technology. At present, foreign firms should aim to assist China in developing new sources of animal protein. This could include direct sales of livestock, inputs of technology for the artificial insemination of livestock, dairy farm and flour mill construction, and prawn breeding aquaculture projects.[15]

Fast food and packaged food play a greater role in the Chinese diet. Having achieved a high degree of expertise in these areas, U.S. companies have been competitive. Kentucky Fried Chicken (KFC) has set up a 500-seat version of its fast food chain in central Beijing. The venture serves an average of 6800 patrons per day and the venture's owners predict $2.5 million in annual sales. Executives at KFC's parent company (R. J. Reynolds) say the Beijing venture "has been profitable from day one," invoking the envy of less fortunate China venture managers. The sign in the window reads: "So good you lick your fingers," and will soon be hanging in Shanghai and other Chinese metropolitan areas.[16]

Many firms that have provided small-scale machinery and product lines that are easy for the Chinese to assimilate into existing food processing factories have achieved success. Coca-Cola currently operates joint venture bottling plants in eight major Chinese cities and has formed Shanghai Shenmei Beverage and Food Co. to supply its soft drink concentrates to bottlers. Pepsi Co, Inc., produces ten million cases of soft drinks annually with its joint venture partner, the Guangzhou Beverage Factory, as well as seasonings, sauces, and other foodstuffs through a separate joint venture partnership. Beatrice Foods and Heinz have also made inroads into the market through joint ventures.

Military Technology and Arms Sales. China's defense acquisitions fluctuate wildly year to year: the country purchased $100 million worth of military hardware in 1977; over $200 million in 1980; only $50 million in 1983; $300 million in 1985; and under $150 million in 1986. China's current needs include naval technology, anti-tank and anti-aircraft weaponry, avionics, fighter jets, helicopters, and munitions factories. Military sales to China by U.S. firms have grown in monetary value and scope, as export controls enforced by the U.S. government have been progressively relaxed since 1978. In 1986, a $550 million deal included a number of U.S. firms (GE and Westinghouse among them) for the purchase of avionics and fire control systems for China's Shenyang J-8 II fighter. Baldwin Aircraft International of the U.S. recently sold $1 billion worth of surveillance jets and Boeing is presently negotiating to sell CH-47D Chinook military helicopters. One factor to remember: China has fast become a net arms exporter and this fact will slow the export approval process by the U.S. government for all arms-related technology transfer agreements.

China as a Market for Consumer Goods/ Health Products

The Chinese were permitted to slake a long-suppressed thirst for Western consumer goods when the Chinese government decentralized the import/export function of the Ministry of Foreign Economic Relations and Trade (MOFERT) in 1984. The action triggered a buying spree in which roughly $9 billion of the country's cash reserves purchased an array of automotive and electronic products (mostly Japanese) in less than two years. The resulting government crackdown on foreign exchange spending and higher import restrictions has severely curtailed sales of products such as radios, color televisions, and videocassette recorders. Illegal black-market trading of these goods tends to bristle Chinese sensitivities about reopening this once-lucrative market. Yet, the market will remain charged by rapidly growing urban and rural incomes and the fact Chinese consumers increasingly demand in their households the "four essentials"—a television, washing machine, refrigerator, and videocassette recorder.

Trade officials restrain imports of consumer goods by requiring foreign traders to sell to consumers through a Chinese foreign trade corporation (FTC). No direct consumer marketing is allowed. Japan's strong presence in all of China's provinces has produced the highest yield in this market. For those U.S. producers that offer the right product for Chinese needs, sales can be remarkable. The U.S. manufacturing company, Turbo-Tek, recently sold 14,000 of its Turbo-Wash hand-held sprayers to China in a single month. Originally designed for washing cars, the Chinese use the spray gun for household cleaning chores. As the firm's president, Fred Reinstein, boasts, "Our sales in China are just unbelievable."[17] A U.S. trading firm, WSJ Incorporated, has attempted to link trade deals between South Korea and China, buying appliances from Korea, putting a WSJ label on them, and selling them in China.[18] Ventures like this can be profitable, but are risky for U.S. firms because the Japanese have access to lower priced goods manufactured in Southeast Asia and more flexibility in structuring deals with Asian partners.

Pharmaceuticals. China has a sustained interest in creating a full-fledged pharmaceutical industry. Recent agreements for a capsule plant, another to produce pharmaceuticals cooperatively, and yet another to manufacture diagnostic test kits reflect the nature of the sector: limited direct sales of pharmaceuticals, but many opportunities to produce health products to be sold in China. The same can be said of cosmetics, hair products, and soaps.

China as a Site for Service Industries

As in other Pacific Rim nations, China's trade officials impose strict regulations on service sector ventures,[19] including those in banking, insurance, shipping, accounting, and legal services. Foreign attorneys cannot officially practice law in China; U.S. insurance companies have avoided the country since government-backed Chinese companies maintain a monopoly of the insurance sector; and foreign banks cannot perform any of their normal functions, including lending funds and guaranteeing loans, except on an experimental basis in selected SEZs. Although they suffer annual losses, these banks maintain offices in China at a cost of $500,000 a year. Adding insult to injury, Chinese officials believe the banks must be making profits or they would have packed up and left. Distrustful of the accounting books of these foreign banks, Chinese tax authorities plan to tax their "deemed income."[20] Some of these bank subsidiaries have not survived.

Progress in the opening of China's advertising market partly offsets the overall bad news about the service sector. Advertising agencies from around the world now devise promotional angles to help their

Income, Consumption, and Cultural Characteristics of the Chinese Populace

Item	Unit	1985	1985 as % of 1978
Income of rural and urban residents			
Income of peasants:			
Net annual income per capita[1,3]	Rmb	398	297.0(262.1)
Income of staff and workers:			
Average annual wage per capita[3]	Rmb	1,148	187.0(138.3)
Annual consumption per capita[2]			
Per capita consumption of all residents	Rmb	407	232.6(177.1)
Grain	kg	254.4	130.1
Cloth	meters	11.67	145.3
Daily consumer goods, value of retail sales	Rmb	93.5	324.7
Living-floor space per capita[1]			
Urban areas	meters^2	6.7	159.5
Rural areas	meters^2	14.7	181.5
Transportation			
Bicycles per 100 persons		21.4	277.9
Buses per 10,000 persons in cities		3.9	118.2
Savings			
Savings deposits per capita (year end)	Rmb	155.2	708.7
Culture			
TV sets per 100 persons		6.7	2,233.3
Radio sets per 100 persons		23.1	296.2
Tape-recorder sets per 100 persons		3.5	N/A
Books and magazines per person per year	copy	16.4	184.3
Retail, catering, and service trades			
Number business units per 10,000 persons	unit	102.6	789.2

The trend in China is toward more consumption and a higher standard of living for larger numbers of Chinese. Farm income is up nearly 300 percent since 1978; for factory workers, nearly 200 percent. Retail sales are up 325 percent as the number of businesses in China has swelled eightfold. There are now 7 TVs and 23 radios for every 100 Chinese. The dim spots are that only 16 out of 10,000 persons attend college and wages are still too low to generate a consumer market for foreign products commensurate with the size of the population.

NOTES: 1. Figures obtained from household income and expenditure sample surveys, calculated on basis of number of persons in the household.
2. Annual consumption of grain and cloth includes both direct consumption by residents and the consumption by catering trade, food, and clothing industries. Cloth also includes that for public use.
3. The parenthesized figures are change rates with increase in price deducted.

SOURCE: *Statistical Yearbook of China, 1986*, State Statistical Bureau, People's Republic of China.

clients sell to the Chinese. In 1986, $200 million was spent on product promotion using Chinese media, 10 percent of that going for foreign products.[21] As state allocations for government-sponsored media have come under the budgetary hatchet, Chinese media organizations have been forced to encourage foreign companies to advertise, even to the extent of having hosted a major advertising conference in May 1987, in the Great Hall of the People. Presently, the advertising industry grows by 50 percent per year. China's 680 domestic agencies pulled in $163 million (in Chinese currency) in 1985 and advertising experts expect this figure to triple by 1990.[22]

Advertising by American firms on Chinese television began when the Central Chinese Television purchased 64 hours of American programming from CBS in the mid-1980s. During these hours, U.S. firms such as Boeing, Kodak, Procter & Gamble, and IBM advertised on television in China for the first time.[23] In 1986, Walt Disney Company traded 104 episodes of Mickey Mouse and Donald Duck cartoons, to be aired in China over the course of two years, in exchange for two minutes of commercial time per program, worth about $20,000 a minute.[24] A plethora of Chinese-language trade directories and journals published by Western companies now saturates the Chinese commercial landscape, including versions of *Business Week, Scientific American, Discover* magazine, and scores of others. Chinese radio, television, and newspapers cater to foreign advertisers as well. Many opportunities for U.S. firms exist in the sector, but foreign corporate advertising needs may be better addressed from offices in Hong Kong or the U.S., closer to the home office of the client.

Construction Contracts and Building Materials.

In welcome contrast to Japan's virtually impenetrable financial sector, the People's Republic has utilized foreign construction firms on large and small projects with increasing frequency since its inception in 1949. The heyday of the market was in the 1970s when China acquired an array of whole plants that it paid for with lump sums of hard cash. By 1980, the Chinese reoriented their construction projects involving foreigners to encourage technology transfer and worker training. Purchases of turnkey plants were cut back and Chinese contractors were put in charge of large construction projects. Domestic contractors now accept bids from domestic and foreign subcontractors capable of handling one or more "small packages" of engineering and construction work that make up a larger construction project. American firms have entered joint ventures with Chinese firms as a way of positioning themselves to win large contracts. Their optimism has begun to wane as such agreements have failed to materialize. Many of these partnerships have been abandoned. Yet the plant and service contract market continues to surge ahead, amounting to $4.45 billion in 1986, up from only $239 million in 1982.[25]

China as a Site for Tourist Ventures

Foreign-operated hotels and other services for foreigners have multiplied since 1978 as swarming tourists and throngs of international business people became a common feature of China's major cities. Some of these hotels have been profitable, both in revenue as well as in benefits to the international image of their parent companies. However, since many major Chinese cities have encountered a hotel glut, some of these ventures are in trouble. Because hotel projects sap local areas of raw materials such as steel and cement, in addition to foreign exchange, government authorities have tried to discourage further hotel construction by curtailing loans for such projects. While the government allowed to flourish a new system of land leasing to foreigners who want to build hotels and other commercial sites, it also claims that it wants to restrict approval of foreign real estate projects.

After the land leasing system started in Shanghai, in 1987, dozens of other cities jumped on the bandwagon to auction thirty- to fifty-year land leases to foreign interests for hard cash. One typical deal involves the lease of a 1.3-ha site in an economic and technical development zone (ETDZ) near Shanghai for fifty years at a total cost of $28 million. That represents about one-thirteenth the current land value in Tokyo. Profitable leasing deals obtained by foreign hotel builders infuriate foreign partners of earlier joint venture hotel deals signed in the early 1980s. In those agreements, the venture duration period was set for ten to fifteen years, hardly enough time to accrue the profits projected for new projects built on leased land.[26]

The hotel construction boom has also spawned country clubs and golf courses, whose target patrons include foreign business people and top-brass Chinese officials. Party Secretary Zhao Ziyang, an avid golfer, has led the country's golf craze and acts as honorary chairman of the China Golf Association. The first golf course was built near Guangzhou and designed by Arnold Palmer. Its success has driven city officials in all major tourist centers to follow suit and begin construction on their

Growth of Tourism in China Since 1978

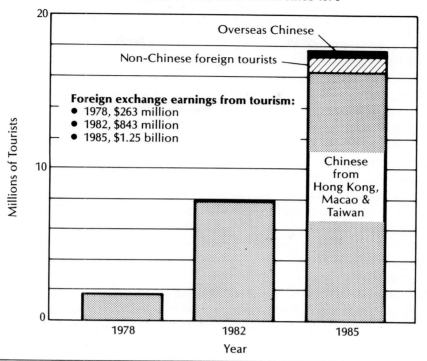

SOURCE: *Statistical Yearbook of China, 1986*, State Statistical Bureau, People's Republic of China.

own fairways, putting greens, and clubhouses. The Japanese have built both the Beijing Golf Club and the Beijing International Golf Club, finding incentive, to be sure, in the fact that country clubs in Tokyo charge up to $500,000 in membership fees. China's golf craze may not promise direct sales of golf clubs, balls, clothing, training videos, and so on, but cooperative manufacturing of golf paraphernalia, as well as other sporting goods, has certainly piqued the interest of U.S. companies.[27]

THE UNORTHODOXY OF CHINA BUSINESS

In 1935, Charles Moser wrote in a Department of Commerce publication that foreign mercantile pioneers in the China market "have learned that vast populations do not necessarily mean vast markets." His reasoning was irrefutable: The Chinese lacked buying power to purchase significant quantities of foreign goods since most of the population existed in a state of dire poverty. There were also the barriers of language and customs between Chinese and foreigners. Poor communications and transport services, by coolie-back or canal junk, made delivery problematic. The added expense of irregular taxation and petty exactions made upon the foreign merchant at every provincial border and customs house led Moser to conclude that "the China merchant who has brought his foreign goods into treaty port with costs, freight, and duty paid, often finds his major problems still ahead of him."[28] More than a few embittered China traders might claim that the same is true of China trade today. To be sure, many of the earliest stumbling blocks to successful trading in China are as formidable today as they were fifty, and even 100, years ago.

Ample business opportunities in the China market certainly exist, but there is nothing easy and fast about it. The most vexing of all the obstacles to achieving sustainable sales, as Moser suggested, remains the country's long-time lack of buying power relative to its huge population, which is still 80 percent rural and very poor. Chinese consumers have little or no access to foreign exchange to buy imported goods. Because China's economy is extremely vulnerable to foreign economic interaction, Chinese officials are also concerned about inflation and the flight of foreign exchange currency out of the country. China also guards its domestic market since access to it is the country's major bargaining chip in dealing with multinational firms. The central government controls access to its market through a system of state-controlled import and export organizations, as well as tariff and non-tariff barriers. It allocates foreign exchange quotas for the purchase of imports to certain localities according to priorities set in the national economic plan. These allocations can vary from year to year. For example, in the case where foreign exchange reserves become depleted, localities may be restricted from spending their usual allocation on imports.[29] The import potential of any locality is thereby linked to its export performance and indigenous foreign exchange earnings. Two tariff increases in 1985 were part of a general tightening over foreign exchange management and spending. The average increase was 44 percent, though in some investment areas where preferential treatment is given to foreign firms, the rates have dropped into the 10–30 percent range. The new tariff structure is both a tactic to control domestic and national FTCs, and a device to limit domestic sales by foreign companies.

China's tariffs are split into two categories: (1) minimum tariffs that are applied to Hong Kong, Macao, and other countries that have signed commercial agreements with China, and (2) general tariffs that apply to all other countries. Tariffs on machinery and materials that China lacks tend to be low, between 3 percent and 6 percent. For consumer products, tariffs and surcharges can amount to over 200 percent of the product's original price. Exemptions are made on goods and materials used by companies with foreign capital participation and those used in the manufacturing of products for export. Import tariff rates tend to vary from region to region according to the whim of individual customs officials.

Nontariff barriers to the market range from those inspired by the Chinese government to those that are natural limitations of the country's highly bureaucratized marketplace. Import licensing restrictions imposed on Chinese end-users continue to vex foreign traders seeking China deals, especially in provinces far removed from China's coastal areas where importers enjoy more buying authority. Government-imposed licensing regulations in priority areas can change unpredictably, catching suppliers off guard. More than a few firms have dedicated huge quantities of human and financial resources to pry open a market niche only to see it shut down a year or so later by government fiat. The harshest licensing crackdown came in early 1986, when China curtailed the issuance of import licenses for microcomputers. After selling more microcomputers in 1985 than in all previous years combined, sales of microcomputers to China plummeted to zero. The list on page 26 of goods requiring import licensing could be updated on a monthly basis.

China's morass of industrial bureaucracy represents a significant nontariff barrier to potential customers and slows the task of locating buyers who are both willing to spend precious foreign exchange on imported products and able to obtain the appropriate import licenses. Without detailed organization charts of central and local government bureaucracy, identifying key acquisition decision makers in the Chinese bureaucracy can result in costly delays. A dearth of information regarding the needs of Chinese consumers and industrial units only makes problems worse for the foreign trader.

Moreover, the country's prime objective to become an export manufacturing site on a par with South Korea and Singapore diminishes the potential for sustained sales of imported goods. Since adopting an export-led industrial strategy in 1979, the People's Republic has

List of Products Subject to China's Import Licensing Control

Motor vehicles
Motorcycles
Vehicle cranes
Electron microscopes
Electronic color scanners
Open-end spinning machines
X-ray cathode testers
Copying machines
Air-conditioners
Computers
Pocket calculators
Video recorders
Cameras
Duplicating equipment for recording
    and video tapes
TV sets
Radio-recorders
Refrigerators
Washing machines
TV kinescopes
Tape recorder mechanisms
Radios
Watches
Electric fans
Bicycles
TV assembly lines
Radio-recorder assembly lines

Refrigerator assembly lines
Washing machine assembly lines
Air-conditioner assembly lines
Motorcycle assembly lines
Minibus assembly lines
Steel
Rubber
ABS resin
Sulphuric acid
Polycarbonate resin
Rubber tyres
Timber
Pesticides
Medicinal herbs (15 varieties):
    antelope horn, rhinocerous horn,
    tiger bone, leopard bone, musk,
    cowbezoar, hippo-campus,
    armadillo-scale, cultivated ginseng,
    bantaroi seed, cardamon inferior,
    cardamon, dragons blood, aloes
    wood, and saffron
Tobacco
Synthetic fibres
Synthetic fibre monomer
Synthetic fabrics
Demolition equipment for civil use

SOURCE: *Intertrade*, February 1987.

pursued ties with foreign firms to promote the introduction of its own products in overseas markets, to the distress of foreign marketers. One of the first U.S. firms to source products from China was J.C. Penney, which began buying sweaters and shirts from China's central textile corporation as early as 1980.[30] The author witnessed a typical encounter between American and Chinese business people at a meeting held at the Sloan School of Management at the Massachusetts Institute of Technology (M.I.T.) in 1985. A sales team from Motorola had just completed a presentation of the product lines that it desired to sell to China, including semiconductors and miniature communication devices. Motorola representatives opened the meeting for questions. The attending Chinese delegation had only one question—whether Motorola would be interested in buying silicon from China for production of its semiconductors. The room filled with restrained laughter.

Gaining Leverage in the China Market

In an effort to gauge the marketing leverage points that U.S. corporations have found effective in China, a questionnaire was distributed to U.S. corporations currently selling manufactured goods to Chinese customers. The results underscore the unorthodox, hard-sell nature of conducting direct sales to the Chinese. The following analysis of the responses reveals some of the unique features of the market and how U.S. firms have sought to gain leverage in their dealings with the People's Republic.

Technology as a Bargaining Chip.   Respondents to the author's questionnaire indicated that offering state-of-the-art technology was the most vital factor in successful China sales. All of the respondents claimed that advanced technology was either "important" or "crucial" in selling to China, the highest rating given to any of the criteria tested. Those firms offering the technology that will assist China in accomplishing its import substitution objectives are finding the market remarkably accessible. While this may sound like a rather simplistic quid pro quo, it is not as easy to accomplish as it may appear. The process of technology transfer to China is slowed by the fact the U.S. government must approve advanced technology exports to Communist countries. The management of technology, once it is acquired by China, presents its own complex problems. Many U.S. firms lack the necessary preparation to assist China in assimilating technologies or to correctly assess China's exact technological needs. Others simply lack adequate incentives to do so.

Recently, many important projects have been going to European firms because of their willingness to transfer technology under more flexible arrangements. Italian, French, West German, and United Kingdom companies often view technology transfer to developing countries in a different light than Japanese or American firms. From the characteristically European perspective of Tom Hans-Gerd Neglein, a board member of West Germany's manufacturing firm, Siemen's: "One-way knowledge transfers are not money-losing propositions. Worldwide, transfers are generating substantial business for [Siemen's] growing services divisions."[31] This board member realizes that by locating his technology in China early, China may grow more dependent on the company's backup service and spare parts. Many firms hesitate to

What does your firm consider crucial to succeed at selling products in the People's Republic?

	Not Important	Important	Crucial
"State-of-the-art technology and superior quality"	0%	64%	36%
"Knowledge of specific needs of the end user"	4%	64%	32%
"Old-friend status among Chinese in a position to influence decision to purchase"	14%	59%	27%
"Firm/brand name recognition among Chinese industrial managers and officials"	23%	59%	18%
"Low-bid price"	22%	69%	9%
"Flexibility in payment terms/financing"	28%	72%	0%

SOURCE: Author's survey (see appendix for complete form of this questionnaire).

transfer technology to China, fearing that China's recently modified patent law may not offer sufficient protection against dual use of sensitive technologies or an effective means by which compensation could be sought if technologies are misused. Yet such transfers seem to be a central means of leverage in China's burgeoning market. In the words of David Simpson, vice chairman of Gould Electronics, foreign firms planning a long-term relationship with China "must provide the Chinese with the seeds of their technology."[32]

Understanding End-User Needs.

The most important criterion for successful selling in China is the advanced technology that a company offers through its product line. The second most important criterion is the knowledge of the Chinese end-users' needs that a foreign firm demonstrates in marketing its product line. In China, serving the customer means understanding the specific manufacturing capabilities, equipment preferences, and financial position of particular Chinese enterprises. Unfortunately, as mentioned earlier, pertinent information about Chinese enterprises is difficult to find without spending time and energy scouting opportunities in person, in China. Few, if any, reputable market analysis organizations exist that can gather together enough relevant customer preference information for a foreign firm to properly promote its products. Product marketing has traditionally been handled by FTCs on behalf of the foreign supplier. In reports produced by Chinese sources, a large population is often mistaken for large numbers of potential buyers. To avoid this mistake, any *preinvestment* activity in the China market should be directed toward feasibility studies and product-usage surveys rather than initiating a corporate presence in China, which can be much more expensive and will likely produce only negligible returns.

Informal Contacts.

Preinvestment in China might also include the strategic cultivation of contacts among China's trade officials and participation in trade seminars, technical seminars, and trade fairs by company representatives destined to be expatriated to China. Questionnaire respondents also indicated that the market is a "who-you-know" market, and those with old-friend status among acquisition decision makers tend to sign contracts.

China shares with East Asian markets a high level of bureaucratic involvement in its distribution sector. Foreign sellers must fit into what has been called the "iron triangle," which involves a government oversight entity, an end-user, and an FTC.[33] Foreign firms must obtain approval of sales from key provincial, municipal, and factory-level officials. Entrenched producer-distributor relationships are often based on *guanxi*, personalized business relationships based on informal favor-giving, which can exclude a new product from the market even though it may be better, cheaper, and more available.

Company Reputation.   The Chinese buy from those foreign firms that they recognize from pre-revolutionary days or that have an excellent brand-name reputation. Thus, the old pioneer firms in China, such as General Electric, Mobil Oil, and Siemen's of West Germany, have a head start in their marketing efforts over newcomers with less name recognition among Chinese industrial end-users.

In developing good reputations among Chinese customers, companies have placed a high priority on keeping their products serviced once they have been sold. Many firms have gone so far as to set up service centers which are run by Chinese personnel. Other firms have offered to run these service centers themselves, seeing product service as extremely important to future sales. One successful U.S. trading company, U.S.-China Industrial Exchange, Inc., has adopted a "serve-every-customer" philosophy. Through its China service center, it hopes to reap the benefits when the company's reputation grows through China by word-of-mouth.[34]

Low Price.   The common perception of Chinese buying priorities is that low price is key to selling in China. Foreign traders of all nationalities indicate repeatedly that the Chinese will not buy unless the price is rock bottom. Oddly, only 9 percent of the twenty-seven firms responding to the author's questionnaire rated low price as crucial to sales. Sixty-nine percent of the respondents, however, indicated low price was indeed "important."

In their attempts to circumvent China's inability to pay cash for imported goods, foreign firms have tried numerous stratagems, including compensation trade arrangements and barter deals. For some firms, leasing equipment to the Chinese is the answer. Three Japanese firms, including C. Itoh and Co., have recently formed Yellow River International with four Chinese companies and a French concern. The plan is to set up an equipment leasing company in Henan Province to import machinery, plants, and assorted industrial equipment to lease to the People's Republic at low interest rates. The company predicts $200 million in business in its first five years.[35] Two U.S. companies involved in leasing in the People's Republic include Security Pacific Bank and Equitable Life Leasing.

Preferential Financing/Terms.   Questionnaire respondents ranked concessionary financing behind all the other selling criteria tested. Nevertheless, after the foreign exchange drain on the Chinese economy in 1984–85, it has become imperative for foreign firms to offer creative packaging of credit and loan guarantees in order to win "big project" contracts.

Venturing in China

American corporations have discovered, albeit reluctantly, that acquiring usable information on Chinese buying patterns and specific end-user needs is akin to the task given to Sisyphus of Greek mythology, who was made to push forever a stone ball to the top of a hill only to have it roll back upon him. American marketing executives also find selling technology to Chinese disconcerting, since the Chinese rarely can pay for it outright. Finally, U.S. companies have found the task of networking among procurement decision makers while building a sound corporate reputation in China expensive and sometimes impossible unless they take their China involvement a step further. In rapidly expanding numbers, U.S. corporations have found it necessary to set up collaborative or solely owned ventures in China in order to gain critically needed leverage strength in the market. Whether the involvement is in manufacturing, distribution, or a service, these corporations have decided that the problems of market access can best be surmounted by deepening their relationship with the Chinese through a China venture. Unable to offer large-scale government-backed financing, or compete with Japanese soga sosha companies in terms of price, corporate America has begun to realize that its most direct and sustainable avenue into the China market is one of equity investment in China-based enterprises. This requires the transfer of technology, the sharing of management expertise, and joint ownership. As such, many U.S. firms have discovered that selling to the China market requires venturing in the China market.

Establishing a production facility in China greatly enhances a foreign firm's marketing effort there. In a growing number of cases, foreign joint venture partners have successfully negotiated contracts stipulating that a significant percentage of their production may be marketed in China: Coca-Cola markets soft drinks, Kodak sells film, Gillette markets razors, Nabisco sells food, Foxboro sells industrial controls, Volkswagen sells automobiles, and Hitachi sells television sets. Often, continuing sales of parts and components can be made to the factory where licensing of technology takes place. The presence of the foreign firm in the Chinese economy can help to expand the direct sales of the parent company's product lines. Foreign firms operating China ventures can contact Chinese industrial end-users directly, often bypassing the pro forma contract between a foreign firm and a government-controlled import/export agency that is still required. For example, because of its status as a domestic factory, China Hewlett-Packard (CHP) can sell its China-made products to Chinese end-users directly for foreign exchange or Rmb, whichever it chooses. Even more impressive, CHP has been included in the Chinese system of production quotas, in which the government buys a certain percentage of the factory's annual production, thus generating consistent Rmb profit for the joint venture partners.[36]

Market access tends to increase with corporate flexibility. Foreign business partners willing to accept a portion of payment in compensation trade and oversee the training of workers and the marketing of production will find their Chinese partners more receptive to accepting a higher percentage of production for domestic sales. One might recall from the analysis of the China market presented earlier how often Chinese trade officials make it a condition of direct sales that foreign firms source a portion of the total set of purchased equipment within China. Auto manufacturers have found that a key leverage device in entering agreements involves the localization of parts and components manufacturing in China.

Modes of venture leveraging can take other forms, as well. Some firms have found they can penetrate the market by offering services and training to the Chinese. Service centers have other direct benefits, such as increasing product applications, facilitating software exchange, and developing a larger customer base. Perkin-Elmer, a U.S.-based machinery manufacturer, has utilized its service center to make direct sales of its products.[37] Honeywell, which sells computer systems in China, is another firm that stations a high ratio of service personnel in China; over half of its forty personnel in China are working in customer service.[38]

Remember, however, that an inherent part of China's approach to foreign joint ventures is to require that they balance their foreign exchange accounts, which can be difficult since Chinese renminbi currency is nonconvertible in world money markets. For this reason, joint ventures must successfully export a large percentage of their production, sometimes leaving little to sell to the domestic market. The revenue joint ventures earn from exports must be used to pay workers' salaries, buy raw materials, pay dividends to partners, employ foreign staffs, and import machinery and parts. Consequently, only exporting joint ventures can obtain the foreign exchange to permit the foreign partner to remit any earnings abroad. By demanding that a large percentage of the goods produced by joint ventures be exported, the Chinese government has implicitly limited access to local markets. In short, venturing in China may remedy some of the problems associated with China marketing by enhancing a foreign firm's ability to leverage for market access. However, the multiple requisites of operating in China cannot be ignored.

STRATEGIC APPROACHES TO INVESTING IN CHINA

Defining a corporate approach to investing in a China venture is a matter of in-house formulation of strategic objectives and is quite divorced from the ground-level realities of selling a product in China. There are a variety of reasons that firms set up subsidiaries and collaborative ventures overseas. Some firms are looking to lower overhead in their export manufacturing; some are searching for fresh sources of raw inputs; some set up in foreign countries to access foreign technologies or markets, and so on. The same holds true for China, with some notable differences.

How should a company position itself in China, as opposed to Japan, South Korea, Taiwan, and other Pacific Basin countries? By looking at the corporate strategies that American firms currently follow in Asia, a corporate planner can begin to develop an appropriate China market strategy. An appropriate China strategy recognizes the potential (hidden and apparent) of China's market and indigenous industrial capabilities, embodies a long-term commitment, and is designed not only to exploit opportunities in China, but to tie together other elements of the firm's global strategy.

Corporate Strategies Pursued in the Asia/Pacific Region

Strategic planning for a China venture should begin with a close look at the corporate strategy that your firm is pursuing in the Asia/Pacific region already.[39] Strive for continuity between your China and Pacific Rim approaches. American corporations pursue eight different corporate strategies in the Asia/Pacific region. Before speaking in specific terms about China venture strategies, let us glance briefly at these eight Asia strategies.

Manufacturing for Export.

An export platform strategy aims to increase the price competitiveness of a product line by cutting the cost of production. This end is attained by employing cheaper labor, renting cheaper land to place a factory, locating where taxes are low, etc. In this strategy, as taxation has outstripped wage in importance as a percentage of production, companies have been locating throughout Asia on the basis of preferential regulations concerning taxes, fees, and rental rates. Overhead may also be cut when firms locate close to their markets, since they can reduce transportation costs. In this way, they can also acquire cheaper, locally sourced raw materials. This approach is used by U.S. companies in Taiwan and the Philippines where export zones offer an exceptionally attractive setting for offshore subsidiaries. A more recent application of this strategy is in Thailand, where wage rates are the lowest in the Asia/Pacific region.

Developing and Exploiting Natural Resources.

Companies in resource-poor nations often make investments overseas as part of their quest for new sources of raw production inputs such as coal, oil, lumber, rubber, copper, and uranium. Often, resource exploitation projects in Asia find their funding through government loans and aid packages made available by the Asia Development Bank, the World Bank, and other international banking institutions. The added costs of pursuing this strategy usually involve infrastructural development to facilitate the transportation of raw materials from the interior of the source country to the receiving country.

Sharing the Burden of R&D.

Under this investment strategy, a firm usually forms a joint venture partnership with a counterpart that possesses the in-house resources and/or government backing to share the expense of developing a new product that it cannot afford to develop on its own because of high cost and high risk. In Asia, this strategy is growing in popularity as the cost of developing technologically sophisticated products skyrockets, and without a lessening of the inherent risk that the new product may fail in the marketplace, even with a concerted R&D effort behind it. Also, the increasingly modular nature of global industrial systems (in which separate parts of a complex product are developed by different countries) demands that firms share and coordinate their technological endeavors with widely dispersed business partners.[40] For example, the exorbitant cost of developing new airliners has prompted Boeing to follow this investment strategy in Japan, where it has teamed up with a consortium of Japanese companies to share the burden of developing its 757 and 767 aircraft.[41]

Holding Ground in a New Market.

As a result of the development of new technology and the acquisition of older technology by Asian nations, these once noncompetitive nations are quickly entering the fold of the world economy as producers of manufactured products. To maintain market share in the face of growing economies-of-scale in Asia, many U.S. firms have entered venture agreements simply to hold ground in emerging markets where, before long, indigenous producers will have acquired similar technology to produce the products on their own. Many times, this strategy involves technology transfer via licensing. For firms that have no presence in a burgeoning Asian market, licensing may be a way to lessen the negative effects of not participating directly in the market, especially if its competition has a secure presence already.[42]

Acquiring New Technology.

When the parent firm cannot afford to develop new technology, it can opt to form a joint venture with an overseas firm that has already developed it, in an effort to acquire that technology. This pursuit may be urgent if the newly developed technology represents a radical breakthrough that threatens the competitiveness of the firm's present product lines. As technological innovation becomes more globalized, many firms will enter Asia simply for technological survival; that is, if they don't, their products will soon become obsolete.[43]

Transplanting Corporate Rivalry into a New Market.

In this investment strategy, competition between corporate rivals—for example, Pepsi and Coke, or Xerox and Fujitsu—is superimposed on a new playing field. Often these firms set up wholly foreign-owned subsidiaries as part of a battering ram approach that seeks a share of a new market. These companies must be sure to protect their technological know-how from spreading into the recipient country, which would create an undesired competitor.

Co-opting the Competition. What happens when an Asian company acquires, steals, or simply develops technology that is identical to that on which a multinational corporation currently bases its competitiveness? What happens when that company suddenly floods markets with low-priced, high-quality goods produced with that technology? In an effort at damage control, a multinational corporation may choose to acquire control of the Asian company through stock ownership and/or equity joint venture. This investment strategy has been popular among U.S. automakers, who have been losing ground to Japanese and Korean automakers. General Motors' joint venture with Toyota, for example, was formed, in part, so that GM could co-opt Toyota's share of the U.S. market.[44]

Penetrating a New Market. The most popular investment strategy pursued in Asia aims to capture new markets by setting up operations in-country, behind tariff and nontariff barriers, via any number of different business forms. To gain access to the market, the foreign firm must offer the necessary concessions. These often include transferring advanced technology, sourcing supplies from domestic sources, exporting a certain percentage of production, and offsetting a percentage of production to indigenous producers.

Corporate Strategies Pursued in the People's Republic

No one doubts that participating in China's investment opportunities entails great risks. For this reason, most of the firms entering China and making financial commitments are large multinational corporations that already have a worldwide network of subsidiary companies and factories. (Responses to the author's questionnaire indicate that the average U.S. joint venture partner in China exports to seventy-four developed and underdeveloped countries and employs a total of 32,543 workers worldwide.) For these companies, entry into the China market has been simply part of their expansion process as they seek new markets around the world. They enter China because it offers potentially substantial returns as the last market frontier in the world.[45] At the same time, they recognize the exploratory nature of their China ventures and, hence, they rarely locate critical production facilities in China. They choose to pay a high price to secure a presence in China while pursuing short-term opportunities that require modest amounts of capital investment and limited exposure. Most firms have postponed key undertakings, but show a commitment to developing fruitful business relations. One Chinese publication cited the cases of thirty multinational corporate subsidiaries whose investments in China were not based on seeking large profits, but were rather just a testing of the waters.[46] Once rooted in the market, they can test their products and gather information about the Chinese business climate, as well as develop contacts with important Chinese decision makers. In learning the Chinese way of doing business, they are also appraising the quality of Chinese labor and the sanctity of investment regulations, while obtaining a certain amount of access to the domestic market.

The majority of foreign firms that have pursued China opportunities through direct investment have done so under a strategy aimed solely at penetrating a new market. On the other hand, in terms of the monetary value of total foreign investment in China, the most important strategy remains one of development and exploitation of resources, especially petroleum reserves in the South China Sea. (It should be mentioned that a number of multinational corporations responding to the author's follow-up questionnaire indicate that their main reason for forming joint ventures in China was, indeed, to access a new market. However, because many of them produce consumer products made with perishable materials, such as cigarettes and foodstuffs, their secondary reason for choosing China was that it is an important source for the raw materials that they require to make their products.) There appear to be few, if any, U.S. firms entering China to acquire new technology, share the burden of R&D, or co-opt the competition. However, these will be the approach modes of the future in China. Also, few U.S. firms have set up in China solely to export to world markets on a large scale. Many firms have been forced to export a certain percentage of their production to gain market access in China, however, and scores of very small Sino-foreign enterprises have been formed in SEZs with the objective of exporting light industrial products and foodstuffs to Hong Kong and Macao. Unlike Taiwan and Japan, China seems ambivalent toward the creation of an attractive investment environment for offshore export manufacturing. Although it advertises itself as an attractive site for export manufacturing, foreign investors have discovered that Chinese labor is expensive relative to skill level and that because China lacks the necessary support industries—service backup, quality control, and available components—success is sometimes virtually impossible. (See Chapter 2 for further discussion of support industries.)

CORPORATE AMERICA'S APPROACH IN CHINA

Most American firms in China have set up ventures in order to build a low-risk bridgehead into China's domestic market. By making direct investments in the form of a joint venture or coproduction agreements, U.S. firms believe they can get closer to the Chinese market than by merely licensing their technology to a Chinese factory. In many cases—especially joint ventures in special economic zones (SEZs), factories built specifically to replace imports, and joint venture firms that transfer high technology into China—U.S. firms have been allowed to sell directly to the domestic market.

Over 90 percent of the U.S. firms with investment in China that responded to the author's questionnaire indicated that they entered China specifically to sell to the market.

These strategic investments may also take advantage of Chinese labor and inexpensive start-up costs and may be motivated by a desire to get closer to certain raw materials. Firms sometimes leverage a commitment to a joint venture in return for guaranteed supplies of certain materials.

Two other strategic imperatives are played out by U.S. firms in the People's Republic. Both are related to maintaining market presence in China, and so fit into the general category of penetrating the China market. They are: (1) transplanting corporate rivalry, and (2) holding ground in a new market.

Transplanting Rivalries to China.   Essentially, firms in this category have entered China to gain a foothold in the market before other firms in the same line of business do so. Also, some multinationals fear that if they do not enter China now, the best Chinese partners may be taken by their competitors. By opening its doors to foreign firms, China has allowed, both implicitly and explicitly, the entry of multinational competition within its borders.

By seeking out a position in the China market, multinationals are responding to two possible types of competition. The first is home country competition, where China becomes the site for the playing out of competition among other domestic firms and themselves.[47] The American computer manufacturers Wang Laboratories and Hewlett-Packard currently vie for China sales through their joint ventures. From Japan, Sanyo and Hitachi do the same as they compete for shares of China's consumer electronics market. The second type is transnational

Why did your firm enter China?	
"To sell products in China"	92%
"To export from China"	18%
"To utilize lower cost labor"	11%
"Other reasons (unspecified)"	7.5%

NOTE: Some respondents cited more than one reason for entering China; therefore, the total percentage adds up to more than 100 percent.

SOURCE: Author's survey (see appendix for complete form of this questionnaire).

competition, where competing firms from different countries transplant their rivalry into China. Many U.S. firms realize that Japanese and European firms could prove insurmountable world export competitors in the long run if allowed to capture the China market, especially if China's modernization program develops to its full potential. American Motors Corporation (AMC), now owned by Chrysler, and Volkswagen set up early automobile manufacturing joint ventures in China attempting to gain strong footholds in the market by agreeing to source domestically made components. Much the same trend occurs in the telecommunications and aerospace sectors.

Holding Ground in China.   Some American firms enter China ventures primarily to protect and defend market share that they assumed safely belonged to them. As a firm's competitors enter the market, the prudent company might choose to hedge its China prospects by participating in a venture that promises to position the company firmly within the Chinese industrial economy. Also, the firm can lock down a well-qualified Chinese venture partner before its competition does. By being on the inside, some firms avoid import restrictions set up to offset the purchases of foreign goods. These firms believe that their presence in the market may offer an attractive advantage if import restrictions in their product lines are tightened, since this action would reduce the competitiveness of rival companies selling to China. *Business International* has termed this strategy "protection against PRC [People's Republic of China] protectionism."

In addition, many firms have established service-oriented businesses in China as a means of safeguarding market share, following their product sales or joint ventures into China to cultivate satisfied customers. Foxboro, one of the most often cited joint ventures, set up a sales and service arm in order to expand its market, but more important, to dispel any notion that dealing with a foreign firm would be a liability in terms of service and maintenance. Foxboro officials wanted to demonstrate that dealing with the Foxboro joint venture would be an asset in comparison with dealing with other foreign firms without an equity presence in the People's Republic.

Developing China's Resources.   Few countries in the world can claim such a rich endowment of natural resources as that possessed by the People's Republic. Many U.S. companies involved in petroleum, coal, and mineral development have entered China as part of their world exploration and development endeavors. Chinese raw materials are not altogether a good bargain, however, because of infrastructure deficiencies that add overhead. For example, Occidental Petroleum has begun work on the Antaibao mine in Shanxi Province, but many experts doubt that the company will be able to export the coal at a competitive price since it must pay for needed transportation facilities and added coal refinement to bring the coal from the mine up to world-class quality. Another resource that attracts foreign investment to China is the South China Sea, one of the last frontiers of unexplored offshore oil. China depends on petroleum as its most lucrative export industry. Unfortunately, the country's onshore oil wells seem to be running dry. Advanced onshore and offshore oil drilling expertise is badly needed.[48] Since China opened its sea tracts to a global sweepstakes, most of the major oil companies have entered into exploration contracts with China. Foreign oil consortia have spent over $2 billion searching for oil off the coast of China, though the terms that the Chinese offer are not as good as those offered by Malaysia. The most noteworthy discoveries have been by Chinese firms, however, in Liaodong Bay north of Bohai, with reserves of an estimated 900 million barrels, and in the south. Agip-Chevron-Texaco, Phillips, Japes Huanan, and Amoco all made first-time discoveries in 1987. The contractual deals signed in 1985 between foreign oil companies and the Chinese have all been for the exploration and development of 3,800–5,100 kilometers of survey/seismic lines, with thirty-year durations, and worth between $62 and $160 million each.[49] Foreign interest has declined due to both the drastic weakening of oil prices in 1986, and, more importantly, the revelation that another

Saudi Arabia does not lie submerged in the South China Sea. American companies entered into long-term contacts with China, obligating them to train Chinese workers and to transfer technology. These contracts have proved disappointing at best.

Recently, China has offered new onshore oil tracts to be explored in ten southern provinces. Foreign interest has been subdued since this oil would be difficult and costly to refine, involving secondary and tertiary processing. Some oil company representatives confirm, however, that China has softened on contract terms with foreign oil companies because it is realizing that the high cost of doing business in China has drained away foreign oil company profits.

Strategic Horizons: Planning for China's Global Role

American executives and business pundits speak often, and sometimes loftily, about the globalization of U.S. companies in the late 1980s. Corporate America has responded to calls from the global wild because so many of its foreign competitors have already staked out a global presence. Even China is moving, albeit slowly, in a global direction by investing overseas, increasing trade with a growing number of countries, and interacting with the world's financial institutions. As China's role in the global economy widens, setting up ventures in China will become more important as a part of a foreign firm's international marketing and manufacturing strategy.

The significant question for U.S. corporations over the long term, and the one more closely linked to corporate global strategies, is how a firm's presence in China can be leveraged to gain a competitive advantage in other markets. As opposed to strategy focusing primarily on China's domestic market, a global strategy needs to be based on certain critical assumptions about the success of China's modernization drive and its ability to achieve stated technological and economic goals. Assuming that China will establish a highly visible presence in the global economy, firms should be seeking a long-term relationship with China that could combine various research and production assets of both parties to develop and manufacture competitive products to be sold in regional and international markets. American firms can articulate two additional business strategies in China that address the needs of a globalized corporation.

Co-opting Chinese Competition.   As Chinese companies become competitive, a few multinational firms will desire a controlling stake in them which they seek through part ownership. These firms have entered China not only to compete among themselves or protect market share, but also to stay abreast of their Chinese industrial competitors.[50] Recognizing that China's R&D and industrial sectors have made headway in certain areas, a select number of firms have already decided to plug into these developments, hoping to build strong working relationships with the most dynamic and advanced units in the Chinese economy. Both U.S. and Japanese firms have concluded that as China becomes more competitive in export markets it will become imperative to be operating inside the country. In this way, these firms believe they can shape the growth of the Chinese economy and influence the course of future developments in their particular industry.

Sharing the Burden of R&D with China.   In the near term, the People's Republic will foster more sharing of R&D endeavors by allotting revenue earned from exports for cooperative projects that they are willing to help finance. Possible project areas that will certainly produce opportunities for American firms desiring to split the cost of R&D will include aerospace, nuclear power, satellite communications, and superconductivity. This type of collaboration may also take place in the development of software designed especially for the Chinese business and manufacturing environment. Wang and Visidata have already participated in Shanghai in this area. As China achieves technological capability in these same areas foreign firms may, in the future, discover that they will acquire some advanced technology from China.

AMERICA'S CORPORATE ENCOUNTER IN CHINA

Through experience and expanded academic research on the People's Republic, U.S. corporations have come to better understand the central objectives of China's open door policies. They have entered China with an awareness that the notion of China being technologically backward, economically stagnant, overcentralized, and hopelessly gridlocked in bureaucratic Communistic squabbling no longer matches many of the realities of China under Deng Xiaoping's reform policies. More important, they realize that the Chinese business climate is built upon, and part of, Deng's reform programs. Throughout the American business community, earlier fears that China might revert to Soviet-style centralized, anti-foreign policies, which were in place under Mao, have been largely replaced by a growing sense of security in China's current policies and commitments. More and more U.S. firms have gone into China as part of their global marketing strategy and to secure a more predictable export market in the People's Republic.

Since nearly all of the U.S. firms that have entered China via ventures have done so seeking market position, or hoping to hold onto market share, it comes as no surprise that U.S. firms most in need of new markets to bolster their position vis-à-vis their competitors have entered China in search of corporate renewal. Throughout the 1980s, many U.S. firms have experienced slumping sales as the result of Asian and European competition and world recession. In many cases, firms have entered China believing that market opportunities there would improve their overall profits and ameliorate cash flow problems. Interestingly, many relatively weak U.S. firms have entered China in hopes of exploiting the market ahead of their competition. They do so by leveraging for an advantageous position in the China market by taking greater risks in China than their more successful rivals. They offer more technology, more training, and are willing to accept less equity share in joint ventures while accepting more locally sourced raw materials and components. In some cases, these firms lack the necessary experience in managing equity joint ventures in developing countries as minority partners.

In some industries, China has attracted U.S. corporate stragglers—those at the back of the pack. For instance, a comparatively small computer firm, Wang Laboratories, has set up a manufacturing venture in China while IBM and Digital Equipment Corporation have resisted manufacturing joint ventures or technology transfer arrangements in China because they can sell computers directly to China based on their superior technology. (Meanwhile, IBM has formed numerous joint ventures in Japan.) In the automobile industry, AMC, a tottering U.S. automaker, entered a joint venture in China as a minority partner (AMC was acquired by Chrysler five years after entering the venture). Although AMC possessed significant experience in conducting overseas operations in developing countries as a minority partner, the size of the company ($3.3 billion in 1983) was minute compared with Ford ($44.5 billion in 1983) and General Motors ($74.6 billion in 1983). These larger companies have bypassed China and entered into ventures with Japan and Korea.

This is not to suggest that some of America's most successful firms are not entering China and setting up ventures. Many have done so, whether in pursuit of market position, to hold ground in a new market, or to square off against their competitors on a new battlefield. Indeed, America's leading oil companies are set up in China exploring for oil and mineral resources. Small U.S. firms, too, have gone into China in a start-up mode, hoping that their investment comes to fruition as China's modernization program gathers steam. These firms are not necessarily weak, they are merely small. The maneuverability associated with being small may offer these firms advantages not seen by multinational corporations. But unlike larger firms, they do not have the capital needed to sustain a long-term presence and endure minimal returns in the short term.

In many industries, especially those in which foreign firms seek both market access and a new source of raw materials, China has attracted both large and small U.S. firms. For example, Squibb, ranked thirteenth among U.S. pharmaceutical companies in 1983, has formed a drug manufacturing joint venture with China. Though relatively small, Squibb has venture experience in developing countries. At the same time, one of the giants of the industry, Johnson & Johnson, has also formed a joint venture in China. In the food industry, one finds an array of large and small U.S. firms entering joint ventures. Some firms, such as Coca-Cola, have used their strength to leverage for sole ownership of their China ventures in order to protect their proprietary know-how (in the food industry, to protect recipes) from being acquired by the Chinese.[51]

The combination of these trends has lent a speculative aura to the business of China venturing. The weaker firms vie for market position by offering concessions, while the big guns tend to hold off on entering manufacturing ventures—unless they need raw materials from China—and concentrate on direct sales into the market.

The competitive pressures of the China market often cause U.S. firms to bypass preliminary stages of market investigation, technology licensing, and direct sales to China—opportunities which may have offered more benefits than a joint venture with a Chinese partner. There have been some failures, but quite a few marketing successes as well. Some U.S. firms have succeeded in securing contracts stipulating that their percentage of sales to China's domestic market of joint venture production should increase each year. Other firms have devised methods of profit repatriation through countertrade, component purchasing, or soliciting foreign exchange allocations from Chinese authorities.

Diversifying Market Approach. Some of the most successful U.S. companies doing business in the People's Republic have expanded their mode of operations to include activities in more than one facet of the China market. A few joint venture partners have initiated trading-house operations, conducting countertrade in order to repatriate profits earned in Rmb; others have made investments in Chinese supplier factories to increase their China-sourced inputs; and a few have moved from mere selling of production to co-development of products designed specially for the China market. The converse is true as well. Firms that formulate strategy based on a single strategic imperative to the exclusion of others—for example, entering the China market because of the fear that one's competition will—while failing to scout opportunities, gauge market characteristics, and consider all the meddlesome difficulties of doing business in China are often the same firms that go belly-up in China.

Negotiating a deal in China often takes years to consummate, so many U.S. firms have pursued a strategy of diversifying their approach in China to maximize their profit potential. Some firms employ Hong Kong middlemen to penetrate one facet of the market while at the same time having an industrial office representative in China to service another. Others maintain multidivision offices in China. For example, Gould, Inc., splits its China staff into five groups—minicomputers and imaging systems, industrial animation, instrument systems, electronic components, and defense systems.[52] Unison Pacific Company divides its China staff into two groups, one handling investment in China and the other handling training and direct sales in China.[53] Bechtel's diversified approach to the China market includes training and consulting on the Dayawan Bay nuclear power plant, participating in the design and construction management of a Shenzhen hotel, and conducting engineering work at the Three Gorges hydroelectric project. In a market that runs very hot and suddenly cold, the strategy of diversifying the approach to the market seems well advised.

Even so, U.S. corporations have not succeeded in gaining widespread access to the China market. Highly disillusioned as a result of their initial experiences in the People's Republic, some firms have concluded that participation in the China market at this time may not be worth the high price. Some observers claim that the approach taken by U.S. firms to the market may not be effective for a number of years, but will eventually succeed. Others insist that U.S. corporate ineffectiveness may be occurring at the global strategic level and also at the level of the business relationship between American and Chinese partners. Some observers suggest that the U.S. corporate representatives in China have failed to learn effective business practices within the Chinese framework.

Success of the Japanese Approach. Unlike European and American firms, which are often willing to enter cooperative manufacturing agreements and transfer technology, Japanese business interests in China have depended mainly on direct sales of goods. The growth of the China market since 1980 has provided Japan's export-oriented economy with a valuable new market. The China market offers Japan's soga sosha unique opportunities; they can source raw materials throughout China in exchange for a vast array of Japanese manufactured products that they market. Acting as responsive middlemen in a burgeoning market, Japanese trading firms are also well placed to set up countertrade agreements, structure creative solutions to pricing and payment problems on the Chinese side, and strike quickly when new marketing opportunities arise. The first soga sosha in China, Nissho Iwai Corporation (NIC), focuses on setting up extremely complex transactions involving China, Japan, and third countries. In one deal worth $12 million, NIC shipped processed marine products from third countries to China National Cereals, Oil, and Foodstuffs Import/Export Corporation's Tanggu factory. From there the products were exported to the Japanese market. NIC amassed a $2 billion transaction volume with the People's Republic in 1986–87.[54]

The second, less intense phase of Japan's approach involves transferring into China its competing manufacturing firms that produce high-demand household consumer goods. The Chinese can now choose between a number of Japanese product lines. This move is in response to rising tariff barriers imposed by Chinese trade authorities on imported consumer goods. Many Japanese firms that produce restricted items are now positioned inside the tariff barriers looking out. Some of these equity-based ventures include Hitachi, set up in 1981 and producing color television sets; Sanyo Electric Company, Ltd., operating two ventures in Shenzhen that produce radios, televisions, and tape recorders; and Canon, which is furnishing parts for copiers in Zhanjiang, in Guangzhou Province.[55]

Although other Japanese firms, including Ricoh, Toshiba, and Matsushita Electric Industrial Co., Ltd., have established joint ventures in China, the Japanese have shown an aversion to setting up joint ventures there. The Chinese have complained about this lack of Japanese commitment, claiming that the Japanese only want to sell to China, thus worsening the trade deficit between the two countries. The Japanese, however, view the Chinese business climate as still too risky for large investment commitments. The reasons they cite are China's incomplete infrastructure, its high cost of electricity and water, and the short duration permitted for joint ventures.[56] Japanese firms have pursued a strategy of reduced operations and are patiently waiting for some of the most critical problems in the China market—conversion of profits, insufficient patent laws, and inaccessibility to the domestic market—to be ameliorated.[57] Nonetheless, Japanese firms are pursuing the opportunities that currently exist in China—namely, direct sales of industrial and consumer goods, assembly agreements, construction assistance, technical renovation consultancy, and technical assistance on supplied components. Clearly, Japanese firms are more interested in selling directly to China than in making direct investments there, even though this type of investment is increasing in the late 1980s as part of Japan's strategy of relocating its labor-intensive industries in low-wage countries in response to the appreciation of the yen. They are not convinced, however, that China is a viable site for manufacturing complex products for export. Instead, Japanese firms have turned their attention to Europe and the United States in their search for profitable manufacturing sites.

American Business Expectations and Responsibilities

In light of China's unique business atmosphere, the primary challenge to American firms in the People's Republic is to balance their expectations of China venturing with the realities of doing business there. At the same time, they must attempt to reassure Chinese leaders, partners, and trade officials by enunciating their corporate responsibilities to China and their commitment to playing a constructive role in the country's modernization program. As a general backdrop to the following

Primary Expectations Held by U.S. Firms Entering the China Market

▶ *Market access.* First and foremost, the expectation of U.S. firms to serve the China market is a direct outgrowth of carefully determined export strategies. Once established in China, these firms deem it essential that they gain access to all the markets they can serve. They expect not to be discriminated against by unfair treatment which could hinder them in dealing effectively with competition within China.

▶ *Stability in investment policies.* Some degree of stability is desired by U.S. firms, especially in those policies affecting their technology, investments, and personnel. They perceive a need for predictability on the part of Chinese government policymaking that affects foreign business in general, for example, taxation, tariffs, and visas. They also expect equal treatment and fair competition in negotiations and related business dealings.

▶ *Effective patent protection.* The right to effective protection for patents, technological know-how, trade secrets, and software also includes guarantees of confidentiality of technology and control of its dissemination. Further, firms expect limited competition for the use of technological assets while obtaining reasonable compensation for the use of such technology. Despite China's relatively undeveloped patent law, many firms insist on exclusivity clauses in their contracts with the Chinese, which many times detracts from their attractiveness as potential partners. Some firms insist that the transfer of their technology to China will occur only in factories in which the foreign firm is an owner or co-owner of the factory.

▶ *Legal protection for personnel and business investments.* Most firms realize that civil law (including tort law) is relatively undeveloped in China. However, they expect China's Law of Joint Ventures and statutes applying to foreign nationals in China to protect both their investments from expropriation and their expatriates from unfair treatment.

Responsibilities to China Perceived by U.S. Companies

▶ To introduce to China the best applicable technologies, expertise, and management skills. In addition, to train Chinese personnel, compensate them fairly, and offer them opportunities for self-advancement and promotion.

▶ To help design and provide adequate working facilities for the utilization of their technologies and skills. Also, to transfer their production and assembly knowledge in order to make the China venture as efficient as possible.

▶ To pursue China ventures with a long-term view, which requires patience and ethical practices. They realize the important role they play in contributing Western expertise to the development of China.

chapters, it might be interesting to preview the broad expectations of the China market that are commonly held by American executives (see the charts on the facing page and above).

China's long-term intention, as viewed by many U.S. corporations, is simply to develop its capabilities to export goods into international markets. After establishing a corporate presence inside China, many foreign firms have found the Chinese tentative, cautious, and pragmatic when it comes to actually buying foreign products. Recent corporate frustrations have also raised the question of whether the Chinese view their business relationships with foreign multinational firms as permanent, or as short-term business interactions to be curtailed once China meets its economic and technological modernization objectives. From this vantage point, the relationship between corporate America and China will remain uneasy until the basis upon which the foreign business community and China relate to each other is more clearly defined.

Foreign Investment in China: A Stocktaking

The main purpose of our policy of opening to the world is to import advanced foreign technology and managerial expertise and attract funds. In doing so, our ultimate aim is to improve the quality of our own products, to increase our capacity for self-reliance, and to speed up China's modernization.

Tian Jiyun
Vice Premier
January 6, 1986

For many Chinese, foreign trade prior to the Communist Revolution (1949) has been associated with a long history of exploitation of China's territory, security, economy, and cultural well-being. Historically, Sino-foreign trade has been marked by short periods of open, limited trade followed by longer periods of vehement Chinese opposition to commercial interaction with foreign traders. The images of exploitation of the Chinese populace and manipulation of its leaders are not soon forgotten in the Chinese collective psyche.

The intention here, however, is not to examine the motivations behind foreign exploitation of pre-revolutionary China. But it is important for present-day investors to realize that foreign investment* in China did not

---

* Please see the China Venture Lexicon on page xxiii for a definition of the term "foreign investment" as used throughout this book.

begin with China's opening in 1978, and therefore should not be viewed as existing in a historical vacuum. Although foreign trade with China has existed for centuries, under the tribute system, foreign participation in China's economy began at the conclusion of the Opium War (1839–1842) when Chinese ports were forced open to Western trading companies under a series of unequal treaties that drew harsh and debilitating concessions from the Chinese.[1] By 1902, total foreign investment in China had topped $500 million; by 1936, it had grown to $2.68 billion.[2]

Sensitive about their past experience with foreign nations, the Chinese allow foreigners to participate in their economy while maintaining strict protection of their national sovereignty and independence. From the Chinese perspective, interaction with foreign business interests must contribute directly to the national objectives of the People's Republic, and investment projects must be fully consistent with current policy goals. Chinese leaders are uneasy, and unwilling at times, to trade off political control of their affairs in return for economic and technological assistance to support their country's modernization drive. Their uneasiness tends to be most intense in regard to wholly foreign-owned ventures in their economy, since they fear such ventures allow foreigners to freely exploit Chinese labor and resources.

The victory of the Communists in 1949 signaled the beginning of a new phase in China's dealings with the outside world. In the early 1950s, attention was focused primarily on industrialization, including large-scale projects in iron, steel, nonferrous metals, and machinery. In their attempt to industrialize, the Chinese gave top priority to construction of facilities to produce automobiles, energy, chemicals, tractors, and aircraft. Desperately needing economic and technical assistance on which to base its development, China sought loans from the Soviet Union. In fact, just two months after the Communists took control of the country, Mao Zedong traveled to Russia to speak with Joseph Stalin about Russian economic aid to China. The result was both an agreement on loan provisions and the Treaty of Friendship, Alliance, and Mutual Assistance (ratified in February 1950).[3] During the following six years, over 150 complete sets of equipment and machinery were ordered from Russia for the development of airports, railways, power plants, agricultural renovation, educational and scientific research projects, and many other projects. By the end of the decade, 304 sets had been contracted. In 1960, however, Nikita Khruschev reacted to the widening rift between the Soviet Union and China by terminating all contracts with China and withdrawing all Soviet technicians and advisers. Though Chinese leaders were committed to continuing many of the projects after the Soviets departed, numerous projects had to be abandoned. By 1964, a year ahead of schedule, China had repaid the Soviet loans, which were given at a rate of 1 to 2 percent over two to ten years. Mao's experience with Russia intensified his push for self-sufficiency in Chinese industry and was responsible for the country's policy orientation during the years of 1960–78, which emphasized technological self-reliance and independence from foreign nations.

Throughout the 1960s, China diversified its list of supplier nations, spending $300 million to acquire production technology and equipment for the renovation of its chemical, machinery, electronics, metallurgical, and light industry sectors. In the years 1965–68, an additional fifty complete sets of equipment and eight whole plants were purchased from Japan, United Kingdom, France, West Germany, Switzerland, Italy, Netherlands, Belgium, and Austria.[4] Some of the larger plant acquisitions included those for the production of polyethylene, porous silica, vinyon fiber, refined oil, and synthetic ammonia.

In the late 1960s and early 1970s, however, the Cultural Revolution halted most acquisition activities and many projects had to be shelved. Nevertheless, China did import a sizable number of fertilizer and chemical plants from the West in the early 1970s.[5] After the Cultural Revolution, the death of Mao, and the demise of the Gang of Four in 1976, foreign contacts picked up at a rapid pace. The renewal of Sino-foreign communication coincided with the onset of the "four modernizations," which included an emphasis on reintegrating China with the world economy.

Between 1977 and 1978, a legion of Chinese delegations traveled abroad, visiting foreign factories and research institutes. Many of these delegations entered into working agreements and contracts with foreign firms for the purchase of numerous whole plants and substantial amounts of equipment. A number of the projects were either canceled or delayed, however, because of either a lack of funds or inadequate feasibility studies.[6] This was a serious setback for advocates of greater openness to the West, as it became clear that many of the problems generated by China's rather laissez-faire approach to these projects had cajoled state planners into spending 70 percent of the country's 1978 foreign exchange budget on only 22 foreign construction projects. It was at this time that foreign investment came to receive attention as a means not only to acquire needed foreign engineering services and turnkey plants, but also foreign technology, capital, and management expertise.

CHINA'S POLICY TOWARD FOREIGN INVESTMENT: A MODEL FOR UNDERSTANDING

For the purpose of historical perspective, this chapter treats the period of China's Open Door Policy (1978–88) in three distinct phases: 1978–81, 1982–84, and 1985–88. Within each of these phases, five sequential stages can be discerned as part of a revolving cycle of policy-making and investment fluctuations. The five stages within each time period are described briefly in the following order: (1) Chinese policy focuses on offering various concessions to the foreign investment community, including tax exemptions and more access to the domestic market; (2) a surge in foreign investment follows as investors respond to the concessions put forward; (3) foreign investors realize problems exist in the investment climate and voice complaints; (4) the rate of foreign investment decreases, joint venture commitments drop, while technology transfer projects decrease in number; and (5) an internal debate occurs in China as to how the investment climate can be improved to attract more foreign investment—a discussion that takes place against a background of deep concern for national self-reliance and independence. At the conclusion of the fifth phase, the pattern appears to begin again. As a consequence of internal debate within China about how to improve the investment climate, more concessions are issued.

Of course, it is not the purpose here to prove that this cycle has occurred in exactly the same way for each of the three phases of foreign investment since 1979. Rather, the model is presented because it is useful in gaining an understanding of the context in which foreign investment has progressed in the People's Republic during this period. The model also helps one to identify and understand some of the contradictions at play in China as its leadership formulates investment policy.

The first apparent contradiction concerns the differences between the objectives held by foreigners and those held by the Chinese regarding China market investment opportunities—specifically, the Chinese attempt to push foreign investment into certain preselected sectors

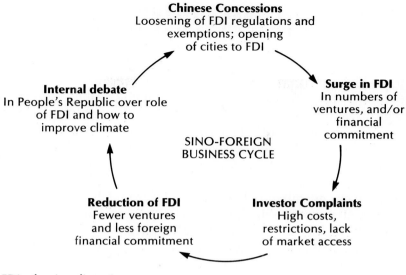

Chinese Concessions
Loosening of FDI regulations and
exemptions; opening
of cities to FDI

Internal debate
In People's Republic over role
of FDI and how to
improve climate

Surge in FDI
In numbers of
ventures, and/or
financial
commitment

SINO-FOREIGN
BUSINESS CYCLE

Reduction of FDI
Fewer ventures
and less foreign
financial commitment

Investor Complaints
High costs,
restrictions, lack
of market access

FDI = foreign direct investment

while foreign investors have sought attractive economic pull factors. The resulting dichotomy of expectations has an effect on the type of concessions the Chinese offer and the investments foreigners are willing to place in the People's Republic. Second, by looking at the nature of internal debate concerning foreign investment policy, one can better appreciate the political tug-of-war that has grown up around the open-door policy—an ongoing war of words among a spectrum of Chinese, ranging from risk-takers, who push for reduced protectionism over home industries, more competition with foreign goods, and more participation by foreign businesses in an improved investment climate to traditionalists, who fear inflation, shortages, inequality, and debt, and wish to maintain China's insulation from foreign goods and business practices.[7] Third, the open-door foreign investment policy has led to internal contradiction inside the Chinese government, where announced policy is difficult to implement at the grass-roots level. Finally, the playing out of this policy has been a human and national drama as two diverse and radically different societies come together to hash out complex international business deals, one side lacking experience yet overly proud, the other the epitome of business experience yet perceived as insensitive to the cultural and sociopolitical conditions of the host business environment.

PHASE I (1979-81):
CHINA FEVER TURNS TO FEAR

China's door opened to the world in the late 1970s with a sense of urgency. Throughout this period, oversight organizations and various management agencies were formed to accommodate the absorption of foreign investment and advanced technology. A program of preferential treatment was inaugurated and basic investment laws were ratified. In effect, China had taken the basic steps to create a climate for foreign investment. The ratification of foreign investment laws began in 1979 with the promulgation of the Law of Joint Ventures. Sino-foreign joint ventures were encouraged because they were perceived as the best method of absorbing foreign capital and technology while retaining the greatest degree of control over Chinese workers.

The law defined the joint venture (*hezi jingying*) as a venture established between a foreign investor and a Chinese entity, including enterprises and government institutions. A board of directors selected by each side manages the venture. Board membership is agreed to in a contract, with the president required to be Chinese and the vice chairman foreign. Essentially, a joint venture can be defined as a limited liability company in which the foreigner must hold at least 25 percent interest.[8] Theoretically, the foreign side could control as much as 99 percent of the venture's equity. Profits and losses are distributed according to equity shares, the foreign side typically contributing technology and equipment, rights to industrial properties, and foreign exchange, the Chinese side usually supplying land rights, buildings, raw materials, and renminbi (Rmb) currency. By granting legal-person status to joint ventures (as well as to wholly foreign-owned ventures), the Chinese guarantee that these ventures cannot be expropriated or nationalized because, in theory, they are regarded as Chinese nationals, not foreign entities.

China's experience with joint ventures did not start in 1979 with the Law of Joint Ventures, however. In 1950–51, four so-called joint-stock companies between China and the Soviet Union (three in Xinjiang and one in Dalian) were formed as part of China's search for economic and military aid after the Korean War. These joint-stock companies amounted to joint operation of a plant by two governments rather than by private corporations. The Soviets supplied the plant and equipment, the Chinese supplied labor and materials. The Soviet Union clearly took advantage of China in these dealings, since China had borrowed the funds necessary to purchase the equipment, some of which the Soviets had originally expropriated from the Japanese.[9] For instance, the joint-stock company in Dalian was a shipyard that had been part of a naval base that the Soviets had taken from Japan.

The first modern joint ventures were evaluated on whether they would help industries such as tourism to earn foreign exchange. Four of the first six joint ventures approved were in the service sector and were of limited duration. Service sector ventures, such as hotels, catering, and restaurants, required limited raw materials from China, as well as hard cash, while having little impact on overall Chinese political/ psychological sensitivities about opening to Western business.

The China Rush. When China opened its doors to trade, entrepreneurs and managers in the West, whose businesses had been hurt by competition from abroad and economic recession at home, thought they had found a ready-made market for their products. But China investment fever did not take hold of the U.S. business community until Fox Butterfield, a respected China scholar and journalist, reported in the *New York Times* (October 1, 1979) that Gu Mu, a high-level Chinese official in charge of construction, and Rong Yiren, the president of China International Trust and Investment Corporation (CITIC), had announced that foreign investors in China would be "guaranteed" profits from joint venture enterprises at a rate above what they could expect in other foreign countries. Scores of pioneering foreign firms, especially Japanese, European, and American, swarmed into China's largest cities in search of ground-breaking deals even before laws concerning patents, profit repatriation, corporate taxation, and business forms other than the joint venture had been defined or put into Chinese law. In April 1980, ES Pacific Development and Construction Co., Ltd., set a tone of unbridled optimism when it signed a deal to construct the Great Wall Hotel in Beijing. The U.S. firm committed $35.28 million on a joint venture to be terminated in only ten years. Of course, the bulk of negotiating activity, which began in 1979, did not show up in the form of large numbers of approved joint venture contracts until 1982–83.

At the outset, most of the early foreign financial commitments were centered on the oil industry. Many foreign oil companies viewed China as an alternative to the increasingly unstable and unpredictable Middle East. By the end of 1984, the United States, through thirteen oil companies in twelve contracts, committed $679 million in actual capital contributions; Japan committed $810 million; and the European Economic Community (EEC) committed $600 million.

Joint development (*hezuo kaifa*) of oil resources in the People's Republic takes place in two stages: geophysical exploration, in which the foreign company incurs all expenses and risk; and exploitation of resources, wherein investment risks and rewards are shared by the foreign and the Chinese side. As negotiated, the Chinese retain a proportion of the output (the X-factor), which is separate from incurred expenses. The remaining output is divided between both partners.[10] The arrangement also allows China to offset the purchase of advanced equipment with future output, reducing its financial risk.

Early Investor Complaints

Almost immediately after start-up of the first series of joint ventures, a storm of complaints began to subdue China trade excitement. Foreign investors quickly realized that Chinese factories, even with foreign technology, suffered from overall lower productivity than in other Asian countries encouraging foreign investment. The reasons for the lower productivity were manifold: redundant personnel, surcharges on Chinese wages, lack of transportation and communication networks, and the high cost associated with bureaucratic red tape or excessive compartmentalization, which slows the approval process and acquisition of raw materials. An inadequate infrastructure to support foreign investment compounded the problem, drawing frequent complaints from Chinese and foreigners alike. The chronic shortages of building materials, power supply, water, and sewage hook-ups caused delays in plant construction and renovation, and disrupted operations once production started. In addition, foreigners discovered that with little or no formal business standing in the People's Republic, gaining access to everything from raw materials to specific services and tools proved extremely frustrating, time consuming, and expensive. Finally, problems associated with financial aspects of doing business in a foreign environment were exacerbated by the absence of financial services geared to the needs of the foreign investor, and by restrictions on the extent to which foreign banks could offer these services to foreign companies doing business in China.

Nowhere were these early complaints made more vociferously than in matters concerning taxation. Tax laws are ambiguous, incomplete, and are said to be subject to the vagaries of local Chinese officials. Basic tax laws were published at the time, but withholding tax was often something to be negotiated against what locals considered fair.[11] The interpretation of the tax law tended to vary from one area to another. Although it was designed to fill gaps in China's tax legislation, the Foreign Enterprise Income Tax Law (put into effect in December 1981) only helped to add to the ambiguity since it did not include non-equity ventures such as cooperative production and compensation trade agreements.

The nineteen articles of the enterprise tax law outlined basic principles only. Although they represented an important beginning in the formulation of a body of tax law, they did not allay the fears of investors. Legal tax avoidance and illegal tax evasion were generally perceived by the Chinese to be one and the same—tactics foreigners use to sidestep Chinese administration of foreign ventures.[12]

Under the Corporate Income Tax Law for Chinese-Foreign Joint Ventures (which was ratified in 1980), the income tax rate was set at 30 percent, with a local surtax of 10 percent of income tax, bringing the total tax to 33 percent. The tax burden on an investor does not stop there, however. The following list enumerates the various other forms of taxation on joint ventures and foreigners who live and work in China.

1. *Industrial and commercial tax.* This amounts to a sales tax levied on each processing stage. The tax can vary from 1.5 percent (for necessities) to 69 percent (for luxuries) of the value of the specific transaction. The percentage of the tax depends on how essential the particualar item or service is to the subsistence of the average Chinese citizen.[13]
2. *Commerce and industry tax.* This is a 5 percent retroactive tax on the total volume of business. In an attempt to negate the retroactive portion of the tax, some investors have protested that their offices in China are not actually doing business.[14]
3. *Import regulatory tax.* Established in July 1985, this tax is designed to discourage certain consumer imports and is payable in addition to customs import duty. For example, motorcycles carry an added tax of 20 percent, videocassette recorders and color televisions an added 70 percent, and calculators an added 80 percent.
4. *Residents tax.* Each person who stays in China more than ninety days in any one year is required to pay this tax.

5. *Building tax.* Promulgated in 1986, this is a tax on the build-ing(s) foreigners rent in China.
6. *Motor vehicles tax.* This tax is applicable to residents who im-port a car, boat, etc.
7. *Social security tax.* For those firms employing Chinese labor, this tax can be as high as 30 percent of payroll.[15]
8. *Office equipment tax.* Regulations published in 1980 made it clear that office equipment could be taxed as much as 100 per-cent, driving home the point that setting up an office presence in China would be an expensive proposition.[16]
9. *Land-use fees.* The Foreign Land-use Measures, issued in 1980, set fees to be paid by foreigners and their Chinese partners for the use of land that their factories occupy. Fees vary widely from 5 to 300 Rmb per square meter, depending on the locale.[17]

This early collection of complaints did little to dampen the general mood of excitement about China's newly opened investment climate. But in early October 1980, truly disheartening news hit the world press. The first factory built in the People's Republic with foreign participa-tion, a wool-spinning mill in Zhuhai, had shut down. The general partners—Novel Enterprises Ltd., and Macao Textile Ltd.—were throw-ing in the towel on their $2 million compensation trade investment because, as the head of the Macao interest stated in a letter to Zhuhai authorities, "the China side had failed to meet its contractual obliga-tions in producing woolen products of sufficient quality."[18] As it was reported in the *Financial Times*, the suspension of operations by the Macao company was a development "confirming the worst fears of prospective foreign partners."[19] In their letter to Zhuhai authorities, Macao owners detailed the specifics of the failure and placed respon-sibility squarely on the shoulders of the Chinese, citing overall Chinese inefficiency, lazy workers, and lackadaisical trainees. In addition, it was noted in the letter that the lack of incentive for Chinese managers was the result of the identical wages being paid to supervisors, foremen, and workers alike. Chinese managers were also criticized for a lack of response to the owners' suggestions, an inability to fire workers, a scar-city of building materials, and most important, an inferior quality of production.[20]

The Chinese response was swift. Two articles in the *People's Daily* stated that the problems at the mill were managerial, not equipment-related, and "should be seen as a warning" that Chinese factories need to improve management skills in Sino-foreign ventures.[21] The changes that were considered, as stated in the articles, included granting managers more autonomy to hire, fire, and discipline workers, to select workers by examination, and to offer higher wages through bonuses.[22] Although the factory was reopened after several weeks, the impression was set: managing ventures in China was not the relatively straightforward task it was in other Asian countries such as Taiwan and the Philippines.[23]

China's investment climate woes did not subside with the restart of the wool-spinning mill in Zhuhai. China's leaders were still faced with slumping growth and a growing trade deficit. Barely two months after the problems in Zhuhai were made public, plans were announced to halt scores of new construction projects—many involving foreigners—as part of a policy of economic readjustment. The biggest casualties were the contracts with Japanese and West German firms to develop the massive Baoshan Steel Works outside Shanghai. In addition to the steel works, the Chinese also scuttled four enormous petrochemical complexes that were to be built with heavy foreign input. When combined with the Baoshan agreements, these contracts amounted to $2.6 billion.[24] In reaction, Japan dispatched foreign economic expert Saburo Okita to the People's Republic to warn the Chinese that cancellation of major industrial contracts could diminish confidence in the People's Republic as a trading partner.[25] Okita rejected China's proposals to resell equipment already delivered as well as the idea of mothballing the equipment for later use.[26] Although the People's Republic paid tens of millions of dollars in compensation to Japan and negotiated a three-year extension of their contract with West Germany, the Baoshan incident and contract cancellations in 1981 served to sour the mood among both Chinese and foreign investors regarding co-managed ventures and large financial commitments to industrial projects. Oddly, a number of U.S. investors pulled out of their Chinese negotiations in response to the problems West Germany and Japan were having.

The cancellations reflected both the problems encountered in China's readjustment policy and the fact that Chinese leaders were not in total agreement on how to most effectively direct China's relations with the foreign business community. Moreover, China's economic readjustment policy coincided with the country's opening to foreign investment. The cuts in capital construction, brought on by the sluggish growth in China's industrial sector and the country's inability to boost exports of manufactured products, had to be compensated for if China was to continue its efforts at rapid modernization. Foreign direct investment was the only option available to increase capital availability, upgrade technology, and boost exports. Clearly, readjustment had not been altogether smooth or complete. In Shandong Province alone, construction on 240 projects, all of which were valued at over 1 million Rmb, had been canceled or suspended from 1978 to 1980.[27] But in February 1981, the U.S. consulate general in Shanghai acknowledged that the control of capital construction was far from being won; there were still 1,300 projects under construction, each valued at over 50,000 Rmb, that would require 300 million Rmb to complete. Apparently, local Chinese resistance to the construction cuts was fouling the cutbacks.

Fueled by a national aversion to foreign debt and fears of a growing trade deficit, Chinese leaders decided to step up the investment acquisition program in an effort to attract low-interest loans and foreign capital for economic modernization. However, exactly how foreign loans and capital should be utilized was the subject of an ongoing debate at various levels of the Chinese bureaucracy, and can be viewed in part as the cause of switchbacks in China's foreign investment policy during the early years of the open-door program.

The issue pivoted on what would be the most rational use of foreign investment. The notion of using foreign capital at all was a sensitive issue among traditional Chinese, many of whom placed utmost importance on Chinese economic self-sufficiency—to the exclusion of foreigners. In 1980, the question of why foreign capital should be used was the subject of great debate in the Chinese press. Proponents of the use of foreign capital stressed that to speed up modernization and offset lacking construction funds, foreign capital should be utilized as part of the state plan, in conjunction with domestic funding. They also stressed that foreign capital should be used to fund only those enterprises that produced export commodities, thus earning needed foreign exchange.[28] This tended to skew project approval away from infrastructural projects and toward those aimed solely at exporting. At the time, however, the People's Republic actually possessed the necessary foreign exchange reserves to increase domestic spending on modernization, and enough foreign exchange in reserve to make significant loans to other foreign nations.

In spite of the reserves, a loan-taking policy was initiated in 1981 with the issuance of General Secretary Zhao Ziyang's *Government*

Work Report, in which he declared: "To speed up our economic construction, it is definitely necessary to utilize as much foreign capital as possible, and first of all to utilize low-interest loans and loans offered on relatively favorable terms."[29] The regime, in a decisive turn away from Maoist economic policies, committed itself to a long-term financial strategy that would include international borrowing and soliciting economic aid.[30]

The loan-taking policy, however, was marked by extreme caution and trepidation among many Chinese about allowing the country to fall into indebtedness to foreign nations. There was constant reference in the Chinese press about China's financial credibility among nations and how that standing would be threatened if total indebtedness rose above 20 percent of the country's foreign exchange export earnings. Consequently, cautious borrowing was encouraged under the principle of "whoever borrows, repays"; that is, the ultimate responsibility for repayment is placed on the enterprise that takes the loan. However, it was also stated that if enterprises experienced difficulty repaying loans, they could request the state to remit or reduce their tax liability. Because taxes represent a major portion of a Chinese enterprise's yearly expenditure, safety-valve measures could only encourage enterprise managers and local bureaucrats to take loans (which were low-interest loans to begin with) for projects which lacked necessary preplanning, feasibility work, or economic viability. Many enterprises acquired new equipment but found that sufficient supplies, fuel, etc., were unavailable.[31] Ultimately, the loan-taking policy encouraged rash importation of foreign equipment. Once again, infrastructural projects were downplayed because the criteria for granting loans were based on small capital need, foreign exchange creation, and capacity for large accumulation.

The trend was toward including foreign capital projects in the state plan to ensure that strict control was maintained over the use of foreign funds and that a surefire strategy was followed regarding the use of foreign investment. The Baoshan debacle forced Chinese trade officials to take what Rong Yiren termed a more "structural approach" to partnerships with foreign investors. Rong also stated that although any form of investment can be discussed with foreigners, a detailed, step-by-step feasibility study should be conducted on joint projects.[32] It was concluded that the problems at Baoshan found their origin in faulty feasibility work, which had overlooked unresolvable infrastructural problems. Interestingly, the Chinese blamed Japan, the principal supplier of equipment to the project, rather than themselves, for the project's problems.

The need for control over foreign funds in the People's Republic paralleled the need to control foreign exchange held by foreign firms doing business in China. Regulations adopted in 1978 had declared that enterprises in the People's Republic with foreign partners, or with foreign capital, must deposit all foreign exchange receipts with the Bank of China and pay all foreign exchange disbursements from those accounts. Further, all transactions within China would be allowed in the form of people's currency (Rmb) only. Consequently, projects with foreigners were approved largely on the ability to earn foreign exchange.[33]

The investment mood worsened in October 1980 when Xue Muqiao, an adviser to the State Planning Commission, warned Hong Kong businessmen that trade between China and foreign equipment manufacturers would be falling off because of infrastructural difficulties (especially in power and transportation) associated with capital-intensive industrial plant development with long lead times.[34] He said that both the United States and China were waiting to see the results of current experimental joint venture/countertrade agreements before signing new deals.[35] Xue also acknowledged that investor interest in China was down (in 1980) in both compensation trade and joint ventures, which brought additional warnings that China may not have the measures in place to actually guarantee profits to foreign investors.[36]

By 1981 joint ventures were being re-examined by all parties. The reason, as stated by a high-level official from CITIC, was that joint venture expansion was draining the limited capital the state had to offer for industrial construction. As a result, new emphasis was placed on compensation trade and processing arrangements because these agreements would upgrade factories and did not require foreign exchange.[37] The foreign investment figures for 1981 bear out this assessment and illustrate the effect of cutbacks and cancellations on investor commitment: joint venture investment fell to $20 million in 19 ventures in 1981 from $177 million in 20 ventures in 1980.[38]

The best refrain to this phase that could be offered was that investors should not give up. In his farewell speech, U.S. Ambassador to China Leonard Woodcock prophesied that the 1980s would be a tough decade for China, but that China venture investors should keep the faith. He predicted with cautious optimism that "China will turn the corner."[39]

PHASE II (1982-84):
RENOVATION OF EXISTING ENTERPRISES

By early 1982 the People's Republic had altered considerably the somber mood among foreign investors. In what was called a major new bid for foreign investment and advanced technology, Chinese officials opened 130 industrial projects to foreign investment. China announced that it was seeking $900 million in investment for these *key point* projects, and promised that reliable supplies of raw materials and financial resources would be provided by the Chinese counterparts of these ventures. This promise was backed by the fact that the projects were sanctioned by, and included in, the national plan. Only five of the projects were new, however; the rest involved renovation or technological transformation. This announcement amounted to an entirely new foreign investment policy—one directed toward renovation (as opposed to turnkey plant acquisition) of China's nearly 400,000 existing factories. The largest projects included plants designed to produce cement, a joint venture to produce color film, another to produce photographic paper, and a soda-ash plant. These key point projects were chosen from 280 proposals, ranging in process from light to medium industry, including consumer goods, textiles, building materials, telecommunications, and electronics. What was most notable about the selections was that large capital-intensive and infrastructural projects, such as those in energy development, transportation, and agriculture, were excluded.[40]

The key to the new strategy was China's intention to boost foreign exchange earnings through exports. And in light of China's perceived foreign exchange difficulties and its fear of indebtedness, foreign investment was viewed as the best method by which advanced technologies could be obtained and applied in order to produce for export.[41] From this point on, the door was opened more to acquire and localize advanced foreign technology than to liberalize trading.

The new approach represented a restart of foreign investment in the People's Republic. The mood was further brightened by two other developments. First, early in 1982 the Chinese successfully renegotiated a $400 million contract with West Germany's Schloemann-Siemag Company for the resumption of construction at Baoshan Steel Works. Second, China resumed its purchasing of industrial equipment from Japan, signing a $15 million contract for three polyester fiber plants.[42] By 1982, most of the provinces of China were advertising investment projects in over 1,000 enterprises, which was a foreign investment drive for $5.3 billion of so-called surplus Western capital. The program intensified when provincial areas tried to take advantage of liberalized investment restrictions in attracting the funding that the state was unable to dole out since the 1981 reconstruction spending cuts.[43]

The requirements of the renovation program reinforced the opinion that the Sino-foreign joint venture was the best way to achieve technological transformation goals. The reasons for this, as one Chinese writer clearly stated, were that joint ventures called for joint capital, joint operation, joint benefits, and joint liability.[44] In addition, because the program involved improvements in plant layout, scheduling techniques, inventory control, personnel management, quality control and testing procedures, and the management of technology, renovation could best be engineered through the close working relationships associated with joint ventures. They were viewed as the most cost-effective and time-effective method of gaining hands-on access to foreign technology and managerial practice. Such an approach also would prevent the emergence of foreign enclaves within the industrial economy.[45]

Nonetheless, joint ventures were approved largely on the basis of whether they could export production successfully. Although the Chinese issued no formal regulation as to the percentage of production joint ventures must export, they required them to balance expenses with foreign exchange earnings from exports, which represented a de facto export requirement rigidly enforced by the nonconvertibility of China's own currency on world markets.

New Business Forms Gain in the South

As part of the aftermath of Baoshan and the selective approval of key point projects, the number of joint ventures dropped in 1982. As joint ventures producing nonessential goods were cut, the effectiveness of the existing export producers was being scrutinized. Many joint ventures were believed to be too complex and frustrating for both sides, and of no help in meeting dire infrastructure needs. While the need for plant renovation focused increased attention on the joint venture as the best format for achieving this objective, diverse new forms of cooperation were being encouraged for smaller manufacturing projects, especially those in the special economic zones (SEZs). These joint business arrangements included cooperative ventures, compensation trade arrangements, and processing/assembly arrangements, as well as various forms of countertrade and barter. The scarcity of foreign exchange had made these forms increasingly attractive. Throughout 1981, while the number of joint ventures dwindled, overall foreign investment actually rose by 20 percent, including 127 small cooperative production ventures (worth $1.2 billion) accounting for nearly all of the total. In that year alone the monetary value of cooperative ventures had quadrupled.[46]

Cooperative ventures (*hezuo jingying*), also called contractual joint ventures (*qiyeshi heying*), feature a number of similarities to the joint venture. The Chinese typically contribute land, buildings, existing equipment, labor, and raw materials while the foreign side contributes cash, technology, equipment, and materials. They differ from joint ventures in that the foreign firm holds no equity and the distribution of profits and losses is based on a negotiated contractual agreement, which also spells out the rights and obligations of each partner. The partners manage cooperative ventures jointly, and share output and profits according to the contract. Although the cooperative venture requires government approval, it is less complex legally and less permanent than the joint venture.[47] Most cooperative ventures involve small manufacturing arrangements with Chinese from Hong Kong and Macao. Some large cooperative ventures, however, exist as well, such as Occidental's coal and natural gas agreement.

Compensation trade (*buchang maoyi*) arrangements are made such that the Chinese purchase equipment and technology on credit and compensate the foreign partner later with what they produce using the imported equipment and technology. The responsibility rests with the foreign partner to market the product overseas. Compensation trade agreements became overwhelmingly popular in 1980. Feng Tienshun, the head of the foreign investment bureau of the Foreign Investment Commission, announced that these deals involved well over $100 million in foreign equipment in that year.[48] By 1982, 888 compensation trade arrangements had been approved; by the end of 1984, 1,371; by 1985, 3,030.[49] Most of these deals involved textiles or other light industries, and two-thirds of them were arrangements between China and Hong Kong firms. Compensation trade deals offer obvious advantages to the Chinese: Chinese factories get updated technology—without foreign exchange expenditure—and Chinese-made products enter world markets, raising China's reputation as an exporter while earning foreign exchange. The Chinese side also acquires experience in international marketing, packaging, quality control, and product design. For the foreigner, the compensation deal may represent an entry-level foothold in the China market. Problems do arise, however, when the Chinese are slow in delivery or unable to produce quality goods (as we saw in the Zhuhai wool-mill case).

Countertrade (barter) deals, wherein one commodity is simply traded for another, are usually struck between China with the Soviet Union and Eastern Europe (a few projects of magnitude have also been arranged between China and Western countries). The biggest countertrade deal was a thirteen-year Sino-Japanese arrangement that involved the exchange of Japanese electronic plants, coal smelters, and fishing equipment for oil, coal, and output from the Chinese factories utilizing the equipment. A smaller countertrade deal was made with General Motors, in which GM traded truck engines for a quantity of China tours which GM used as sales incentives for dealers.[50] Countertrade grew in importance as the foreign exchange problem worsened. The Ministry of Foreign Economic Relations and Trade (MOFERT) set up a countertrade bureau to coordinate an effort to supply countertrade goods in a consistent manner. These deals are easy for the Chinese planners who have control over the necessary resources to justify and approve because they are self-liquidating.[51]

Special Economic Zones

In August 1979 Fujian and Guangdong became the first provinces authorized to set up SEZs in China. Guangdong set up three zones in the cities of Shenzhen, Zhuhai, and Shantou; Fujian set up one zone in Xiamen. These two provinces were granted greater autonomy in some aspects of economic decision making, in addition to other privileges, because of their proximity to overseas Chinese in Hong Kong and Macao. Eventually, SEZs were granted the right to offer their own unique set of regulations to foreign investors. These zones tend to get priority access to raw materials, have more freedom to offer their own financial banking services, and can issue their own export licenses on some goods. As originally conceived, an SEZ would be an isolated bastion of capitalism on the mainland, where investors could enjoy the benefits associated with Hong Kong—in other words, closed areas where market forces and international pricing, rather than state planning, would govern transactions.[52]

In this sense the zones were viewed as a buffer between the economic systems of mainland China and those of Hong Kong, Macao, and Taiwan, and ultimately as part of a grander strategy to unify all these areas with the mainland.[53] Politically, China hopes the zones will show that the two-systems idea that top Chinese leaders have prescribed for Hong Kong will prove workable, that is, socialism and capitalism co-existing under the sovereignty of the People's Republic.[54] Chinese leaders also believed they could depend on the zones to keep unwanted foreign goods and values from spreading uncontrollably throughout the interior provinces. In this sense, however, the policy backfired. The effect of concentrating foreign direct investment in SEZs brought about the rapid expansion and sophistication of resident Chinese consumers and entrepreneurs, exposing them to foreign goods, finance methods, culture, and values. It was not long before adjacent provinces desired similar advantages. The notion of maintaining a separation between SEZs and the inner provinces soon became generally untenable as jealousies hindered cooperation among various officials.

The SEZs offer the foreign investor a series of attractive incentives in a number of areas which are secured in published regulations. The following is a list of just a few of the attractions in the SEZs:

Personnel
- foreign firms can employ foreign staff managers
- foreign personnel pay no taxes
- Chinese workers can be hired and fired

Competitiveness
- foreign firms are exempt from import/export duties and from after-tax profit remittance
- access to Chinese partners is facilitated by various industry-specific development companies, which assist foreign investors

SEZs vs. Hong Kong
- tax rates in SEZs are 15 percent vs. Hong Kong tax rates of 18.5 percent
- wages in SEZs are 75–80 percent lower than in Hong Kong

Taxation
- exports from SEZs are exempt from Consolidated Industrial Commercial Tax
- monies deposited in Shenzhen banks are free from taxation
- interest on loans is not taxed
- sales tax on products sold in SEZs will be returned after approval by tax authorities[55]

One of the zones, Shenzhen, has achieved comparatively miraculous growth. Almost overnight the once tiny fishing village was transformed into a metropolis, featuring skyscrapers and an entrepreneurial-minded population of 330,000.[56] From 1979 to 1985, 3,700 contracts were signed there, amounting to $3 billion in pledged investment ($700 million actual), or 20 percent of the national total for that period.

Overseas Chinese.   The rapid growth in SEZs can be attributed largely to the overseas Chinese, who have been enabled via the zones to take advantage of familial connections in South China and initiate ventures quickly and smoothly (although Hong Kong and Macao firms have remained uninvolved in oil-related foreign investment). Overseas Chinese can claim responsibility for the majority of Sino-foreign ventures and cumulative foreign investment to China. When one considers the role Hong Kong middlemen play in selling Western products from Hong Kong, the crucial role of overseas Chinese becomes clear. (One Hong Kong trader indicated during an interview that he had sold 400 American-made X-ray machines to China in 1985 alone!) The increases in foreign investment during the period from 1979 to 1987 can be attributed primarily to investment inputs in the SEZs from Hong Kong and Macao. Most of these ventures are small in terms of total value and do not represent high-technology transfer, but they have been set up in startling numbers.

Over 80 percent of China's joint ventures include overseas Chinese as partners. They own 75 percent of the wholly foreign-owned ventures in China, and most significantly, their investment accounts for 60 percent of the total number of cases of foreign investment in China as of 1985 (Western Europe accounts for 13 percent; Japan, 7 percent; United States, 7 percent). Overseas Chinese have been the clear front-runners in foreign investment, especially in Shenzhen, supplying 90 percent of the investment there during the period of 1982–84.[57]

Breakdown of Investment in China Ventures by Countries and Size

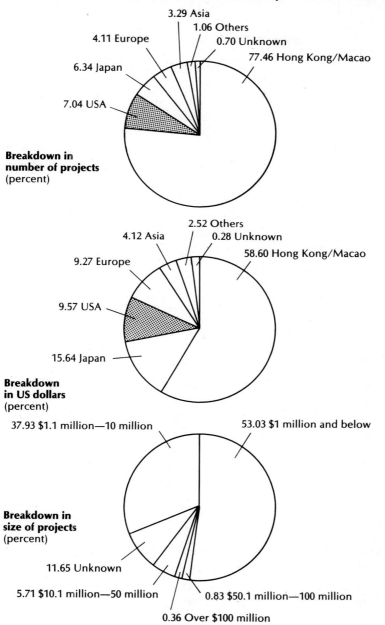

3.29 Asia
1.06 Others
0.70 Unknown
4.11 Europe
6.34 Japan
7.04 USA
77.46 Hong Kong/Macao

Breakdown in number of projects (percent)

2.52 Others
0.28 Unknown
4.12 Asia
9.27 Europe
9.57 USA
15.64 Japan
58.60 Hong Kong/Macao

Breakdown in US dollars (percent)

37.93 $1.1 million—10 million
53.03 $1 million and below
11.65 Unknown
5.71 $10.1 million—50 million
0.83 $50.1 million—100 million
0.36 Over $100 million

Breakdown in size of projects (percent)

SOURCE: *South China Morning Post*, by permission, 1986.

Renewed Investor Complaints and Foreign Investment Policy Reassessment

Investor complaints continued to surface in 1982. The complaints were centered on an ongoing and intensifying concern over long negotiating periods, bureaucratic interference, and investment law that was thought to be lacking. Specifically, China had failed to promulgate a body of corporate law that could offer desired safeguards to investors regarding repatriation of profits, taxation of various forms of business enterprise other than joint ventures, and acceptable arbitration procedures in case of disputes.[58] Added to the list of frustrations were financial regulations that allowed foreigners to make deposits in banks outside China, but stipulated that they submit quarterly reports on the use and disbursement of these accounts, even if the accounts had nothing to do with an investor's China activities.[59] In some cases, frustration turned to resentment among foreign investors because of China's unwillingness to offer a significant share of the domestic market to investors. Foreign investors also resented China's refusal to assist many joint ventures with loans or other forms of credit, saying that the country was too poor to accept high-interest commercial loans, when in fact many business executives understood China to be itself a net lender to other nations.[60,61]

By 1984 the Chinese had begun to reassess their foreign investment policy in light of these complaints *and* to notice that their intentions to renovate Chinese enterprises with foreign technology and management techniques were not being realized as rapidly as they had hoped. Aside from offshore oil, most of the American investment (est. $2.6 billion) in China up until that time had been concentrated in low-risk, low-technology, light-industrial or commercial client projects.[62] Some of the joint ventures had been formed in textiles, light industry, hotels, and the service sector, while the fewest had undertaken manufacturing. This cautious approach was also the mood at a Shanghai International Trade and Investment Corporation (SITIC) symposium for 2,000 Hong Kong businessmen, where it was reported that there was an "investment intention fever" but little actual commitment because investors were overly cautious. The writer covering the symposium argued that foreigners invest money in investment environments where they anticipate profit-making, that they have not come to China merely to do charity work, and that China will have to improve its investment climate if it is to compete with other countries for foreign investment.[63]

In the past, policymakers had generally overlooked, or had little appreciation for, the risk that foreign investors perceived in the China market. Recently, in their efforts to reduce those risks, central Chinese authorities have attempted to convince local officials and enterprise managers that foreign investors should not be exploited, or squeezed, in order to extract from them the short-term benefits of foreign exchange inputs and equipment. The short-term contracts that the Chinese pushed for, it was argued, bred an ideology on the part of the investor that would not facilitate long-term technology transfer.[64] In Communistic fashion, local Chinese were catechized on the merits of utilizing foreign capital. However, many locals resisted its use on protectionist grounds, believing that domestic industries would be hurt if foreign-invested factories began competing with domestic enterprises. In reality, the import cuts that resulted from protectionist policies helped to lower machinery imports by 43 percent in 1982 compared with a similar period in 1981; imports of U.S. machinery and equipment fell 59 percent in 1981. An article in the *People's Daily* at the time urged that importation of equipment that was also produced domestically must be strictly forbidden.[65]

The local-level resistance to working with foreigners and to carrying out renovation with foreign investment was denounced in the press as an attempt to seal off the China market to foreign participation in an effort to avoid international competition.[66] The various arguments used to convince local Chinese to utilize foreign investment included reference to the success of factories using foreign capital, the export potential of new technology, increased efficiency, and mutual benefit. Low-interest loan offerings were also continued incentives for enterprises that renovated using foreign capital, with an added emphasis on feasibility studies to offset the tendency noticed in 1984 for projects using such loans to be unworkable. For example, the *China Daily* reported that in Tianjin, because of the irrational distribution of funds and arbitrary approval of loan packages, fewer than ten of the eighty-seven key projects that were approved to receive loans from the People's Bank in 1983 were actually qualified for such loans. Most of these projects were ill-conceived and suffered serious delays in start-up.[67]

Conciliation and Concessions.   In an effort to improve the investment climate, Chinese leaders implemented policy changes in 1984 which had an immediate and tangible effect on the character and quality of foreign investment in China. In a tone of conciliation toward foreign investors, it was announced that more cities would be opened to foreign investment, and efforts to accommodate foreign investment would be intensified. One Chinese Foreign Ministry official repeated an old refrain (on condition he not be identified) that China would "guarantee profits to all those enterprises that come to China."[68] As Vice Premier Yao Yilin advised foreign investors in his 1984 New Year's speech: "If you fail the first time, please don't feel upset. Come back for another try."[69] CITIC executive director Jing Shiping announced that China was looking into further concessions, including greater market access, longer duration for joint ventures, and greater freedom for local governments to conduct business with foreigners.[70] At management symposiums throughout China, it was promised that duplicitous and self-serving practices by the local bureaucracy would be remedied.[71] It was made clear that firms transferring technology would be rewarded with flexibility in taxation and be allowed to sell some, if not all, of their production to China's domestic market if they produced import substitutes.[72] To facilitate Sino-foreign cooperation, economic consulting offices began to sprout up in major Chinese cities to assist in negotiating venture contracts and arbitrating disputes.

In July 1984, China made a decisive move toward decentralization of the management of foreign investment and provided more opportunities for foreign investment in China by targeting fourteen coastal cities for investment. These cities were: Dalian, Tianjin, Quingdao, Yantai, Shanghai, Ningbo, Guangzhou (all of which have good facilities); and Quinhuangdo, Lianyungang, Nantong, Wenzhou, Fuzhou, Zhanjiang, and Beihai (all of which are undeveloped).[73] In fact, these cities were all former treaty ports which were forced open by foreign imperialist countries in the nineteenth century.[74]

The "fourteen open cities" represented some of the most productive areas in the country. They contained 8 percent of the country's total population, yet accounted for 23 percent of total industrial output and 40 percent of its exports.[75] As planned, preferential treatment for investors in these cities would be similar to that offered in the SEZs. It was hoped that approximately $1.5 billion would be raised for 207 projects, two-thirds of which would be technology-oriented.[76] The cities were also granted the right to establish economic and technical development zones (ETDZs) outside city centers, which could offer tax rates of 15 percent and waive the 10 percent profit remittance tax. The ETDZs were set up to concentrate foreign investment in four cities—Tianjin, Dalian, Shanghai, and Guangzhou—ultimately to create exports.[77]

The most crucial development in decentralizing trade and investment management was the policy of granting provinces and municipalities the right to approve a foreign investment project unilaterally, without central government approval, if it was under a specified dollar value. For example, Shanghai and Tianjin could approve projects valued at up to $30 million.[78] This figure was informally cut back later to $10–15 million, based on the current economic conditions in each city.[79] Guangdong, Fujian, and Dalian could approve projects valued at up to $10 million.[80] In addition, key enterprises, such as Dalian Shipyard, were empowered to approve projects valued at up to $3 million.

Foreign trade was further decentralized as local foreign trade corporations (FTCs) were allowed to operate more independently from MOFERT. Provinces were also permitted to set up local trust and investment corporations modeled after CITIC, which undertook liaison activities with foreign firms. In four of the opened cities, Tianjin, Shanghai, Dalian, and Guangzhou, the policy worked to attract impressive amounts of foreign investment. The ten other cities, however, had their autonomy revoked because of infrastructural deficiencies, lack of experience in dealing with foreign firms, and corruption among some Chinese officials in charge of Sino-foreign transactions at the provincial and municipal levels. Though China's pronounced objective of completing 207 projects in fourteen newly opened cities would prove too optimistic, discernible gains were made in pulling in foreign investment.

Foreign Investment Soars in the Provinces

The combination of investor concessions, increased market access, and competition among China's provinces to create an investment climate attractive to cautious foreign investors helped to increase foreign investment in 1984 by 50 percent over 1983; joint investment experienced a 466 percent increase in the same period.[81] In 1984 a remarkable 741 joint ventures were approved.[82] And, in general, the provinces realized the benefits of using foreign capital as exports increased in light industries and textiles where foreign technology was implemented. For instance, in Nanjing Province, it was found that for every dollar of foreign funds used in development, approximately two dollars worth of Rmb in production value was realized.[83]

A few of the provinces experienced veritable deal madness in 1984. Fujian Province, for example, signed 118 contracts with foreign firms from January to September (which was twenty-six times the figure for the same period in 1983), including fifty-one joint ventures, fifty-three cooperative ventures, and eight compensation trade agreements. These contracts included ventures with General Electric and Reynolds Tobacco Company, and a venture with Kodak that involved the production technology for photographic film.[84] In addition, the province signed eighty-eight technology import deals in the first half of the year.[85] In turn, Shanghai attracted $530 million in pledged foreign investment from eleven nations, including sixty-five joint venture agreements. A number of other oil-related joint ventures were initiated by offshore oil-drilling companies and the firms supplying them, in the hope that such cooperative undertakings would lend an advantage in bidding on offshore contracts.[86]

During this boom period, over sixty Sino-American joint ventures were approved, many of which had been in the negotiating stage for several years. The approved ventures produced such diverse commodities as computers, baby food, cotton, cigarettes, silk, solar cells, hotels, jeeps, and photographic materials. In short, the period of 1983–84 represented a watershed in China's economic development. The international business community was deeply impressed by the country's ability to attract and utilize new and varied forms of investment. One factor contributing to this success was a trade surge in 1984 which increased the total value of imports and exports in 1984 to $49.97 billion, a 22.4 percent increase over 1983. In the same period, trade with Japan also rose by 36.3 percent, with the United States by 50.6 percent, with Hong Kong by 27.7 percent, and with the Soviet Union by 73.3 percent. This trend continued in 1985 as total trade hit $73 billion, an increase of 20 percent over 1984. As this second phase came to an end, the foreign investment picture was decidedly upbeat as hundreds of foreign firms engaged in negotiations with the Chinese, intent on positioning themselves within the China market. Financially, the Chinese were in better shape as well with $14.06 billion in foreign exchange revenue earmarked for spending on further modernization and offshore oil development.[87]

PHASE III (1985–88): A FOREIGN EXCHANGE CRISIS AND FURTHER CONCESSIONS

As 1985 began, hundreds of foreign firms were poised for the China business payoff. But quick gain would elude them. In that year, the repercussions of China's 1984 decentralization of import and export regulations and a growing trade deficit were felt in the economy. Since 1978, the People's Republic had treated foreign exchange conservation as a national priority, so when Chinese trade officials realized that in the course of a year (between 1984 and 1985) foreign exchange coffers had been drained from roughly $19 billion to $10 billion, the country went into a state of shock. Foreign trade corporations, as well as enterprises and corrupt officials, had abused the new freedoms of importation to seek foreign capital and purchase consumer goods and equipment (mainly from Japan) only to resell them to Chinese consumers at often tremendous profit. (In Hainan Island, the unauthorized importation of $500 million worth of Japanese cars resulted in several executions.) During 1984, Chinese banks were encouraged to make further low-interest loans to local enterprises as part of a system of increased incentives to managers and workers. Unfortunately, these loans were indiscriminately granted, which caused a further drain on foreign exchange reserves. The problem was made more severe by a widening trade deficit—from 1.27 billion Rmb in 1984 to 14.9 billion Rmb in 1985.[88] Concurrently, the textile trade (from which China earns much of its foreign exchange) was experiencing slow growth and the price of oil (from which China anticipated earning the largest percentage of its foreign exchange revenue) had virtually collapsed.

The government responded by reclaiming control over foreign exchange markets and the import/export functions of local FTCs. New restrictions on access to foreign exchange by Chinese enterprises led to a number of instances where Chinese partners were forced to renege on signed contracts with foreign partners in cases where the Chinese could not obtain the foreign exchange they expected. In 1985, reports surfaced of six-figure contracts being canceled because of sudden restrictions, as well as a number of company failures in Hong Kong associated with breached Chinese contracts.[89]

Foreigners and Chinese participating in joint ventures were affected as localized government control over the examination and approval of foreign exchange loans made by local branches of the Bank of China was withdrawn. Further provisions to aid local and foreign capital projects were reduced. The relevant entities that had supported Sino-foreign ventures financially were required to obtain (and balance) foreign exchange by their own efforts, which placed increased financial pressure on the foreign partners.[90] Despite the greater autonomy granted to certain localities, as during the period of 1982–84, there were new stringent controls put in place over the allocation and use of foreign exchange, which were reflected in the strengthening of MO-FERT's administrative control over the management of foreign investment.[91] As MOFERT took control, massive cuts in imports were undertaken (especially those from Japan), and the approval process for import licenses was expanded. All stages of conducting business in a China venture were affected by the crisis. For example, an approval at the local level to purchase the equipment and implement the start-up for a project would often be vetoed at a higher level.

The crisis reached critical mass when foreign firms attempted to repatriate their profits. These problems were acutely felt in those ventures in which import substitution was the primary purpose. These ventures were set up under the assumption that the Chinese would be able to pay for at least a percentage of the factory's production with foreign exchange, making the venture economically viable. Moreover, the foreign exchange crisis impinged upon the ability of foreign firms to raise funds in China or recoup any of their profits. Many of the pioneer joint ventures had to rely primarily on imported kits and components because they could not locate reliable, high-quality domestic parts and components. These imported kits had to be paid for with foreign exchange. As it got harder for China to convert Rmb profits into foreign currency, the balancing of foreign exchange within Sino-foreign ventures became problematic, if not impossible, without the foreign partner subsidizing the venture.

In July 1986, the Chinese government surveyed the foreign investment enterprises (FIEs) in nineteen provinces and cities (including Tianjin, Guangdong, and Fujian provinces, and the city of Beijing) and found that these ventures had experienced a cumulative deficit of $579.7 million. One of the reasons for the high deficit was a lack of bank support and cash flow to the ventures. For example, foreign enterprises spent $1.28 billion for imported parts and raw materials in 1985 but only generated $472 million in exports. Many of these joint ventures, in reality, had been selling to the domestic market.[92] Chu Baotai, a deputy director at MOFERT, said the shortage of products from joint ventures meant that a higher price could be found for them within China rather than in export markets, so joint venture boards directed products into the domestic market. However, the profits from these domestic sales accrued in the form of nonconvertible renminbi.[93] (It is difficult to know whether the decision to sell to the domestic market was influenced by the Chinese side looking for the highest price, the foreign side seeking access to the domestic market, or both. Whichever it was, the repatriation problem was deeply affected by restrictions on foreign exchange allocations, and the burden to support ventures suffering imbalances lay on the shoulders of the foreign partners. See Chapter 6 for more on renminbi repatriation schemes.)

The well-publicized problems that AMC had experienced with foreign exchange were hardly unique. Firms such as Hitachi of Japan (which operates a color television manufacturing facility in Fujian), Peugeot of France (which operates a joint venture to assemble automobiles in Guangzhou), and Squibb Pharmaceuticals (which operates a drug manufacturing joint venture in Shanghai) encountered similar difficulties because of their need to import large quantities of parts and materials.[94] By the end of 1985, foreign exchange was being allocated for technology transfer and export projects only; foreign firms were urged to transfer more technology for less compensation. Participation in joint ventures became more risky as local governments took more control over the financial aspects of these ventures, and export rules concerning the percentage of production to be sold overseas were tightened. In short, the ability to balance foreign exchange became the overriding criterion for approval of new Sino-foreign ventures.

By the end of 1986, the so-called contraction policy was moderately successful in controlling the foreign exchange disequilibrium. This success was, in part, the result of China's state control of the economy, which allows for swift amelioration of financial problems associated with government-controlled entities. By July 1986, the contraction policy devalued the Rmb by 13.6 percent, the sharpest yet, in order to prod exportation and lure new foreign investors with a more attractive exchange rate.[95] The trade deficit, a dropping rate of tourism, and falling oil profits were also cited as reasons for the devaluation.[96]

In March 1988, a more cautious decentralization of import and export policies was initiated through regulations that create a contract system between MOFERT's subsidiary FTCs at the local level and the ministry itself at the central level. Large purchases by FTCs now require approval directly from the State Council. In essence, local government and trading entities have reclaimed much of the freedom to import and export that they had in 1984, and skeptics fear a repeat of China's buying binge. However, the new system guarantees reporting of purchases to higher levels and should prevent rampant buying, economic corruption, and foreign exchange depletion.[97]

Intensified Investor Complaints

A barrage of complaints—some old, some new—surfaced again in the foreign business community in 1985–86. Without going into great detail, these problems included a lack of access to the Chinese domestic market; a lack of foreign managerial control in China ventures; difficulties with repatriation of profits and dividends; difficulty in gaining the protection of proprietary information; poor infrastructure support for China activities (power outages, shipping delays, etc.); uncertain supply and cost of production-related imports; and uneven quality of locally sourced components and raw materials. Another source of difficulty had to do with the process of decentralization within China's planned economy. By granting of greater autonomy to local areas such as Shanghai, Tianjin, and Guangdong, few foreign firms had the slightest notion of which individuals or organizations had the final authority to approve agreements and sign contracts. All of these problems were associated with doing business in China, and they were not perceived as commensurate with the high cost of entering the market and setting up an office and staff presence in the People's Republic.[98]

Between 1985 and 1987 the cost of doing business in the People's Republic continued to skyrocket. For example, the cost of hotel office and living space for staff increased 85 percent in one six-month period. Leases were unfair, typically requiring a year's rent to be paid in advance with increases possible at any time. A small office with living quarters, when added to a year's salary for one executive representative stationed in China, cost close to $250,000 a year for most firms. Exorbitant charges characterized every facet of the business environment. As one Chinese writer freely admitted in 1986, heavy charges exacted by so-called departments in charge, under all sorts of pretexts, had seriously damaged China's investment climate. Moreover, the method by which foreigners were charged was an irritant as well. For instance, water and power fees were charged not by the amount of water and power used, but according to the caliber of water pipes and the load capacity of transformers, respectively.[99]

Most disconcerting, however, was that the Chinese had set up a dual price system by which foreign businesses were charged higher prices than Chinese businesses for services, food, raw materials, parts, transportation, and labor. In one Chinese periodical, a writer admitted the system gave rise to price gouging by local-level officials when dealing with foreigners.[100] For example, in the city of Xiamen, foreigners were paying 100 percent more for telecommunication installation and 500 percent more for telecommunication service than the local Chinese.[101] On top of this, foreign businesses were often the victims of locally enforced fines and penalties, including those made against individuals who failed to report taxes, evaded taxes, or were overdue in paying their taxes. In mid-September of 1985, twenty-seven Hong Kong and Macao enterprises were fined for failing to register as companies doing business in China. All of them had been renting rooms at the local hotels as companies set up for trade liaison purposes. All twenty-seven enterprises had been involved in such a practice for more than six months, some of them as long as four years. The fines were imposed under the *Regulations Concerning the Registration of Representative Offices in China* by foreign enterprises.[102] Foreign investors felt themselves squeezed from all directions. The situation brought into focus the question of whether Chinese at the local level would ever accept foreign companies on an equal footing.

In another development that appeared to the foreign investor as an additional disincentive to doing business in China, the debt/equity ratio for joint ventures was raised in 1986 in an attempt both to increase the level of foreign capital to the People's Republic and to raise state tax revenues. For example, a one-to-one debt/equity ratio is now required in joint venture investments valued at $3–10 million. The ratio is lowered as total investment increases, yet no borrowing is permitted on joint ventures or wholly foreign-owned ventures valued at less than $3 million.[103]

All in all, with the comparative opportunities for foreign investors in Asian countries such as Taiwan, South Korea, and India, China became an increasingly unattractive place to do business in the period of 1985–87. Further diminishing China's attraction were the efforts by U.S. companies to develop new technologies and production processes that would bring certain parts of the production process back on shore, thereby avoiding the complexities of doing business in places such as China.[104]

By 1986 the ramifications of the disgruntlement began to appear in the form of declining foreign investment and a proliferation of published complaints in the world press. The decline in foreign investment was the first such decrease since 1978. Foreign investment commitments in 1986 were roughly one-half of what they were in 1985. It was at this time that the investment climate received its most critical blow. In April 1986, AMC announced that its Beijing-based joint venture would have to halt production because of unresolved foreign exchange problems.[105]

An aura of negativism descended upon the foreign investment community following AMC's announcement. A U.S. corporate exodus from China was even mentioned as a possibility in the *Wall Street Journal*. The real possibility arose that the doomsayers in both China and the foreign business community might be proven correct in predicting that Beijing would be unable to manage the investment policies promulgated in its open-door policy. Interviews conducted in Beijing in July 1986 confirmed that a large number of the big-name U.S. firms in the People's Republic seriously considered pulling out. Many of the firms that did not consider deregistering from the market were American oil companies. They perceived little benefit in walking away from investments in oil exploration worth tens of millions of dollars. Although some firms packed it in, most simply cut back their China operations and charted a course of retrenchment. Of the 1,691 foreign corporate offices established in China, twenty-six were shut down in the first half of 1986, while in others the staff was significantly reduced.[106] As Chinese officials were well aware, the office closings augured an ominous trend since they had not occurred before.

Improvements in Investment Climate

Nevertheless, in 1985–86, Chinese policymakers made a concerted and effective effort to brighten the investment climate by pushing through a number of policy changes and by ratifying new laws. In January 1986 China issued a set of regulations concerning wholly foreign-owned investments which formalized its willingness to accept this type of investment. In effect, wholly foreign-owned ventures (*duzi jingying*) are established and owned by foreign companies on Chinese soil. The foreigner manages the venture independent of the Chinese; there is no sharing of risks or expenses and no sharing of profits. These ventures are regulated only to the extent that all equipment and technology installed in the factory must be deemed by Chinese import officials to be advanced.[107] Hong Kong firms own most of the wholly foreign-owned factories, which are most prevalent in the SEZs. As of 1987, American companies owned and operated fewer than ten such firms. Nearly all wholly foreign-owned ventures in China, however, are geared to the production of textiles, foods, and simple electronics with an average start-up cost of $50,000.

In early 1986 the Chinese also increased the number of investment incentives applicable to certain sectors and geographic regions. The incentives for investing included:

- land-use fee exemptions in Shenzhen SEZ;
- free-port policies in Xiamen SEZ (including direct trade with Taiwan);
- certain tax holidays, land-use exemptions, and preferential treatment for foreign business investing in Kunming and Shenyang provinces;
- positive developments in the Shanghai area, including specific foreign exchange support for high-technology joint ventures and other joint ventures that sold to the domestic market, as well as general progress on the level of skill and experience of the labor force, and the adoption of a complete set of labor regulations.

In the oil exploration sector the incentives included:

- new tracts made available together with new incentives to explore them, particularly for foreign companies whose drilling was unsuccessful in the initial contract areas;
- import and harbor development made available;
- preferential treatment terms for foreign partners, similar to those in the fourteen open cities, such as tax holidays, tax reduction, automatic tax-free profit remittance, long-term contracts, accelerated depreciation of fixed assets, exemptions from customs duty, and taxes on imports of materials and equipment.[108]

Further incentives included tax exemptions for joint ventures: a 50 percent tax exemption over three years, and a 30 percent tax reduction over ten years for low-yield joint venture projects such as agriculture, forestry, animal husbandry, and breeding. Also, duties and general taxation were cut on equipment for joint ventures.

Foreign pressure also prompted the Chinese to extend the lifespan of Sino-foreign ventures. New, more flexible regulations permitted joint ventures to operate for up to fifty years, rather than the previous limit of thirty years. Many firms had been pushing for *unlimited* joint venture arrangements. One could conclude from the new venture-duration policy and guarantees of more independence to wholly foreign-owned firms that the Chinese leadership was becoming comfortable with foreign business in China and that it hoped to convince foreign investors that the country's investment climate would improve.

Also in January 1986, the State Council promulgated a set of new regulations on foreign exchange balancing by foreign joint ventures to help ameliorate the problems experienced by many foreign firms. The regulations opened up several new possibilities for dealing with the foreign exchange problems in those cases where exports were not available at the time or where import substitution was the main purpose of the venture. The new provisions sanctioned foreign exchange trading between foreign joint ventures, but the effectiveness of this method in solving the repatriation dilemma, as well as others outlined in the provisions, will not be known for a few years. (See Chapter 6 for details on the provisions.)

Attempts have also been made to coordinate foreign investment activities at the administrative level. One such move has been the establishment of a *leading group* for managing foreign investment, headed by State Councilor Gu Mu, under the auspices of the State Council. As with several similar State Council level bodies, this group was empowered with broad responsibilities in terms of monitoring and managing China's overall investment environment. The leading group includes representatives of the commissions, ministries, and financial institutions in charge of foreign investment issues. It appears Beijing has recognized that foreign investment decision making needs to be more centrally orchestrated to be evenly implemented at ground level.

Another propitious event occurred in June 1986 when the State Economic Commission set up a business coordination center to help Sino-foreign joint ventures solve their internal problems. From this office, joint venture complaints are communicated directly to high Chinese state officials. The resultant pressure from this level of central government would, in theory, speed local bureaucratic approval methods, which are typically stalled by intradepartmental quibbling. Similarly, Shanghai's foreign trade commission undertook the task of assisting joint ventures under its jurisdiction in exporting their production of light industrial products.[109] In Shanghai, where 126 separate "chops" (stamps of approval) were once needed to approve a project, the process of approval of joint ventures and solving foreign investment problems has been speeded up by streamlining the administration of foreign investment and establishing a coordinating service center related to foreign nationals. This organization, like others springing up across China, is evidence of China's acknowledgment that the country lacks the trained personnel for dealing with the financial and managerial problems associated with Sino-foreign ventures. China has also recognized that discrimination against foreigners by the Chinese at the local level is, in part, the result of a lack of information about Beijing's policy and its limitations.

The State Council also responded to foreign investor complaints by issuing the twenty-two articles of the *Provisions of the State Council for the Encouragement of Foreign Investment* on October 11, 1986. These provisions are being put into effect at the regional level through provincial legislation. In addition, a number of key provinces and municipalities have issued their own complementary investment incentives and new regulations to enhance their own attractiveness to foreign companies. The city of Shanghai was the first to respond with a body of new investment regulations which, among other things, were designed to improve the investment climate, facilitate the absorption of foreign investment, introduce advanced technology, and improve product quality and exports in order to earn more foreign exchange and develop the national economy.[110] Also, a series of sixteen guidelines was issued at the end of March 1987, thirteen of which have been formally promulgated as of March 1, 1988. These guidelines streamline and greatly enhance the effectiveness of an array of regulations concerning the following areas:

- hiring, firing, and wages of Chinese labor;
- debt/equity rules;
- Bank of China loans and loan guarantees;
- customs charges, taxation, and foreign exchange balancing methods;
- exportation of Chinese goods purchased by foreigners in China; and
- conditions governing the eligibility of foreign ventures, exporting from China or transferring technology, to receive special privileges.[111]

According to regulations issued so far, qualifying ventures can expect a variety of benefits, including reduced taxes and lower fees that companies pay to the state for land and labor use, abolition of customs duties on imported goods needed to produce export products, and greater authority to hire, fire, and make decisions about production and other business matters without approval from government bureaus. Another provision allows ventures to recruit their own employees and gives the Labor and Personnel Ministry the right to investigate disputes and to order transfers. The rules also allow investors to refuse to pay unreasonable charges and to appeal cases of alleged price gouging to a grievance board working under the powerful State Economic Commission. They also go to some length to ensure that services such as water, power, transport, and communications are provided at the same cost paid by Chinese enterprises.

More specifically, the new provisions delineate two types of enterprises eligible for special treatment upon certification by MOFERT. The first of these is the productive enterprise, which can export 50 percent of its output and earn a foreign exchange surplus after deducting all of its foreign exchange expenditures. The second type is an enterprise possessing advanced technologies supplied by overseas investors that can be used to develop new products and upgrade or replace old products.[112] The new regulations appear to have three main goals: (1) to use preferential measures in such areas as taxation, loan availability, and labor cost in order to guide the investment direction of export-oriented and high-technology enterprises; (2) to lower different kinds of fees (e.g., land-use fees) so that products made by foreign-owned firms are internationally competitive; and (3) to protect the autonomy of foreign-invested companies, and to tackle the problems of complicated procedures and worker inefficiency.[113] Firms that fit into these categories are now qualified for certification at the local level, thus ensuring that they receive the benefits offered in the new provisions. Some foreign firms have become certified and report improvement in the Chinese response to their problems. For instance, Foxboro has recently secured repatriation of its Rmb earnings through Shanghai financial institutions. Earlier the firm had depended on a *guanxi,* or back door, repatriation scheme involving the selling of Rmb for foreign exchange through a willing Shanghai banking entity. This implies that the new provisions may institutionalize many of the back-door methods foreign firms have resorted to in order to do business in the People's Republic. By November 1986, twenty-four technically advanced and export-oriented enterprises had received certification in Beijing alone.[114]

The State Council provisions could have their greatest impact on the regulation of personnel management practices. The regulation of personnel practices has been a thorny issue for most foreign firms in China. In most cases, despite Chinese claims to the contrary, foreign firms have been severely restricted in hiring and firing workers and in determining their own wage and bonus levels. (Chapter 6 will go into greater detail on the hiring/firing of Chinese personnel.) In late 1986, the State Council provisions were reinforced when the now reorganized Ministry of Labor and Personnel announced a series of specific measures which would expand the rights of foreign-owned firms to oversee the hiring, wages, bonuses, and welfare of their workers.[115] The ministry's announcement was an implicit acknowledgment by leading Chinese officials that judgments about workers' performance and behavior can best be made at the enterprise level.

Another implication of the provisions is that exorbitant fees charged by the labor agency FESCO (Foreign Enterprises Service Corporation) will be brought under stricter control. The provisions go a long way toward placing the burden of responsibility on local government entities to ensure that foreign-owned enterprises remain unfettered by the bureaucracy that plagues many Chinese enterprises. However, one tends to wonder what will happen to nonexport producing and low-technology Sino-foreign joint ventures (such as hotels, restaurants, and textile factories) in China's new investment climate. Could these ventures be left to fend for themselves in an already difficult environment? Will local officials charge inflated prices for services for these firms while restraining themselves when dealing with privileged ones, thus turning a dual-price system into a triple-tiered system?

FOREIGN INVESTMENT ASSESSMENT THROUGH CHINESE EYES

The cumulative capital investment into China since 1979 has surpassed investment totals in most other Asian countries. The total capital invested during the period of 1979–86 equaled $24.88 billion, of which $6.9 billion was foreign investment and $18.19 billion entered the People's Republic in the form of loans.[116] Not only has the open-door policy increased the rate of foreign participation but it has also encouraged the diversification of investment into various business forms, including joint ventures, wholly foreign-owned ventures, compensation trade deals, cooperative production, assembly and processing, and joint oil development. Clearly, the trend has been away from concentrating investment in joint offshore oil development and toward other sectors and geographic regions.

Foreign Investment Policy Performance

In 1986, foreign investment was down 48 percent—commitments equaling $3.3 billion. By the end of that year, the Chinese press reported that the amount of foreign investment entering China was unsatisfactory, and that most investments focused on nonproductive sectors such as tourism, real estate, light industry, textiles, consumer goods, and building materials. The preferred sectors—manufacturing and projects involving the transfer of high technology—had attracted only small amounts of foreign investment. The overwhelming majority of foreign investment was in labor-intensive and low-technology projects. The policy was said to have missed the mark in assimilating advanced technology, having allowed the spread of enterprises with poor export capability, poor capability in earning foreign exchange, and enterprises which were domestically oriented rather than export oriented.[117] Although the areas of energy, computers and electronics, transportation, communications, food processing, and building construction have been given a high priority under the Seventh Five-Year Plan, the country has been largely unsuccessful in attracting foreign investment into these sectors. Most foreign investment in the People's Republic has been concentrated in light industry, real estate, and tourism rather than larger infrastructural projects. Between 1979 and 1984, hotels, apartments, and office buildings accounted for over 40 percent of the total monetary value of investment in joint ventures. Roughly 60 percent of these joint ventures are tourist hotels,[118] the reason being that foreign exchange can be amassed in these ventures directly from foreign purchasers and guests, thereby avoiding the problem of repatriation.

Another distressing issue has been the lackluster performance of China's SEZs, which were set up to attract foreign firms, increase and upgrade exports, and to assimilate foreign technology and managerial expertise. By the end of 1985, the SEZs had attracted $1.17 billion in foreign investment, about 20 percent of all investment in China.[119] A vast amount of investment had contributed to infrastructural development in the zones, but export growth had faltered since foreign ventures in the SEZs were not sufficiently geared to supplying international markets and SEZ-produced products were of uneven quality and poor design. In addition, SEZs are fraught with economic corruption associated with their close proximity to Hong Kong and Macao, and their relatively lax regulations concerning import licensing and project funding.[120] In another report the SEZs were said to be unsuitable for spread-

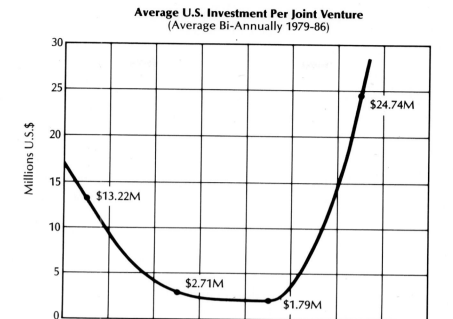

Average U.S. Investment Per Joint Venture
(Average Bi-Annually 1979-86)

SOURCE: Compiled by the author from various sources including *South,* Department of Commerce publications, and the *China Business Review.*

U.S. side. These deals came to fruition in 1985–86. Calculating from Chinese government figures, American partners in U.S.–China joint ventures committed, on average, about $5.6 million per venture between 1978 and 1987.

NEW OPPORTUNITIES IN CHINA (1989-2000)

Chinese leaders recognize the seriousness of the unresolved problems in the country's business climate. Foreign pressure to correct these problems has produced many tangible results. In a stream of similar articles appearing in the *People's Daily* in 1986, Gu Mu characteristically congratulated China's investment policies for attracting a total of 6,000 joint ventures (3,000 of which have started up) while defining the three aspects of China's investment climate at the root of the salient problems, which are still unresolved. First, he admitted that the People's Republic lacks experience in conducting international business. Second, the country is finding it difficult to mold an old system of time-wasting bureaucratic procedures into a more efficient system of supply and demand. Third, Gu cited China's incomplete investment laws and regulations as a cause for foreign investor discontent. In an article in *Intertrade* (June 1985), it was written that four necessary adjustments would have to be made to improve the investment climate: (1) further improvement of the infrastructure, despite the fact that recent huge inputs in the infrastructure have shown little improvement in the investment climate; (2) the liberalization of investment polices, including more tax breaks and exemptions; (3) streamlining of agencies involved in foreign trade to reduce red tape; and (4) improvement of information dissemination among Chinese trade officials so policies can be carried out after promulgation.

Nevertheless, most foreign businessmen say that the basic issue—Can foreign joint ventures sell in China's domestic market and take profit from those sales out of the country?—has been ignored, even in new provisions and guidelines announced in 1986–87. In the 1990s, however, the foreign investor community may witness the transformation of China's investment climate fostered by a loosening of restrictions on foreign investment. The Chinese, most significantly at the local level, are beginning to change their view of the role of foreign investment in their country. In the past, locals did not appreciate the risk foreigners were taking by investing in the People's Republic—and that these investors had come to China with profit-making motivations. The failure of China to address this perception problem was indicative of the political sensitivity associated with allowing foreigners to benefit by doing business in their country. By 1986, a full-fledged propaganda program was under way in an attempt to offset a steep drop in foreign investment and project approval. A typical quote, in this case from *People's Daily*, was: "All our government agencies, enterprises, and cadres must cherish, support, and help Chinese-foreign joint ventures and should never discriminate against them, put obstacles in their way, treat them unfairly, or try to take advantage of them."[124]

The fear that foreigners might eventually come to dominate the Chinese economy was countered with the argument that the country's economy is simply too vast for such domination to occur, and that the approach to foreign capital and technology acquisition should be one that includes the notion of "letting others benefit before we do."[125] Most of the apprehension existing among Chinese officials and enterprise managers at the local level had been fear of being defrauded by foreigners, which encouraged local administrators to be overly stingy."[126] Hence, local Chinese administrators were urged to curtail "evil practices" of arbitrarily apportioning expenses to be paid by enterprises run with foreign investment, to stop breaking promises, and to refrain from laying obstacles in the way of foreign joint ventures.[127] Chinese units were encouraged to stop ignoring joint ventures and to assist and support them, reducing the exorbitant and unpredictable charges foreigners must pay and improving the treatment they receive doing business in China.[128] Foreign firms are increasingly sensitive to global competitive pressures and the need for acquiring additional production inputs—other than cheap labor—in their overseas operations. As a result, their willingness to place key technologies in China is lacking. With China's continuing shortage of skilled technicians, its lack of protection for proprietary information, and its unwillingness and inability to pay for imported technology, the foreign investor remains uneasy.

Moreover, the Chinese still appear quite unwilling to assist Sino-foreign joint ventures financially or offer them protection from local bureaucratic entities, which these firms must have in order to prosper in the People's Republic. As one U.S. businessman put it: "The Chinese at some point are going to have to make the commitment to use Chinese government resources to support" the foreign exchange needs of Sino-foreign joint ventures.[129] Most feel, however, that China has not offered the elements attractive to foreign investors in a consistent manner—financial transactions are fraught with red tape, workers cannot be easily relocated if needed, and multilayered bureaucracy impedes production efforts, even for the Chinese. Nevertheless, China will eventually ratify the crucial incentives offered in other Asian countries when they discover it is possible to do so without significantly disrupting their own economy. All signs point in this direction.

Undoubtedly, the Chinese government has begun to take a much more prominent role in officially sanctioning the profit motivations of the foreign companies that had pledged, as of July 1988, over $9.5 billion in 11,500 ventures in China. As Philip Caldwell, a senior managing director of Shearson and a director of Ford Motor Company, has said, "I can't think of anything more important to an investor than to have the host establish profitability as the key element in an investment."[130] The rate of new projects approved in the first half of 1988 (2,134 investments in all) was up 180 percent over the same period in 1987; meanwhile, the total output of Sino–foreign joint ventures nearly doubled in 1987 alone.

And so, in the waning months of the 1980s, foreign interest in the China market has intensified again. Yet, as the veterans of China trade reiterate, the challenge of the market is not so much in making adjustments to the vagaries of China's investment climate as it is learning to do business the way the Chinese do business. To this we must now turn our attention.

Negotiating and Organizing a China Venture

The complexities of doing business in the People's Republic demand that U.S. companies enter the country with a clear set of objectives as to what they expect to accomplish in the short and long term. Without such a clear perspective on goals and expectations, the likelihood increases that disappointment and frustration will quickly set in. Moreover, lacking such an explicit agenda places foreign firms in a relatively disadvantageous position with their competitors and their Chinese counterparts. It is essential to be realistic, well informed, and farsighted when beginning your China venture. Otherwise, the entire process of negotiating and organizing a venture will be fraught with uncertainties and a host of vexing problems.

Until 1979, only very formal, highly controlled channels existed for the foreigner to approach the Chinese. For years, the Canton Trade Fair was the sole venue for introducing trade goods.

As recently as 1982, foreign companies had to choose among the various foreign trade corporations under MOFERT to gain access to China's economy. With time, and the ratification of China's investment statutes, the process of entering the China market has grown more standardized and systematic. Today, multiple paths exist for foreign firms seeking partnerships with Chinese industrial enterprises.

Once the decision has been made to enter the market in the form of a venture (as opposed to direct exports), where does a firm begin in its search for the proper partner on the Chinese side? Of all the potential entry points, which ones offer genuinely beneficial connections with a viable counterpart in China? No golden axioms or hard-and-fast rules exist for locating the "perfect" partner. However, by looking at the past experience of firms in China, one can begin to surmise the appropriate items to consider and the relevant questions to ask during a firm's search for a Chinese counterpart.

Specific options for market entry, partner selection, negotiating tactics, and contracting should be governed primarily by the objectives driving the foreign company into China (as opposed to simply following Chinese objectives). For instance, most offshore manufacturing firms who intend to establish a production base in China should be thinking in terms of a broader strategic imperative; that is, to create new business activities or link existing ones to the Asia-Pacific region. Guided by a regional strategic perspective, some of these firms can use their presence in China as a key element in their overall strategy for competing with Japan in third-country markets. These firms can locate new sources of raw materials in the region at a competitive price, secure low-cost labor, and utilize efficient transportation facilities to move finished products rapidly from China to the firms' overseas markets. On the other hand, firms that desire to sell directly to the China market may want to tailor their China ventures to qualify for the special treatment offered to "technologically advanced" and "import substituting" foreign investment enterprises (FIEs). These firms will find that they must dedicate more time to careful research of the investment climate if they are to determine the most advantageous location, the most appropriate technology to transfer to China, and the standards their factories will have to meet to qualify for special status. As a final example, the firm that enters the China market in a defensive posture, that is, aiming to hold ground against the possible domination of the market by a competitor, may develop an entry strategy with the objective of starting small, keeping costs down, transferring as little technology as possible, and merely learning all that it can about the market for later, possibly larger, endeavors. These firms might want to collaborate with lower profile Chinese companies, especially if they possess non-traditional access to foreign exchange. Most important, it should be recognized that a firm's overall venture objectives may find expression in a set of expectations that may, or may not, interface readily with those held by its potential Chinese partner. Under such circumstances, it is in the best interests of the U.S. firm to anticipate these different goals, and different approaches, before making any significant investment of resources.

POINTS OF ENTRY IN THE BUSINESS RELATIONSHIP

Sino-U.S. business partnerships often originate in an unorthodox manner because of China's provincial, fiefdom-like organizational structure that puts a premium on personal connections. A number of American companies have simply stumbled into China by coincidence. The catalyst may have been a company executive meeting a Chinese economic official at a trade convention, and then running into him again later at another location, perhaps in China. Or it might have been a Chinese-American in the firm, through a connection with a relative in a remote Chinese province, who brings an opportunity to the attention of his or her boss. Or a telex arrives one day from a Chinese factory expressing a desire to visit the company's facilities and discuss possible cooperation in a venture.

Many of the early pioneering deals were put together as the direct result of the personal motivations of American executives who saw great promise in the China market. Some of the early firms were led into China by veritable crusaders who boarded the first plane to the mainland the day the door was opened. Some American executives (John Marshall of 3M, Armand Hammer of Occidental Petroleum, and Todd Clare of AMC, to name a few) had been enthusiastic about "the mainland" for years, especially if they had previously dealt with East Asia and had since become top executives with the power and position to usher their firms into China. Interestingly, the Chinese had similar true believers on their side. These individuals, either through their educational training or by having relatives in the United States, served as advocates of strengthening links with American industry.

The case of the 3M corporation illustrates this situation. 3M's entry into China depended on the convictions and first-hand experience of John Marshall, who commandeered the company's initial China activities. For the most part, the entry strategy used by 3M employed no consultants, did not conduct extensive investigations, initiated no company conferences, and did not present plans to a board of directors for a vote of approval. The decision to enter the China market was followed by the shifting of 3M's China office from Zug, Switzerland, to the company's main headquarters in Minneapolis, Minnesota. One reason for the shift was that 3M believed its proposals would be more credible to the Chinese if they emanated from headquarters rather than a remote subsidiary. Entering the China market required extensive coordination among the company's multiple divisions and subsidiaries; it was judged that this coordination could be best implemented through the firm's headquarters. Another factor in 3M's decision was the notion that, over time, in-house expertise could be enhanced by exposing all divisions of the company directly to the China market. The company recognized early on in the process that the Chinese prefer dealing directly with a foreign firm's head office, rather than its agents and representatives. The company felt, correctly, that its products could not be sold without the conviction and commitment of its home office.[1] The 3M case also underscores a point made later in this book that when boards of directors, stockholders, and underinformed company executives get involved in the direction of a firm's China strategy, preconceived biases, faulty images, and misperceptions can impair a company's approach strategy.

High-level corporate diplomacy has served as a stimulus behind some Sino-U.S. joint projects. In 1985, Hewlett-Packard opened a joint venture that had its origin in talks held between former Premier Zhao Enlai and former U.S. Secretary of State Henry Kissinger. Other agreements were linked to the ongoing bilateral science and technology cooperation accords between the two countries. In 1979, when the Sino-American Science and Technology Cooperation Agreement was signed, an explicit objective of the U.S. science adviser and his staff was to ensure that commercial ties grew from expanded science and technology cooperation. Unfortunately, only a few such projects have emerged as of 1989, mainly because of the nature of government-business relations in the United States. However slow this effort was to materialize, the basic intent was there from the start.

Today, contacts can be made at a variety of different levels. This makes the selection process much more complex, but it does allow for more intimate working relations between the foreign firm and its specific Chinese counterpart. In spite of a certain reimposition of control by the central authorities regarding foreign economic and investment relations, MOFERT no longer coordinates all of the access routes. For better or worse, the cast of characters grows daily as those provinces and cities in the interior compete with China's coastal cities for potential investors and foreign partners. This competition still exists despite the decision of the leadership, in early 1988, to stress the development of China's coastal areas.

The decision to enter China must take into account the size and type of the project to be undertaken as well as the specific organizations that have responsibility for the implementation of the venture. A project involving extensive infrastructural improvements or multi-province coordination of Chinese government agencies requires approvals from a myriad of central and local officials. From the outset, such a project should have the backing of an influential government-entity counterpart that will facilitate all project-related activities. If the project requires large inputs of foreign exchange on the Chinese side, an investment entity such as CITIC or one of its provincial counterparts might be an appropriate point of contact, since these agencies control large sums of foreign exchange and have close ties with the Bank of China.

As a firm approaches the China market, it must seek to build an appropriate partnership network. The choice of a relevant set of allies, however, can be accomplished only after a firm has set forth its specific needs and objectives. Foreign executives need to understand that the relationship between their firm and their Chinese counterpart will vary depending on where the Chinese entity is positioned within the People's Republic bureaucracy, how modernization reforms affect its independence, etc. For example, the interaction between a foreign firm and a Chinese trade/consultancy organization and between the same foreign firm and an industrial ministry generally will have little in common. The Chinese government structure tends to define organizational responsibilities in a very narrow fashion when it comes to foreign linkages. As such, each relationship must be evaluated on its own merits and developed with a set of specific goals in mind.

To establish a network of business connections and create a good reputation among Chinese customers, Western companies typically set up an office presence in the China market. This is done at the very beginning if a firm needs to position itself close to its prospective end-users. Trading firms, for example, require a more visible presence than others because trading involves constant interaction with suppliers, distributors, and a variety of other entities. Office presence is expensive, however, and not always the most cost-effective use of resources. The majority of firms doing business in China still do so from their Hong Kong or Tokyo offices. Most small firms merely selling to China still operate from within the United States. Obviously, while operating from outside China may be sufficient for some firms, it may also prevent them from staying current on the latest business scuttlebutt or maintaining the maximum attention of their Chinese counterparts.

Many companies locate large numbers of people and technical staff in Hong Kong while stationing just a few in Beijing. At one point, IBM had stationed fifty families in Beijing, but recalled some staff to Hong Kong when the firm's China sales plunged in 1985. Some firms, such as Digital Electronics Corporation, have tried to keep their staffs in China to a minimum. Digital, however, has found it necessary to establish a service office along with a smaller operations office in Beijing because of expanding sales of its computers. Mobil Oil works through a Hong Kong office because balancing foreign exchange is too difficult if the company goes into China directly. In a recent survey of eighty-seven U.S. companies based in Hong Kong, 50 percent indicated that they conduct sales in China via Hong Kong. Seventy-one of the respondents said that they located in Hong Kong to gain access to Asian markets in general. In other words, many U.S. firms are penetrating the China market and other burgeoning Asian markets from their comfortable offices in Hong Kong, and will continue to do so at least until 1997, when Hong Kong becomes part of the People's Republic.[2]

For the average firm, an office in Hong Kong indeed holds several advantages. First, Hong Kong offers office space that is less expensive than in China. Some firms simply base their operations in Hong Kong and make frequent trips to the People's Republic. For the same cost of renting an office in Beijing and stationing an expatriate there for a year ($250,000–$300,000), a firm can send a small team into the People's Republic from the United States twice a month for the whole year at $10,000 per visit. In addition, appreciable profits continue to be made by foreigners who ally with Hong Kong businessmen to invest in cooperative ventures in the People's Republic. This sort of venture has gained in popularity as China has decentralized economic decision making and the SEZs have developed a more functional business infrastructure.

Second, the role of Hong Kong may be more important to foreign firms as a next-door source of management personnel, financial services, and components, which can be utilized in operations within the People's Republic.[3] In addition, Hong Kong reigns supreme as a way station for Chinese goods ultimately bound for third countries (re-exports). Hong Kong will likely become a conduit for goods exported by joint ventures in China to other nations in Asia.[4] Heretofore, it has also served as a vehicle for facilitating China trade with Taiwan and South Korea, especially on the import side.

Office presence in China certainly does not represent a panacea for finding the right venture partner. This can be accomplished through a number of avenues. A proven method is the direct communication of proposals to potential Chinese counterparts who are introduced by a Chinese consulate business officer in the United States, or a U.S. consulate business officer in China. There are numerous examples of Chinese-American firms in the United States being approached directly as potential business partners. This fact was confirmed decidedly in the questionnaires distributed by the author, wherein 59 percent of the responding firms indicate that they entered the China market after the Chinese solicited their firm directly. This was especially true for small firms that produced machinery or parts and components for manufacturing processes. Evidently, information concerning their products and technologies had been previously obtained as part of an intensive, orchestrated effort by Chinese factories and/or technology import corporations. The Chinese also purchase space in major periodicals and newspapers to advertise projects open to foreign participation and invite foreign executives to attend technology and product fairs throughout China. In some instances, these advertisements go unseen by U.S. firms, which is unfortunate because these fairs differ from exhibitions in that they are specifically joint venture fairs in which Chinese municipalities and provinces solicit foreign partners directly.

In the case of Cummins Engine Company, the China National Technical Import Corporation (TECHIMPORT), an agency under MOFERT, invited a Cummins delegation to China in July 1978 to discuss a technology transfer project. It was no coincidence that the China National Machinery Import and Export Corporation (MACHIMPEX), another subordinate to MOFERT, had purchased ten Cummins engines from the company's Manila office a few months earlier. In 1979, soon after the Cummins delegation visited China, the Chinese contracted with the Japanese firm Komatsu to license their technology to produce bulldozers in two factories in China. The connecting link in the strategy of courting both of these firms was that Komatsu powers its vehicles with Cummins engines, which it licenses from Cummins Engine Company. Because Komatsu could not sublicense the Cummins diesel engine technology in China, the Chinese were highly motivated to offer Cummins preferential treatment to entice the company to transfer their engine technology.[5] This case also points out the importance of monitoring the finished products and components China purchases and what products come under licenses to be manufactured there. Certainly, a vast number of U.S. firms fail to realize that some of their products and technology are being sold to China as part of finished goods assembled by other companies around the world.

The Myth of Trading Company Liaisons

Though Hong Kong offers the foreign firm many benefits and comforts, there exists a widespread misperception that by going into China through Hong Kong representatives, a U.S. firm will gain an absolute advantage. Indeed, some Hong Kong representatives can offer valuable connections in the People's Republic. However, if a U.S. firm enters the China market through a Hong Kong subsidiary or partner, it may offset some of the clout that the firm, through its reputation, may wield among Chinese leaders. The Chinese greatly respect American business people and engineers, and consider an American presence in China a sign of great sincerity and commitment.

A firm should not assume that a Hong Kong negotiator's common-culture link can necessarily overcome the regional loyalties and idiosyncrasies of various parts of China. Officials working in Beijing are not always impressed by the use of Hong Kong negotiators. For one thing, Cantonese-speaking traders from Hong Kong do not always make the best speakers of *putonghua* (Mandarin Chinese). There is a traditional Chinese saying: "Don't be afraid of the heavens; don't be afraid of hell; just be afraid of a Cantonese trying to speak Mandarin!" Another drawback to using Hong Kong negotiators concerns the past dealings between Hong Kong businessmen and their Chinese counterparts. There may arise certain doubts in the minds of Chinese officials regarding the integrity and reliability of the Hong Kong representative. While there is often no basis in fact for this kind of perception, it nonetheless may be a problem worth considering.

Another common practice that leads to problems is the use of a Hong Kong trading firm as an intermediary between potential foreign and Chinese partners. One firm made the mistake of transferring the main responsibilities for supervision and control of its manufacturing contract with China to a Hong Kong trading company that had no experience with either the specific equipment in question or the qualifications for selecting the Chinese factories that would manufacture the equipment. The U.S. firm, therefore, was not involved directly with the end-user in the People's Republic, leaving quality specifications largely unmonitored. As one might expect, the ensuing equipment malfunctions led to the collapse of the enterprise with concomitant losses to the U.S., Hong Kong, and Chinese companies.[6] This is not to downplay the value of contacts with trading entities; they are often useful in establishing initial contacts. Including them in the implementation of a contractual agreement and plant operations, however, generally spells trouble later.

Institutional and Extra-Institutional Approaches

If the Chinese press is any guide, more and more investment companies in the People's Republic exist primarily as brokers for foreign firms seeking Chinese partners. These companies differ from their counterparts in the West in that they are government operated; however, their income is based on commission. If they have a direct link to the potential Chinese partner, they may have a vested interest in selecting that partner, though it may not be the most ideal one available. On the other hand, such companies make potentially good business partners if they are close to the decision makers in the People's Republic and have access to foreign exchange, such as CITIC and its provincial subsidiaries. (See Appendix for a list of Foreign Exchange Guarantors.) Caution should be observed, however, by foreign firms that are unfamiliar with these new business entities. They should avoid being drawn into a partnership billed as "quick and easy." These silver-lined opportunities quickly tarnish when the Chinese partner does not deliver all that was promised.

Some of these new brokering entities include foreign trade companies forming joint ventures with foreign firms; investment and trading corporations seeking revenue-creating partnerships; and consulting companies—e.g., CONSULTEC and VENTURETECH—specializing in linking up foreign high technology firms and Chinese partners. Some of China's larger factories also have been granted the power to seek foreign investors unilaterally. As long as these enterprises have approval from their superiors, this may be a channel worth considering—though one should not ignore the need to establish and nurture the partnership network.

CROSSING CULTURES AND POLITICAL SYSTEMS: CHOOSING THE APPROPRIATE PARTNER

The ultimate goal for a foreign firm in China should be to establish as much direct contact as possible between itself and the Chinese factory in charge of the proposed production. Successful firms interact with managers, factory directors, and engineers rather than depending on tenuous relations with bureaus and ministries.[7] These firms also integrate sourcing, manufacturing, and distribution as closely as possible. Unfortunately, even after these alliances or partnerships are built, the foreign company is still at the mercy of the departments in charge, the various liaison agencies, and the local foreign trade corporation.

The selection of an appropriate venture partner, whether for a joint venture or a nonequity-based venture, is quite simply the most important factor in the successful implementation and operation of a project in China. Locating potential partners has become less difficult than in the past and the foreign company has more choice in the matter. Today, most firms initiate a concerted search for a partner rather than depending on a Chinese introduction.

Before making an official tour of China, foreign firms should feel no obligation to commit to one or another Chinese partner. Do not be pressured into a commitment prior to making an assessment of the alternatives. Keep agreements simmering with five or ten potential Chinese partners simultaneously. Sift through a number of options before deciding on a specific partner, avoiding the glossy trade brochures being published by various Chinese organizations that offer one-stop services to the China market. Remain flexible until a Chinese partner emerges who possesses the appropriate qualifications or who can at least meet the basic conditions for success.

The rules for locating a good partner in China are not firm, yet some useful guidelines do exist. First of all, finding an ideal, high-quality partner remains problematic because many of the factories chosen to be partners with foreign companies are nearly always deficient in several critical areas—management, worker skills, shop-floor technology, and sourcing. All partner alternatives involve trade-offs of one sort or another. Finding a partner for a manufacturing joint venture entails the most risk when the venture represents a direct threat to an existing Chinese industry. On the other hand, some firms seek a lower-profile Chinese partner that merely assembles products, for no other reason than to establish a company presence in the People's Republic. For others, the search is for a partner to build quality exports at a lower cost, while upholding the reputation of the parent company's product line. Nike, a sports shoe manufacturer, had to terminate arrangements with four different Chinese factories in 1984, trying to find one capable of manufacturing its shoes as cheaply as Taiwan and Korea, while maintaining quality. The company's objective in China was to produce 25 percent of its shoes in the People's Republic; it had to settle for 5 percent.[8]

Key Issues in Partner Selection

The answers to these questions define the nature of a potential partner and its degree of operating independence.

- What type of access does the partner have to China's domestic market?

A foreign firm should request a marketing history of the Chinese enterprise to ascertain the prevailing market for the enterprise's products and how much this market might be expanded if higher-quality products are introduced. Market access often remains circumscribed even for enterprises that have upgraded production using foreign technology. Firms should not assume that new markets in distant provinces will automatically open up for joint venture enterprise. They should attempt to find out the potential for attracting new customers given prevailing market boundaries. They should also be sensitive to the existence of economic blockades between provinces and bureaucratic jurisdictions that can prevent the free exchange of goods and services.

- Does the enterprise serve a market that is likely to remain strong?

    In the People's Republic, remember that government policy shifts and changing consumer preferences can significantly alter the nature of current and future demand. A good example involves a project in Shanghai that uses American technology to produce glass bulbs for black-and-white television tubes. With the rapid upsurge in demand for color televisions, and the government policy of establishing domestic manufacturing for color televisions, this project is in trouble—even taking into account demand for black and white televisions in rural areas. Take the time to look into the nature of the current customer base served by the Chinese enterprise partner. Do customers buy the enterprise's products because of their high quality, low price, or out of loyalty to the partner? Will they develop an aversion to products made by a Sino-foreign joint venture?

- Are competing enterprises planned and does your partner wield the political clout to keep these enterprises out of this area?

    Become aware of the existing distribution system that the partner relies upon. Because of the emphasis China places on both diversifying its foreign joint venture partners and developing indigenous manufacturing capabilities, it is possible that a domestic source of the same or a similar product will appear in a short time. In one extraordinary case, a zipper manufacturing joint venture formed by China and Hong Kong—Lanzhou Xinglong International Enterprise Co.—carried out an initial feasibility study and found that in 1983, only eleven zipper factories existed in China. Both partners predicted huge sales. But two years later, 105 zipper factories (twenty of them Sino-foreign joint ventures) had driven up supply of zippers in China elevenfold, saturating the market and bankrupting the venture in 1987, two years after start-up.[9]

- How much weight does your partner have in securing needed supplies and raw materials?

    Foreign firms often assume that necessary manufacturing inputs will be readily available or easily acquired. In many instances, neither assumption is true. Even if the needed inputs can be acquired, they may not meet U.S. specifications. (See Chapter 6 for more on sourcing in China.)

- How far and how fast has the enterprise moved in keeping step with the economic reform program? Will its leaders move forward decisively in this effort over the long term?

Foreign firms, for the most part, should seek out Chinese enterprises that possess a high degree of autonomy. These enterprises can maneuver more easily within the structure of China's emerging industrial economy. If supplies or raw materials do not materialize from traditional sources, these enterprises have the ability to go elsewhere to obtain needed inputs.

Clearly, not all of China's enterprises share equal enthusiasm for the new economic reforms. Some are reluctant to break the "iron rice bowl" because for them this represents security and minimizes much of the uncertainty that tends to be associated with the reforms. While at one extreme there are enterprises led by exuberant entrepreneurial managers, there are also others at the opposite extreme that are basically ignoring the reforms. (See Chapter 5 for more on enterprise reforms.)

- Is the enterprise run by "ideal" managers? The ideal manager not only understands the expanded autonomy offered to the enterprise but is willing to capitalize on it. Is he or she familiar with multiple points of access to the supply and distribution system?

A Chinese manager must be sought who has a vested interest in building an alliance with a foreign firm and is open to having a direct relationship with the people on the foreign side.

- Does the general manager have a technical education background? Has he or she any conception of Western corporate management?

In some cases, a joint venture director may not even have been a factory director in the past. The appointed director may have little grasp of corporate management in a Western sense.

- Does a unified relationship exist among the chief engineer, the party chief, and the factory manager?

If so, this unification represents the smooth synthesis of the political, organizational, and technological aspects of the management in the factory. Look carefully at the interplay between the *de facto* and the *de jure* leaders of the enterprise. Find out who controls the day-to-day operations of the factory and where it gets its operating budget.

- Will the Chinese factory be able to assimilate the foreign technology package planned?

Evaluate the technical competency of the chief engineer. This individual is responsible primarily for the technological aspects of the enterprise, which will include manufacturing, quality control, research, and maintenance. The chief engineer also helps prepare the feasibility studies for technology importation. Solicit the potential partner for help in conducting feasibility studies so as to gain a better appreciation for how the Chinese assess the key elements needed to make the project a success.

As noted, Chinese officials tend to introduce foreign executives to enterprises most in need of technical upgrading; they may be incapable of absorbing advanced technology for lack of managerial experience, poor infrastructure, or a dearth of skilled workers. Chinese unwillingness to divulge all the necessary details about the partner's specific capabilities and resources makes the process difficult. Obviously, repeated investigative visits by foreign technicians should be conducted. Rockwell International had to shop around until it found a technically competent plant for its textile machine project. The plant Rockwell chose had been building high-precision parts for weapons, and therefore was capable of fine tooling and meeting precision requirements.[10]

Government Partnerships.   In some cases, success in China may depend on whether the venture includes a Chinese government entity such as an industrial bureau or department, as either a formal or informal partner. At times, high-level local officials serve on these government bodies; their involvement in the business relationship lends clout to the project, and cuts communication time with the government to a fraction of the norm. Forming a partnership with a Chinese government entity may offer certain strategic advantages, especially if it is brought in as a minor third-party partner for the purpose of gaining clout among Chinese decision makers. Third-party partners often contribute foreign exchange or provide a mechanism to swap Rmb for foreign currency. Hewlett-Packard, for example, focuses its energies on developing a direct working relationship with one of China's most powerful industrial ministries, the Ministry of Electronics Industry (MEI), which is joined in the partnership by the municipal electronics bureau of the Beijing city government. Hewlett-Packard credits the preferential treatment it receives to the company's cooperation with a highly subsidized factory. In this case, high-level officials from MEI organize, plan, and attend meetings. This partnership affords Hewlett-Packard direct access to high-level government officials.[11]

Who should be the third party and how much equity should they be required to bring to the venture? While equity contribution is important, knowledge and political clout are even more valuable. A third party can bring all three to the venture. For example, the joint venture involving Volkswagen of West Germany and the Shanghai Automobile Corporation includes minority participation by the Bank of China and CITIC. Both of these organizations bring to the venture needed foreign exchange and high-level access to officials should problems arise. Their presence has helped rather than hindered the operation of the venture, proving the strategic advantage of including them from the start.

MATCHING OPPORTUNITIES WITH THE APPROPRIATE BUSINESS STRUCTURE

The precise legal form a firm chooses for cooperating with a Chinese enterprise grows out of a combination of the strategic imperatives driving the China activity and the location-specific factors that might affect the operation of the venture. As the literature in the field of international management makes clear, ownership and control are not synonymous (especially when operating a venture in a developing nation). The foreign firm can control a venture effectively while holding a minority equity position. Conversely, the host government or the local firm can also control it effectively while holding 50 percent or less of the equity. Thus, the critical issue in China centers on a form of business venture that will provide the desired avenues of control when and where necessary. Be cautious, however, about pushing too hard for a desired arrangement before examining the trade-offs. For example, although the People's Republic is on record as permitting a foreign firm to establish a wholly owned venture in China, the reality is that the venture is likely to receive less than wholehearted support at all levels.

The Chinese strongly urge solely foreign-owned factories to introduce advanced technology to China—especially technologies to produce exportable products—often as a precondition to approval. The regulations also encourage these ventures to export 100 percent of their production (though cases exist in which the foreign company has lobbied for a large percentage of the enterprise's products to be sold on the domestic Chinese market). While foreign investors are offered more decision-making power and less Chinese interference in wholly owned factories, they experience no greater ease of access within the bureaucracy. In theory, the management of a wholly owned China venture appears rather simple, often three managers handling sales, finance, and production, respectively. However, such ventures are not protected by joint venture tax treatment. In many respects, the Chinese consider them "representative offices," and, as such, assess them at a tax rate far above what joint ventures must pay. Wholly owned factories are in the 20–40 percent bracket plus 10 percent,[12] though this may change, says one manager of an important U.S. wholly owned factory that is pushing hard to be taxed as a joint venture.

Chinese officials often do not want to take the risk of involving themselves in a venture of this type without a large bureaucratic consensus behind them, despite official pronouncements to do so. The endeavor of going it alone in China generally brings worse problems and higher costs than joint ventures. Marketing and distribution tend to be more arduous. Without the leverage and influence of a local partner, many local Chinese will take advantage of foreigners, charging them higher rates for factory space, services, and labor, and then competing with them for export sales. Nonetheless, owners of wholly foreign-owned enterprises do experience more independence over setting wages, hiring and firing workers, and other production details.

In theory, wholly owned factories should offer increased operating autonomy. A new set of regulations governing wholly owned ventures released in 1986 was, in large part, an attempt to balance government control over foreign investment in China with the desires of foreigners to have more control over their business operations in the People's Republic. Although the 1986 regulations have lessened interference in the affairs of wholly owned firms, government entities within China still monitor and inspect these foreign entities, requiring them to report to relevant departments as to their production plans and business activities. Two articles in the 1986 regulations clearly state that (1) the administration of industry and commerce will "inspect and monitor" the investment situation of wholly owned ventures (Article IX), and (2) the production and business programs of the wholly owned ventures shall be reported to the Chinese authorities (Article XI). It remains to be seen whether the Chinese government will strengthen or loosen control and supervision on foreign-owned ventures in the near term. Zheng Tuobin, minister of Foreign Economic Relations and Trade, said at the National

People's Congress meeting, in March 1985, that it is necessary to "strengthen control and supervision over wholly foreign-owned ventures." Zheng, speaking on behalf of the State Council, also said that such ventures, formed without Chinese participation, should be subject to more stringent requirements than joint ventures.[13] While his comments were criticized by other Chinese officials, it is fair to say that his views reflect the underlying concerns and apprehensions of a large number of China's leaders.

Given the operational problems for business ventures in the People's Republic, the trend for U.S. companies entering the China market has been to set up small manufacturing firms geared more specifically toward exportation. Smaller, more manageable operations tend to grow and diversify, while grandiose projects often miss start-up deadlines, drain the parent company of resources, create negative press for both partners, and only succeed in highlighting the deficiencies still prevalent in China's manufacturing sector. The maxim "Plant seeds and let them grow" applies to both small and large foreign corporations, since all-important experience in the China market is not a function of the size of the foreign firm. A practitioner of the aforementioned maxim is the Boston-based Gillette Company, which operates sixty factories in thirty countries. As Michael C. Hawley, vice president of operations services for Gillette worldwide, pointed out: "We [Gillette] had the ability to mount an operation anywhere in the world, but no one [at Gillette] had built any experience in China at all." Gillette started small by setting up a joint venture in Shenyang (Shenmei Daily Use Products Co.) with forty-five employees, manufacturing *Rhino* razor blades. By 1987, the venture employed 100 workers. Today, Gillette has expanded by adding a subassembly plant producing applicator stems for the company's *Liquid Paper* correction fluids.[14]

The "small is beautiful" trend has been intensified by China's favorable treatment of export-oriented and technologically advanced FIEs. The benefits (summarized in Chapter 2) available to firms qualifying for special status have become, albeit slowly, more tangible and predictable. Thus, firms considering the China market may want to study the possibility of planning their projects such that they become certified to receive concessionary treatment. An FIE that can export 50 percent of its production and balance its foreign exchange account (and submit an annual report proving so) will theoretically qualify as an export-oriented FIE. If the FIE brings in technology that is unknown or rare in China, or that will produce a new product or upgrade an existing Chinese product, it will likely be deemed technologically advanced by MOFERT. Keep in mind, however, that this status is reviewed yearly and can be revoked if similar technology is subsequently acquired by Chinese entities, thus terminating benefits. The starting point for pursuing either of these strategies is to solicit the very latest information available from MOFERT and visit its local affiliate at the proposed location of the factory. As of March 1988, only 226 FIEs had attained "technologically advanced" status, which is only a fraction of the FIEs in China eligible for certification.[15]

Differences Between Joint Ventures and Cooperative Ventures

One underlying motive behind the new measures encouraging investment is simply to promote the growth of joint ventures, as opposed to other forms of nonequity investment made by foreign firms in the People's Republic. The cooperative venture, on the other hand, affords a more flexible arrangement because of its simpler legal structure and its informal business environment. Generally, the nature of these ventures is impermanent and not as precisely defined as an equity joint venture. A cooperative agreement is often treated as a preliminary stage of technical transfer.

In manufacturing, it may be best to establish a cooperative venture at the beginning. This arrangement is well suited to foreign investors because they can minimize their equity at risk and are not solely involved in trying to manage the business.

Import Substitution Strategy.   Foreign firms pursue an import substitution strategy in hopes of selling to China's domestic market for foreign exchange rather than Rmb. However, as outlined in the *Measures Concerning the Substitution of Imports with Products Manufactured by Chinese-Foreign Joint Ventures*, ratified in 1987, the foreign exchange input by the Chinese will only be issued on a temporary basis. Import substitution status is guaranteed to twelve products that China will need over the long term, including acrylic, pig iron, and aluminum. Other products require approval by the State Planning Commission at the central or local level. The Chinese also insist that these projects localize production progressively and source some supplies from China while ensuring that the goods produced meet international standards in price, quality, and service backup. Criteria ap-

plied to import substitution proposals include long-term need for the products and advanced technology. As with other forms of special status, import substitution certification could be retracted if Chinese entities begin producing similar products.

In pursuing an import substitution deal, U.S. firms should also (1) prove to the Chinese side that significant savings can be made, and (2) show that the manufacturing process can be localized rapidly. An exhaustive investigation stage should culminate with a feasibility study to gauge local-level interest in the project. Present the plan to local equivalents of the Foreign Economic Trade Commission. Once a local partner is secured, get a local FTC behind the project. Then go about convincing local government officials to push for approval at the central government level, where most of the red tape is involved. In 3M's import substitution approach to the China market, John Marshall outlines several guidelines that bear consideration by those companies planning to sell in China.

- Select products that fit China's pressing needs rather than those promising easy exportability. (3M ascertained that electrical generation, distribution, and telecommunications were serious priorities in China; hence, chose to manufacture electrical tape and connectors.)
- Select products from company divisions that have international orientation. (3M chose product lines, in part, because managers associated with them sold the products around the world.)
- Select products already produced in the Far East by your company, and from which you may draw experience.
- Select products, as 3M did, that are simple to start up, easy to scale up, and require minimal front-end investment.[16]

3M's approach involved assessing the investment climate, defining objectives, and presenting a proposal that had little regard for such Chinese priorities as exporting and technology transfer, or the fact that China had ratified no law governing wholly foreign-owned ventures in China. The company proposed a wholly owned factory that would sell 100 percent of its production to the domestic market, and transfer no technology. Holding to these requirements, the firm nailed down a successful agreement.[17] The 3M strategy follows a bold, "three no's" approach: *no* technology transfer, *no* export guarantee, and *no* Chinese ownership. They reached an agreement by leveraging the company's solid management reputation, which meant offering management training, and offering the product to be manufactured in the People's Republic as an import substitute.

NEGOTIATING A CHINA VENTURE

A number of unique features make negotiating and organizing business ventures in the People's Republic different from traditional Western business interactions. Much of the uniqueness derives from differences between the Chinese and their Western counterparts in the perception of time, human nature, and business relations. The combination of well-developed negotiating and bargaining skills and the distinct cultural differences will present the Western business executive with a novel experience when arranging a venture in China for the first time.

In the following sections, some recent negotiating problems are analyzed. Although experience provides clear lessons, every joint venture encounters its own set of apparent and unforeseen impasses. The Chinese seem at no loss in finding subtle and shrewd ways to pressure foreign representatives into making concessions. Nonetheless, one goal common to all negotiation, whether it is a joint venture or a licensing agreement, is the equitable sharing of rewards. A successful venture contract makes the risk on the Chinese side commensurate with their contribution and/or equity share in the venture. The fundamental concept of shared risk should be addressed directly in the agreement for multiple areas. Heretofore, the Chinese have had little incentive to participate in ventures that share risks along with the rewards.

Although Chinese officials produce a wealth of new investment legislation, most regulations remain negotiable. In a real sense, these guideline regulations represent a central part of China's strategy in dealing with multinational firms. The best response to the Chinese approach is to pursue a strategy of continuing attempts to leverage for concessions. A cardinal rule of negotiating in China: Ask the same questions and make the same demands that would be appropriate in any other developing country with a difficult investment climate. In general, firms should treat China on the same terms as any other country, demystifying the country's business atmosphere by defining fundamental demands before entering the process of negotiation. As agreement nears, do not allow those demands to be subordinated. Hold onto your original purpose. If your firm entered China seeking access to the China market, fight for that privilege in your contract. Oddly, many firms that enter negotiations with this intention end up agreeing to export 100 percent of joint venture production from China in order to get approval. In reality, they know that this agreement cannot be met. It was not their original intention to engage in such export activity.

The Negotiation Process

The process begins with initial meetings in which the Chinese side is represented by several organizations; for example, representatives from construction and development corporations, an import/export office, and various technicians and engineers from relevant factories. Also present, in all likelihood, will be key players from a ministry-led corporation in the relevant field of endeavor. Early discussions usually center on assessing the technical capacity and competence of each party. At this time, the foreign side ascertains the manufacturing capability of the Chinese factory. In the second meeting, the Chinese side may propose that the two parties begin working out the details of a complex venture, possibly a joint equity or cooperative venture. The foreign side often obtains samples of parts and components the Chinese propose using, and ships them home for testing to gauge the production competence of the Chinese factory.

Initial negotiating sessions offer the foreign company a chance to compare the priorities held by each side regarding the terms of potential business cooperation. In some ways, the "needs and wants" will be more similar to other investment climates than expected. In other areas there will be a marked difference. In any case, this early stage should be used by foreign firms to formulate a running list of both their own needs and wants and those of the specific Chinese counterpart with whom they are negotiating. Obviously, the nature of these priorities varies on both sides according to the objectives of the firm and the goals of China's economic planners. Only by establishing priorities can negotiators pinpoint disparate objectives held by each side and find points of leverage in ongoing negotiations. The table on page 116 shows what this comparison of objectives might look like for a joint venture or a cooperative production agreement.

Needs and Wants Compared

Foreign Side	Chinese Side
Sell to domestic market	Export output or substitute imports
Contribute to venture in noncash items	Contribute to venture in noncash items
High total valuation of transferred technology	Low total valuation of transferred technology
Payment and dividends in foreign exchange	Foreign side to be paid with product/Rmb
Guarantee on future sales of equipment with 5–15 percent commission on all sales	No secure guarantee on future purchases and 1–5 percent commission on selected sales
One-time transfer of dated technology	Ongoing transfer of current technology
Strict confidentiality of technical know-how	Sharing of technical know-how
No transfer/training of R&D capabilities	Transfer/training of R&D capabilities
Foreign management and leadership	Foreign management with Chinese leadership
Exclusivity in China	Inability to guarantee exclusivity to venture
Localization as quality standards are achieved	Rapid localization
No selling of Chinese-made products to existing export markets	International marketing rights for production
"Buy-back" production priced according to low-wage hourly rate	"Buy-back" production priced according to international market prices
Production to meet high standards if brand name is to be used	Production quality less important
Long venture duration	Short venture duration (15–30 years)
No commitment to assist Chinese side in exporting production	Foreign assistance in exporting production
Compensation for value of venture at time of liquidation	Distribution of assets according to equity share at time of liquidation

Defining Points of Leverage. The Chinese recognize that they cannot yet bring much to the bargaining table in order to leverage the foreign firm into making attractive concessions. Yet, this is rapidly changing. Elements of leverage that the Chinese buyer can now offer include: limited foreign exchange conversion; partial access to the domestic market; greater access to groups of skilled workers; and greater access to the established distribution system—the kind of things that help facilitate profitable business. Nonetheless, the Chinese still simply cannot put cash up front to purchase an item as might be the case in Taiwan or South Korea. China's main point of leverage remains its ability to control the terms of the contract; lacking a consistent avenue to apply leverage over a broad spectrum of agreement, China's negotiators have to approach agreements with foriegners on a case-by-case basis. Only in this way can they wield leverage in specific negotiations. In defining a foreign firm's points of leverage, two questions must be answered before entering negotiations in China under any of the various corporate strategies discussed in Chapter 1. (1) Can the foreign firm afford the expenses associated with entering its desired China venture? and (2) Is the firm clear on what it can, and is willing to, offer the Chinese? Briefly, firms must consider all of the following possible concessions that the Chinese may request of the foreign firm in exchange for concessions by the Chinese side:

- Transferring technology, rights to know-how, documentation, and trademarks
- Establishing a production line, including manufacturing and quality testing
- Supplying components in semi-knockdown (SKD) or complete knockdown (CKD) form with all or partial payment in product
- Training in assembly, production, management, quality control, and marketing
- Willingness to buy back output if standards can be achieved by Chinese factory
- Continued support in the forms of updating of technology and R&D training
- Assisting in exporting Chinese production to world markets
- Willingness to attempt application of Chinese-made components in factories outside China.[18]

Drafting the Contract

The nitty-gritty of negotiations, of course, is the hashing out of a suitable contractual agreement. China contracts vary in type and function in much the same way that they vary in other developing nations. Contracts made with FTCs tend to be standardized in form, while *non-FTC contracts* follow no standard form.[19] The different types of contracts include those for the purchase of equipment, the sale of Chinese goods, the licensing of foreign technology, and those for the more complex collaborative ventures. *Turnkey contracts* require the foreign party to provide the equipment, designs, and materials; the training for technicians; the managers; and the workers to build the plants. The foreign partner often subcontracts many of the tasks to other companies and assumes the responsibility and the risk entailed in coordinating the project. Once a complete processing facility produces a specified output under the conditions of contract, the responsibility of the foreign firm is terminated. Guarantees on specific pieces of equipment are the responsibility of the original manufacturers. Recently, *dynamic licensing agreements* have become a customary format for China venture contracts. Consequently, contracting has become more lengthy and complex. The final contract between China and Racal Electronics (U.K.) contained "nineteen chapters, twelve appendices, and occupied three feet of shelf space."[20]

Let us take a hard look at the negotiable points of a typical Sino-foreign contract—clause by clause. The experienced overseas negotiator will see immediately how contracting in China differs in some respects from that in other investment climates, and in others is quite similar. The contract format used normally applied to a technology licensing agreement that involves the transfer of technology and know-how, equipment sales, training of Chinese workers, and prescription for the ongoing "dynamic" transfer of technology and know-how. (Chapter 6 covers the elements which must be included in a more complex joint venture or wholly foreign-owned contract, such as labor management, salaries, and sourcing of raw materials and components.)

Definitions.   Contracts begin by defining the language of the agreement. These would include the *contract product*, which is the exact type and model of the product to be manufactured and its replacement parts, components, or assembly for use in the maintenance or repair of the product. The *verification product* refers to the first contract product manufactured in the Chinese factory containing a specified percentage of locally sourced components, which is used for quality assurance inspection and testing. The exact nature of the *technology* must be defined. This usually includes drawings, specifications, know-how, and other data referring to the maintenance and marketing of the contract product. Finally, *net sales price of the replacement parts* is defined as the freight on board (FOB) published price in the city where the foreign partner is located, excluding packing, insurance, freight, and related charges.

Transfer and Use of the Technology.   In this section of the contract, the two parties outline the procedures for delivering the written technology and where the contract products and replacement parts are to be manufactured in China. The foreign partner must require the Chinese to manufacture products and parts in strict accordance with the written technology furnished, without making changes in their specifications or manufacturing process. The Chinese side must guarantee that the workmanship and material be in conformity with the quality standards of the supplying firm. The foreign party may choose to supply detailed information on specialized equipment and measuring devices necessary for quality inspection. Finally, the two parties agree in this section as to what percentage of the contract product can be sourced in China, estimate the price of components and parts to be supplied by the foreign partner, and define the components and parts that cannot be locally produced by the Chinese.

Foreign firms should not rely on existing patents for technology protection in China, because effective patent protection for industrial property is a relatively new addition to China's growing body of foreign investment legislation. Foreign technology is better protected in China than before, yet technology contracts must contain additional protective clauses and stipulations concerning royalty, confidentiality, and application.

Countering Chinese pressure to transfer state-of-the-art technology can be accomplished with proposals offering simple technology at first and then upgrading it on a periodic basis. This strategy sets the stage for a long-term partnership and encourages the Chinese partner to protect the technology from misuse or secondary transfer into possibly competing Chinese enterprises. Foreign firms might also gain leverage by offering the Chinese partner a foreign exchange percentage of export sales of products produced by the licensed technology.[21] The foreign side must stress that it is in the interest of both parties to protect the technology because the competitiveness of the product on domestic and export markets affects the financial success of the venture.

Training and Consultation.   Technology transfer contracts customarily involve training of Chinese technical personnel. The contract agreement must include the exact nature of such training— the number of Chinese to be trained, months of training at facilities in the United States, traveling and living expenses, etc.—in addition to the nature of ongoing technical consultation at the Chinese facility by foreign technical specialists and coordinators. The parties may also agree to authorize representatives to conduct periodic meetings to discuss the status of implementation of the training contract.

Verification and Acceptance.   This section of the contract outlines the future plans for testing finished products before they are marketed, and delineates various penalties in the event that contract products fail verification tests. This section also stipulates that technical personnel from both parties shall be present at such tests; in most cases, agreement is made that products will be tested in the field as well as the factory. The parties may outline plans for ameliorating technical problems in products through joint study and evaluation. The cost of such a joint effort is usually borne by the party responsible for the deficiency. If the contract product passes verification tests, the two parties will often sign a verification certificate that permits the products to be marketed.

Marketing Rights.   In this section, the foreign party grants the Chinese side various exclusive or partial rights to manufacture and sell the contract products and parts in China and other foreign countries. The foreign partner often agrees to assist the Chinese in marketing efforts (if such assistance is requested) at a mutually agreed rate of compensation.

Trademark, Infringement, and Confidentiality. The two parties must work out various issues concerning the use of a foreign firm's trademark, protection of proprietary information, and the use of the foreign company's brand name in Chinese catalogs, packaging, and other literature for use in selling or promoting the contract products or parts. Typically, the Chinese maintain the secrecy of the technology, agreeing to disclose its contents only to employees whose duties require them to know and to authorized third persons, as necessary, to manufacture components.

Price and Terms of Payment.

The initial fee to be paid to the foreign firm in exchange for written technology is set forth in this section. Also negotiated at this point are the terms of payment and the royalties paid to the foreign firm for both contract products and replacement parts manufactured in China and marketed by the Chinese. Royalty percentages may vary for different markets. For example, government-to-government sales may carry a lower rate of royalties than sales made to foreign countries. Terms of payment should include all stipulations pertaining to letters of credit, shipping, insurance, etc.

Negotiators be forewarned, the Chinese bargain hard on licensing fees, royalty payments, and terms. Deals can be structured to require the Chinese to pay 10 to 20 percent of the total licensing cost up front, but unless the technology is a top priority, the Chinese may push to pay for it with renminbi.[22] Foreign firms should negotiate for royalty payments on all sales of products using their firm's technology, whether the sales are domestic or export. Fujian-Hitachi has such an agreement, receiving 6 Rmb for each television set it sells inside and outside China. The Japanese demand was prudent indeed, as the joint venture has failed to export production consistently, yet has sold well domestically.

Regarding sale price, firms should leave themselves room to maneuver. They should avoid stating a "fair" price at the outset of negotiations and holding to it even when the Chinese side is asking for price concessions. Regarding profit margin, the Chinese partner cannot allow the foreigner too broad a profit margin without risking accusations of allowing foreign exploitation. In the oil industry, a lot of negotiating time is spent on pinpointing the X-factor, or what is a reasonable profit for the foreigner to accrue. One standard in setting profit margin used in the past has been a 15 percent after-tax profit on total turnover; this figure was applied in Schindler's contract to produce elevators in Shanghai.[23]

If the foreign partner intends to buy back production from the joint venture, the foreign partner should attempt to purchase finished products at a price based on the hourly rate needed to manufacture them, in addition to securing the right to resell the products at a higher price (for example, 20 percent or higher). However, the Chinese push for prices of buy-back production to be set according to the international price of the product, thereby removing a potentially profitable element of an agreement for the foreign partner.[24]

Purchase of Equipment and Raw Material. Another way the foreign partner generates profits from a joint venture is by getting an agreement from the Chinese partner to purchase all future equipment and raw materials from the foreign partner. By buying and reselling such supplies at a marked-up price to the China venture, the foreign partner accrues a 5–15 percent commission profit. The author's interviews with venture managers suggest that some of the large manufacturing joint ventures that suffer well-publicized repatriation problems compensate their losses with commissions and direct sales associated with the ongoing equipment needs of the venture.

Arbitration. In contracts with the Chinese, arbitration clauses emphasize the settling of disputes through "friendly consultation between both parties." In cases where the two parties reach no agreement through negotiation, this clause stipulates that an arbitration committee—consisting of one representative appointed by each party and a member of a third nationality agreed upon by both parties—should convene at a mutually agreed upon location. Often, parties agree to settle disputes under the auspices of an arbitration institute or organization in a third country. In most cases, however, the Chinese will only agree reluctantly to this option.

Additional Issues to Be Contracted

Other issues pertaining to more complex ventures such as joint ventures and wholly foreign-owned ventures, which involve equity contributions by foreign and Chinese partners, should be negotiated.

Contribution. Joint venture contracts include stipulations as to the contributions made to the venture by each partner. Negotiators soon discover that the Chinese insist on large foreign cash contributions to a venture. On the other hand, contributions to joint ventures from the Chinese partner usually consist of noncash items such as land use, existing buildings, and construction materials, all of which are difficult to price accurately and easy for the Chinese to overvalue. The actual ownership of land, of course, cannot be contributed by the Chinese because all land belongs to the state. Flexible land-use rates can be granted, however, depending on the intended use, infrastructural requirements of the venture, and the costs incurred making the site suitable for the venture.[25]

Deciding on Equity Split.

The Chinese are easing requirements that stipulate that their side should hold the major portion of equity in a joint venture. The minimum equity to be held by a foreign partner remains at 25 percent of the original investment, but some foreign firms control 50 percent or more. It may soon become possible for a foreign firm to increase its equity share over time through additional investment and total buy-outs of joint ventures. Wella Hair Products of West Germany, for example, has a joint venture contract in which the firm's equity increases, yet the norm is a preset, two- or three-partner equity split. This arrangement is typical of Beatrice Foods' joint venture in Guangzhou, in which CITIC hold 10 percent, the Guangzhou Foodstuffs Industrial Company holds 40 percent, and Beatrice Foods Co. holds 50 percent.[26]

In structuring the equity split, foreign firms should not assume that by giving the Chinese side a larger share of the venture the Chinese partner will solve problems in a way decidedly more beneficial to the joint venture.[27] In situations where equity increases in its favor, the foreign firm should negotiate to define precisely how its influence over the venture's operation will be increased commensurately.

Duration of the Venture.

Firms should also negotiate a *buy out* provision to cover the termination of the joint venture. Negotiators should force the Chinese to pay a premium on the assets left behind in the People's Republic, especially on the "going concern" value. This clause may make it easier to leverage for a duration extension at the close of the contract.

The Chinese like to keep joint venture durations short, which adds risk to ventures involving the transfer of sophisticated technology. Negotiators must clarify exactly what the fate of the assets, technology, and machinery will be after the termination of the joint venture. In January 1985, the maximum duration permitted was increased to fifty years. The majority of ventures, however, fall into a category of ten- to twenty-year durations, a short time indeed to recoup a China investment. Chinese policymakers appear increasingly flexible about venture duration, recognizing that time limits create a negative attitude among potential investors. Related to the duration is the fate of imported tech-

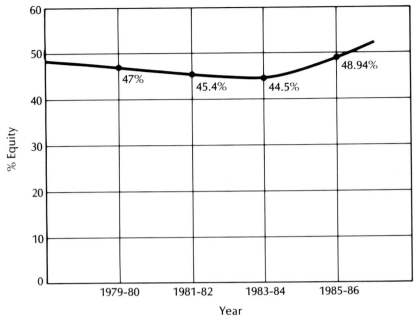

Average Equity Share (%) for U.S. Partners in U.S.-China Joint Ventures

---

SOURCE: Compiled by the author from various sources including *South,* Department of Commerce publications, and the *China Business Review.*

---

nology and machinery at the time of liquidation. How is equity to be divided? Negotiators must be prepared to handle this uncharted territory.

Exclusivity.   The Chinese find it difficult to offer guarantees of exclusivity, yet special attention should be paid to getting local bureaucrats to adhere to their assurances that they will not establish competing ventures within discomforting proximity. Squibb Pharmaceuticals opened a plant in Minhang, outside Shanghai, to manufacture Captopril, an antihypertensive drug. Neither partner realized that another local drug company was to begin marketing a "knockoff" of the same drug at one-third the price. When Mitsubushi Transport joined in an amusement park venture in Guangdong Province, the company was not expecting that more than twelve other such parks would spring up in the same area in less than three years. The company was forced to delay loan repayments because of competition.

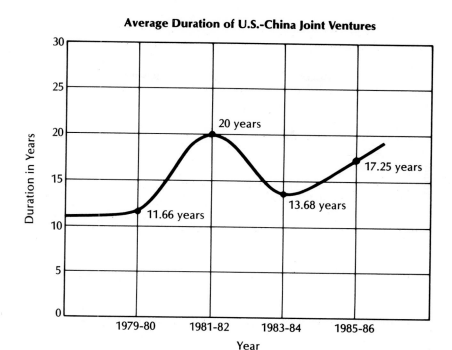

Average Duration of U.S.-China Joint Ventures

SOURCE: Compiled by the author from various sources including *South,* Department of Commerce publications, and the *China Business Review.*

Characteristics of Various Sino-Foreign Joint Ventures in Operation

Name: **Great Wall Hotel**
Location: Beijing
Participants: (Chinese party):   China International Travel Service—
                               Beijing Branch
               (Foreign party):   ES Pacific Development and
                               Construction Co. Ltd., [USA]
Field: Tourist hotel
Total Investment (US$): 72M
Foreign Equity Share: 49 percent
Foreign Investment (US$): 35.28M
Date of Approval: April 21, 1980
Duration: 10 years

Name: **Shanghai Foxboro Co. Ltd.**
Location: Shanghai
Participants: (Chinese party):   Shanghai Instrument Industry Company
                (Foreign party):   Foxboro Company [USA]
Field: Manufacturing of automatic instruments and meters
Total Investment: (US$): 10M
Foreign Equity Share: 49 percent
Foreign Investment (US$): 4.9M
Date of Approval: April 12, 1982
Duration: 20 years

Name: **Sino-French Joint Venture Winery, Ltd.**
Location: Tianjin
Participants: (Chinese party):   Tianjin Municipal Vineyard
                (Foreign party):   Remy Martin, France
Field: Winery
Total Investment (US$): 533,000
Foreign Equity Share: 38 percent
Foreign Investment (US$): 202,500
Date of Approval: May 20, 1980
Duration: 11 years

Name: **China Tianjin Otis Elevator Co. Ltd.**
Location: Tianjin
Participants: (Chinese party):   Tianjin Lift Company
                (Foreign party):   Otis Elevator Co. Ltd. [USA]
Field: Elevator manufacturing
Total Investment (US$): 500,000
Foreign Equity Share: 30 percent
Foreign Investment (US$): 150,000
Date of Approval: December 1982
Duration: 2 years

Name: **Parker-Hubei Seals Co. Ltd.**
Location: Wuhan, Hubei
Participants: (Chinese party):   Hubei Automotive Industry Corp.
                (Foreign party):   Parker-Hannifin Corp. [USA]
Field: Rubber seal production
Total Investment (US$): 990,000
Foreign Equity Share: 49 percent
Foreign Investment (US$): 485,000
Date of Approval: December 6, 1981
Duration: 20 years

Name: **Guangmei Foods Corporation**
Location: Guangzhou, Guangdong
Participants: (Chinese party): CITIC Guangzhou Food Industry Corp.
 (Foreign party): Beatrice Foods Company [USA]
Field: Beverage and milk products
Total Investment (US$): 10M
Foreign Equity Share: 50 percent
Foreign Investment (US$): 5M
Date of Approval: December 1981
Duration: 15 years

Name: **Fujian Hitachi Television Co. Ltd.**
Location: Fujian
Participants: (Chinese party): Fujian Electronic Import and Export Corp.
 Fujian Investment & Enterprises Corp.
 (Foreign party): Hitachi Ltd.
 Hitachi Sales Corp.
Field: TV production and assembly
Total Investment (US$): 2.4M
Foreign Equity Share: 50 percent
Foreign Investment (US$): 1.2M
Date of Approval: December 5, 1980
Duration: 15 years

Name: **Beijing Jeep Corp.**
Location: Beijing
Participants: (Chinese party): Beijing Municipality CNAIC
 (Foreign party): American Motors Corp. (recently acquired
 by Chrysler) [USA]
Field: Automobile manufacturing
Total Investment (US$): 51M
Foreign Equity Share: 31.35 percent
Foreign Investment (US$): 16M
Date of Approval: January 1984
Duration: May be extended

Name: **Sino-American Shanghai Squibb Pharmaceuticals, Ltd.**
Location: Shanghai
Participants: (Chinese party): National Pharmaceutical Administration
 Shanghai Trust and Investment Corp.
 Shanghai Pharmaceutical Administration
 (Foreign party): E.R. Squibb & Sons Inc.
Field: Pharmaceutical production

Total Investment (US$): 6.32M
Foreign Equity Share: 50 percent
Foreign Investment (US$): 3.16M
Date of Approval: May 1982
Duration: 20 years

Sources: Guide to Foreign Economic Relations and Trade in China—Investments in China Issue; and various publications, such as *South, Asian Wall Street Journal,* and *China Business Review.*

Why Negotiations Break Down

Negotiations often break down over the issue of profitability for the foreign partner. Foreign negotiators are in agreement that something must be done about each of the following:

- diminishing profits and dividends resulting from high withholding taxes
- little or no cash compensation for training Chinese workers and technicians
- undervaluation of technology
- Chinese unwillingness to allow commissions for the foreign partner on sales to the domestic market
- absence of any guarantee of future Chinese purchases of equipment or spare parts to be paid in foreign exchange
- short duration time which makes it impossible to recoup original investment

Other factors leading to breakdowns in negotiations include:

- uncertainty as to the repatriation of profits
- unsecured market access
- excessive cash capitalization requirement on the foreign partner (especially if the foreign firm is small)
- Chinese intolerance of foreign partner attempts to reduce equity share in an effort to lessen the total cash contribution to the venture

Capitalization.   The foreign side should address its concerns that Chinese capitalization consists of land and factory buildings at inflated prices. Usually, the Chinese limit the total amount of technical and managerial contribution by the foreign partner. This makes it difficult for smaller foreign firms with fewer cash assets to enter joint ventures in the People's Republic. The Chinese apply the ceiling to prevent foreign firms from padding the value of their technology, equipment, and training, and to encourage foreign partners to bring in foreign exchange. Also, the Joint Venture Law stipulates that additional contributions of technology and know-how must be valued by qualified public accountants and accompanied by patent certificates.[28] Typically, the U.S. side attempts to input technology for as much capital as possible, though the regulations state that no more than 15 percent of the foreign contribution to a joint venture may be in the form of technology license and royalty. Because the Chinese often calculate their contribution to the venture to "coincidentally" equal 51 percent of the total venture investment, negotiators should push for exact cost estimates from the Chinese before announcing capital value estimates of their firm's technology to be transferred.

Almost all foreign firms must also bring in hard cash to joint ventures in China. Foreign partners usually attempt to minimize their cash contributions, however. This is more plausible in coproduction arrangements because these ventures allow for more emphasis to be placed on division of labor rather than on equity.[29] Also, the foreign partner will find it easier to receive cash or production output in return for training, management transfer, etc.

As an example of the last option, let's review the case of a Singaporean firm, which we will call Alpha Company. This firm negotiated an agreement with two different Chinese entities desiring the same technology. The negotiations for the first project, a joint venture, broke down over issues related to a poor return of investment for the foreign firm—no compensation for training, high cash contribution requirement, low commissions, overvalued production used to compensate the foreign partner, and a low ceiling on the percentage of foreign investment to be in the form of technology. After this effort fell apart, the same firm began negotiating a cooperative deal with another Chinese partner. The second deal proved profitable because the foreign firm was able to leverage, in the absence of the joint venture laws, for cash compensation for training, guaranteed cash purchases on equipment and spare parts over the life of the contract, and sizable commissions on all sales. Over the three-year duration of the coproduction contract, Alpha was able to accrue a net profit of $395,000. The table of income and expenses for Alpha Company on page 132 illustrates the prudence of remaining flexible in terms of business form and active in pursuing a

Options at an Impasse

▶ *Abandon the entire project.* Cut off communication and correspondence; cut losses and begin searching for another Chinese partner.

▶ *Delay the project.* Wait for the Chinese to improve the deal; maintain letter correspondence only; remain frank and firm on minimum requirements; maintain a holding pattern while keeping a close watch on moves of the competition.

▶ *Proceed with agreement.* If pursuing a defensive strategy, when the Chinese partner is asking for too much cash investment, begin looking for other partners to share investment risk. Contact additional partners, on both the U.S. and Chinese sides (e.g., CITIC).

▶ *Proceed with modified venture agreement.* Scale down the size of investment to lower the cash requirements. Again, if cash investment is a problem, reduce the total value of investment. The Chinese may foot the bill for the difference or go for the smaller deal because it may be easier for them to get approval of the project if it is scaled down.

▶ *Negotiate another type of agreement.* Propose an agreement in a different business format. Many times, a joint venture is constricting because the Chinese require the foreigner to abide by local and central regulations, when in fact they would accept terms more beneficial to the foreign party if the venture were put into a compensation trade or processing/ assembly arrangement.

▶ *Offer different deal to another Chinese partner.* If modifying the agreement and changing its structure doesn't help, shop the deal elsewhere.

Chinese partner that can meet the minimum requirements held by the foreign firm.[30]

Creating "Organic" Contracts

The critical factor to keep in mind during the contracting stage of a China venture commitment is that the contract represents a dynamic relationship which involves many trade-offs and unwritten commitments. The document must be adaptable to the changing interests of the Chinese and foreign parties over time. China's less than favorable compatibility problems associated with technology transfer have prompted Chinese negotiators to emphasize long-term commitments in their foreign contracts. In short, China does not accept the "quick kill" contract.

The contract that China does favor is an *organic contract*, one which stipulates a continuing collaboration between parties as a succession of performance clauses are achieved by both sides. For example, a foreign partner chooses to upgrade ten-year-old technology if and when its Chinese counterpart does certain things, for instance, opens up new lines of distribution into additional provinces of China, or makes arrangements for Rmb conversion to foreign exchange on a regular schedule. The Chinese partner, on the other hand, demands that the foreign counterpart buy back a certain percentage of production if and when the Chinese achieve a specified standard of quality and rate of production. In the same vein, the foreign firm agrees to utilize Chinese-made products in the production of finished goods at its factories outside China, or to include these products in its overseas marketing strategy, in return for guarantees of sales of spare parts and raw materials to the Chinese side. Adding another facet to the contract, the Chinese enterprise asks that the foreign partner expand manufacturing training to include R&D training if and when the Chinese side successfully train their own personnel to take over the manufacturing training program. Moreover, an equitable organic contract takes advantage of the function between market access by the foreign company and technology acquisition by the Chinese. That is, an escalating percentage of production is sold to China's domestic market in return for additional technology or updated technology.

Ultimately, creative foreign negotiators learn to build flexibility and expansion into their China venture contracts by mixing available

Alpha Company's Cash Flow in Its Coproduction Venture

Contract duration: 3 years

Inflow:	1ST YR	2ND YR	3RD YR
Training fee of $50,000 less withholding tax ($10,000)	40,000	—	—
Trading profit on sale of equipment at 15%	150,000	—	—
Profit from sales of spare parts at 20% markup	54,000	108,000	108,000
Additional profit for the first $100,000 sales from Chinese factory as compensation payment for training (less $50,000 cash paid above)	100,000	—	—
Total Inflow:	**344,000**	**108,000**	**108,000**
Less Total Outflow:			
Marketing and administration cost to foreign partner	32,000	32,000	32,000
Salary for instructors and machine time	24,000	—	—
Costs of inspection trips	5,000	5,000	5,000
Cost of upkeep of capital equipment and repair costs	10,000	10,000	10,000
Total Outflow:	**71,000**	**47,000**	**47,000**
New Cash Flow:	**273,000**	**61,000**	**61,000**

Net Profit of Venture to Foreign Firm After Three Years: 395,000

SOURCE: A. N. Hakam, "Negotiations Between Singaporeans and Firms in China: The Case of a Singaporean Electronic Firm Contemplating Investment in China." Paper presented at The Chinese Enterprise Conference held at the Manchester Business School, U.K., June 1–2, 1987. By permission.

business forms, building in performance incentives, and moving ahead only when both sides attain successive levels of achievement. Only in this way can both sides truly share the risks and the rewards of a China venture. And only in this way can both sides avoid entering into what Raymond Vernon of Harvard once termed "the obsolescing agreement."

Renegotiating Contract Terms.   The specter of having to reopen the negotiation of a contract, which may literally have taken years to close, can be nothing less than traumatic for a foreign negotiator. The Chinese often attempt to renegotiate the financial terms of contracts, especially licensing agreements, during the start-up phase of a venture. Some U.S. executives interviewed questioned whether their Chinese partner ever intended to honor his contract in the first place. A request for renegotiation often follows the project start-up, especially if the Chinese begin to encounter serious problems installing and assimilating licensed technology. When agreements impose constraints on the flexibility of the Chinese partner in a venture, the partner will seek adjustments to the contract. Firms should be prepared for this to happen. They should be flexible and use the occasion to leverage for something in a trade-off. They too should attempt to take advantage of the Chinese perception that the contract is renegotiable. Moreover, the foreign firm should periodically make demands that might involve changes in the agreement to its advantage, such as lowering the percentage of production to be exported, decreasing the number of unskilled workers, and so on.

Many firms have had similar experiences, confirming a Chinese propensity to renegotiate after the conclusion of an agreement if they discover the original contract terms to be to their disadvantage or out of alignment with "the spirit and principles" initially forged by the partners. In one case, in which an American partner reminded his Chinese counterpart that his request was in violation of their contract, the Chinese responded, "If you keep referring back to that agreement we'll never get anything done!"[31] Of course, since the business environment is largely unfamiliar to the foreign partner, the firm itself might also want to renegotiate various aspects of their original China agreement. In this sense the problem of renegotiation in China may be a blessing in disguise. Renegotiation, in fact, is closely linked to the concept of organic contracts. The contract allows for adjustments along the way as long as the short-term demands of each partner are being satisfied.

GAINING AN EDGE IN CHINA NEGOTIATING

Over the past five years, Sino-foreign negotiations have become much smoother affairs than in the past, as the Chinese become increasingly comfortable entering business agreements with foreign interests. Chinese negotiating teams possess a much deeper understanding of foreign companies, international markets, and foreign technology.

Defining the Limits of Agreements

For most Americans, the end product of a negotiation is the contract; we tend to define our level of participation in a venture according to what is explicitly stated in that contract. The Chinese, however, perceive negotiating as part of a process rather than as a goal-oriented activity; they view the signing of an agreement as the starting point of a relationship rather than an armistice. To the Chinese, a contractual agreement represents more a pledge to cooperate throughout the life of a business relationship than a simple, one-time transaction; a beginning point for future demands by one side rather than the end result of the process of two sides voicing demands and offering compromise.[32]

The relationship might involve aspects of a partnership unfamiliar to Western business practices, such as exchanging technical and managerial expertise, additional training of workers and technicians, and trips for Chinese to the foreign firm's home factory. True to this definition of an agreement, the Chinese often request uncontracted "favors" after a seemingly inclusive contract has been signed.[33] These favors, such as extra services at no extra charge, put pressure on foreign representatives and sometimes create animosities between the two partners. Foreign firms, on the other hand, rarely pursue special favors from the Chinese negotiators. The solution seems to be for the foreign side to define its level of participation at the outset, and then nail down what is to be expected of each partner in terms of commitment to the business relationshp. To offset Chinese pressure for gratuitous services, a foreign engineering firm based in Shanghai offered the Chinese a contract package it had used previously in various Third World and Eastern Bloc countries that outlined the exact nature and method of work to be done. However, despite its "mutually beneficial" orientation, the agreement was rejected—mainly because the personal relationships among the players had not been fully established.[34] (The importance placed on personal relationships in business is a cultural trait as well as a utilitarian point of leverage for the Chinese negotiator.)

Hidden Identities and Agendas

Because of the size, complexity, and fluidity of China's government structure, foreign executives must feel their way in the dark to acquire a solid working understanding of how the respective departments and bureaus involved in the proposed venture interlink. The foreign firm's ignorance regarding this underlying network of bureaucratic relationships and contact points complicates what in the West is a fairly straightforward process. These same competing interests surrounding a Sino-foreign agreement may make themselves felt repeatedly after the agreement has been implemented. Here again, if the boundaries of the business relationship are not firmly established at the beginning, the relationship itself will be subject to intense manipulation once a venture is under way. Bear in mind that the Chinese negotiator views a deal in a wider context—social, political, and economic—than the Western negotiator. The Chinese negotiator must first build a consensus of support from diverse and politically disparate individuals. This explains why the Chinese negotiator's behavior, at times, tends to suggest that the negotiation is a zero-sum proposition, wherein any gain on the foreign side translates into a loss for the Chinese side. Under such circumstances, so-called cooperative relations can often start off on an adversarial basis. Consequently, foreign firms are more likely to succeed in China when their negotiators have set up from the start a win-win situation, highlighting the specific tangible benefits to both sides at the outset. Foreign firms must seek out and create cooperative solutions to problems. Do not allow a negotiation to devolve into a win-lose situation.

Although meetings usually begin with an exchange of business cards and handshakes, the true identities of the real Chinese decision makers may remain unknown indefinitely. Also, the number of Chinese participants may swell over time, while the foreign side generally depends on the same team throughout. Ascertaining precisely who the key players are and how much influence they wield is difficult since some persons may vanish only to reappear at a later banquet. What often appears to be a group of redundant players may represent the plethora of relevant Chinese organizations associated with the project, each taking measure of the proposed agreement and the potential foreign partner. The puzzle can be best assembled through sustained and cordial discussions with the officials and directors with whom you are dealing. Through the creation of a running list of key players, one can formulate conclusions as to how they interconnect. One key objective is to identify the sequence of the decision-making process within and among the major organizations that surround your proposed venture, or, for that matter, the sale of your goods and/or technology. Factory directors usually diagram the interlocking governmental institutions affecting their enterprise for the foreign executive who asks. As new players come into the picture, ask them where their organization fits into the decision-making arrangment. If asked, most Chinese officials will provide this information.

However, the foreign negotiator has to be more perceptive in pinpointing the persons within each Chinese organization who have influence over the approval process of a project or sale. This process includes informally interviewing members of the Chinese negotiating team, taking note of seating arrangments at meetings and banquets, and keeping alert to gestures and offhand remarks that evidence levels of deference between members of the Chinese negotiating team. With a more complete understanding of the role of each individual and organization affecting a proposed venture or transaction, the foreign firm can better address problems by pushing the right levers at the right time and contacting the right people in the appropriate organizations.

Adjusting to Negotiation Setting

Once involved in negotiating a project in China, the foreigner enters an environment where many of the elements of a negotiation appear familiar but the style is unusual, at least by Western standards. The foreign party is typically outnumbered by a ratio of about five to one. Although the foreign team usually is empowered with high-level decision-making authority, the career negotiator on the Chinese side of the table possesses little, or no, power to make unilateral decisions.

Indeed, negotiating in China entails a continuous performance by all parties; foreigners for Chinese and Chinese for other Chinese. Compared with the process in the West, it is an extremely personalized business encounter, involving days of formal and informal conversations, factory tours, site visits, and banquets. A foreign representative is evaluated in terms of how he handles himself in every situation. Be warned, even though personalizing the business relationship can enhance communication and mutual understanding, the Chinese also see it as an opportunity to obtain proprietary information about the foreign firm, its size and past endeavors, the price and marketability of its products, its experience in China, etc. The Chinese, however, do not expect Chineseness from a Westerner. In fact, some group meals take place in dining rooms divided by partitions, where foreigners are served Western-style food on one side and the Chinese eat Chinese-style on the other. Banquets are another matter. Formal toasts are important at these occasions. When the conversation drags, avoid speaking among yourselves while ignoring the Chinese hosts. Avoid innappropriate or sensitive conversation subjects such as current Chinese politics, abortion, divorce, sex, corruption, etc. Instead, be well versed in topics of interest and relevance to China, such as Chinese history, art, literature, etc.

Controlling the Pace of Negotiations

At times, Chinese hosts set itineraries and plan business agendas without consultation with their foreign counterparts. Foreign negotiators are usually shuttled from factory to meeting room to banquets on a strict schedule arranged by a Chinese liaison organization—in many cases, a local FTC. The typically short stay of foreign executives in China works in favor of the Chinese, who like to pace negotiations to their advantage. In the final days of negotiation, the Chinese are known to ask for price reductions and last-minute changes in the contract terms, which they often succeed in getting since the foreigners are about to leave China.

The Chinese test the patience of foreigners for several reasons. Often they stall for time to get higher-level approvals, to kill a deal without losing face, or simply to intimidate the foreigner into making concessions on the contract. They often produce "wild cards" as the departure date for the foreigner approaches, such as a large price increase, a suddenly discovered local export tariff, or a major change in the terms of proposed technology transfer. Whatever their reasons, it is important not to exhibit anger. (Foreigners who lose their composure are not trusted.) Respond to Chinese delays with a strategy of patience. Don't be afraid to express a willingness to return home without a signed contract. Invite the Chinese to send a delegation to the United States to continue the negotiation. Take control of the pace of negotiations by

---

Advice for Negotiating in China

▶ Conduct preliminary negotiations through the mail; send documents ahead of the visit so there are no surprises.

▶ Set time and money spending limits for each potential agreement. Know when to quit and move on to another potential partner.

▶ Do not allow the parent Chinese organization to trap foreign representatives into opting for a Chinese partner with whom they are not completely satisfied in order to bring home a contract.

▶ In overseas negotiations, Americans often ignore the importance of (1) developing personal relationships and (2) earning the trust of their counterparts.[35] American negotiators excel in the art of persuasion, but those bound for China should also make it an objective to achieve the status of *lao pengyou*, an "old friend of China."

---

holding a preliminary discussion at the outset of the visit to define the scope of the trip and set an agenda with the Chinese. This guards against sudden changes halfway through the visit. At this early meeting, identify general mutual objectives and articulate auxiliary plans if initial intentions prove unworkable. Also, firms can schedule their stay in China to be open-ended.

GETTING ORGANIZED FOR VENTURE START-UP

Organizing a venture in the People's Republic requires a high degree of preparation, in-house organization, and sensitivity to Chinese capabilities and deficiencies. The task can begin with the formation of a specialized "China Venture Group" within the parent company and dividing up responsibilities among teams of top managers and technicians who carry out the implementation of the project in China, including the smooth transfer and translation of technical documentation, the installation of equipment, the training of Chinese workers and managers, and in the case of a joint venture, the transfer of a suitable management/production system. In addition, a well-organized venture helps to alleviate communication problems by including Chinese-speaking managers and technicians in the transfer process.

In the case of Cummins Engine Company's transfer of diesel engine technology to the Chongqing Engine Plant, the Chinese side had formed eight separate groups to facilitate the transfer and manufacturing process. The groups were composed of bureaucrats from Techimport, the Ministry of Machine Building Industry, and top officials and engineers from the Chongqing Engine Plant. One group consisted of engineers from the Chongqing Fuel Systems Plant, a supplier of the Chongqing Engine Plant. Two of the groups were in charge of: (1) dealing with outside commercial issues, (2) organizing the training program, (3) supplying technical assistance, (4) researching market profile of Chinese end-users, (5) formulating a ten-year production plan, (6) introducing Cummins to the Chongqing Engine Plant operational structure, and (7) establishing methods of communication.

Another group handled the following: (1) materials management, (2) purchased part management, (3) CKD kit management, (4) marketing and after-sales service, (5) product adaptation, (6) application engineering, and (7) product engineering. Yet other groups assessed the capabilities at the Chongqing Engine Plant for the proposed manufacturing process and formulated manufacturing plans which were discussed later with manufacturing experts from Cummins.[36] The ability of teams from both sides to work together effectively and openly, to a large extent, governs the outcome of organizational efforts leading to start-up.

Feasibility Studies

More than in other places, China demands that additional preparatory work be conducted before start-up. Traditionally, the Chinese are largely unconvinced of the value and necessity of feasibility studies, although this is changing. The Chinese view these studies as possibly jeopardizing future contract deals. Their enthusiasm for groundbreaking is extremely high, however. After their problems with Baoshan Steel Works, Beijing Jeep Corporation, and Fujian-Hitachi, China realizes that feasibility studies are essential. The debate now centers on who should pay for them.

Physical Plant.   The Chinese usually bring foreigners to exist-ing factories or sites that are in great need of upgrading. Negotiators should make serious inquiries regarding the location of the proposed venture. The following considerations are vital in conducting feasibility studies:

- Is there sufficient infrastructure at the site?
- Does the existing factory suffer frequent power outages as do the majority of Chinese plants?
- How much additional electricity will the joint venture require and will that amount be available?
- What is the status of surrounding communication, road, rail, and port transportation systems, and what demands will the joint venture place on them?
- What will the total costs of improvements be and will local Chi-nese agencies be willing to contribute?
- What are the current availability and quality of raw materials in the site area?

Obtaining verified answers to these questions will reduce unantic-ipated costs. Seeking such information, however, may entail conduct-ing feasibility studies that fly in the face of Chinese assurances. One case illustrates the prudence of early information gathering. A Sino-American joint venture was designed to manufacture pharmaceutical capsules utilizing water from a nearby lake that the Chinese guaranteed was clean. It was not, however, and the U.S. partner was forced to install a water purification plant. Then the company discovered that local power outages were common, which soon jeopardized the manufac-turing process. The U.S. partner was compelled to install the appropri-ate backup generating equipment. These problems resulted in unantic-ipated higher costs to the U.S. partner, yet it seems both could have been avoided.

Feasibility studies should be undertaken by qualified institutes and consultancies, particularly on larger projects. The Chinese now require a joint feasibility study to be completed that looks into raw material supply, expenses, labor availability, profit projection, foreign exchange needs, and return on investment. The feasibility study has grown in importance in terms of getting the overall venture approved, with Chinese partners having to justify both partner and technology selection.

Locale.   All too often, the foreign partner has little say in the choice of an appropriate site for the factory, because the decision is commonly made by central and local bureaucrats. Yet the selection of a site is vital and should include the foreign party and other experts who can judge potential locations objectively. Begin the process by asking to visit several possible locations and use the following criteria in making a final decision:

- Does the city have a well-developed industrial base that could manufacture product lines complementary to the joint venture's product lines?
- How Westernized is the area? Are local factories and business entities exposed to Western companies and business practices?
- Does the area have any historical linkage with the outside through trade and other contact?
- How open are local decision makers to new business forms outlined in foreign investment policy and what application of these techniques exists in the area? Are city leaders, especially the mayor, positive about foreign investment and will they actively assist enterprises with foreign participation?
- Does the city offer the necessary infrastructure?
- How does the area compare with others in terms of privileges for foreign firms such as tax exemptions and market access? For example, by locating in the Minhang-Shanghai ETDZ, Xerox was allowed to sell 100 percent of its copiers to the domestic market for the first five years of the venture.[37]

FINANCING CHINA VENTURES

The majority of joint ventures seek their funding through Hong Kong banking institutions because the Bank of China has shown a reluctance to share the financial risk of initiating joint ventures. The Bank of China is not keen to lend to joint ventures for initial assets; instead, it concentrates more on short-term working capital loans. Typically, international banks want a guarantee from the Bank of China or other Chinese financial institutions authorized to guarantee loans. The Bank of China guarantees only the portion of joint venture equity share held by the Chinese side; the foreign side must find its own guarantor.[38] However, 75 percent of all Sino-foreign joint ventures have received some Bank of

China funding. Equity investments by the Bank of China are made in ventures as well, under the auspices of the bank's investment arm, the Bank of China Trust and Consulting Company. Between 1983 and mid-1986, the company had invested $270 million in 133 joint ventures. The China Investment Bank and CITIC are other Chinese organizations that the foreign firm should solicit for possible equity participation in China ventures.[39]

European banks are exhibiting a willingness to fund some of the largest U.S. joint ventures in China. More American banks may choose to fund projects in the China market through subsidiaries set up in Hong Kong—following the lead of Security Pacific Bank, which has opened a subsidiary called Bank of Canton in Hong Kong—rather than setting up operations in Beijing, where many U.S. banks have gutted their operations for lack of business. Only a handful of U.S. banks directly finance Sino-American joint ventures. The few that do, attract hundreds of applications for joint venture projects, most of which are already beyond the negotiation stage with the Chinese.

The present funding range of $50,000 to $100 million is available to U.S. firms with joint venture agreements already signed with the Chinese which meet a relatively stringent set of risk-reducing criteria. Of course, these criteria vary according to the amount of funding required, the past experience of the bank or institution in China, and the idiosyncrasies of the personnel in its Asia affairs department.

Criteria for Financing

Field of endeavor.   Potential financiers view technology transfer projects as high-risk ventures for two reasons: (1) technology venture products are too expensive for sufficient numbers of Chinese customers to purchase, even when authorized to do so; and (2) the questionable quality of high-tech products made in China makes them difficult to sell to export markets.

Local business environment.   U.S. banks want to know whether the local business environment is sufficient to support the joint venture. They make this determination based on a series of questions: Is the joint venture practical within this specific locale? If skilled employees are not available in the factory's locale, do municipal regulations in the area allow employees to be located by way of labor advertisements? (The difficulty of this varies as to location.)

Finally, does the area possess the export capability to transport production to outside markets?

Market: Domestic and International. Creditors take a hard look at the markets the parent company already serves in the United States. A firm's market projections must indicate ready markets for the projected percentage of export product from China. Unless the parent company's reputation is extremely strong, a firm producing China products without ready markets will find potential creditors unwilling to finance their production.

Also under consideration is the attractiveness of a product line to China as either a potential export or an import substitute. Firms involved in joint ventures producing import substitutes for the China market have an obvious advantage in ready markets, and thus can project instantaneous sales. In this case, creditors will consider the percentage split between production for domestic sales versus export sales.

Creditor's equity percentage. Are other financial institutions involved on the U.S. or Chinese side? If other creditors are involved, their experience and history of funding joint ventures in China will be a consideration.

Project size. There is an inclination among U.S. creditors to avoid overambitious projects and concentrate on joint ventures in the $1–10 million range.

Business background. Creditors will investigate the background of the specific type of business and its interrelationship with the province and municipality in which the joint venture plans to produce and market its products.

Endorsements. The level of Chinese approval and the number of significant endorsements is also given some weight in the creditor's decision.

Proposal Preparedness.

The great majority of proposals from U.S. firms soliciting funds for joint venture projects in China contain a general description of a production idea, but little detail on China's business atmosphere. Most market projections are based on the firm's experience in other, less difficult overseas investment climates. Surprisingly, interviews with banking executives indicate that many of these corporate ideas are ill conceived in terms of China's unique market, often containing totally exaggerated sales projections for the locality in which they plan to sell in China. Many cases exist in which the venture plans of a U.S. partner receive rapid approval by an overenthusiastic Chinese partner, who views the venture as an easy way of obtaining foreign exchange and foreign technology, without serious consideration of product salability or the venture's future ability to repay its creditors. The U.S. side, excited by the "quick hit," approaches the financial institution ill prepared. One bank official at the China department of a U.S. bank said bluntly, "Ninety percent of the China joint venture proposals we receive are garbage—we don't even look at them."

The proposals sent by U.S. firms to financial institutions usually consist of a full description of both the proposed project and the background of the U.S. firm, but little material related to the operation and history of the factory on the Chinese side. Proposals should describe the product to be manufactured and exported, and the import ratio. Firms should also attempt to convince the funder why the product will be profitable. The downfall of many proposals is that they rarely contain verifiable information about the marketability of production in specifically defined areas of China, down to the municipality level. Financiers interpret this fundamental problem as a lack of understanding of the China market on the part of the U.S. firm. Loan officers are highly suspicious of the Chinese tendency to accept U.S. proposals that bring in dollars and technology with little risk-sharing on the Chinese side.

With few exceptions, proposals for funding contain letters of approval and signed contracts between joint venture partners, but few of them show that a significant number of Chinese managers and officials—from many different levels of local and central leadership— endorse the project and plan to generate support for it. This may be acceptable in SEZs, where approval by one aggressive city mayor or other high official may be sufficient to unify and mobilize local suppliers, labor organizations, export transportation companies, etc., to ensure the success of a young joint venture, but this is rarely the case in areas outside the SEZs. Without the energetic support of a large number of Chinese up and down the local administrative hierarchy, the venture may fail simply because of its isolation and neglect in the business infrastructure. In any viable proposal, local and regional support should be confirmed by the inclusion of letters of endorsement. To many firms, the high cost and frustration of selling the joint venture concept to relatively low-level, nonessential players is perceived as superfluous. Many of these same firms, however, discover later that their joint ventures suffer from time-consuming operational problems because they failed to secure the outside support of local officials, suppliers, and other entities affecting the efficiency of the venture.

Banking officials are well aware that many ventures fail without these vital connections. They stress that any U.S. partner in a joint venture will have to deal at some time after start-up with officials from various organizations including MOFERT, Chinese banks, CITIC, and others. They advise that U.S. firms seek out these players before start-up and form the personal relationships which will offer vital assistance later. China is no different from anywhere else in the sense that you cannot conduct business in a vacuum. Bankers consider proposals which include endorsements from top-level officials down to local managers in a much more favorable light than proposals without these endorsements. Another criterion could be added to the list: How well has the U.S. partner performed so far in influencing the Chinese business system through the ground-laying of *guanxi* relationships?[40]

Proposals should indicate how many Chinese approve, endorse, or are involved positively in the project. The great majority of proposals usually contain Chinese approval at two levels only: (1) one high-level approval, such as that of a mayor of a city; and (2) an approval from the head of the factory entering into the joint venture. These two levels might be enough in a SEZ, but in cities such as Wuhan, Xian, and Urumchi, two-level authorization and endorsement would not be enough. In these places, multilevel approval and assistance will be necessary from Beijing through provincial and municipal levels.

The Importance of Shopping Around

Bank officials take a hard look at the investigative work U.S. firms carry out before they sign a joint venture contract. Loan officers, in their own research, ascertain how many potential Chinese enterprises were considered before choosing the best one. They research such questions as: Did the U.S. firm contact U.S. embassy commercial officers in China in order to solicit potential partners? How many factories did the U.S. firm tour? Has the firm taken full advantage of U.S. government assistance, consultants, and trade liaison services on both sides?

Bank research supports the notion that many firms find a single partner and hold steadfast. This occurs, perhaps, because the Chinese foreign trade corporations tend to promote specific factories which

China's Financial Decision-Making Structure

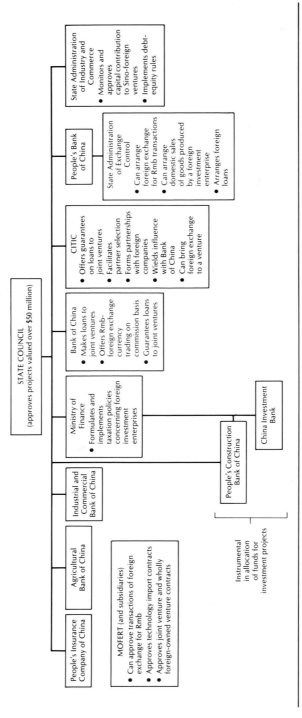

China's financial structure promotes a tightly knit, "old boy" solidarity when collaborating with foreigners on financial matters. Two general elements of project financing frustrate the investor: (1) obtaining loans for initial start-up, and (2) balancing foreign exchange after start-up. Foreign investors seek loans from the Bank of China (BOC) often in conjunction with foreign banks. However, through an exclusionary system of loan syndication, the BOC has made it difficult for foreign banks to participate in loans to foreign investment enterprises. (CITIC can offer the necessary leverage to get loan guarantees.) Balancing foreign exchange accounts can be accomplished by swapping Rmb earned from domestic sales through organizations such as MOFERT, the State Administration of Exchange Control, or the BOC. (See Chapter 6, profit repatriation.)

SOURCES: China International Consultants, Inc., *The China Investment Guide*, and the table compiled by John Frisbie in *China Business Review* (March–April, 1988, 34, 35).

need foreign help in promoting their exports. To counter this steering, foreign firms should demand to see as many potential partners as possible. The challenge is to obtain financial and market information from factory managers who may be instructed not to divulge sensitive figures. Before this information can be collected, however, U.S. firms have to build a bond of trust between themselves and their potential partners. This takes time, but it is essential to obtaining funding from risk-averse lenders.

Thousands of miles from Beijing, television antennas fashioned out of long branches rise above mud-brick homes on a state farm. In a few Chinese cities, six out of seven families now own a television set.

*"Demand proletarian internationalism and support all the oppressed
nations and people in the struggle to oppose imperialism, colonialism, and
hegemonism, and fight for liberation and social progress."*

*After a series of preliminary
agreements, Chinese and foreign
parties sign final contracts.
American negotiating teams
often become discouraged when
the Chinese partner later
requests a renegotiation of
contract clauses.*

*Newly constructed skyscrapers
tower above central Shenzhen,
a special economic zone where
Chinese and Western cultures
blend.*

A typical Chinese negotiating room with sofas, tables, tea cups, thermoses of hot water, and a banner depicting the annual output of the adjacent production unit.

Fast-food services and food-processing technologies have become vital to fueling China's faster-paced urban population.

Crowded television and appliance stores reflect how Deng's open-door policy has increased China's appetite for consumer goods, alarming many traditional Marxists.

An American agronomist discusses possible joint venture project objectives with managers of a state farm. For proposed beef farming, a strategy of land reclamation is planned that will produce grass and fodder. Joint venture development, especially in outlying provinces where infrastructure remains undeveloped, is slow and can be fraught with problems.

American executives peruse finished products in a showroom at a Chinese textile factory.

American representatives converse with trade officials at a typical Chinese business banquet. Fifteen to twenty dishes are served including eel, squid, mutton, seaweed, pork liver, turtle soup, and freshwater shrimp. In addition to kiwi wine and local beer, numerous toasts are made with Maotai, a clear, 180-proof liquor made from sorghum and sipped from a tiny porcelain shot glass.

A new free market in Hefei, Anhui, is symptomatic of China's changing policies concerning free enterprise. Individual rural households can now sell their surplus production at higher prices to the state or at local markets.

Subterranean river water emerges from the base of a cliff, rushes through a hydroelectric power plant, and flows onto the Tarim basin of Xinjiang Province to be used in irrigation. Energy development and conservation will remain a top technological priority in the People's Republic well beyond the year 2000.

Understanding China's Business Culture

Doing business with China's vast bureaucracies continues to frustrate and bewilder the Beijing sojourner today, as it did a century ago. After all, the Chinese invented bureaucracy over two millennia ago, and in the interim they have perfected all of its excesses.

Kenneth Lieberthal
Michel Oksenberg
(as quoted in *China Business Review*)

The Chinaman [sic] may love you, but you are a devil all the same. It is most natural that he should think so. For generation upon generation China was almost completely isolated from the rest of the world. . . . Then the foreign devil burst upon the scene—a being as antagonistic to themselves in every way as it is possible to conceive.

Herbert A. Giles
1911

Lying in state in his glass-covered tomb in Tian'anmen Square, Mao Zedong would probably be aghast if he had witnessed Deng Xiaoping's reform policies take root in China. The recent reforms amount to a frontal assault on the social and economic programs associated with Mao, going so far as to include a principal role for foreign companies as participants in the country's modernization drive. As such, those foreign firms that have responded to the China challenge are vulnerable to the political ebb and flow of the reform program. To succeed in China, therefore, these firms must manage their China activities in conjunction with the reforms. They must not lose sight of the process of change that constitutes the crux of the economic modernization effort. American corporate executives must recognize that China's reform program defines the parameters in which the Sino-foreign corporate encounter takes place. The

155

foreign business person fully apprised of how the Chinese decision-making bureaucracy works will be able to maneuver within it to capitalize on opportunities while avoiding the danger implicit in remaining aloof from the swift changes under way.

CHINA'S INDUSTRIAL LANDSCAPE: MAO ZEDONG'S LEGACY

I remember once saying to a Chinese factory director that "Mao was a great man." The director looked away nervously, and then said, "Yes, up until 1950." He was implying, with characteristic Chinese subtlety, that Mao's greatness was achieved when he mobilized Communist armies and chased Chiang Kai-shek's Nationalists off the mainland to seek refuge on the island of Taiwan. After 1950, this factory director believed, as many Chinese do, that Mao had led China down a road of perpetual revolution that turned out to be a cul-de-sac of isolationism from the rest of the world.

To avoid dependence on foreigners, Mao had stressed the importance of self-reliance and encouraged the development of indigenous economic and technological capabilities at all levels. The pig-iron foundries constructed in many Chinese towns during the Great Leap Forward (1958–60) were representative of this orientation. Mao emphasized decentralization of the industrial base, with each locality being asked to produce a broad array of basic goods under the umbrella of a series of self-contained local administrative entities directed by the Chinese Communist Party (CCP). Under this strategy China proved, though at some cost, it could indeed produce industrial goods without appreciable help of foreign companies.

Unfortunately, one important result of these policies was massive inefficiency. China basically struggled at the wrong end of the economies of scale. In spite of China's massive reform efforts that began in 1976, the Chinese have made little progress in ameliorating the long-term ill effects of Mao's political and economic legacy. Deeply entrenched vestiges of Maoism continue to thwart progressive change in China's industrial structure and foil its attempts to modernize and improve its international competitiveness. Though China's overall production capacity is large, most factories operate at a fraction of capacity because they lack incentives or pressures to do otherwise. Nearly all

Chinese factories still suffer from insufficient working capital and limited access to technology due to foreign exchange limitations. Efforts to break the iron rice bowl with employment and wage incentives have achieved only modest success as many workers and managers prefer the security of the past to the uncertainties associated with a market-led system.

Moreover, Maoist policies stimulated only modest technological progress. Until Mao's death in 1976, China's approach to technological modernization had focused in large part upon procuring key equipment in limited quantities from abroad and attempting to reverse engineer the designs. Once the embodied technology was understood, modifications to fit local needs could be made. At times, certain products were "sinicized" in order to avoid direct copying from the West. Embellishing the "Chineseness" of such products was considered to be politically appropriate. Mao's overall industrial strategy also contributed to the dispersion of factories in similar sectors across China (third-line industries), which constrained technology transfer and caused perpetual energy and material shortages. For instance, China had over 250 auto factories in the early 1980s, yet some of them produced fewer than fifty vehicles per year. Development of a workable infrastructure to support technological exchange in both industry and agriculture across provincial boundaries was also limited. As a result of these past policies, China remains technologically incapable of competing in most areas with the other fast-rising East Asian economies.

Mao's localized industrial strategy also resulted in the hoarding of manufacturing supplies at all levels of production. Local bureaucrats vied for control of inputs and output in order to wield near monarchical control over their local production units. The coordination of productive efforts across provincial borders became virtually impossible. Ultimately, his "road to socialism" has led China's industrial economy to a state in which prerogatives issued at the local level often preempt national directives emanating from the central level. Beijing's basic policies continue to be undermined or subverted at the provincial level, delaying many of China's most crucial reform initiatives.[1]

Byzantine Bureaucracy

The repercussions of adopting the Soviet model of central planning in 1949 continue to be felt today, mainly in the form of a gargantuan network of governing bodies, agencies, institutions, and societies. Dense bureaucracy has existed in China for centuries, but reliance on a central planning model accentuated the role of government and gave great impetus to the burgeoning presence of the CCP in all spheres of life.

Heretofore, our impressions about China were that there existed a planned economy, organized and monitored at all levels by the government in Beijing. In reality, one finds that Chinese bureaucratic organizations often work at cross purposes, competing with each other rather than cooperating. The various elements of the Chinese system actually cooperate in only a handful of isolated cases involving high-priority projects, such as in the advanced weapons field, superconductivity, and microelectronics. Historically, there has been only limited collaboration between industries except on critical military projects. Resources are rarely pooled in a system of ingrained self-sufficiency. Centrally organized efforts to create horizontal economic linkages, while reflecting Beijing's intent to decentralize industrial decision making, actually reveal the absence of appropriate structures, channels, and incentives to do so. The great majority of decision makers are motivated more by regional prerogatives than by central government objectives. This means that the majority of decisions made within the system tend to be the product of bargaining and negotiation rather than careful orchestration by central planners.

China's system of administrative hierarchies, or fiefdoms, limits the possibility of an efficient economic system. As Lieberthal and Oksenberg have written: ". . . Almost every arrangement in China depends on the cooperation of different units that have no power of command over each other."[2] Without sustained interaction among subordinate agencies, new economic initiatives often wither from lack of vital organizational support structures. This "vertical" nature of authority is depicted in the organizational chart on page 159.

Before discussing Chinese business culture further, a brief overview of China's current bureaucratic hierarchy is in order. The State Council, which is responsible for the major decisions of government, occupies the highest level of a four-tiered system of administrative control. Below the State Council are various planning commissions that formulate and oversee the country's industrial and financial policies. The third level of government consists of the ministries—agricultural and industrial—that implement state plans within specific sectors of the economy. The ministries accomplish this through a full complement of similarly affiliated bureaus at the provincial and municipal

China's Four-tiered Bureaucratic Hierarchy

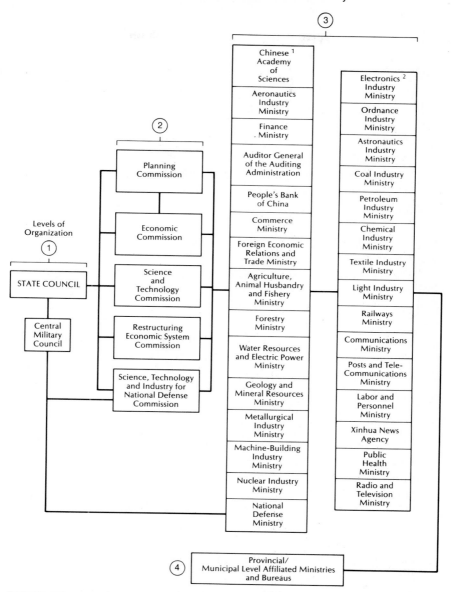

NOTES: 1. The CAS reports to the State Council, but is organizationally different from other ministries.

2. The Ministry of Electronics Industry and the State Machine-Building Industry Commission have been merged recently to form the Machine-Building and Electronics Industry.

levels—the fourth tier of China's bureaucratic system. The State Council also oversees several types of foreign trade entities. The largest entity, MOFERT, runs the national trade corporations of China. There are also numerous FTCs that report directly to the ministries and other high-level bodies such as the Chinese Academy of Sciences. The third level consists of local foreign trade commissions (e.g., a Shanghai FTC or a Guangzhou FTC). Some of the changes announced at the Thirteenth National People's Congress, held in Beijing in March 1987, however, require that many of the local branches of the national FTCs report directly to their local governments rather than to Beijing.

The State Planning Commission and State Economic Commission (merged in 1987) develop import plans which are carried out through numerous provincial and municipal import/export entities under the oversight of MOFERT, which is also responsible for approving, monitoring, and supervising the operations of foreign-owned enterprises. In addition, MOFERT implements and enforces the laws, provisions, and regulations related to technology transfer. Local planning commissions devise annual and long-term economic plans for their respective regions. The State Science and Technology Commission is responsible for formulating and implementing science and technology policy; the State Educational Commission is responsible for administering China's key colleges and universities; the National Defense Science, Technology and Industry Commission is responsible for military science, technology and industry affairs.

Because of their vertically defined boundaries, many of China's ministries tend to display a distinct unwillingness to share technology, manufacturing capability, or production experience with their counterparts in other related sectors. Recently, however, Chinese leaders have undertaken a program to transform their existing administrative structure for managing industry. Economic factors are being used increasingly as the criteria to define organizational structures. Hence, the MEI was merged with the State Machine-Building Industry Commission to facilitate internal cooperation and technology transfer. This merger occurred in spite of the strong opposition of both units. Such a top-down approach to industrial administration characterizes most sectors of the economy. A number of prevailing irrationalities in the economy, such as shortages of key production inputs and price problems, suggest that it will not be easy to fully abandon this general approach.

Center-Local Friction

Provincial protectionism continues to be a major obstacle to greater economic integration. Provincial leaders obviously want to generate profits from production units within their administrative authority, sometimes doing so by barring the movement of goods, imposing export duties, or forcing products to move through "turnpikes" (that is, collecting tolls on their way from the province to the outside).[3] Unlike some of the inland provinces, China's coastal cities have a long legacy as foreign enclaves and trade entrepôts with more developed transportation systems and communication networks intact. In recent years the Chinese leadership has recognized this fact and has targeted several of the coastal cities as their country's main link to the outside world. The growing stature of these cities makes the city mayors extremely powerful, in some ways even monarchical. Local policies in these cities often discriminate against not only foreigners but even Chinese from outside the immediate region. Similar types of obstacles or blockades exist with respect to the diffusion of technology. What becomes clear is that local authorities can successfully resist the will of the government if desired, in ways that foreigners would not believe possible from what has been, heretofore, their impressions about the authority of the Communist Party in China.

A good example of the conflict between the center and localities is illustrated in the relationship between Shanghai and Beijing in the electronics industry. Coordination and redundancy are critical problems in this relationship. The intense rivalry between the central ministries and the localities focuses on the desire of each to create and maintain its own capabilities and prerogatives. China's electronics industry is composed of several key ministries. Prior to the reorganization in April 1988, the primary ministry was the MEI, which had jurisdiction over a series of major manufacturing and research facilities. Beginning in mid-1985, the electronics industry underwent a significant decentralization. The MEI relinquished direct managerial control over all but two of its 177 enterprises. Numerous enterprises in the electronics industry are still managed under the principle of "dual leadership," wherein central and local authorities have an equal voice in enterprise affairs. Factories operating in the electronics industry may have as many as ten different forms of local and central administrative oversight, making it difficult to form clear-cut lines of decision making.[4] Even so, because of their continued reliance on the center for both overhead and project funding, enterprises and their associated bureaus at the provincial and municipal levels, such as those in Shanghai, cannot totally disregard the wishes of Beijing.

The increasing imbalance of power and authority between provinces is also reflected in the country's borrowing policies. International banking institutions push China to accept loans since China has a high credit rating. On the Chinese side, provincial leaders have been granted the authority to take loans unilaterally, without central level approval. All provinces of China greatly desire foreign exchange loans at attractive interest rates, believing their chance to take such loans may not last forever. Economic disparity between provinces fouls the program, however. Obviously, the impetus on the part of international banks is to push loans into China's richer provinces, rather than the poorer ones, since the poorer provinces lack the ability to generate foreign exchange to repay the loans. So too, China's central government requires that provinces possess the foreign exchange to cover any loans they take. This tends to eliminate the poorer provinces from receiving borrowed funds. In the end, few loans are made to the underendowed provinces for development projects, worsening their economic position relative to the better-endowed, usually coastal provinces. On the other hand, the poorer provinces do not lack political power and clout in the central government. In some cases, they resist Deng's reform program which they perceive as benefiting some provinces to the exclusion of others. Often, they apply the brakes on reforms in their areas, or at least, vulgarize them relative to Beijing's original directives.[5]

Guanxi Allocation of Supplies

Similarly, goods and services tend to flow poorly across provincial borders. China's system of supply and demand is based on an informal distribution network whereby the movement of goods and services occurs within a weblike series of channels. Agreements are consummated by people in positions of power and influence who are connected through professional, familial, and/or political linkages. Surplus supplies can be bartered as goods in high demand are offered. The Chinese business environment epitomizes the adage: "It's not what you know; it's who you know." Although this system has worked for centuries throughout Asia, it constrains the progress of many initiatives because of the absence of the appropriate informal relationship.

The trading of goods and services through inside connections has spawned an economy that depends increasingly on dealing with local government and "unofficial" suppliers in a gray market rather than through official channels. In cities such as Guangzhou, for example, vying for influence within the bureaucracy and among distributors by doing favors and offering thinly disguised gifts is the best way to gain leverage. The monetary value of goods is subordinated, at times, to the clout one has within the distribution network in terms of *guanxi*. Even today, guanxi relationships form the backbone of decision making, promotions, and resource allocation in China. Guanxi relationships can be described as ingratiating personal relationships that impose multiple obligations on the respective players. Among the Chinese, these guanxi relationships can stem from the town in which one's parents were born, the university one attended, or a direct familial tie.

Insider favoritism and informal reciprocity tear at the fabric of the ultimate intention of Deng's reform program. The country's dependence on guanxi-style networking tends to reduce, if not nullify, those regulations concerning internal trade and economic exchange issued by Beijing. It is the reason why managerial positions are filled with family members, friends, and coworkers rather than those who are simply well qualified. It also explains why many university students studying abroad are the offspring of high officials. Guanxi also interferes with fair competition and skews the supply system. Nonetheless, in a system where uncertainty remains high and dependence on formal institutions is still unpredictable, guanxi relations can make things happen when and where they otherwise might not.

Administrative Interference.   The currency of an informal barter system is the goods, services, and foreign exchange that the enterprises produce. As one would expect from this system, official meddling in the affairs of Chinese factories is rampant, as party cadres and bureaucrats move to acquire goods and services with which to barter. Chinese enterprises have found it difficult to take advantage of new economic freedoms because they remain caught in the stranglehold of impetuous local officials. Enterprises that produce economically strategic goods that are in great demand, such as bicycles and televisions, experience the most intrusion since these goods can be traded by local officials for needed resources in another province. For example, the city of Shanghai can leverage other provinces to obtain resources to fuel its manufacturing in exchange for supplying a quota of television sets. Unfortunately, many enterprises must pay deference to the internal guanxi barter system as a means of obtaining scarce resources whose delivery cannot be guaranteed by the state.

THE REFORM PROGRAM: IMPACT OF DECENTRALIZATION

In 1978, after almost three decades of Communist rule, China had to face up to a variety of serious economic problems. Industrial growth had slowed significantly and the output of agricultural products was barely keeping pace with China's population increases. State-owned enterprises reported average losses of 20 percent in 1985, which led to a reassessment of the state's ability to manage and operate these enterprises.[6] Moreover, serious doubts about the future existed among growing numbers of Chinese who remained embittered and disillusioned after the Cultural Revolution. Questions arose in the minds of millions regarding the ability of the party to lead China's modernization or to generate further improvement in the standard of living of the people.[7]

China's economic development path was put on a new course after the meeting of the Third Plenary Session of the Eleventh Central Committee of the CCP in December 1978. At this meeting, it was decided that major structural reforms in the economy were necessary to produce a sustained pattern of economic growth. Since 1978, China has launched a number of major reforms in its industrial economic system. The main characteristics of the overall reform program include: (1) revamping the taxation system, which allows enterprises to retain a proportion of their profit; (2) economic decentralization in which local governments and enterprises retain greater decision-making autonomy and control; and (3) emphasis on light industry by encouraging collective enterprises, especially in small townships. Deng Xiaoping's reforms also included an overhaul of the Chinese management system, the selected introduction of free markets, and labor reforms such as piece-work bonuses and wage increases. Concurrently, in the rural sector, the *household-responsibility* system was implemented to stimulate agricultural production and help curb the swelling of urban populations.[8] Agriculture was decollectivized, and attempts were made to revitalize the rural economy by allowing price increases for food staples. The individual household became the smallest unit of production. By allowing the diversification of the rural economy and an appreciable degree of privatization, China's agrarian sector received a needed stimulus to increase output and improve overall productivity.

Associated with the reforms has been an astounding rate of growth in China's overall industry during the 1980s. The total growth rate of heavy and light industry in 1981 equaled 3.7 percent; by 1985 growth had reached 17.7 percent.[9] In terms of industrial strategy, in most cases, mandatory planning has been replaced by guidance planning. As Audrey Chan has described, guidance planning uses "economic levers such as pricing, taxation and credits to guide enterprises in fulfilling the state plan."[10] (However, mandatory planning is still being enforced for those products relating to national defense or considered essential to maintaining the standard of living of the Chinese people.)

As control has been decentralized down to the localities, many of China's large industrial ministries have been dispersed and their affiliated enterprises have been either set off on their own or control over them has been decentralized down to the local level. In the auto industry, for instance, direct central control has been relinquished and local automobile corporations can conduct business more independently. The Thirteenth National People's Congress further decentralized day-to-day administrative authority over the economy by placing increased emphasis on the *production responsibility* system. Moreover, many Chinese cities, which historically had been squeezed by the central government for tax revenue, have been brought under the system of *baogan*, a financial contract arrangement between Beijing and these cities that designates the amount of city revenue to be returned to the central coffers—a target commitment that the central government desires each city to generate annually. Any additional income accrued by a city can be retained for purposes of upgrading its own infrastructure. This system creates additional incentives for cities to increase production, amass revenue, and invest in their own industrial well-being. The set percentages are designed to decrease, so that cities get to retain a larger proportion of their earnings. Baogan is part of the movement toward making China's localities more responsible for their own welfare and development.

Overview of Chinese Policies Since 1949

Policy Area / Period	Industry	Agriculture	Military
1949–1952 Rehabilitation and Consolidation	Former nationalist enterprises remain state enterprises; foreign holdings become state run; Chinese capitalists continue to control their plants	Land redistributed to individual households	Reliance on USSR for protection and arms
1953–1957 First Five-Year Plan	Major investment in heavy industry; virtually all industry brought under state plan; large wage increase for urban workers	Collectivization of agriculture to level of agricultural producing cooperatives; some traditional inputs; little direct state investment in agriculture	Build up a professional military modeled on the Soviet Red Army
1958–1960 Great Leap Forward	3-tier arrangement; heavy industry under central control; light industry under provincial control, less sophisticated industry under commune control. "Backyard steel furnaces" to increase output in heavy industry.	Formation of communes; no increase in direct state investment in agriculture	Lin Biao becomes defense minister; people's war and political training grow in importance relative to highly technological warfare
1961–1965 Readjustment and Recovery New Economic Program	Many local factories closed down; policy of building on the best and directing resources to industries in coastal cities and the northeast	Beginning of direct state investment in agriculture; communes reduced in size; agricultural equipment factories built earlier begin to come on line	PLA demonstrates that it is both "red" and "expert," serves as a model and staffs new political work departments

Period	Industry	Agriculture	Military
1966–1969 Cultural Revolution	Disruption in factories due to political turbulence, no change in investment	Little change in policy; strong emphasis on self-reliance	PLA takes on many administrative and police functions; continues to be "red and expert," but some units or commanders are found to be politically unreliable
1970–1975 Transition	Industry support to agriculture; cellular economy with shift away from complete self-reliance at lowest levels; trend toward more imports of foreign equipment and technology	Limited direct state investment; more local industry to generate revenue for agriculture	Shift away from "Two Enemy" strategy to tilt towards the U.S.; PLA continues to serve as reserve of labor and equipment for civilian functions; continued emphasis on people's war and nuclear deterrent
1976–1978	High levels of capital construction particularly for heavy industrial plant; imports of foreign industrial equipment and technology equipment and technology	Calls for rapid mechanization and modernization but limited state investment	Gradual reduction of PLA's non-military functions; beginning of emphasis on professional military ethic
1979–1984 Readjustment	Cutback in capital construction; shift toward investment in light industry; relatively more autonomy for enterprise managers	Introduction of household contract system; commune loses political function; resurgence of free market	Relegation of defense modernization to 4th on list of priorities; lower defense budgets following incursion into Vietnam in 1979; gradual evolution of doctrine to "people's war under modern conditions"
1985–present	Push ahead with technical transformation of industries; introduction of further economic reforms; emergence of small private companies and entrepreneurs (minban gongsi)	Expansion of private plots; proliferation of free markets throughout the country; reemergence of rural industry; strengthening of small towns (spark plan); leasing of land.	Emphasis on technical modernization of the military; improvement of professional and technical training; selective import of foreign military technology

Unforeseen Repercussions

In the first decade of reform, despite China's sustained high level of industrial growth, many unforeseen consequences of the new policies have surfaced that cannot be ignored. Some regions of China are simply not as prepared as others to accept the market-oriented economic levers embodied in the responsibility program. The experimental fashion of many of the economic reforms results in their implementation in some regions to the exclusion of others; some of the crucial reforms presuppose integration and cooperation across provincial borders when such cooperation simply does not exist. Progress in one area in China is not always duplicated in another area. Some areas naturally are excluded from the decentralization privileges and benefits. Jealousies abound and interprovince turf fighting is exacerbated by the provincialism generated in many cases by Mao's self-sufficiency programs. Furthermore, local politics have a significant effect on the pace and scope of the reform implementation process. Available knowledge regarding specific reform initiatives suggested by Beijing is extensive in some areas, while in others it is lacking. In general, information concerning the nature, purpose, and methods for adopting specific reforms tends to dissipate the further it travels from the center, so that by the time local managers and officials receive the information, much of its content and urgency is trivialized. So, too, failure to implement certain reforms goes largely unrecognized and unpunished in most cases. Positive benefits may come to the local leader who initiates certain changes, but little negative effect has yet to befall the local leader who ignores them.

The reforms are not only geographically uneven, they have also been implemented in an inconsistent fashion; that is, some elements of the reform program have been enacted more quickly than others. China's decision to move forward with the decentralization of authority in enterprises—as opposed to price reform—is the best example of this inconsistency. Obviously, enterprise performance and the price of goods produced are linked in such a way that it is difficult to conceive an enterprise exercising true autonomy if the price of its inputs and outputs remain fixed by the government. (The responsibility system has not included replacement of the current system in which the government still fixes most prices, interest rates, and exchange rates.) There is a good reason for this, however. Discussions about reform of the pricing system bring to the surface historical fears of rampant inflation. And, since modernization is viewed by the Chinese as an upgrading of the people's quality of life and prosperity, any inflation is considered necessarily a direct threat to hard-won wage increases. Inflation is also treated with great seriousness because of recent events in Poland. Both the People's Republic leadership and the masses see rapid price increases as destabilizing, and, therefore, a potentially lethal threat to the gains of modernization.

This fear of inflation forces the government to continue subsidizing vast numbers of enterprises, which only promotes management inefficiencies. Though bankruptcy has been discussed, enterprises are rarely permitted to fail, so they too lack motivation to truly succeed. Should scores of enterprises fail, millions of Chinese would be put out of work without the benefit of unemployment insurance. Such a state of affairs would put a gash in the Chinese social safety net—a politically unacceptable outcome. The bulk of reform has been implemented in such a way as to minimize disruption of traditional patterns of egalitarianism.[11] The country's current economic policy is, in essence, a "hurt nobody very badly" strategy. While such an incremental approach has its benefits, it also has some serious costs.

Impact on Local Economies.

In some major cities, such as Wuhan, where the divestment of enterprise authority has been carried out on a large scale, a severely detrimental economic chain reaction has followed. As enterprises increase output to take advantage of new opportunities, goods are produced that quickly flood regional markets. The massive influx of lower-price, higher-quality goods pinches local industries that produce similar products. Fast to respond to their new privileges, township-run industries begin producing more output and soon hurt the state-run enterprises, threatening workers with possible wage cuts and underemployment. Most important, some state and private enterprises collude to resell goods in short supply for additional profit, pushing up prices. At the same time, transportation and communication lines are overloaded and energy capacity is strained as companies further mobilize to increase production and marketing. Almost overnight, these local economies begin to reel under uncontrollable economic pressures. In some cities, the enterprise reforms have sent local economies on a collision course with other facets of the modernization program. Often, the brakes must be applied. Since the early 1980s, the central government has pushed forward and then retreated sharply several times as it has sought to find the right balance between relinquishing and asserting its control.

Intensified Competition Among Enterprises

In response to the reforms, many of China's long somnambulant enterprises have risen up to take advantage of new opportunities in a competitive and often fractious manner. Many of China's leading ministries have splintered into large corporations specializing in one subsector of an industry. Without direct ministerial oversight, many of these newly formed corporations are less willing to cooperate than to compete. As markets are opened to freer competition, serious questions have arisen as to what type of competitive tactics will be tolerated and what impact the dynamics of competition will have on strategic industries traditionally under state control. Under the reforms, these industries vie for access to raw materials and try to attract foreign investors for needed capital and technology. They often flood the domestic market with similar products and undertake redundant projects with foreign firms—in many cases, the latter projects are not export-oriented but are primarily aimed at the domestic market.

For instance, the China National Automotive Industry Corporation (CNAIC) sprang out of the former Ministry of Machine Building in 1982. Given corporate status, CNAIC's role was to centralize and coordinate China's auto industry by directing resources to the major automobile factories. Its ultimate objective, which is now almost complete, was to form several large automotive manufacturing complexes. Before CNAIC could implement an overall coordination plan, it had to face extensive pressures from a newly centralized auto industry that felt discriminated against compared with other sectors which were decentralized. The ensuing debate on whether control of the auto industry should be in central or local hands resulted in a seesaw effect on the implementation of reforms in the auto sector. In this industry, each plant received components, which were manufactured in satellite factories, specific to its particular vehicle. This supply route tended to isolate one plant from another.[12] Unfortunately, most of the smaller factories had formed a tight relationship with local governments. They depend on the local government for certain critical inputs, for which they reciprocate by supplying the local government with finished goods. Thus, while the central government may see great progress in dissolving small, self-contained factories, the local governments are reluctant to see them dismantled or brought under the influence of a higher level of officialdom. As one Chinese official remarked in an interview, "These factories cannot exist in a vacuum—either they belong to us [the local government] or to them [the central government]—they must belong to somebody!"

The uneven nature of the decision-making authority has created especially difficult times in the electronics industry. The government is attempting to break down the vertical decision-making apparatus and formulate a system of horizontally linked branches of responsibility. The delegation of authority has run into snags at the bureau and enterprise levels. A survey of 400 electronics industry enterprises in Shanghai indicates that little decentralization of authority has occurred in medium and large enterprises. The explanations given for the failure include: (1) unwillingness of local officials to give up their authority; (2) poor organizational flexibility, hence an inability to adjust readily to less rigid working regimes; and (3) an inability or unwillingness on the part of many manager cadres to grasp the political fundamentals of reformist decentralization.[13]

In regard to linking up with foreign firms, similar problems occurred in China's petroleum industry, which has been encouraged strongly to forge links with the leading international oil companies. Originally, the Chinese avoided organizing the industry around one master ministry. They divided up the activities for offshore oil development among a variety of organizations loosely grouped under three centers of power: (1) the Ministry of Petroleum Industry (MOPI) and its subsidiary, China National Offshore Oil Corporation (CNOOC); (2) various regional authorities; and (3) other corporate or ministerial organizations which provide offshore oil-related equipment or services. Because MOPI and CNOOC cannot provide all the services needed to develop China's oil resources, foreign firms have had to deal with multiple ministries and companies outside of MOPI's influence. As one observer has noticed, most projects "need approval by bodies other than the Ministry of Petroleum."[14] In addition, many of China's ministries supplying the offshore sector are interested in gaining access to the large sums of foreign exchange being spent by the foreign oil companies pursuing petroleum in the South China Sea. As a result, stiff competition and rivalry occur among those Chinese ministries which occupy essential positions on the periphery of the oil sector. Since most Westerners assumed these organizations to be under the auspices of MOPI and CNOOC, it was difficult to understand the reasons and underlying sources for the competition. The result has been continued concerns about the security of supplies and sources as well as costly delays in project operation. As many Chinese industrial entities attempt to exercise their new freedom to participate in complex transactions and partnerships, their lack of prior experience or knowledge surfaces quickly. Many entities appear too willing to take risks, possibly because they remain attached to the old system in which the state will pick up the tab if serious management mistakes are made.

Uncoordinated dealings with foreign firms have also taken their toll with regard to the import of foreign equipment and technology. The decentralization of import and export responsibility has often created serious problems of import duplication. Since 1984, for example, China has imported over eighty assembly lines for the production of complete color television sets. While China's capacity for manufacturing complete sets is quite high, its inability to produce sufficient quantities of high-quality components and accessories forces enterprises to import parts to maintain production levels. To compound the problem, the assembly lines originate from so many different countries that component specifications vary widely, causing significant domestic production of color televisions to remain problematic.[15]

NEW APPROACHES TO AMELIORATE PROBLEMS

Chinese leaders have found it difficult to break down the self-sufficiency mentality of small-scale enterprises. As a result, the effort to form a cooperative industrial system structured around large-scale specialized factories has run into many difficulties. The industrial linkages present in Japan, Taiwan, and South Korea, whereby end-product manufacturers "pull" along the component industries by upgrading technology and skill levels, are barely discernible in China. Unlike in Japan, unified coordination and collusion among government organizations and business interests—that is, a form of "China, Inc."—has been elusive. China's government acknowledges that it needs to provide more room for increasing local initiative among factories, encouraging them to innovate and increase production. At the same time, the government also has to safeguard against excessive deviation from its larger objectives regarding particular industries. The government will have to decide on a balance between the amount and type of industrial competition it can tolerate and what the economy as a whole can endure. The problem has been to develop a coherent national strategy for both reform and overall modernization while at the same time decentralizing control. The quandary remains: Where should the locus of authority lie? Striking this balance continues to vex Chinese planners.

In the last few years, China has tried to overcome some of the major impediments to cooperation in the economy by establishing leading groups to forge horizontal integration across geographical and administrative regions. In most cases, leading groups represent an acknowledgment by Beijing that the vertical system of planning and organization is not performing well. Chinese leaders hope the leading groups subdue unnecessary competition and encourage coordination between enterprises and ministries across vital industries. In theory, leading groups have extraordinary clout because they are headed by the country's highest officials. For example, the leading group for the electronics industry was led by then-acting Premier Li Peng. By working through the various government commissions, especially with respect to the allocation of resources, the leading groups provide general direction for new policy initiatives or set standards where they may be lacking.

Consolidating Enterprises

One of the key objectives of the economic reforms is to break the symbiotic and, at times, parasitic relationship between the Chinese factory and the central or local government agency that has jurisdiction over it. Official policy encourages enterprises to establish cooperative relationships by grouping together and collaborating on a formal basis. This attempt to break the rigid control over smaller factories held by local supervising agencies and governments is being made in conjunction with other program objectives, such as developing new products, increasing productivity, setting industrial standards, and fostering greater competitiveness for entry into world markets.

Expanding economic cooperation among selected Chinese work units would clearly result in higher efficiency in certain sectors. For instance, reform of the country's transport and communications systems might be accomplished more efficiently and effectively by the formation of cooperative networks that have the authority to distribute profits, form alliances, and participate in joint projects, in the hope of breaking down the barriers between units within different administrative structures and in different fields.[16]

To help enterprises free themselves from the stranglehold of the bureaucracy, they now receive official encouragement to enter into formal and informal relationships with each other. These new attempts at cooperation between Chinese enterprises come under various definitions. A "loosely knit" affiliation describes a situation where one concern has influence over a less powerful concern, but holds no shares in the other; a "closely knit" enterprise is a relationship where one company co-owns the other; "half-knit" enterprises participate in a relationship where one owns some share of the other. In a loosely knit relationship, one enterprise may control the production output and distribution of another concern, while the smaller concern's personnel and accounting remain under the auspices of its parent ministry or bureau. Occasionally, smaller firms desiring to increase their clout move from a loosely knit relationship into a closely knit one, because they perceive advantages in surrendering control to a larger entity that yields wider influence in more than one province or region. This strategy is often part of an effort by managers to reduce the influence of the local government upon their enterprises. If wholly controlled by another factory, the smaller concern will likely enjoy greater security as well as increased investment by the larger firm and possibly greater access to the markets (domestic and international) targeted by that firm.

In addition, some ministries (and their affiliated corporations) have also begun to form alliances with each other in an attempt to circumvent the constraints imposed by China's vertical industrial structure. An example of alliance-building is the collaboration between the Ministry of Geology and Mineral Resources and the former Ministry of Petroleum Industry to develop China's oil and gas reserves "after decades of bureaucratic estrangement that often led to duplication and waste."[17] The two ministries established coordinating groups to formulate programs for joint prospecting and production, data exchange, recovery and extraction, and personnel training. The ministries also circulated a communique urging subordinate institutions and factories to "discard departmentalism and establish closer ties to speed up oil and gas prospecting."[18] In the past, prospecting had occurred in the same fields. When oil was discovered, the ministries would vie for control of these areas, concealing data from each other.

Corporate Conglomerates.   China has also initiated the formation of industrial conglomerates (*jituan*) in another move against self-contained industrial relations. In the electronics industry, there are now four computer conglomerates that have been created, the most significant being the Great Wall Computer Corporation in Beijing. (The others are located in Shanghai, Guangzhou, and Shenyang.) Patterned after IBM, each of these corporations is endowed with a full complement of services including R&D, production, service, maintenance, and sales. Their fully integrated organization is designed to cut across vertical barriers within the system (i.e., they exist independent of state-run distribution networks, sales agencies, etc.). While the Great Wall Corporation's experience has not been without its problems, the fact is that its creation represents a fundamentally new type of organizational amalgam—one that may set a trend for the future in other sectors.

Another interesting example under this program involves the Aeolus Automotive Industry Corporation. Aeolus took the initiative to revamp its management and then transfer technology to the Hubei Wuhan Valve Works, which was described by the factory's deputy manager as "on the brink of collapse." Aeolus has since linked up with 168 companies, the majority of which were faltering; now most are thriving. The Aeolus Corporation spans twenty-four provinces, has direct relations with the State Council, and can circumvent the CNAIC in Beijing. Aeolus also has the power to sign foreign joint venture agreements and source raw materials unilaterally.[19]

The aim of Chinese leaders is that conglomerates such as Aeolus and the Great Wall Computer Corporation be given complete authority to obtain approvals for various projects and to do so more rapidly, be granted unencumbered access to the domestic market and raw materials, and be better able to cross provincial distribution lines. They will also have ample foreign exchange to import equipment and license technology. In this way, they may team up with foreign firms more easily in efforts to upgrade component suppliers and set new design standards.

Some critics fear that conglomerates could develop into monopolies, however, leading to hostile takeovers and the demise of smaller companies. After all, their main goal is to establish a strong market position vis-à-vis all competitors. The Great Wall Computer Corporation, for example, accepts member factories and research units from all around the country. Nonetheless, they do offer the prospect of overcoming many of the past bureaucratic impediments to industrial performance.

The Chinese have also worked toward the creation of production alliances (*lian heti*) which help enterprises cross vertical boundaries within the economy. These have been formed particularly in the textile industry in northeast China. For example, a design institute, a dyeing factory, a cloth printing factory, and a sewing factory will merge to produce new apparel as part of one operating unit. As *lian heti* emerge throughout the country, one will witness an increased ability of certain industries to traverse the vertically segmented administrative organization of the economy that has traditionally prevented cross-functional cooperation.

Economic associations have been formed as well, gathering together large numbers of enterprises to create the clout needed to bypass ties with various departments at the central, provincial, and city level that choose the source of their inputs and designate the destination of (and earnings from) their output. In Wuhan, 1,300 machine-building enterprises that were individually attached to over forty management departments formed such an association and have cut costs and become more competitive as a result.[20] As with many of the other new organizational forms that have emerged, however, it remains unclear how they will relate to their counterparts in other localities or in other sectors.

Divestment of Foreign Trade Structure

The performance of industry and trade have been traditionally separate functions in China. New efforts are under way to combine the interests of the industrial enterprise with those of the FTC, thus forging a more direct link between production and marketing activities in specific areas such as the promotion of exports. Reduced controls over the inputs and output of factories encourage Chinese enterprises to pursue closer contacts within the country's distribution system and the international marketplace. Although some large state-owned enterprises had established their own import/export organizations, the management of their import/export activities remained subject to the authority of administrative departments outside the enterprise. Until recently, FTCs were the sole conduit through which trading transactions could be made between China and the outside world. There was often a lack of coordination between what was needed for export or import and what could be produced on the factory floor. Under these conditions, there was little chance of Chinese industry being responsive or competitive in the world economy.

During 1986, as discussed in Chapter 2, MOFERT required all FTCs to undergo substantial reorganization and consolidation. Like other forms of enterprise coming under the umbrella of reform, FTCs are now primarily responsible for their own profit and loss. The new system places local FTCs under the control of government entities at the provincial, municipal, and county levels. For large purchases, however, MOFERT still maintains its leading position. In addition, increasing numbers of factories have been granted the authority to make import decisions for themselves, particularly to conduct negotiations with foreigners. Of course, MOFERT still must approve the final contract, except in special cases where the factory has the permission and the foreign exchange to cover the cost of the purchase. Localities and factories are allowed to retain an increasing portion of their foreign exchange. They also have increasing discretion over how they use it, within certain limits (e.g., a cap on total transaction cost). However, this does not necessarily mean that the local FTC once affiliated with MOFERT will be any less powerful. In fact, local FTCs may be more powerful, not as representatives of Beijing, but more powerful within the bureaucracy of the locality. While the level of overall planning has been significantly decentralized, the autonomy of the Chinese enterprise has not been increased to an equivalent extent.

To further overcome these problems, there has been a blossoming of corporations since the early 1980s which are jointly managed by large industrial enterprises *and* FTCs. As one writer says, the managers of these ventures "participate more directly in the management of the enterprise and act on behalf of the production enterprise in managing all of its export/import business. . . . [They] participate in bringing in technology, equipment, components, and raw materials needed by the enterprise for the development of production."[21]

The more direct links between foreign trade activity and factory production have increased responsiveness to the domestic and international market and quickened decision making as fewer numbers of approval levels are required to handle the trade activities of the factory. These joint management groups also help to identify potential consumers and act as liaisons between foreign vendors and the enterprise as it pursues plant renovation. The integration of industry and trade in these joint entities was initially controversial in China. One faction believes that the enterprise should have the freedom to market its own production and not be tied at all to the formal trading system. Indeed, the addition of new players in enterprise affairs could form yet another obstacle for factory directors as they attempt to gain full control over their enterprises. Nonetheless, the changes clearly constitute an improvement over the situation in the past.

Proponents of these ventures claim that enterprises simply do not possess the knowledge to market successfully overseas. Based on the author's research, this tends to be true. Yet, if FTC entities maintain control over foreign trade, it is unlikely that enterprise managers will develop the necessary insight to assess the international market. In addition, it has been very difficult, in some cases, for a large number of enterprises to form joint management groups to integrate production and trade because of "administrative interference." As one Chinese writer declared:

> In order to prevent grass roots enterprises and trade enterprises from joining together, some leading industrial units hurriedly established representative offices in industrial enterprises and factories, and interfered in the management of the factories. [These units] still want to retain the single corporation that takes care of everything from production to supply to marketing, from human to financial to material resources, and from domestic to foreign trade, and hope that through this single corporation they can control enterprises at a grass-roots level throughout the country.[22]

In many respects, the entire system of local foreign trade administration is superfluous and could be removed altogether. In theory, if the present reforms in the foreign trade sector were to move even further in the direction of decentralization, the national FTCs—TECHIMPORT and others—would become increasingly irrelevant, if not obsolete. In their absence, the State Planning Commission, the State Economic Commission, and MOFERT would only get involved in large, transprovincial projects (such as a railroad or communication line) that require extensive coordination of resources and/or facilitation of decision making across disparate administrative regions of China. The major impediments to the dismantling of the foreign trade structure, however, include concerns over foreign exchange spending and limited knowledge of the international market for goods and technology.

ECONOMIC POLICY AND COOPERATION WITH FOREIGN FIRMS

Numerous factors have motivated the People's Republic to accelerate its modernization drive and secure assistance from outside: a Chinese desire for a higher standard of living; the rise of other rival East Asian economies including Taiwan; a growing hunger for more sophisticated products; and a growing fear that the technological gap between China and the rest of the industrialized world is widening. Most Chinese managers and bureaucrats, ironically, consider cooperation with foreign firms secondary to exploiting the opportunities of a ravenous domestic market. Chinese policy decisions have not been very effective at linking the objectives of foreign investment to the country's modernization program. Although decisions regarding specific foreign investment projects are not without rhyme or reason, there seems to be a lack of an internal logic or strategy by which Chinese policymakers tie together China's industrialization with the activities of foreign firms. That is, a strategic perspective regarding issues such as import substitution and export production appears to be missing. Although Beijing has developed a policy of promoting exports for generating more foreign exchange, local areas often establish import substitution projects with foreign firms to sell primarily to the domestic market. As one Chinese writer has said: "There is neither a perfect and elaborate import substitution strategy nor are there plans for shifting to an externally oriented development strategy."[23] Many projects, especially those aimed at increasing local content, suffer from a lack of coordination among relevant agencies of the bureaucracy, in great part because China's investment bureaucracy has developed around entities like CITIC whose main principle is to attract foreign firms. Once those firms come to China and new dilemmas arise, the buck gets passed to other authorities who may be unprepared to deal effectively with foreign investor problems.

Current Attitudes Toward Foreign Business

The impact of Western cultural incursion on Chinese society plays some role in fostering a mood of trepidation and reluctance among influential Chinese about pushing the door open further to foreign ideas and relinquishing control over the economy through greater power incentives for potential foreign investors. Merchants have always been mistrusted in China, partly because the merchant class occupied a low rung on the Confucian order of social classes. These feelings were reaffirmed for many Chinese when China opened its doors to foreign business and Western investors did not come running. In many cases, a "Chinese versus foreign" mentality persists to this day. The present-day corporate sojourner to the People's Republic likely encounters a Chinese business partner whose image of foreigners is derived from a historical legacy that has left Chinese society uneasy about allowing widespread foreign participation in the country's development. One result is China's cold, pragmatic approach to cooperation with foreigners, whereby China utilizes foreign technology and know-how as tools for realizing modernization goals while keeping contact, communication, and long-term commitment to foreign nations to a minimum.

The history of foreign abuses in China clearly justifies Chinese reticence concerning binding interaction with foreigners. For better or worse, current foreign involvement in the People's Republic remains set against a not-so-distant past of foreign domination of China and exploitation of its people. Resentment still exists toward those foreign nations that participated in a number of historical blights in China. For example, China remains uneasy about its relations with Japan after centuries of exploitation and war atrocities. It remains uneasy toward the United States for supplying military aid to Chiang Kai-shek during World War II and more recently to Taiwan. China also remains uneasy toward the Soviet Union for its almost vindictive economic pullout from China in the late 1950s and its subsequent military build-up along China's border.

To the detriment of those seeking business opportunities in China today, the long-standing apprehension and distrust of foreigners is a key facet of doing business in China, one that cannot be completely ignored. Sino-foreign ventures can sometimes be stigmatized as "capitalist"—where a few privileged Chinese receive special benefits. Some Chinese fail to realize that these enterprises pay taxes and reinvest in themselves just as Chinese factories do and that the Chinese managers in these ventures receive roughly the same pay as other Chinese managers.

Isolation versus Participation.

The outspoken Chinese can be divided into several camps regarding the extent to which the country should permit the introduction of Western ideas, culture, and values into China. One group, which generally leans toward a more isolationist mode, calls for a renewal of traditional culture, fearing that China's national culture is being engulfed by foreign culture. Persons of this persuasion apparently feel that all aspects of Chinese life have been adversely affected by foreign goods, ideas, and social traits. They rail against the symbols of Sino-Western contact such as "jeans fever," "tourist fever," and "disco fever." It is not an overstatement to suggest that many Chinese remain horrified by the idea of an extensive foreign presence in the People's Republic, believing it entails corruption of officials and a sharp break with traditional and socialist values. Many of these same people were behind the short-lived assault on foreign influence in 1983 called the "spiritual pollution" campaign.

Unable to launch a direct attack on the open-door program itself, the movement represented a last-ditch effort to halt further Westernization by instilling the population with greater national patriotism and a new belief in the purity and sanctity of Chinese culture. More than anything, it was an attempt to purge China of things essentially foreign—fashions, values, and free market competition. Yet, even as the "anti-bourgeois liberalization" campaign in 1986–87 waged on, entrepôts such as Shenzhen SEZ became more Western every day. Appearing in these cities were skyscrapers, motorcycles, banks, night clubs, country clubs, and curio shops selling foreign soft drinks and cigarettes. Many young people in China's larger cities remain fascinated with foreign music, clothes, and ideas. Learning English has become a national pastime.

Opposite the isolationists are those who fear that China could fall further behind the developed nations by remaining isolated from the world. These "participationists" urge China to expand foreign contacts, use foreign technology, and seek out more foreign investment. Most important, they believe that Western values cannot be separated out from Western technology. Concepts such as democracy go hand-in-hand with the high technology achievements of the West.

The reality in China is that these two groups represent the opposite ends of a broad spectrum across which the majority of Chinese probably are scattered evenly. Limiting the analysis to those in the larger cities and among those who are educated, however, reveals that the majority is congregated around the center. In other words, most Chinese are skeptical about opening up their society. While this may change as the younger generation assumes the reins of authority, the impression is that cross-cultural interaction will continue to be a problem for most Chinese—at least until China is able to see the gap between itself and the rest of the industrialized world close.

Accommodating Foreign Business with New Laws

The Chinese are making serious headway in their attempt to institutionalize their approach to dealing with foreign firms. In theory, the evolving set of rules is designed to normalize the procedures by which foreign firms can enter the China market. Chinese leaders realize the need for developing a body of workable commercial law if their country is to protect itself from foreign exploitation and attract larger quantities of foreign direct investment, including advanced technology.

Recognizing the high degree of leverage that can be gained from making and then revising the rules of Sino-foreign business transactions, the Chinese structure flexibility into many of the regulations that govern foreign investment. The Chinese have come to see that the legal trappings of Western business practice are indeed necessary to attract multinational corporations. However, the Chinese do not want to regularize their approach to foreign firms to the point of becoming totally predictable. As suggested, the Chinese want to leave a large element of flexibility in their codes and regulations to allow for exceptions. They feel that if their regulations are too precise it will constrain them in their ability to manage foreign firms. Despite what appears in the press, the Chinese do not seem prepared to offer most firms the guarantees that they would like. To the unbiased observer, it is commendable that the Chinese have withstood foreign pressure to offer more investment guarantees. At the same time, foreign investors would be foolish not to demand those guarantees.

For centuries business transactions within China have taken place without the binding legality associated with a Western-style contract.

China did not have a body of applicable law regarding foreign investment before the Regulations on Joint Ventures in 1979. Moreover, the concept of legal recourse in China is not well developed, or even accepted as a normal means of settling disputes. Historically, the Chinese have resolved business conflicts face to face. Therefore, it follows that settling disputes in China generally results more from mediation than arbitration by a third party or a court trial. The nature of most Chinese regulations leaves interpretation of laws largely up to the government body closest to the case. As stated in one U.S. Consulate circular, this allows for "varied interpretation and application to fit circumstance."[24] By keeping language vague in most regulations, the Chinese leave room for minor adjustments. Although China has promulgated a vast array of new laws and regulations over the past five years, the opinion of most foreign business executives is that China's legal atmosphere remains uncertain and incomplete.

Until recently, Chinese jurisprudence contained only limited civil law (i.e., tort, bankruptcy, and copyright law). Recognizing the possible value of such laws, China ratified general principles concerning civil law in April 1986, with a broad treatment of civil concepts important to potential foreign investors such as copyright, deformation, mortgage, and bankruptcy.[25] As more cases involving foreign firms are mediated, a growing body of precedent will enhance the efficacy and consistency of the legal environment. Interviews with American lawyers in Beijing, however, indicate that precedents are rarely used in disputes and an official public record of cases is not available. Few cases have gone to a Chinese court of law for arbitration. Most cases are solved through mediation only, each treated as a "special case."[26] Variations in the administration of laws and the inability to obtain advanced rulings on specific aspects of contracts pose great difficulties for the foreigner who encounters a business problem. Furthermore, new laws often affect older laws retroactively. As one U.S. lawyer based in China stated, shifts in legal policy that affect signed contracts are inevitable.[27]

Secret Rules and Guidelines.   Formulating and ratifying new laws in China is a painstaking process involving every level of bureaucracy. As such, many of the regulatory provisions that govern foreign ventures remain hidden from foreigners. These internal guidelines—referred to as *neibu* documents—often become law in refined form after the Chinese have tested them in the field. Though a foreigner may not be permitted to see such regulations, they are legally binding. This encourages suspicion and mistrust.

The existence of *neibu* guidelines makes it impossible for foreigners to know their legal rights fully or to protect their property in China. To no one's surprise, foreign investment tends to flow faster as China ratifies more formal laws to protect foreign business interests. Many investors claim, however, that the legal climate in the People's Republic does not regard their interests in an objective fashion on crucial issues and generally creates a business situation that favors the Chinese. In effect, China's legal framework not only facilitates investment but works to keep out those foreign firms that are not truly committed to gaining entry to the China market under the terms defined by China.

Chinese Decision Making on Foreign Projects

At the level of the industrial enterprise, the unevenness in the pace and momentum of the reforms plagues both foreign and Chinese executives alike. For their part, Chinese bureaucrats remain unsure about how much weight they carry should they support projects involving foreign firms. The Chinese seek to be "united in dealing with outsiders instead of scattering their forces and giving outsiders the opportunity to take unfair advantage. . . ."[28]

In spite of some recent changes in cities such as Shanghai, all foreign projects are subject to a system of tiered approval in order to avoid costly economic and political mistakes. A sizable number of projects are preplanned by a small group of high-level officials in Beijing and other cities who wield control over the allocation of funds to implement plans. Projects with foreign entities differ as to type, size, priority, and origin. Their common characteristic is the bargaining power of the Chinese government over their implementation and operation. Thus, foreign firms wishing to participate in the China market must be well prepared to consult, negotiate, and conduct business with government bureaucrats or other partners closely linked to formal government organizations.

Bureaucratic Behavior and Foreign Projects

Chinese bureaucrats, like those in other Asian societies, usually attain their privileged position through family connections, professional qualifications, and membership in professional and social societies.[29]

Through skillful maneuvering, prudence, knowledge, and most important, personal connections with counterparts higher on the totem pole, the most successful officials in China wield their authority from positions in key decision-making bodies such as the Party Politboro, the State Council, and the State Economic Commission.[30] Inherently, Chinese government decision making is highly personal and compartmental at all levels. Since a decision that bears rotten fruit can result in dismissal, officials working in the system often appear diffident, contentious, and even insecure. This, in turn, lends a certain instability to the overall functioning of Chinese bureaucracy. Certainly, it promotes caution in individuals rather than temerity, rank consciousness rather than initiative, while compelling the solitary bureaucrat, when confronting a foreign project proposal in need of approval, to hesitate and hedge until his colleagues give their consent as well.[31,32]

When a Chinese bureaucrat makes a final decision to move forward on a project, he assumes responsibility for the outcome. Consequently, the fear of making a bad decision tends to slow down the decision-making process as officials generally seek the safety of consensus decisions. There is a saying in China: "Those who have authority don't want responsibility; and those who will accept responsibility have no authority." An illustration of the problem follows. An official fairly high in the decision-making chain leaves for a month overseas with a delegation. A memorandum arrives from a foreign firm at his office needing his signature (or "chop") before it can move on to the next person for approval. Under standard operating procedures in China, no bureaucrat involved in the process will take responsibility for the memo and sign off on it. Thus, it will collect dust for a month waiting for the return of the absent official. Furthermore, in all likelihood, the official has not chosen to leave someone in charge.

In many cases, there is little real incentive for Chinese bureaucrats to involve themselves in foreign projects at all. Similarly, there is little incentive for either Chinese managers or bureaucrats to align themselves with a foreign firm in China. They are exposed to many risks should the project fail, yet receive few tangible rewards should it succeed. Foreign negotiators should anticipate the risks involved in a specific foreign project from the Chinese point of view. Becoming too friendly with foreigners or looking out for one's own interests too vigorously can be dangerous for an official in the People's Republic.

In light of all this, lengthy decision-making processes and vagueness on the part of the Chinese are not so much an attempt to frustrate foreigners as they are part of an effort by Chinese managers and officials to avoid making mistakes in their dealings with foreigners. As suggested, serious mistakes in foreign business relations can be extremely damaging to the position and integrity of a Chinese official or manager. In many cases, Chinese bureaucrats are powerless to make decisions of any magnitude without full discussion with their superiors. In point of fact, it is often hard to find the one person on the Chinese side that can make decisions on the spot because such a person probably does not exist. Western management encourages responsible leaders; Chinese bureaucracy encourages conformity and protection of individuals from responsibility. Excessive caution creates bureaucratic lethargy in the decision-making chain, while the "old-boy" system of promotion allows for a significant degree of official incompetence. Officials are rarely demoted, even if they make mistakes. They often hold positions beyond their capabilities.[33] The face of Chinese bureaucracy is changing, however. Younger people, possessing technical credentials better suited to particular positions of authority, are being recruited to revitalize China's administration. Unfortunately, many of these new entrants soon become frustrated by their fellow bureaucrats who would remain indifferent to the reforms.

So why are some bureaucrats willing to involve themselves in a Sino-foreign venture in the first place? Some possible answers follow:

- To bring any number of benefits to their organizations (e.g., foreign trips, foreign goods, increased employment, or training by a foreign firm).
- To bring in foreign exchange, which could earn them a promotion, or be used as leverage in creating other deals in China based on foreign exchange/Rmb conversion exchanges.
- To gain clout over higher-level officials for themselves and their organization since the authorization of Sino-foreign ventures needs consensus approval from many people, all of whom will associate the proposed project with the person who is pushing for its implementation.
- To exhibit their active and sincere commitment to a stated policy of cooperation with foreign firms which win the approval of supervisors.[34]
- To receive reciprocal favors. (Reports from U.S. executives indicate that low-key corruption on the part of numerous officials in contact with foreigners is on the upswing. Bribes in cash, secret bank accounts in Hong Kong, and surreptitious product trading

through consultancy "fronts" are all occurring to some degree in the People's Republic as they do elsewhere.)[35]

Obviously, some members of the Chinese bureaucracy use their privileged position to take unfair advantage of foreign business people. Marco Lobo, a foreign manager working in China, wrote in a letter to the *Far Eastern Economic Review* that he experiences "daily frustrations at the hands of the spoilt elite who have come to expect certain advantages in dealing with foreigners." This foreign manager, like others interviewed, believes that "as the decentralization policies continue to evolve and corporations and workers become more performance-oriented, the elite will have to show their true worth."[36] Both the quality and quantity of Chinese officials involved on a given foreign project will, however, depend on the project's size, location, and monetary value.

Types of Projects

Projects with foreign participation in the People's Republic can be classified into three basic categories: (1) the direct sale of equipment; (2) the transfer of technology involving limited foreign participation and collaboration, and (3) foreign investment involving the contribution of capital and/or equipment by a foreign company. In terms of preplanning and approval, foreign projects can be similarly divided into three groups. The first contains those projects preapproved by the central government. In this case, the sponsoring organization of the project guarantees access to the necessary funding (including foreign exchange) to undertake the project. These usually involve large infrastructural projects. The second category of projects includes those not yet formally approved. The Chinese participating in this type of project submit proposals within the system and compete for funds. The third type of project is created by a tender offer from the central government for which Chinese organizations and their foreign partners bid competitively. All of the groups may include projects of varying size. Projects are divided into two groups according to size—*small projects* (under $5 million), and *large projects* (over $5 million).

Choosing a Project.   In selecting projects, the foreign company should first answer the following key questions:

Matrix of Project Types

	Centrally Initiated (and funded)	Locally Initiated (and funded)
Large Project (>US$5 million)	1	2
Small Project (<US$5 million)	3	4

Sino-foreign projects fall into one of four general categories: (1) Large projects that are centrally coordinated; (2) Large projects that are locally coordinated; (3) Small projects that are centrally coordinated; and (4) Small projects that are locally coordinated. Project type (4) will usually be most easily and rapidly approved. Project type (1) will likely be the most dilatory, as it will require multilevel approvals and central-local collaboration.

- Is the project considered a national project or a local one (i.e., who is the project going to benefit?). And, who will have oversight responsibility?
- Is the project large or small?
- Where is the funding for the project coming from? Is the funding guaranteed or coming from outside?

The last question is probably the most important, since it tends to condition the first two. Some projects have money, but increasingly in the form of loans rather than grants from the government. In one sense these loans may represent an indirect subsidy. They may be allocated in the form of foreign exchange but are to be paid back in Rmb. Nonetheless, in most cases, they ensure that more attention is paid to the project on the part of the participating Chinese factory because of the loan repayment requirements. In general, small local projects that have funding coming from the locality are much easier to initiate, from the perspective of the foreign firm, since they ostensibly involve less intervention by Beijing. Conversely, large projects, externally funded by sources such as the World Bank, the Asia Development Bank, and the United Nations, tend to be complex undertakings involving multiple bureaucratic interests all competing to have the lead on the project, especially if it is an attractive project.

Creating Push and Pull for Project Approval. As a project moves through the latter stages of negotiation, both sides of the venture must join forces to get the project approved; that is, convincing high officials in the central government to create "pull" for the project, while convincing local officials to "push" the project through the bureaucratic steps necessary for final approval.

Turning back again to the 3M strategy, we find a prime example of the push-pull approach. The strategists at 3M had to remain active selling their project even after preliminary approval at two different levels—in Beijing at the national policy level, and in Shanghai at the local business level. In order to convince the Chinese of its openness and goodwill, and the viability of a solely foreign-owned factory on Chinese soil, 3M invited them to visit similar factories, including a 3M subsidiary in Mexico. After witnessing such factories in operation, the officials on the tour issued immediate approval of the 3M project in Shanghai.[37]

A Small-Project Case Scenario

The procedures that a Chinese factory must follow in purchasing equipment from abroad as part of a small project involve passing through a maze of bureaucratic obstacles at several decision-making levels. In the electronics industry, when a factory decides to buy foreign equipment, a special subunit known as the "technology introduction office" assumes primary responsibility over the acquisition process. A meeting is convened that involves, among others, the chief engineer, the finance department, the planning department, the factory director, and members of the technology introduction office. The chief engineer plays a critical role at this meeting, since he possesses the power to authorize or disapprove the equipment purchase under consideration.

Once all of the relevant persons in the factory have reached agreement, the technology introduction office prepares a written document of two separate parts. The first part amounts to an acquisition proposal (*jianyishu*) and briefly describes the equipment to be imported, the potential suppliers, associated costs, and desired benefits. In effect, it is a justification for the project. The second part contains a thorough feasibility study (*kexinxin baogao*), including an explanation of how the cost/benefit projection was determined. It also includes a plan for payback of the loan if the project money has been borrowed.[38]

In response to pressure from government authorities, enterprises are required to conduct feasibility studies as part of the decision-making process. In the electronics industry in Shanghai, for example, feasibility studies related to the acquisition of foreign equipment and technology must answer the following questions: (1) why is the technology desired?; (2) what benefits will the technology yield?; (3) how long will it take to recapture or repay money spent on the technology?; (4) what will the return be?; (5) who will be the foreign partner (or foreign source of the technology)? and (6) how does the price compare to other sources? In other words, the Chinese counterpart in a Sino-foreign project has to present a complete analysis of all facets of the project.[39]

The feasibility study then comes up for review by the "umbrella" corporation under which the importing enterprise sits. Discussions at this level are followed by recommendations. Even if the acquisition proposal totals less than $2 million—the ceiling set by the state for the corporation's acquisition autonomy—it still is required to report its plans to the local electronics bureau. The bureau, in turn, is empowered to override, nullify, or demand modification of the proposal as it chooses. If the bureau opts to exercise its veto powers, the entire proposal process may have to be repeated from the start. If the total cost of an acquisition proposal amounts to over $2 million, the bureau's formal approval is required. If the amount totals less than $5 million—the ceiling set for the autonomy of the bureau itself—it must report to the level of the municipal government (e.g., the local economic commission), especially in cases involving the import of restricted items such as television production lines. If a proposal totals more than $5 million, the bureau must submit its decision directly to the central government for authorization. While a case is under consideration in Beijing, the ministry and/or the State Council special leading group may play a major role in moving the project toward final approval or disapproval.[40]

Clearly, the larger the project, the more likely the central government will assert its prerogatives. Moreover, the greater the number of decision makers between the end user and the foreign firm, the more difficult the project will be to manage.

A Large-Project Case Scenario

A case study by Sally Stewart and Yeung Yun Choi concerning the Hexian Paper Pulp Project in Guangxi Province depicts the decision-making and review process for a project which was large enough to have been included in the Seventh Five-Year Plan (1986–90). The twelve steps listed below summarize the approval process. These steps represent an overview of how Chinese decision makers and foreign negotiators push and pull for a large project at the central and local levels, gaining approval for the project at the state planning level, and forming a consensus of decision makers at the local, provincial, and central levels to move the project forward.

1. The initial decision to develop the paper plant was made by a bureaucrat in Hexian County.
2. The Guangxi Department of Forestry next lent its support and conducted an investigation of local resources.
3. The Planning Commission of Wuzhou Prefecture collaborated with Hexian County government on the further development of the proposal.
4. The Guangxi government, represented by the Guangxi Planning Commission, approved both a feasibility study for the project and a grant to the Guangxi Bureau of Light Industry to carry out the study.
5. The Guangxi Bureau of Light Industry sent a representative to the State Planning Commission, negotiated the technical details of the project with foreign firms, and conducted an informal visit with the United Nations Development Program (UNDP).
6. The Ministry of Light Industry approved the proposal, introduced foreign interests, and "agreed to make the formal application for the grant from the UNDP."
7. The State Planning Commission approved the project and made arrangements for its presentation to the National People's Congress.

After money had been obtained to conduct the feasibility study:

8. Foreign experts and personnel from the Guangxi Bureau of Forestry and the Guangxi Bureau of Light Industry together conducted another feasibility study.
9. The feasibility study was then submitted to the Guangxi Planning Commission along with recommendations from the Guangxi Bureau of Light Industry in an attempt to gain a final decision.
10. A final draft of the feasibility study was then sent to the State Planning Commission for approval with a recommendation from the Ministry of Light Industry. If approved, the project would be included in the Seventh Five-Year Plan and would thereby be carried out.
11. The Guangxi Planning Commission is responsible for those decisions regarding the use of funds supplied by the central government and makes decisions as to who will be responsible for project implementation.
12. Foreign exchange must be allocated before the project can proceed. In this case, the Swedish government may be a source of low-interest loans for the project, especially if Swedish firms are to participate.[41]

As this case illustrates, foreign firms should seek out projects in which an influential Chinese decision maker has a particular vested interest, or is going to take a strong interest. If the project is strategically important to the country's modernization program, it will invite the attention of high-level leaders who are likely to view the project's failure as detrimental to the country and therefore, will be more willing to intervene if there are problems.

BUSINESS RISK AND THE REFORM HORIZON

Mao Zedong wrote that the contradictions between idealism and materialism can be "resolved one after the other by the socialist system itself."[42] Today a growing list of critical social, economic, and political issues—all growing pains of the modernization program—are whipping up debates within China's leadership. The prospect of the socialist system resolving these debates without fundamental adjustments in the nature of socialism itself is looking more doubtful the wider China's door opens to world economic and cultural forces. Moreover, the reforms and the presence of foreigners in the economy have created new political and social cleavages. All of these add up to business risks for the foreign firms participating in China's reform-oriented economy.

China's Economic Vulnerability

For better or worse, the Chinese remain constrained by the vulnerability of their own economy in terms of their willingness to offer the significant concessions that foreign firms would like to see. If Chinese leaders were suddenly to accede to foreign calls for such things as greater allowances for profit repatriation and broader access to the best supplies, there might well be a tremendous outflow of foreign exchange. Foreign joint ventures might even come to dominate important areas of the Chinese economy. Both scenarios clearly are unacceptable to the Chinese. Moreover, if China were to remove limits on foreign capitalization in joint ventures, possibly permitting technology inputs to accumulate beyond the current 15 percent limit, the country might be unable to finance any Sino-foreign ventures at all.

China has already witnessed the detrimental effects of maintaining a dual-currency monetary system, one it created to accommodate the growing foreign presence in the economy. The system of foreign exchange certificates (FEC), originally set up to isolate the foreign community, is causing seemingly unending fiscal problems as well as corruption. The problems stem from the difficulty of maintaining two different exchange rates. To avoid seriously disturbing normal trading, the state must set and monitor both rates while protecting the credibility of the Chinese yuan.[43] However, demand for FEC currently dominates Chinese Rmb, which tends to irritate national pride. In 1983, the Guangdong branch of the State Foreign Exchange Control Bureau offered a reward to anyone turning in any "unit" or individual known to be making a profit from the disparate exchange rate between FEC and Rmb.[44] The possibility of floating the Rmb rate has been suggested as a solution to the exchange rate problem. But the fear of fueling inflation with this action prevents it from being a viable option. (Due to its budget deficit, excess money supply, and credit growth, China's annual inflation rate had reached 19.6 percent in 1987; in the first quarter of 1988, a benchmark nationwide retail price index pinned the annual inflation rate at 11 percent.)

Official Corruption and the Hidden Economy.

The open door has generated a significant increase in financial crime, a foreboding problem in a country as vast and divided by provincial boundaries as the People's Republic. Corruption is on the rise in China for several reasons: the lack of financial control at the enterprise level, the new doctrine of "rich is glorious," and the decentralization of decision making at the import authorization level. The need clearly exists for strengthening the internal regulatory system in China. The newly established Ministry of Supervision, which was created as a watchdog agency, is supposed to help deal with the growing problems. A scholarly journal, *Law in China*, "showed that Tianjin economic crimes involving more than 10,000 yuan increased by 160 percent in the first half of 1985. Additionally, 43 percent of these cases involved malpractice in firms together with institutions and administrative organizations."[45] Another article on the subject described how party officials had become businessmen, engaging in trade in their own name or group. The state accused these persons of taking advantage of the favorable conditions afforded them by their positions. An investigation revealed that they had amassed staggering profits through the resale and speculation of goods.[46] Many Chinese complain openly of favoritism toward those who have connections in the CCP (e.g., getting jobs, acceptance into universities, overseas travel, etc.) and use these connections for personal benefit. In a recent poll conducted by the Chinese Academy of Sciences, 83.7 percent of the urban respondents listed "corrupt behavior of government officials" as the thing they resented most.[47]

Social/Political Tensions

As if economic problems were not enough, student protests demanding democratic reforms broke out in late 1986–87. The party exploited the uprising to regain its lost influence by taking hold of selected lecturer positions and professorships at universities, installing 13,000 of its members as faculty in order to gain firmer control of indoctrination of China's over two million college students. Scientists, journalists, artists, and writers were reminded that their work still should be compatible with Marxism and should not embrace total Westernization.[48]

The swiftness of these changes casts some doubt on the future pace and direction of reforms, especially in the post-Deng era. The Chinese leadership appears to have undergone a fundamental change. No longer will China be guided by a messianic leader similar to Mao.

While much of the centralized government control and discipline is vanishing, vestiges of it will remain for a long time to come. Social goals are now sought in different ways: through economic freedoms, private ownership, and greater reward for job performance. By offering the Chinese people a higher standard of living, Chinese officials hope to maintain social contentment and, therefore, social stability.

At the same time, China's political climate continues to depend on one man, Deng Xiaoping. Deng has been grooming a "third tier" of younger leaders while reducing the power of the military and party bureaucracy. The third tier advanced in power in the closing months of 1987, accompanied by Deng's self-removal from his consolidated position of unchallenged power. Yet the redistribution of power has stoked opposition fires as well as furthering Deng's so-called second revolution. Many influential persons have rallied in an ongoing public debate, claiming China should pursue economic reforms more conservatively and remain more centralized while promoting less autonomy for Chinese trade corporations and enterprises. Moreover, these persons represent a strong and vociferous faction in China that could be a politically influential contingent after Deng's death. They point to official corruption and black marketing as the negative side effects of opening to the West. Unable to wield the political unity to combat Deng openly in the form of a direct challenge, these political dark horses within China will likely resist the reforms by ignoring or obstructing them. In other words, they will drag their feet in the implementation of policies and make China's reform program as difficult as they can. Should significant aspects of the reform program fail, remaining hard-line conservatives could derail open-door economic policies and delay the improvement of China's investment climate.

Most of the traditional Marxists wishing to close the door on foreigners are party relics in their seventies and eighties who want to "turn back the clock on the modernization program," as their critics claim. Some of them once occupied high government positions before they were purged in favor of younger followers of the reforms. In the unlikely event that these groups gain in power and influence after Deng, the risks to foreign firms in China could increase dramatically. Some conservatives are voicing uncertainty about the reforms, most notably during addresses to the National People's Congress. To quell the rising dissent, as stated in *Business International,* Deng "had to vow publicly that China's future lies with communism, not capitalism. . . . This avowal came only months after he claimed that 'a little capitalism' would not hurt China."[49] In the minds of the skeptics of reform, "a little capitalism" has already damaged China.

On the other hand, the popularity of Communism among the Chinese populace has waned under China's exposure to market economies, Western cultural values, and images of Western lifestyle received via the media coverage of international events such as the Los Angeles and Seoul Olympics. Further evidence of Chinese disinterest in Communism was borne out when the once all-powerful political journal *Red Flag* folded in 1988. Its circulation had plummeted to only three million readers, millions fewer than read *Popular Cinema*. A Chinese journalist claimed that at the time of its demise, *Red Flag* had only four subscribers who were not party affiliates, who are required to receive the journal.[50]

Skepticism of political remedies to China's problems has spread. The expectations set forth in 1978–79 for upgrading services, housing, and the Chinese standard of living have failed to materialize. At the core of China's social problems is the dilemma of the traditional family farm. On the one hand, rural workers are being told that their households are now the smallest "units" of production. And to boost productivity, Chinese officials encourage selling on the open market by proclaiming that getting rich is "glorious." On the other hand, families are told that they may only bear a single child, making it increasingly difficult to operate the traditional family farm. With increasing market competition, many Chinese find themselves pushed to the brink of economic disaster. While the government must take care of people who drop through the social net, it also has to be cautious not to recreate the iron rice bowl. In the face of this dilemma, many Chinese have quietly resigned themselves to the fact that some of Deng's modernization goals will not be realized in their lifetimes.

The resultant danger of reform in China resides in the reform movement itself. The currents of rapid change, experimentation, and adjustment sweeping China's landscape adversely affect those foreign firms unprepared to weather these changes. It cannot be overstated that an involvement in a specific industry in China must be thoroughly investigated before making a commitment. The prudent foreign firm has to monitor the past, present, and future effects of the reforms on its particular industry. Considering the unevenness of reforms, the fierce competition, and the changing foreign trade structure in China, foreign firms must question how their industry will be affected by decentralization. Without adequate preparation, a firm may find itself overexposed in a high-risk area. Rather than combating the reforms, foreign firms must be willing and able to ride the wave of reform.

One of the problems in dealing with China under the present circumstances is that it is a society in transition. What is still missing from the modernization program, as China's leaders are articulating it, is what the Chinese industrial landscape is supposed to look like after all the reforms are in place—that is, an "end-state" conception. There seems to be no absence of views about how to best achieve modernization, but there is no consensus on what a modernized China should look like, beyond a general, amorphous conception of China becoming an economically powerful and prosperous country. China appears to be working on multiple problems simultaneously, but how the pieces relate to one another at any one time remains unclear. At times, there appears to be an internal inconsistency in the objectives that are pursued and an overall lack of a strategic perspective of what the modernization program is intended to produce. If asked about the character of the Chinese economy and the management system to be in place in twenty years, Chinese leaders cannot readily explain what they are working toward. Does China still want to end up with a socialist economy? It is increasingly difficult to tell. If China continues to move in the current direction, it is going to end up with a mixed economy, at best. Chinese leaders are clearly cognizant that they do not want to initiate a totally free market system. But, short of that, there is no consensus on how much market force is politically acceptable and economically adequate. Hence, the Chinese say they want a socialist economy that works like a capitalist economy.

Managing the Risk of Investing in China

The on-again, off-again nature of regulatory change in China has caused many U.S. executives to question whether Deng has successfully instilled a long-term commitment to the reform policies among future leaders. The inherent risks of doing business in the People's Republic come not so much from the threat of expropriation of investments as it does from the periodic victimization of profit-making commercial activities that results from constant investment climate changes.

Most U.S. executives interviewed believe that stability will prevail after the Deng era. They are concerned, however, about the status of Sino-American relations and the possible negative effects of a potential political rift between the two countries. Should relations sour, such as over Beijing's sale of missiles to the Middle East, U.S. ventures in China could be used as "instruments of power protection by either the United States or China," which would bring disastrous results for China ventures.[51] Another concern of American executives is that Chinese attacks on "bourgeois liberalization" may reach the economic sphere. There is some indication that this has already happened. Song Tingming, a director for China's State Commission on Economic Reform, recently warned: "Some people want to expand the campaign [for Marxist ideology] . . . from the political to the economic field."[52]

American firms are understandably justified in applying sufficient resources and personnel to the task of monitoring China's political trends and policy. Roughly one-half of the U.S. firms entering China conduct a political risk analysis before undertaking joint ventures in the People's Republic.[53] To manage political risk, U.S. firms have adopted one or more of three possible strategies: (1) protect investments against calamity, expropriations, or civil strife by purchasing insurance; (2) keep investment commitment minimized; or (3) negotiate contract clauses permitting withdrawal from the joint venture under adverse political conditions.[54] Firms such as AMF, Foxboro, Caterpillar, and Dresser Industries have gone so far as to buy insurance from the Overseas Private Investment Corporation (OPIC) to protect their investments. People's Insurance Company of China also offers political insurance to foreign firms, but whether its coverage would include protection against expropriation that might result from major policy shifts is unknown. As one writer said, "the [PRC] can not be expected to give back with the left hand what it has taken away with the right."[55]

In the short term, however, foreign firms will have to face heightened investment risk in the guise of fast-changing, unpredictable laws and regulatory policies affecting their investments. The consistency of Chinese trade policy, the growing vulnerability of the Chinese economy to foreign economic events, and the uneven implementation of the reforms in general have set the stage for further changes in policy in the future. This situation presents all the more reason to get anticipatory clauses into contracts with the Chinese. Even so, contracts could be considered invalid, or suddenly interpreted differently by the Chinese side, if changes in laws or regulations occur. This is a sobering thought. These unknowns can sabotage business strategies and run budgets into the red. For example, those American computer firms that profited from a ravenous China market in 1984–85 witnessed the demise of that market after imposition of official restrictions on the purchase of foreign microcomputers, which was almost tantamount to a total embargo. Many of these companies had previously multiplied their staffs and office space in China in response to the boom times. One American computer firm entered into a service agreement when direct sales of the company's computers suddenly were slashed. Since revenue from direct sales supported the service venture, the agreement quickly became a financial burden.

How should firms plan their China investment over the long term? Pursue a prudent, cost-effective presence in the China market, and formulate plans that keep risk minimized and strategy flexible. Concentrate part of your staff on monitoring China's investment climate; watch China's spending, Deng Xiaoping's and Zhao Ziyang's reforms, attitudes of reform skeptics, and provincial policy shifts; and keep abreast of new cases involving official corruption. Before entering into a venture in China carefully consider whether you can hold out if hidden costs arise because of changing economic policies. Optimally, the management of political risk begins with choosing the right Chinese partner. Stick with partners with apparent state-level ranking within the bureaucratic hierarchy rather than merely local level ranking. Since foreign firms play an important role in China's modernization program, they should be concerned with their own performance within the Chinese system. If the Chinese perceive that foreign firms are not making a positive contribution, the firms could become an object of criticism. Some of that criticism will also be directed at the Chinese who invited them in the first place. On the other hand, should a China venture succeed in China, the firm involved might attain a privileged position. Viewed from an overall perspective, if Sino-foreign ventures enhance Chinese economic prosperity as well as the material standard of the Chinese people, the prospects for a significant political reversal with regard to the open door will be greatly diminished.

Searching for a Safe Niche. One of the unexpected positive outcomes of China's decision to allow the formation of joint ventures with foreign corporations has been the new links developing between these firms and the Chinese enterprise. In some ways the process by which foreign firms are drawing the Chinese enterprise into the world market may have a more significant impact on Chinese enterprise directors and managers than the production responsibility system. The demands of operating in the global marketplace are forcing the Chinese enterprise to change in major ways. These changes should not be ignored.

Securing a position in the China market depends on forging strong links with as many governmental, manufacturing, and R&D entities as possible. Toward this end, foreign executives may find it useful to form collaborative linkages with multiple Chinese organizations and then build up the requisite support structure by gaining the acceptance and backing of higher Chinese officials as the venture develops and achieves its stated goals. This will ensure its survival and viability because the venture has brought benefits (e.g., promotion, prestige, access to foreign exchange, etc.) to the officials associated with the venture. Such linkages, however, depend on the ability of the foreign partner to mesh its strategic and managerial prerogatives with those of its Chinese partners. This is a tall order, however, since few foreign managers fully understand the Chinese enterprise at the micromanagement level, making true corporate linkage between Chinese and foreign entities a rare phenomenon.

Chinese Management Style

There exists no contractual right for the [Chinese] firm's management. The Chinese manager can neither negotiate about pooling resources (labor or capital) with workers, firms, or capital owners, nor can he negotiate directly with suppliers or buyers of his products.

Barbara Krug

[E]very laborer has the right to directly participate in the management and use of the means of production of his own unit. . . . Otherwise, it would be contrary to the position of the laboring people as the masters of the means of production and to the nature of the system of ownership of the means of production by the whole people.

Huang Zhengqi

We chat a lot at the workshop, usually work at a rather casual pace. Many of us are quite addicted to taking a short nap after lunch break.

A worker in Hongzhou

The tensions and uncertainties embodied in China's reforms at the macroeconomic level of the country's industrial landscape strongly influence the behavior of the Chinese manager at the microeconomic level. Partly because of the systemic constraints imposed upon him, the Chinese manager has historically taken a cautious, risk-averse approach to running his enterprise. In many respects, this is still true today. Many Chinese managers lack an appropriate incentive to forge lasting business partnerships with foreign firms. Because of the potential problems, the factory manager in China may see only limited advantage in linking up with foreigners. This makes co-managing ventures in the People's Republic more difficult than in most other countries. Yet, if the foreign venture partner can better understand the idiosyncrasies and underlying motivations of the Chinese manager, the foreigner has a better chance of structuring an arrangement within which both parties can live and work to-gether in an harmonious fashion. Moreover, the foreign manager will be better equipped to co-manage his company's China venture, merg-ing his firm's objectives with those of his Chinese counterpart(s).

WHAT IS CHINESE ENTERPRISE?

The foreign executive experiencing his or her first tour of a Chinese factory is seldom prepared for what he or she finds inside the noisy, cavernous Chinese industrial plant: the apparent chaos on the shop floor, workers asleep at their positions, and the dilapidated factory buildings. Invariably, questions arise in the foreigner's mind: Just what is manufacturing in the Chinese context? What differences exist among the many types of Chinese enterprises? How do they compare and con-trast in operation?

Working conditions in China's factories closely resemble the con-ditions in American and European factories during the early 1900s: dimly lit, the air choked with dust, the noise sometimes unbearable. Though Chinese factories are tightly packed with machinery and workers, the bulk of the equipment appears dormant and large numbers of workers seem to be just standing around. Under pressure to conserve electricity, plants are often rather dark and lack any effective air-cleaning or antipollution apparatus. To their surprise, foreigners often find outdated and obsolete factory machinery kept in immaculate condition by poorly equipped repair personnel, a vestige of Mao's pro-motion of factory self-sufficiency. After visiting a series of Chinese in-dustrial facilities, it is hard to imagine how China can enter the ranks of the industrialized nations in the near future.

The Ownership-Leadership Dichotomy

China's industrial base consists of over 450,000 enterprises. Of the country's total industrial output of 800 billion yuan, over 550 billion yuan is generated by state-owned enterprises. Virtually all of the re-maining output is produced by collectives. The so-called privately owned enterprises still account for only a minor proportion of total production output in the People's Republic.[1]

State enterprises and collectives differ in both their pattern of own-ership and their mode of administration. The relationship between an

Number of Industrial Enterprises by Various Characteristics

Item	Enterprises (10 thousand)		Proportion (%)	
	1980	1985	1980	1985
Total	37.73	46.32	100	100
By type of ownership				
State-owned	8.34	9.37	22.1	20.2
Collective-owned	29.35	36.78	77.8	79.4
Of which: township enterprises	18.66	21.71	49.5	46.9
Others	0.04	0.17	0.1	0.4
By light and heavy industry				
Light industry	22.73	26.69	60.2	57.6
Heavy industry	15.00	19.63	39.8	42.4
By size of the enterprises				
Large	0.14	0.23	0.4	0.5
Medium	0.34	0.56	0.9	1.2
Small	37.25	45.53	98.7	98.3

SOURCE: *Statistical Yearbook of China, 1986,* State Statistical Bureau, People's Republic of China.

enterprise's ownership and management is currently the subject of much debate and experimentation. Various ownership alternatives are being tested in an attempt to increase productivity, improve efficiency, increase the supply of goods to the consumer, and expand production of higher-quality items.

The lines of authority above an individual enterprise can vary drastically. Heretofore, most ministries have managed a series of state-owned enterprises directly; local governments have also had management authority over a set of enterprises as well. If led by a ministry, the operation of the enterprise, including the planning, distribution resources, and sales of the enterprise, has been controlled by various components of the ministry. The ministry asserts its control directly from Beijing. If led by a locality, the enterprise comes under the auspices of a bureau at the provincial or municipal level. Some enterprises, however, are under joint control (*shuangzhong lingdao*). A dual-controlled enterprise, in effect, is under the authority of both the central and municipal government. Such circumstances create friction and obscure the real locus of authority.

State Enterprises.   State-owned entities, such as enterprises and research institutes, theoretically are owned by the people. The largest Chinese factories in both size and output (though not necessarily the most efficient) are administered by the state. These are generally considered the most important enterprises and have first call on skilled workers, foreign exchange, material inputs, etc. The near total social and job security these enterprises offer workers, however, tend to minimize labor productivity and innovation. For obvious reasons, Chinese leaders would like to stimulate improvements and technological progress in these enterprises. To that end they have begun a movement to release a sizable number of them from direct state control. While some enterprises clearly will prosper under these new conditions, it is also certain that some will not. As one enterprise manager remarked during an interview, "There are just too many factors still outside our control to allow us to produce at a higher level."

Collectives.   The number of collective enterprises jumped from about 300,000 in 1983 to 370,000 in 1985. The proportion of state enterprises to collectives, however, has remained unchanged since 1980, about one state enterprise per four collectives.[2] Jointly owned by groups of citizens, collectives often receive the aid of bank loans or government subsidies. They offer the participants some of the security of a state-run business along with the profit potential of a private enterprise. At present, hundreds of new collectives are being established each month, producing everything from foodstuffs and fodder to soft drinks and rice wine. One more recent manifestation of the push toward industrial collectives has been the development of the so-called *minban* companies. In essence, these are joint stock companies organized by a few persons with special competence. A good example is the Stone Computer Company, which was founded by a small group of engineers from the Chinese Academy of Sciences.

Over the past few years, a substantial amount of discretionary power has moved into the hands of factory managers within these collectives. In certain facets of their day-to-day operational decision making, however, many of these managers still must consult local bureaus of supervising ministries for assistance in obtaining commitments for supplies, transportation of goods, etc. Nonetheless, in response to the problems associated with the multiple administrative bottlenecks throughout the economy, the Chinese government has encouraged the spread of collective enterprises. Their flexibility in terms of both organization and decision making allows more timely responses to emerging opportunities.[3]

Most collective enterprises were originally owned by people who pooled assets to create them. As suggested, collectives have become more important because they are tied to traditional forms of management and administration. Recent changes in the collective enterprise management system have been broad based and more extensive in comparison to the state sector, partly because fewer constraints are imposed on collectives than state enterprises. While collectives may not offer their workers the welfare benefits and security they might receive as employees of state enterprises, the basic wage (excluding bonuses and benefits) may be higher. In fact, no ceiling is set on the amount of bonus wage that can be paid to a worker of a collective. (Average total wages are, however, moderately higher in state enterprises.) In principle, collectives downplay traditional worker wage egalitarianism, while encouraging worker competition and aggressiveness.

Since state enterprises receive the majority of government preferences, collective enterprises are often hard-pressed to compete. For example, state enterprises possess better access to investment capital, especially if the funds are coming from Beijing rather than a local province or municipal organization. State authorities tend to focus their investments on enterprises that the state owns as a means of retaining tight control over capital investments. Moreover, Chinese banks generally lend money far more readily to state enterprises because these enterprises maintain a higher, more consistent credit rating. Collectives, on the other hand, are viewed as virtually unsecurable.

Greater access to foreign exchange, via loans from state-controlled banking institutions, enables state enterprises to maintain a higher level of technology. State enterprises also tend to be better endowed with skilled personnel and production resources. Heretofore, they have gotten first choice of promising graduates, who first are made available to the military, second to the university system, and third to the ministries (i.e., the state enterprise system). Only recently have collectives been allowed to bid for Chinese youths entering the job market. Similarly, state enterprises also are placed first in line for needed supplies and raw materials, having the power and leverage to circumvent red tape to rapidly obtain allocations of critical supplies.

Private Ownership. A relatively small number of working Chinese, about 22 million people, now work for more than 13.7 million private, mostly small businesses that handle 14 percent of China's retail sales. According to Chinese sources, 115,000 of these enterprises employ nine or more workers.[4] For the most part, these businesses have not made a significant contribution to the country's economic development, though they receive the dragon's share of foreign press coverage of China's economy. Examples of private ownership include restaurants, travel bureaus, tailors, doctors, law firms, food stalls, service shops, transportation specialists, and handicraft makers. The overwhelming majority of these enterprises involve services such as catering, commerce, and the supply and marketing of goods including household wares.[5] These individual firms have had their greatest impact on the Chinese economy in the distribution sector, such as when local entrepreneurs purchase a truck to facilitate local transportation of agricultural goods to the free market. A handful of these private entrepreneurs are becoming rich, at least by Chinese standards. Most of China's "10,000-yuan households" are in the countryside, however, as are 90 percent of the private enterprises, because of delays in implementing reforms in urban areas.

Since 1987, the government in Beijing has made a strong effort to encourage further privatization of those parts of the economy that the state sector cannot adequately serve. Some new categories of privately owned enterprises have been established. First, a distinction is made between individual and private enterprises: the former employ seven or fewer employees; the latter employ eight or more. Second, private enterprises are classified according to ownership and management categories: (1) individually funded businesses; (2) household managed businesses; (3) joint-stock management businesses; and (4) state enterprises auctioned off to individuals.

Apparently, the main purpose of private enterprise promotion has been to put the rural unemployed back to work and increase agricultural production. China's modernization agenda does not include, as the international press often suggests, widespread privatization of large-scale industry in the near term. In other words, capitalist free enterprise in the People's Republic is accepted by most as a short-term response to specific social and economic problems, rather than as a long-term cure-all for the country's economic ills. Undoubtedly, the Chinese economy is much less centralized and less planned than a few years ago. Nonetheless, planning remains as an important part of the economy, even as the locus of planning has shifted to the local level.

The numerous articles appearing in the Western press exalting China's pronounced capitalist reforms have actually done a disservice to Western corporate executives in their dealings with China's highly bureaucratized, industrial environment. Above all, foreign managers must forge workable partnerships within the state-controlled sector of the People's Republic economy, which is still predominantly based on hierarchical command relationships among officials, managers, and organizations. By no means should the foreign executive enter the market seduced by the hoopla in the Western press. Here again, one cannot and should not ignore the tremendous changes in the People's Republic that seem to be moving the country closer to Western modes of business interaction. Yet, at the same time, the Western business executive must accept the steadfast socialist character and bureaucratic orientation of the Chinese economy. These elements are still solidly in place. No matter how market-oriented China becomes, the foreign investor will have to traverse a highly complex administrative network where his Chinese counterpart is only one of many actors with an interest, direct or indirect, in a particular project or initiative.

CHINA'S MANAGERIAL REVOLUTION

The People's Republic is trying hard to develop the tools needed to emulate the manufacturing pattern of high volume, low cost, and variety that has characterized Japanese success. With recent advances in automation and industrial production processing, labor costs now account for only a small percentage of total production costs. The People's Republic, with its large population, simply cannot contend as a

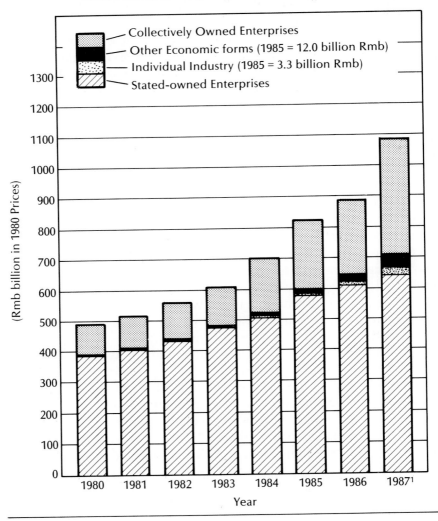

China's Industrial Output by Form of Enterprise Ownership

Collectively Owned Enterprises

Other Economic forms (1985 = 12.0 billion Rmb)

Individual Industry (1985 = 3.3 billion Rmb)

Stated-owned Enterprises

(Rmb billion in 1980 Prices)

Year

NOTE: 1. Estimated.

SOURCE: *Statistical Yearbook of China, 1986*, State Statistical Bureau, People's Republic of China; *China Trade Report*, April 1988; and *Far Eastern Economic Review*, 24 March 1988.

global competitor by offering up masses of inexpensive, unskilled labor to foreign firms in search of low-cost export platforms. The primary solution to China's modernization problems lies in improving both Chinese management techniques and worker skills. In 1978, China's leaders inaugurated a broad program to push Chinese enterprises into the forefront of Asian manufacturing efficiency. So far, progress has been slow to materialize in most of the key industrial sectors.

During the late 1970s, and in contrast to previous thinking, Chinese leaders realized that productivity could best be increased by implementing managerial improvements along with introducing new technologies (hardware and software) into the enterprise setting. In this context, the Third Plenary Session of the Eleventh Central Committee of the CCP held in December 1978 was a milestone in the evolution of industrial management in the People's Republic. At this meeting, China's top leaders revealed a willingness to reconsider many of the policies that were considered inviolable principles of the socialist system.

Beginning with the introduction of new management techniques in 4,000 Sichuan enterprises in 1979 (and in a lesser number of enterprises in Yunnan and Anhui provinces), a new industrial responsibility system was inaugurated, and later introduced in over 36,000 industrial enterprises. These enterprises, while only 16 percent of the total number of state-owned enterprises in the People's Republic, account for a remarkable 70 percent of total profit making among state enterprises.[6] As Party Secretary Zhao Ziyang has stated, a primary objective of the current policies is to give enterprises more independence and operating room as economic entities, establish broader management autonomy, and make managers more accountable for the profits and losses incurred by their enterprise.[7]

Chinese leaders now realize that an economy run by government fiat is a flawed model for efficient production.[8] Zhao Ziyang outlined four major tasks for the reform of industrial enterprises in a 1981 report on the work of the government:

1. to strengthen the economic responsibility system, improve management in enterprises via better planning, control, and business accounting;
2. to promote capable people to leading posts and overcome overstaffing problems through reorganization of work units;

3. to increase worker discipline by implementing a strict reward and penalty system; and
4. to tighten financial control.

In essence, the reforms alter the ideological foundation of what a Chinese enterprise represents within China's socialist economy. The enterprise is no longer merely a production entity fulfilling quotas and turning profits over to the state. Many enterprises now have become fully activated businesses as well as production entities, formulating their own marketing targets and distributing their output without direct government control. They must now issue full profit and loss reports. For the most part, they can also set wages and have greater control over the hiring and firing of their workers. They can also reward good worker performance to a greater extent than in the past. Enterprises have also been given the means for independent expansion and growth, more control over depreciation funds, and more power to procure their own equipment and technology from abroad. Some can even negotiate directly with foreign firms. Taken in its entirety, the management reform program is designed to bring into practice, in most areas, new systems of accounting, quality control, strategic planning, and market forecasting. The full choice of new freedoms include the following enterprise rights:

- to reserve part of factory profits for developing production, improving workers' welfare, and paying bonuses to the workers.
- to expand production with funds accumulated and retain profits derived from expansion for the first two years.
- to retain 60 percent of depreciation funds for fixed assets (as opposed to 40 percent in the past).
- to engage additional production demanded by the market after meeting the production quotas of the state plan.
- to market a portion of their products not acquired by the state commercial and materials departments.
- to apply to export their products and to reserve part of the foreign exchange earnings for the import of new technology, raw and other materials, and key equipment.
- to issue bonuses at the enterprise's own discretion within the range approved by the state (generally not more than four months' average wages of the workers and staff).

- to penalize individuals who incur heavy losses to the state, including workers, party secretaries, and factory directors, because of negligence in work or other subjective reasons. The most serious offenders will be expelled from the factory.[9]

An Overview of Factory Operations

After the CCP took control of China in 1949, it introduced a system of enterprise management patterned after the Soviet Union. The system was characterized by the strong role attached to the CCP. Almost every economic and social aspect of the enterprise came under the purview of the party. At the same time, the factory felt the administrative influence of the government bureaucracy. Production "mandates" were assigned to enterprises and goods were handed over to the state to be distributed. All profits and losses incurred were the responsibility of the state, not the enterprise.

With little in the way of competitive pressures to conduct their manufacturing processes efficiently, most Chinese factories fell victim to a host of operational and organizational problems. Many of these problems continue to plague Chinese factories. To begin with, they suffer from an array of shortcomings associated with poor shop-floor management techniques, such as incomplete quality control, product testing, and inspection. Complicated products are often not tested until assembled. Moreover, most Chinese factories do not operate under any statistically based process control systems. Since there is no inventory cost associated with factory production, there is little concern about excess inventory and no tradition of inventory systemization. In addition, the weak infrastructure and absence of technology associated with transportation of goods prohibit quick response in the shipping of products. As one China scholar has suggested, most Chinese factories are run with a "just-in-case" mentality rather than a "just-in-time" mentality.[10] Chinese factories also have trouble managing high-volume and diversified manufacturing endeavors. Widespread production redundancy creates long lead times from the design to the implementation stage of a new product. Often four or five years is necessary to bring a new product onto the market. Chinese enterprises simply remain unable to diversify products as rapidly as required by an international market flooded with manufactured goods assembled by low-cost labor using foreign machinery in the Pacific Rim nations.

Enhanced Autonomy. Although the management reforms have provided many new freedoms to factory managers, it should be noted that extensive enterprise autonomy has not yet been fully granted in the areas of R&D, training, distribution, technical renovation, pricing, and importation of technology, all of which are governed by state mandate. The enterprise cannot freely conduct its affairs in these areas. This is not to suggest that major adjustments in enterprise operations have not been carried out. Many significant and highly promising changes have been put in place since 1978.

In the past, most working capital was allocated by the state. Governmental agencies simply paid out to enterprises what they believed the enterprises needed to achieve the targets set in the central plan in light of negotiations with the enterprise directors. Investment capital was similarly doled out to enterprises by the state. Today, earnings, loans, and even stock issues have become the primary sources of investment funds used by the enterprise. By retaining earnings and obtaining bank loans, enterprises make decisions directly related to the accumulation and expenditure of capital. In Liaoning, an experiment is under way in which banks can make short-term loans to enterprises in response to varying levels of supply and demand in local areas, thus accelerating capital turnover.[11]

Enterprises also have obtained a great deal more power to conceive and carry out expansion plans, in part because of additional depreciation funds and a new enterprise fund derived from enterprise profits. With greater control over its finances, enterprises are able to procure equipment and raw materials better suited to their production requirements. Unfortunately, these funds also are being used to engage in unauthorized capital construction—a problem that has grown serious at times despite Beijing's efforts to curtail such investments.

The increasing availability of bank loans has placed enterprises in a better position to carry out technical renovation of both plant and equipment. Projects can originate from four different sources: the central government, local governments, a foreign trade corporation, or the enterprise itself. In order to compete, many enterprises pursue multiple avenues of equipment improvement, often buying foreign machinery and know-how to create new or more sophisticated products. From the perspective of foreign firms, the technical renovation program offers a chance to reshape both the structure and operation of a particular Chinese production facility.

New links between FTCs and producers have fostered more efficient and direct connections between enterprises and the distribution system. When raw materials and component sourcing was largely the responsibility of the state, serious delivery problems were incessant because of internal diversion of supplies and chronic shortages. Now, enterprises have some discretion over the source of their supplies, even to the extent of going outside of their regional system to acquire needed inputs, which is sometimes done with the help of the local government. This helps speed up production, lower costs, and remove unwanted bureaucratic interference in the sourcing process. To import raw materials or components, however, enterprises must buy primarily from local FTCs, many of which charge double the rate for imported items compared to the international market price. Having no other method for acquiring such items, enterprises have turned to bank loans for financing, which are fairly easy to obtain, though at an interest rate of 7.5–8 percent.[12]

Many manufacturers can sell their products directly into the Chinese market. In the past, state supply agencies received products from the factory for distribution. Today, enterprises producing consumer products, for example, are largely responsible for initiating collaborative arrangements between themselves and retailers. The introduction of contract law has helped to facilitate the development of these new relationships, providing both buyers and sellers with a greater sense of security.

Ideas regarding product design have been changed as well. In the past, the ministry would gather product ideas from factories under its control. (Sometimes these ideas would come from the reverse-engineering of a foreign product.) After consultation with the ministry, each factory manager would return to his factory to produce the item, ostensibly the same way in each factory. Today, factory managers can initiate the design and production of new products in response to emerging market demand. The trend is for enterprises to deal more directly with their customers.

Historically, quantity rather than quality has been a top priority in Chinese industry. The so-called "Mao jacket philosophy" (which means it doesn't matter what a product looks like as long as every citizen can have one) continues in China today, even though the Seventh Five-Year Plan emphasizes the need for higher quality in Chinese products. In China, the inherent quality problems of domestically produced products are accepted as part of the risk of buying Chinese. Domestic merchandise carries no consumer guarantee. As such, enterprises now advertise their products, especially consumer goods, in order to boost sales. Foreign competition in the domestic market also encourages Chinese firms to promote their products. For instance, Asia Soft Drinks, a Chinese company, dominated the beverage market in the People's Republic until the Beatrice and Coca-Cola joint ventures were established. Today, Asia Soft Drinks has gained name recognition through sustained advertising. According to one manager, Asia Soft Drinks spends $1200 a month for a neon sign in Guangzhou that reads simply: "Please Drink Asia Soft Drinks."[13]

New Role for Managers.   China's reformers recognize that the enterprise manager is the turnkey for China's industrial modernization. Accordingly, his achievements are often held up as heroic. Articles appear in the Chinese press about managers succeeding in the marketplace in the face of numerous obstacles. These news stories illustrate a sort of manager-hero who takes over a factory in debt, gathers market information, comes to understand the demands of his consumers, finds a niche for his products, acts quickly to get the product into the market, works to become number one in his township, and eventually succeeds in exporting his production.[14] It may not be such an exaggeration to cast these persons in such an heroic light. Mobilizing internal factory resources is a difficult task by itself; when one includes success in overcoming the manifold external constraints, the manager who succeeds is indeed heroic in style and spirit.

Management in China still suffers from its Soviet/Maoist legacy, wherein many of management-related activities boil down to what Max Boisot has called "technical problem solving," with the main focus of a manager's attention on attaining short-term production targets.[15] Until recently, the manager occupied a relatively low position in the Chinese decision-making hierarchy. Typically, pre-reform enterprises were headed by a factory director who worked with several deputies, including a chief engineer and a senior accountant. The day-to-day operational responsibilities were distributed between a number of staff departments: finance and accounting, labor and wages, training, planning, personnel, and general administration. In some respects, management reforms force the factory director to assume a greater role in shaping the operation of the factory. The factory director now chairs a committee composed of his senior deputy, chief engineer, chief economist, chief accountant, CCP committee secretary, trade union president, secretary of the Communist Youth League committee, and a representative elected by the Workers' Congress. This committee has a great deal of influence over a range of managerial alternatives and options.

The enterprise responsibility program is best viewed as a system of informal contracting between government entities in charge of factories and selected Chinese managers. The process often begins with the solicitation of bids from numerous managers on specific manufacturing projects. After winning a bid, theoretically on the basis of ability and past performance, the manager agrees in contract to meet certain production targets and quality specifications over the life of the contract, usually three to five years. A number of different contract forms are used, depending on the nature of the enterprise in question. If the enterprise succeeds in meeting the stated requirements, the manager typically can earn a bonus equal to one year's salary; if the factory misses the target, the manager can be expected to receive a reduction in salary of around 5 percent. Often, the newly contracted manager of an enterprise signs contracts between himself and middle managers, and even workers, forming multiple levels of responsibility contracts within an enterprise.[16] In effect, the factory director responsibility system has replaced the party leadership system. This system is in effect in all of China's major cities, including Wuhan, where 80 percent of the factories have adopted the policy.[17]

The new system gives managers greater control over everything from product mix to advertising, product development, and marketing both the quota portion as well as the surplus portion of production.[18] In the past, production schedules were established on the basis of directions from the state. A ministry would inform its factories, either directly or through the channel of a local industrial bureau, as to the amounts they were responsible for producing for the next year. Factory managers could negotiate for a lower quota, if necessary. Today, in most industries, no quotas are issued as such. While the same decision-making hierarchy exists and sets informal expectations, these are seen as "guidance plans" by the factory manager. At one time, factories would produce and deliver production to a wholesaling bureau, never knowing their customers or the final selling price of their product. Today, factories produce against an adjustable quota, but the factory has to find the customers itself.

The road to better management in China has not been without its potholes and cul de sacs. Many managers find taking advantage of their new freedoms extremely frustrating, because of the incomplete and uneven nature of China's economic reforms, as described in Chapter 4. The structural problems of pricing, taxation, and distribution remain a serious impasse to true factory autonomy. In many ways, the vitality of an enterprise depends strongly on the guanxi relationships held by the factory director. A manager may have all the technical skills of his foreign counterpart, but the one with fewer personal connections will not be as effective. Although the Chinese manager is being forced to address new issues like technological innovation, performance-based incentive systems, and production of new products that are responsive to fast-changing world markets, guanxi relations are still important, if not more important, as new competitive pressures emerge.

MARKET-RESPONSIVE MANAGEMENT: A CONTINUUM OF CONSTRAINTS

By allowing greater play of market forces, China's domestic industrial environment has grown more competitive. Not long ago, even defective products could find a market in China's economy of scarcity. In China's current economy, inferior quality will invite failure in the marketplace. Prior to the adoption of new product standards, factory managers could not develop and implement production strategies single-handedly. Their governing ministry handled most of their marketing, finance accounting, and product development. Modern Chinese managers must be familiar with current product design trends, applications, fashions, and packaging.

Essentially, the growing competition among Chinese enterprises has led to a new emphasis on creating products that can dominate domestic markets as well as successfully enter export markets. Enterprise managers have responded to the growing role of the market in a variety of ways. Some managers actually gather market information and formulate long-term market forecasts. When products emerge as high-demand items, numerous factories mobilize to produce them on their own. Possession of good market information allows managers to improve product quality, produce new varieties of products, and offer more extensive customer service. In their effort to target new markets, enterprise managers now carry out fairly sophisticated sales forecasting and customer-demand investigations. Inventory problems in selected factories are starting to disappear as managers find they can move products into the marketplace without state interference. Product lines are being improved and diversified, and more attention is being paid to aesthetics, warranties, and service backup. Greater technical innovation has also come into play as enterprises seek production advantages. Many plants are producing closer to capacity and are using their machinery and labor more efficiently. Recent trends in patent registration confirm that the evolving system is encouraging Chinese enterprises to innovate and protect their discoveries with patent protection.

The enterprise reforms have not resolved all of the marketing dilemmas for factory directors, however. Managers remain principally concerned with maintaining market share within their own domestic market rather than the export market because the monetary rewards for doing so are greater. Even when an enterprise succeeds in exporting production for foreign exchange, 50–75 percent of those earnings must be returned to the central government or local governments. Of the limited percentage which the enterprise is allowed to retain, such foreign exchange must be placed in an account with the Bank of China, and must be used under the auspices of the relevant bureau.[19] The legacy of direct state control over enterprises, combined with the domestic hunger for products, conditions the Chinese manager to maintain a rather short-term marketing perspective. As such, the Chinese manager downplays export schemes and emphasizes selling to domestic end-users—much as American manufacturers behaved during the 1950s and 1960s. Since the domestic consumer and capital goods markets are impulsive, managers pursue short-term goals, and may limit spending on R&D and foreign know-how. In addition, short-term enterprise performance evaluation (in the form of quarterly assessments) encourages short-term behavior on the part of management.[20] The lessons of the past and the uncertainty of the future seem to dictate a quick-fix, short-term managerial mentality.

Based on interviews in the People's Republic, many Chinese managers perceive producing for export as a risk rather than a surefire benefit. Managers seem to equate the opportunity to export production with losing domestic competitiveness, perceiving they are vulnerable to fluctuations in the international market as well as pressures from Chinese government agencies seeking foreign exchange. In many respects, the Chinese managers' response is a rational one, given the far easier task of addressing the local market. Accordingly, most Chinese managers still possess less than full knowledge or appreciation of the international market. The so-called front guard of professional managers who head China's largest state factories, trading companies, and hotels have worked for three decades in a system where the government took profits from the efficient firms to bail out the inefficient ones. If a firm experienced a losing year, state subsidies would alleviate imbalances, and pressure on the manager would be eased. Most managers are concerned about the possibility of having the international market be the prime vehicle for determining their enterprise's efficiency, fearing that their enterprise may not meet the challenge.

Since some enterprises sell literally everything they produce domestically, they often can ignore the task of understanding overseas markets. They take it as an affront that international prices fluctuate. Many factory managers refuse to export their production because foreign distribution of their products remains the task of the relevant FTC, which are not particularly reliable as distributors. Production may sit in warehouses for long periods of time, while the FTC delays payment of foreign exchange owed to the factory until the FTC gets paid from abroad. Most factory managers try to avoid dealing with FTCs any more than necessary because of the rapid turnover in the domestic market.

Surely, part of the international marketing problems faced by Chinese management have their origin in the lack of exposure to the world economy and a dearth of educational programs geared to training management to operate in a globally competitive economy. Blame does not fall solely on the managers, however. As indicated, many obstacles stand in the path of the manager who desires to utilize enterprise autonomy to maximize production—and sell abroad. These obstacles are built into the Chinese industrial system and cannot be overemphasized as primary causes for both Chinese enterprise inefficiency as well as their unresponsiveness to foreign markets. Nonetheless, as decentralization of the Chinese economy spreads, the market mechanisms now in full swing in selected areas will come to play an important role throughout the entire production and distribution network. This will clearly necessitate the emergence of a new type of enterprise manager in China on a broad scale.

Though it cannot be denied that the reforms offer a significant expansion of opportunities, numerous factors continue to impede the initiatives of certain newly responsible Chinese managers. The new freedoms given to enterprises have not lessened the burden of managing a multitude of political, economic, and social forces that impinge upon the activities of the Chinese factory at virtually every level. These include:

- infrastructural deficiencies
- state control of enterprise financial transactions via adjustable taxation
- central and local bureaucratic manipulation of production schedules via quotas
- limited availability of skilled technicians and trained managers
- continued involvement by politically motivated party cadres in key facets of enterprise decision making
- a scarcity of supplies from various distributors.

While there is room for optimism, the overall result of the reforms has been discouraging. Many Chinese enterprises still operate with little vigor or ingenuity, appearing lethargic in comparison with those in some other East Asian nations. Certainly, prior to co-manufacturing with a Chinese enterprise, it is vital to be fully aware of the economic, cultural, and political constraints on the particular enterprise and its directors who could hold back qualitative changes in operating modes. Most problems for the manager seeking to use his new powers begin with contradictions in the lines of authority and delineation of tasks and responsibilities, or, how the enterprise governs itself.

Vertical versus Horizontal Administration

Chinese enterprises are simultaneously administered from inside and outside by internal managers, directors, and cadres, as well as local bureau and central ministerial officials. The structure within the enterprise is an extension of the vertical structure of the bureaucracy that surrounds the enterprise. Each department within an enterprise must report to the general manager of the enterprise as well as its corresponding municipal bureau.[21] For instance, the import department of an enterprise must have links with the local foreign trade commission. Hence, the enterprise is not only regulated, in the Western corporate sense, but it is checked at every level of its organization by numerous external forces. Enterprises must contend with various types of government controls—usually enacted through government-issued directives—and local government prerogatives and priorities that are most often based less upon carrying out Beijing's wishes than on allocating sufficient production and foreign exchange for its own needs. As the central government reduces its role in individual enterprise decision making, local bureaucratic entities seem to be taking advantage of decentralization to meddle in the affairs of the enterprise even more than before.

The manager remains largely powerless to extricate the enterprise from the state's administrative clutches. Multiple government entities are likely to wield influence over the internal functioning and decision making of the enterprise, making it nearly impossible for managers to implement, let alone fully actualize, their new plans and programs. If their plans fail, demotion, or at least ostracism, is quite possible. Directives emanating from outside can be both conflicting and redundant. The Chinese enterprise manager is often forced into a position of trying to please various bureaucrats rather than concentrate on taking full advantage of his enterprise's pronounced autonomy and responsibilities.

Trivialization of Manager Responsibilities. The unclear lines of managerial authority and responsibility force Chinese managers to spend a great deal of time and energy on issues which seem arcane and irrelevant to their economic role. All problems, including maintenance issues of a relatively obscure nature, must be approved by several layers of management.[22] As Huan-ming Ling has summarized, "Managers must oversee not only their enterprises' efficiency and output, but also tend to worker welfare issues."[23] That is, managers find themselves constantly bogged down in dealing with personnel issues such as worker housing, pension funds, and the education of workers' children.

Political Obstacles: The Role of the Party

Along with the vagueness of authority, the position of the CCP represents the most formidable obstacle to direct managerial leadership. Under the current reforms, enterprise managers and party secretaries have entered, in theory, a dynamic relationship of "shared leadership" over factory operations. The CCP no longer solely governs decision making that concerns the economic administration of enterprise operations. This is not to imply, however, that political considerations no longer affect the functioning of the Chinese factory. The CCP secretaries still play an important role in decisions concerning wages, worker welfare, worker rewards, and political consciousness-raising.

The CCP links the enterprise with the ideological interests of the state. Committees and trade unions under the influence of the party are responsible for the political indoctrination of workers through political discussion seminars.[24] Enterprises once were a place of class struggle rather than a place of production. While this has clearly changed, the party has not disappeared; its presence is always felt.

The CCP appears to maintain a sort of referee role inside the enterprise, overseeing worker morale and ideological correctness as well as ensuring that worker benefits are received. The party monitors worker interest and establishes role models for emulation while staying out of financial decision making. Moreover, if the factory director conducts himself in an ideologically suspect or corrupt manner, the party will get involved. Since the factory director may be associated with the CCP, his leadership may be colored by the interests of party officials in the enterprise. Factory directors were once responsible for political guidance in the factory, but now their responsibilities usually end with technical and production problem solving. Based on the author's interviews, it seems that the CCP continues to monitor factory leaders who desire to create performance incentives or undertake innovations deemed by the party to be ideologically out of step. A textile factory manager in Shanghai, for instance, was fired for initiating production of apparel that was too bold—"too Western"—in color, said one Chinese factory manager.

Prior to 1980, membership in the CCP represented the pinnacle of success, an instant guarantee of career mobility. However, the party's attractiveness in offering career prestige and bureaucratic perks has waned with the emergence of new avenues for career mobility in China. The country's "best and brightest" want to go abroad to study. When, and if, they return, they are more interested in forming new businesses than upholding Communist ideology. The party has been forced to acknowledge that the country's modernization drive demands more from its labor force than simply being ideologically "red." Party officials now recognize the importance of technical capability in workers and that the promotion of workers and managers must be based increasingly on skill levels rather than politics. As a result, the CCP has embraced the technically trained factory director who may not be politically cognizant of the party line, but represents someone the party can accept in

ENTERPRISE ORGANIZATION
The Structure of Beijing, No. 3 Knitwear Mill

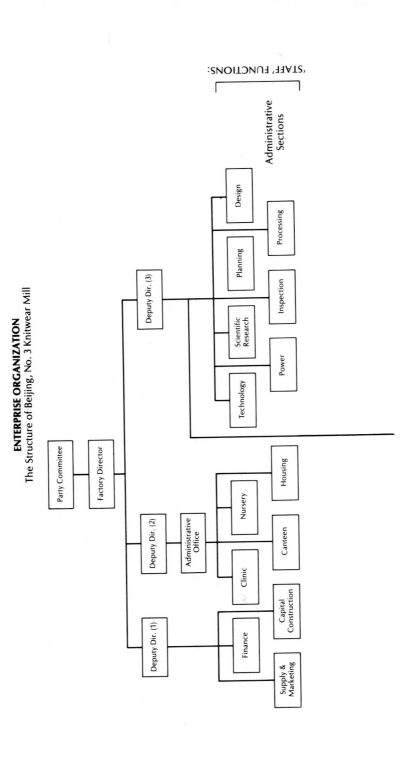

'STAFF' FUNCTIONS:

Administrative Sections

Party Committee

Factory Director

Deputy Dir. (1)

Deputy Dir. (2)

Deputy Dir. (3)

Administrative Office

Supply & Marketing

Finance

Capital Construction

Clinic

Canteen

Nursery

Housing

Technology

Scientific Research

Planning

Design

Power

Inspection

Processing

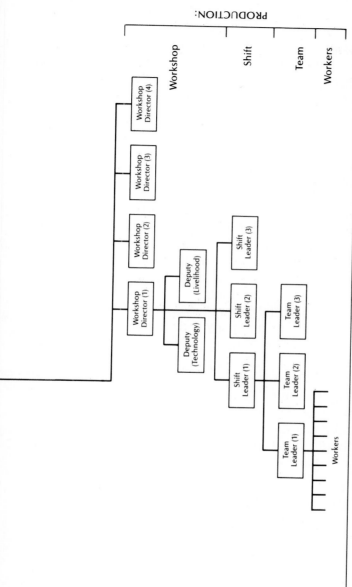

PRODUCTION:

Workshop

Shift

Team

Workers

Workshop Director (1) — Workshop Director (2) — Workshop Director (3) — Workshop Director (4)

Deputy (Technology) — Deputy (Livelihood)

Shift Leader (1) — Shift Leader (2) — Shift Leader (3)

Team Leader (1) — Team Leader (2) — Team Leader (3)

Workers

The Chinese organize enterprises to emphasize vertical, rather than lateral, communication. Characteristically, Beijing No. 3 Knitwear Mill has five functional levels: (1) administrative, (2) workshop production, (3) shift leaders, (4) team leaders, and (5) workers. The enterprise is under the auspices of a party committee and is administered by three deputies working under a factory director.

Of the factory's three organizational "trees," only one deals with actual production; the other two handle supply, marketing, and worker services. Thus,

supply and marketing remain divorced from manufacturing operations. This overburdens Deputy Director #3, who has to organize R&D, product design, quality control, and technology acquisition as well as ameliorate constant shop-floor problems brought to him by all four workshop directors. His responsibilities befit two deputies — one in charge of production; the other, R&D.

Below Deputy Director #3, the presence of shift leaders and team leaders implies middle-management redundancy. Workers need to be brought into more direct contact with workshop directors.

SOURCE: Martin Lockett, "Culture and the Problems of Chinese Management," *Organization Studies*, Sept. 4, 1988, by permission.

order to maintain its own position. The CCP now concentrates on recruiting trained factory directors in its attempt to remain functionally relevant. Without technically skilled members, the organization would lose desperately needed clout. To bolster its ranks, the Communist Youth League has had to cater to more materialistic young Chinese, going so far as to sponsor dances and a computer dating service.[25]

The CCP's power and influence in the industrial sphere is now questioned with increasing frequency. Open criticism of the CCP is expressed today without the fear of political reprisal. The party no longer controls the personnel records of all the managers, workers, etc. Reformers are doubting the usefulness of the CCP in production entities. A steady stream of articles in the Chinese press claim that Chinese industry would benefit if enterprise management and CCP functions were totally separated.

The party still plays a decisive role in decision making within the enterprise, however, because many decisions must be pushed up the vertical hierarchy to formulate a consensus. In essence, the CCP functions largely as a constraint on enterprise autonomy, advocating benefits to political cadres, and criticizing policies that yield too many freedoms to managers. Reports in the *China Daily* describe "managers who have been stymied by antagonistic party cadres, removed from their positions for going too far toward putting 'production in command,' or otherwise brought to heel by insistent party pressures."[26] After all, the Politboro of the Central Committee of the CCP still wields substantial social, political, and economic decision-making authority in the country. By working alongside managers within enterprises, CCP secretaries can influence factory managers and/or resist the changes they are making.[27] While politics is no longer in command, the Chinese work setting is not without politics in its day-to-day affairs.

Confining Covenants Between the Enterprise and the Chinese Economy

The Chinese economy is still characterized by high levels of state inducement and intervention. No matter how much freedom the enterprise may have on paper, its choice of alternatives (e.g., in articulating new production techniques) is still greatly restricted. In effect, the state controls enterprises through its control of pricing, the imposition of import tariffs, the delivery of critical inputs, and by manipulating the amount of revenue enterprises can keep after taxes. The state accom-

The Organization of China's Communist Party

```
                                    CENTRAL COMMITTEE
                                           |
                                           |
        Military Affairs        Central Advisory        Central Discipline
        Commission              Commission              Inspection Commission
            |                                                   
    ┌───────┼───────┐                                    POLITBORO
    |       |       |                                         |
 General  General  General                          POLITBORO
 Staff    Political Logistics                        STANDING COMMITTEE
 Department Department Department                          |
                                              GENERAL SECRETARY
                                                 Zhao Ziyang
                                                      |
                                                 SECRETARIAT
                                                      |
                                           FOREIGN AFFAIRS SMALL GROUP
```

CENTRAL COMMITTEE

Military Affairs Commission

Central Advisory Commission

Central Discipline Inspection Commission

General Staff Department

General Political Department

General Logistics Department

POLITBORO

POLITBORO STANDING COMMITTEE

GENERAL SECRETARY Zhao Ziyang

SECRETARIAT

FOREIGN AFFAIRS SMALL GROUP

Organization Department

General Office

Propaganda Department

United Front Work Department

International Liaison Department

Central Party School

Research Center of the Secretariat

Rural Policy Research Center of the Secretariat

Party Literature Research Center

Party History Research Center

plishes this through a complex system of quotas, taxation, remittances, and state purchases of production. The state's controls run against the independent functioning of the enterprise, thus limiting its ability to respond to new demands or shift production into new areas. Despite the controls that remain, direct economic control over enterprises by the central government has been reduced through the decentralization of enterprise management. The crux of the problem, however, is that all of these restrictions represent serious impediments to enterprise directors seeking avenues for production/marketing flexibility, responsiveness, and competitiveness.

Critics of reform believe that state-led economic control ensures the government a continuous supply of revenue to fund the country's modernization. Too much financial freedom for the enterprise, critics claim, is a threat to China's economic stability. Government representatives also fear that financial exchanges between enterprises and government agencies might be both difficult to maintain and vulnerable to unsavory business practices by unscrupulous administrators seeking to profit from the regulatory problems plaguing the country's vast provinces. Such schemes have included tax evasion, price gouging, arbitrarily issuing bonuses and subsidies, and retaining profits marked to be remitted to the state.[28]

Enterprise Performance.   In the past, Chinese factory performance was measured by the "eight great standards": production volume, quality, cost, labor efficiency, consumption of resources, capital utilization, production value, and profit. But these numbers made little sense in a system of controlled prices and government subsidies. In essence, all enterprises—profitable and unprofitable, efficient and inefficient—"ate from the same big pot."[29] Today the eight great standards are still measured, but overall enterprise profit has become the criterion most closely scrutinized.[30]

A system of taxation-against-profit (*li gai shui*) has recently been applied to industrial enterprises in order to turn over more control of the financial aspects of factory management to enterprise employees. In the past, factories simply remitted all their earnings to the state. Administrative authorities then would issue the factory an operating budget for the following term. In fact, the largest source of income to the state came from factory remittances; it is this revenue that is being replaced by factory taxation. Taxation, however, is not seen as a sure method of guaranteeing the state the revenue it is accustomed to receiving. Profits are difficult to predict and measure, yet can be manipulated. Officials fear that factories will skim profits, falsify rates of production, and hide sales figures to avoid paying their share. The result for management: government officials lack trust in managers to remit their factories' profits in the form of taxes. Since taxes are calculated against a benchmark rate of profit in a given year, the actual rate of taxation is largely left up to the negotiating abilities of the factory manager and local bureaucrats. The manager desires the baseline year to be a relatively poor year; the officials want the enterprise to pay taxes on the factory's best year's production.

Pricing of Output.   Price fixing is probably the most profound constraint on the profitability of an enterprise. China has moved from the old Soviet-style system of government price fixing toward a system of semi-controlled pricing. As long as inflation remains in the economy, the Chinese will continue to resist decontrolling prices in any substantial way. The state still sets most prices, keeping them low on essential raw materials, which tends to help control price inflation but also depresses the factories producing these goods.[31]

During the most recent phase of the modernization program, the pricing of goods has changed significantly. Recently, a system of price "bands" (ranges) was put into effect. In some cases, an enterprise can set prices itself within a designated band, especially for output produced beyond the state quota set for the factory. The pricing of certain goods is now completely uncontrolled. Moreover, enterprises that meet state quotas and have production surpluses can sell directly to the consumer on the free market, or to the state, both at a higher price than they sell under government quota.

As the market becomes more competitive and mature, pricing is being diversified and further deregulated. Taxes will become increasingly unnecessary as a mechanism to manipulate enterprise competition and balance disparate advantages among enterprises, as they were used in the past. However, this is not to suggest that deregulation will spread throughout the economy, but only that a general loosening up is taking place that will change the nature of the production enterprise and the way it relates to the overall economy.

Taken in their entirety, the enterprise reforms discussed so far, however incomplete and uneven they might be, have served to set the stage for a fundamental change in the operation of the Chinese economy. Starting at the microeconomic level, the enterprise has become more independent even though the manager is still encumbered by political and bureaucratic constraints. Today's manager in China has a chance to take advantage of emerging opportunities especially in those cases where the risks and associated penalties are outweighed by the potential for both personal and enterprise gain. Admittedly, these opportunities are not as widespread as one would hope, but they are there.

The fundamental problem is the poor mesh between declarations made by the central government in Beijing at the macroeconomic level and the ability to act on these policies at the microeconomic level. As has been the case in the Soviet Union, the major point of interference comes from the middle bureaucracy that sees itself as the interpreter of central directives. As a result, emerging opportunities are shut off and innovative managers must succumb to the prerogatives of the local bureaucracy, if they are going to survive as managers. Accordingly, local initiative becomes stifled and managers end up even more frustrated than before the reforms.

MOTIVATING WORKERS: THE INERTIA OF DANWEI

The Chinese have extensive experience with motivational schemes to enhance worker productivity. Since 1949, China has employed numerous incentive programs as a way of increasing output. These programs have run the gamut from group incentives to individual rewards, from moral suasion and emulation campaigns to piece rate and stock options. Mao Zedong promoted labor volunteerism based on "emulation drives," which in turn inspired the formation of emulation committees in most of the country's factories.[32] Awards were given for successful imitation of highly propagandized model factories. Since Mao's death, there has been greater emphasis on material incentives. Today's Chinese worker is motivated through moral encouragement and material rewards.

Unfortunately for workers, there have been no significant pay raises in the state sector since 1966. With some exceptions, recent wage reforms have been mostly remedial. Within the state sector there still exists little job mobility. The challenge now is for China to create a new incentive structure so that worker motivation rises and output increases.

Lack of Labor Mobility.

When the Communists took political control of China in 1949, they organized human resources into a system that evolved into the household-registration system called *danwei*. In the system, workers and managers are placed (often permanently) in a specific production unit directly out of school. In effect, a person's workplace and home tend to be one and the same; a place to live, raise children, socialize, grow old, and die. A production unit may be part of a commune, a state farm or factory, or a collective. In general, it is extremely difficult to transfer to another production unit. To change units, a person must have the approval of the new unit as well as that of the old. Furthermore, getting out of a unit is even more toilsome if one is technically skilled, as that unit will resist allowing a much-needed worker or manager to leave.[33] To leave an enterprise, a worker might be labeled aberrant, and thereafter, find it nearly impossible to locate a better position in another factory. Though there now exist more ways of leaving a unit and moving to another one, workers must still obtain releases. A woman wanting to relocate in Beijing describes her ordeal:

> Getting my residence permit transferred to Beijing was difficult . . . [I] had to move on several fronts at once. There is the official . . . that looks after entry to and exit from the city, and there's the unit in Beijing that you want to work for. . . . you have to find somebody who wants to exchange with you. There are a few people who want to leave Beijing. I found some . . . working in the track maintenance department of the railway bureau. . . . These two people made a couple of conditions: firstly, one of them wanted me to help him find a job, a good job, in [my] little town. The other one wanted a flat there. I managed all of this but then the personnel department wouldn't let them go. So I had to think up some way to overcome this new problem. . . . It's no good just spending money: you have to make sure you spend it the right way. The thing to do is to see what they need for their families—you have to use your eyes or make inquiries.[34]

In China, the enterprise fulfills a social role in society as well as an economic one. Chinese workers usually work in the same physical location for most of their lives. Workers enjoy the many forms of security offered them by the factory. The enterprise itself makes up a large portion of a worker's financial and social support system. The typical Chinese factory is a social entity embedded in the fabric of Chinese culture and tradition. In the West, we would consider it to be the ultimate "family" firm. In many ways, the factory is a veritable microcosm of Chinese family organization, guaranteeing the worker not only wages, but also housing, clothing, medical care, living stipend, and education. The worker's basic wage equals only about 40 percent of what employees actually receive. The unit also affords psychological support and a sense of community membership. From an early stage in life, the Chinese worker is inexorably linked to the economic and social structure of his production unit.

In the mind of the enterprise manager, however, danwei prevents workers from being dismissed, which largely deprives him of the power to hire and fire. Generally speaking, jobs in China are guaranteed—lifetime employment has existed since 1949. By offering security and promoting an ethos of conformity and "belongingness," danwei ensures that workers maintain a fairly sedentary lifestyle. Workers and managers remain stationary throughout most, if not all, of their careers. There exists no real job market, no free labor pool, and most factories must employ far more workers than needed. Also, workers will not readily leave their jobs to relocate, making recruitment of appropriately skilled workers difficult. As a result, some industries have too many workers clogging plants and factories and draining off capital into unnecessary wages, while sectors such as the service industry experience underemployment because of a lack of capital and equipment.[35] This overabundance of workers, in relation to work to be completed, leads to rampant worker idleness, absenteeism, low morale, and spreads disrespect for management. Ultimately, overstaffing inhibits a manager's efforts to offer individual incentives, to streamline production activities, or to reduce the ranks of middle managers.

New forms of worker recruitment represent an attempt to circumvent the traditional obstacles of the danwei. One approach involves employment quotas in selected youth categories, such as youths sent to the countryside, recent graduates of secondary school, and other groups not yet rooted to local work environments. These youth groups are often solicited through recruitment advertising. The most successful approach, however, is for individual factories to organize their own new-employee recruitment and then establish ex post facto approval by the labor authorities. In this manner, temporary workers are hired, graded, and paid daily rates. Some of the temporaries may become regular workers after on-the-job training. Because workers are now hired on a labor contract system, they can be dismissed if they violate work rules. (The labor contract system is discussed further on page 232.) Referrals for new workers may be obtained from relatives of workers already employed, by off-site employment offices, or by word-of-mouth networking (the grapevine). In addition, there appears to be a pattern of informal job inheritance, wherein a job may be guaranteed for one child of each retiring worker.

As noted, the danwei system enables enterprises across the economy to provide services and welfare to their employees. Most Chinese are attached socially and psychologically to the security offered by the production unit system. In spite of the recent influx of labor into China's special economic zones, luring them away from their danwei to work for more money or a better job may be problematic. In some cases, Chinese workers choose to remain at a secure job rather than take the risk of leaving it for a higher paying one, especially if they hold a position in a state-owned factory where benefits and stability are greatest. Enjoying the benefits of the iron rice bowl, workers in state-owned factories perceive little advantage in breaking out of the traditional labor system in order to pursue jobs in private enterprise or in a collective where their income and independence could be enhanced. This problem is pronounced for managers of state-owned enterprises. The state enterprises offer security that collectives do not. Some "youth awaiting employment" will wait for jobs in the state sector rather than take a possibly higher paying job at a collective. State enterprises reinforce this tendency by often refusing to take workers who have already worked in a collective. Even some Chinese who have started one-man businesses that make large amounts of money compared to state workers would give up their businesses to go back to the state sector at a lower pay level.[36]

The group orientation of the danwei tends to prohibit nonconformity, and therefore independent moves toward upward mobility. Although "sideline" production in small collectives and households has grown steadily, as has the practice of workers moonlighting at their regular jobs after hours to boost income, given the choice, most Chinese still opt for security and belongingness over free enterprise and independence. Entrepreneurs are viewed with uneasiness in a society that has not forgotten the egalitarian ideals of the past three decades. A recent survey conducted in Shanghai found that individual entrepreneurship is considered risky both politically and economically. Those who are self-employed were perceived as being uneducated and rustic in their behavior. Moreover, entrepreneurs suffer the reputation of being of low social status. Entrepreneurship ranked nearly last as a favored form of employment.[37] Since one of the intentions of allowing the formation of private enterprises in China was also to employ more of the country's estimated 14 million urban youths (18–25 year olds), a sector of the population considered responsible for the majority of the country's serious crime, the negative image of private business endeavors might be expected.

The social role of the factory restricts managers from initiating creative solutions to worker incentive problems. Because of the egalitarian tendency to provide workers and managers with most, if not all, of their basic needs, it follows that enterprise managers prefer using alternative incentive systems in addition to those based on material reward.

Reforming of the danwei system requires fundamental changes in the role of local governments regarding housing, medical care, education, etc. There is little likelihood that China will undertake this effort any time soon, but rather will attempt slow but steady progress in diminishing the efficacy of this system.

Use of Wage Incentives

Workers usually work nine hours a day, six days a week. Wages for workers are based on an eight-grade scale; grade one being unskilled, grade eight, highly skilled.[38] Beijing is seeking to institute a new tenet of "distribution according to labor" through wage reforms. Deng Xiaoping's reforms call for distribution according to the quantity and quality of an individual's work such that an individual's grade on the pay scale is calculated on the basis of on-the-job performance, including his or her technical skill. Wages were once determined according to a scale based primarily on seniority: the higher the worker on the scale, the higher his wage. Critics claimed the system rewarded worker seniority but failed to reward actual performance. By 1978, a points system that rated an individual's performance, skill level, and labor attitude had been developed to supplant seniority as a condition for promotion.

More problems ensued with this system. In 1982 a bonus system was adopted in a new effort to link wages to performance.[39] Net profits now go to bonuses, under a system of distribution according to labor, linking worker reward directly with the profitability of the enterprise.[40] Since skill levels differ across various sectors of the same industry, the bonus system becomes a means to tie wages to performance. Workers who perform well receive a bonus of 10 to 25 percent of their basic wage. The bonus ceilings have been rising since the program was initiated. As of 1987, bonuses stood at 12.9 percent of basic wages.[41] The state encourages bonus-giving by offering favorable taxation structures. However, if an enterprise fails to produce a profit, workers may only receive 80 percent of their base pay and forgo bonuses altogether.

Currently, wage structure in state enterprises consists of four different levels:

1. *basic wage*, which is guaranteed across the country;
2. *supplemental wage*, based on piece rate and extra shift work which rewards individual performance and seniority;
3. *welfare subsidies*, which includes housing, food supplements, utilities, transportation, day care, and hospitalization; and
4. *performance wages*, which are rewarded in the form of "floating" bonuses.

Worker Morale.   Enterprise productivity is often impaired by workers who remain unmotivated while feeling secure in their job, and receive bonuses equal to those given to more productive employees. The problem of worker morale has worsened in recent years. An investigation conducted in 1987 by an institute at the Chinese Academy of Sciences reported that "workers feel they have lost their previous status in society." Although more fortunate workers have entered training programs to become technicians or managers, those who cannot gain access to these programs remain on the job unmotivated to improve their performance.[42]

Performance is still not rewarded anywhere close to that in Western factories. Getting a raise still depends not only on work performance but also on political standing, low absenteeism, proper maintenance of tools, safety in production, attitude, etc.[43] In addition, fringe benefits usually go to cadres. One study done by John Child found that fringe benefits for cadres accounted for 17 percent of their personal income in 1984, while only 8 percent of a worker's personal income was in the form of fringe benefits.[44] Child also found that an employee's age has the most influence on his or her wage. The older the employee,

**Wage Breakdown
in State-Owned Enterprises**

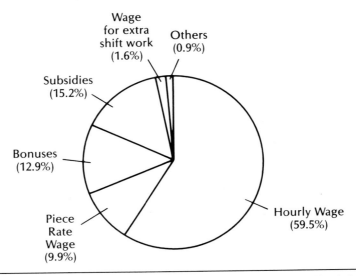

Wage
for extra
shift work
(1.6%)

Others
(0.9%)

Subsidies
(15.2%)

Bonuses
(12.9%)

Piece
Rate
Wage
(9.9%)

Hourly Wage
(59.5%)

SOURCE: *Statistical Yearbook of China, 1986*, State Statistical Bureau, People's Republic of China.

the higher the salary. Job level and length of service in the enterprise each have an effect on a worker's wage, but only about half the effect of age.[45]

THE RISK-AVERSE MANAGEMENT RATIONALE

An array of factors—some systemic, others cultural—encourage managers to avoid entrepreneurial risk. With so many unknowns in the system making outcomes uncertain, managers experience little incentive to do much more than obey government directives in exchange for various benefits. These benefits include more privileged supply of goods, prestige as managers of "model" enterprises that utilize foreign equipment, and more influence among government officials since they may command more foreign exchange because of their factories' ability to export.

Most decisions by factory managers are based on political prerogatives rather than a predilection to increase profit margin. To be sure,

Average Annual Wages in China by Type of Enterprise

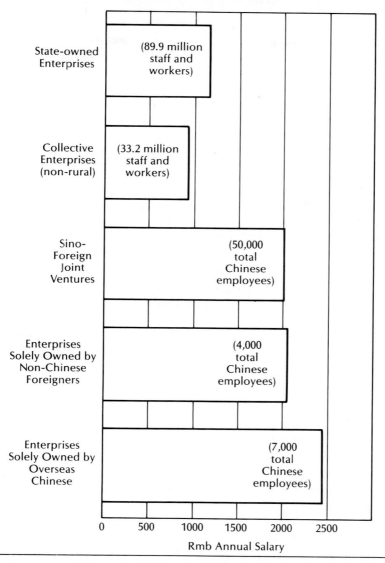

State-owned Enterprises — (89.9 million staff and workers)

Collective Enterprises (non-rural) — (33.2 million staff and workers)

Sino-Foreign Joint Ventures — (50,000 total Chinese employees)

Enterprises Solely Owned by Non-Chinese Foreigners — (4,000 total Chinese employees)

Enterprises Solely Owned by Overseas Chinese — (7,000 total Chinese employees)

0   500   1000   1500   2000   2500

Rmb Annual Salary

Joint venture workers earn roughly twice the salary of the average Chinese employee of a nonrural enterprise. (However, take-home pay may be less disparate since FESCO, China's employment agency that supplies workers to foreign-investment enterprises, often takes a cut.) Oddly, ventures run by overseas Chinese are willing — and permitted — to defray their workers nearly 20 percent more than other foreign investment enterprises.

SOURCE: *Statistical Yearbook of China, 1986,* State Statistical Bureau, People's Republic of China.

the majority of Chinese managers exhibit apprehension at the prospect of taking true responsibility for their factories' profits and losses. Chinese managers feel most comfortable viewing themselves as facilitators, rather than leaders, responsible mainly for relaying information and translating higher commands to the factory floor. While Western managers view their role as decision makers, those in China perceive their role as a relatively small element in the decision-making hierarchy. The principal aim of Chinese managers is to circulate the mandates and instructions coming from above to the appropriate team leaders and workers so that their factories meet their quotas, thereby protecting themselves and their fringe benefits. Chinese managers seek to insulate themselves from direct responsibility via participation in the old system of consensus/ministerial management—the very system that Deng, Zhao, and others are trying to dismantle.

Product demand in China outstrips supply to such an extent that the market has played only a minor role in encouraging managers to try new techniques, develop new products, and manage for excellence. "We can sell anything in China, easily," exclaimed one Chinese manager. When enterprises can easily sell whatever they produce, there is little reason to test ideas or adopt new technology. Most Chinese managers tend to view the adoption of new projects in a negative light. Indeed, innovation and experimentation with novel production techniques carry tangible risks for the manager. First, he may undergo political discrimination from party officials, as often befalls managers tagged as "too-progressive." Second, if a manager becomes a manager-hero, his employees will request additional salary and benefits which could cut into the manager's own income and/or access to benefits. And third, if his enterprise's income is enlarged, the administrative bureau presiding over the factory will gouge deeper into its earnings, reducing the amount of profit the factory may retain for its own use if harder times come in the future.[46] A prudent manager will not necessarily adopt a new project or managerial technique unless compelled by bureaucrats above him.

Conversely, there are numerous sound reasons why managers should not adopt a new project or act to change current management practice. For example, implementing a new project can cause production breakdowns, leading to losses that endanger the life of the factory, and for which the manager will be seen as culpable. This helps to explain why most managers would rather delay implementing specific plans until another enterprise has been successful with a similar project. By delaying the adoption of a new project until the same project is successful elsewhere, the manager can be sure that state authorities will eventually implement such a plan in his factory whether he has requested it or not. Most Chinese managers are conditioned to wait for bureaucrats to carry out projects rather than pursue them unilaterally as a means to increase output or efficiency. Other managers resist innovations simply because they believe that politically motivated decisions made at a higher level will adversely affect the outcome of the effort. For example, if an enterprise begins to produce exportable goods, additional agencies will want a piece of the action and the factory will incur increased interference from outside.

Moreover, there currently exists little reason for a manager to work to increase his enterprise's output since output improvements do not necessarily bring him rewards in either higher salary or job mobility. It does not seem plausible that in a system of profit-loss responsibility, manager incentives can be qualitatively increased without pay incentives. Yet, in January 1987, fourteen of ninety textile factory managers attending a citywide conference in Beijing threatened to resign, mainly because of low salary.[47] Without pay-performance linkage, managers will continue to experience low expectations, passivity, and indifference. They will continue to operate in a mode of seeking "hidden" benefits, pursuing their own interests in the face of the above mentioned constraints. They do this by maximizing resources within the enterprise over which they, rather than external bureaucrats, maintain control.[48] In the end, managers spend much of their creative energies on avoiding system-approved methods for increasing output efficiency so they can concentrate on broadening the personal benefits they can obtain in kind, including preferential allocation of housing, better access to scarce (or rationed) consumer goods, and better living conditions.[49] Managers may even reduce state quota demands on their factory by purposely underestimating its production capabilities in annual production reports. In that way they gain additional leisure time to spend bartering (via guanxi) for goods that the enterprise may need, but cannot procure through normal channels.[50]

All of these behavior modes do not imply that Chinese management is somehow inappropriate given the Chinese industrial system. In fact, Chinese managers should be congratulated for making their system work in China for the past four decades. When exception is made for the fact that managers have dealt with woefully insufficient infrastructural support and chronic unpredictability of supply sources since the establishment of the People's Republic, the country's peculiar managerial system suddenly appears to be a logical response to unique conditions.

To Whom Does the Manager Answer?

The contract responsibility system has created another dilemma for managers: Should their loyalties remain in the interest of the state, or with making a profit for their factory? The question has spurred a political debate, managers falling into a widening gray area between state and enterprise priorities. At present, managers are being asked to set their loyalties with both the state and the enterprise, a position perhaps as untenable as the tension between the manager and the party.

To maintain his position, the manager needs the explicit approval of both state agencies and workers' congresses. Some Chinese leaders claim that the interests of the state should reign over those for profit making, but enterprise workers may not agree since their bonuses are now tied directly to increasing the production output of their enterprise. That is, managerial success in profit making bears directly on the bonuses workers receive.[51] This has the effect of creating an artificial tension that need not exist. This tension is most visible in the realm of manager mobility.

Manager Appointment and Promotion. The appointment of managers was once an area exclusively assigned to the state through the local economic commissions at the municipal and provincial levels. Managerial appointments were made from among the workers who were both politically sound (i.e., red) and, secondarily, technically competent (i.e., expert). Their promotion involved recommendation and discussion among workers, managers, and Communist Party committee members.[52] Today the appointment of managers depends more on a balance of both "redness" and "expertness," yet it is clear that the latter is now much more critical than the former. The entire system has moved toward examination and merit as a basis for achieving management positions. Although most managers are still appointed by local economic commissions, the State Council has decreed recently that managers must come up for election every five years. And it is the task of local workers' congresses to decide, through elections, whether managers should be reinstated. Herein lies the tension. Bemused by inconsistent policies imposed from the outside, many workers have become disillusioned with their directors and have voted against them in director elections. No clear-cut regulations exist to deal with the worker-manager dichotomy. Factory directors are hamstrung. They promise workers high bonuses only to discover that red tape at a higher bureaucratic level reduces the factory's income. Bonuses fail to materialize and workers blame the director, putting him in jeopardy at the next director election.

Full financial responsibility for enterprises has placed workers and managers in a new relationship. In the old days, Soviet one-man leadership, wherein the factory director answered to a government body rather than the party, had been implemented. The system gave prominence to the factory director, who could then work up the ranks to a position of sole decision maker. By 1956, the system was rejected and the party divided powers among management cadres. The rationale was that leadership by one individual was incongruent with Maoist egalitarian ideology. The new emphasis on democracy in Chinese management was designed to keep management from exploiting or abusing the rights of workers.[53]

The change started a tradition of worker influence in the factory through various labor organization bodies such as the workers' and staff congresses, labor unions, and the party within the enterprise. The sharing of control over the administration of such things as production plans, annual budgets, and labor management, while beneficial to workers in terms of seeing that their wages are fair and the workplace is safe, may now be one reason market-driven decision making is today so difficult for the enterprise manager. The advent of new forms of management appointment has changed the perception of the role and qualifications of factory managers. Educational systems have been employed in a system of manager certification. Factory managers are now being asked to pass national exams before being installed as top managers, even though choosing managers via examination runs against the long-held belief among veteran managers in China that managerial experience should be valued more than formal business-oriented education. This may be changing, however, as the management certification policy takes hold. Managers are being motivated to seek more training and increase their skill levels. Younger, well-educated managers are getting top positions. These new managers are introducing more scientific management practices in greater numbers of enterprises. Potential managers are appraised increasingly in terms of technical competence and leadership abilities. It would not be premature to suggest that a professional managerial class is emerging in the People's Republic.

In summary, the manager cannot satisfy everyone in the system as it now exists. As profits rise with improvements in the enterprise, so do the taxation requirements of local governments. Workers get disgruntled when bonuses are canceled because of government skimming of enterprise profits. Furthermore, managers are now involved in the capitalization of the enterprise through contact with equity holders, foreign joint venture partners, and capital sources.[54] Some believe stock issues could improve the efficiency of enterprises, forcing managers to answer to shareholders. Stock-trading companies will not list poorly managed enterprises because the banks' reputations will be put at stake. This creates an incentive for better factory management and fiscal responsibility.[55]

Some feel that the manager-ownership relationship must be revamped in order to tie manager incentive to factory performance. Factory directors tend not to view themselves at present as owners of the enterprise that they administer, seeing themselves instead as representatives of either the state or the workers, or both. Because of this attitude, directors, managers, and workers tend to seek short-term gains for personal benefit, even to the point of compromising the long-term needs and interests of the overall enterprise.[56]

Some leading reform-minded thinkers suggest a mixed system of ownership in state enterprises which could promote individual ownership and incentive to upgrade enterprise performance. Professor Li Ying-ling of Beijing University is convinced that the correct solution is to move toward a stock ownership system with the following characteristics:

1. Government administration would be separated from enterprise management by introducing a stock ownership system;
2. Vertical relationships would be circumvented through the stock ownership system;
3. Individual initiative could be enhanced by offering individual ownership;
4. There would be higher enterprise initiative motivated by stock ownership, and

5. The reform of ownership would become a priority over the re-form of prices.[57] Stock ownership would consist of three cate-gories of stocks: state-owned, enterprise-owned, and individual-owned.

CONTRADICTIONS IN THE RESPONSIBILITY SYSTEM

The responsibility system seems to place an unfair burden on manag-ers as representative leaders of enterprises, when in fact they can hardly be said to wield the authority to truly lead their enterprise. For this reason, the notion of judging managers in terms of output has an arbitrary and highly biased tone. The absence of price-controlled allo-cation of supplies and labor makes any system of measuring the per-formance of enterprises conditional, especially when one considers that profit making is manipulated by state-controlled pricing and sub-ject to fluctuation in the supply of goods. If you judge managers and factory directors in terms of profit performance criteria, without tak-ing into account conditions over which they have no control, final eval-uation of managers will be skewed. As Easson states, "The new respon-sibility system has been imposed upon an economy where there are efficiently operated firms which cannot hope to make a profit and inef-ficient ones which have no difficulty in doing so."[58] That is, some will receive supplies when others will not, some are close to transportation facilities and other services while others are not, and so on.

The most glaring contradictions of the system are embodied in the Enterprise Bankruptcy Law of the People's Republic of China, which was issued in December 1986 to punish inefficient enterprises in a setting of systemic inequalities. By ratifying a bankruptcy statute, the Chinese are attempting, as they have numerous times in the past, to create incentives for workers and managers to revitalize the enterprises in which they work. After raucous debate as to the law's application to collectives, private enterprises, Sino-foreign joint ventures, and wholly foreign-owned enterprises, the law—in its final form—only applies to state-owned enterprises. The law outlines the conditions under which an enterprise can be declared officially bankrupt.[59] Debate over earlier versions of the law showed that many decision makers felt strongly that it was simply too early to punish enterprises that fail to perform against a profit criterion without consideration of the manifold negative influences that impinge upon the profit-making capability of underprivileged enterprises. Indeed, the reasons cited in forcing the first enterprise bankruptcy (of Shen Yang Welding Equipment Factory) included: a lack of skills among workers, large numbers of pensioners to support, frequent changes in management, corruption, and high taxes—not all of which can be blamed directly on the enterprise or its director.[60] Certainly, the danwei labor system and outside bureaucratic meddling play key roles in factory efficiency and inefficiency.

The greatest hope for resolving some of the inherent contradictions in the Chinese manager's situation is through alternative managerial role-structuring based on the application of various models or the evolution of new models for the new Chinese managers.

Management Training: Conflicting Signals from the Models Available

Today, too few Chinese are sufficiently endowed with the tools to implement a new system of management based on sophisticated market forecasting, financial analysis, and personnel management systems. Despite increased training and exposure to Western management systems, few Chinese managers actually possess the experience or education to fully grasp and rapidly implement managerial techniques based on the concepts of profitability and accountability—concepts the vast majority of these managers must better understand.

With few exceptions, management training efforts launched in China so far have largely ignored economic management in order to concentrate on technical management. The result is a scarcity of desperately needed enterprise strategists, economic analysts and professional accountants. For instance, in Shanghai, where technical expertise is relatively high, there are only six high-level accountants and two experts in economic planning and marketing.[61]

The problem of deficient management skills in the People's Republic has a dual origin. First, during the 1950s senior management positions were filled by cadres with political and military experience rather than industrial and marketing experience. Second, many traditional managers were replaced by managers with much less experience during the Cultural Revolution.[62] In addition to their technical illiteracy, many of these appointees not only lacked training but also exhibited little initiative to improve their management skills. Educational levels among managers were low as well, a problem originating with the closure of educational institutions and the persecution of intellectuals during the Cultural Revolution.[63] Chan's research led her to conclude that "less than one half of the managing cadres in China had finished their senior middle-school education."[64] In fact, most enterprises employ chief engineers only. A mere 20 percent have chief accountants; and only 10 percent have economic planning and marketing specialists.[65]

Intense demand for skilled managers in the People's Republic sparked a decisive effort to promote training of managers under an array of training programs. A growing number of Chinese managers are being exposed to Western management practices through a number of different transfer processes.[66] Government organizations, such as the China Enterprise Management Association (CEMA), have formed management education programs. Enterprises have set up educational facilities. Executive training programs and conferences have been conducted. The ideological and political content of all these programs have been toned down gradually. The whole field was slowed by a phobia associated with communicating with foreigners and adopting techniques employed in capitalist countries. Foreign management techniques were first disseminated via restricted professional publications that were circulated among middle- and upper-level cadres.

By 1978, management research associations had been formed for the purpose of transferring foreign managerial techniques. Professional societies were promoting the technical application of management techniques in specific sectors since 1979.[67] CEMA, which was formed in 1979 by the State Economic Commission to promote and diffuse modern management techniques and study questions of domestic and foreign management, is indicative of the institutionalization of professional management training. The organization sponsors workshops and lecture series and publishes a journal containing relevant Western articles on the subject of modern management practice. It is represented in twenty-nine provinces, municipalities, and autonomous regions. The Chinese have also encouraged the growth of Western management training centers throughout the country, sponsored by various developed countries including Japan, the United States, and the European Economic Community (EEC) countries. These collaborative training centers are designed to disseminate Western management know-how through the training of Chinese trainers.

Management Programs Under Way in the People's Republic

▶ The Canadian International Development Agency—a Canadian effort in Chengdu, Sichuan, involving $15 million investment in management education.

▶ The Corporate Management Center in Tianjin established by the Japanese International Cooperation Agency and co-sponsored with CEMA. The program includes the training of management teachers.

▶ The U.S.-China Management Training Center in Dalian established with funding from the U.S. Department of Commerce and the State Economic Commission. (One of the center's most auspicious graduates is Wang Zhaoguo, who has changed position as manager of one of China's largest automobile manufacturing facilities to membership in the Central Committee of the CCP.)

▶ The EEC's Beijing Business Administration Center, offering an M.B.A. program founded with $3 million in investment.

▶ Various international organizations include the United Nations Development Program of the World Bank, which conducts management training.

▶ The Sister Cities of San Francisco and Shanghai have initiated training programs.

▶ Various business symposiums, including one that involves the Xerox Foundation which is currently underwriting a $225,000, three-year lecture series sponsored by Unison International Corporation (U.S.) and CEMA.[68]

Chinese leaders hope this multifaceted management training effort will be sufficiently coordinated to avoid the conflicts that result from a lack of guidance and coordination in the adoption of diverse, and contradictory, foreign management models. The Chinese intend to blend foreign techniques with the distinct qualities of Chinese traditional management style. The aim is to borrow and adapt foreign models, and formulate a homespun management style, albeit one representing an amalgamation of techniques taken from many sources.[69] However, the approach implies that there will be compatibility problems among the diverse management techniques being emulated. At present, no one knows exactly where the management training road is leading in the People's Republic, but all the foreign nations participating realize that the adoption of their country's management systems in China will enhance their marketing position there.

The Role Multinationals Can Play. Managers are also being trained abroad in Western educational institutions as well as by foreign firms that have set up factories in China. Training of Chinese managers has become an essential part of most Sino-foreign joint venture agreements. Teaching management techniques through joint ventures is a great opportunity to enhance one's corporate image in China. Firms that offer the Chinese help in these areas will find themselves attractive as business partners in the People's Republic. Because the Japanese have been slow to offer this form of assistance, U.S. firms may find it advantageous to pursue this direction.

Management training (as opposed to worker training) can be a cost-effective way to sweeten a deal. A training package should include information systems, new management techniques, market research, and performance evaluation, among others. The Chinese are receptive to trade-offs in exchange for management know-how. New demands in terms of accounting, design, competition, etc., combined with political scrutiny from outside in many directions cause manager anxiety, burnout, and possibly failure. The foreign partner can offer the Chinese manager assistance outside their contract in areas of accounting, market forecasting, and organizational planning.[70] Informal training of this sort makes middle-level people look good to their superiors, and forms strong personal relationships for the future. Should the foreign firm place a monetary value on this contribution? Before offering such packages, delineate exactly what should be given away as a sweetener and what should be part of the total contribution to the venture.

Chinese managers must confront a new array of responsibilities, anxieties, and fears. Their reaction to their current predicament directly affects their willingness, and capability, to carry out the management tasks according to the guidelines proposed by foreign business partners. The ranks of good managers in the People's Republic are certainly expanding, yet foreign firms will still have problems finding the ones who have the training, clout, and initiative to break the parasitic relationship between the factory and local government and are willing to work to build independent links between their factory and its foreign business partner.

Operating a Venture in China

Meeting the demands of manufacturing operations in China is no less difficult for the Sino-foreign joint venture, which wields less clout and possesses less experience resolving issues in China, than it is for an indigenous enterprise. Even so, many foreign managers begin the task of managing a joint venture with little appreciation of the inherent problems faced by Chinese enterprises. Even after arriving at their factory in China, many foreign managers entertain the false notion that the profound encumbrances to effective management in China won't affect their company's China venture since it is a foreign-invested enterprise (FIE). They find solace in thinking that FIEs in the People's Republic receive certain privileges that will safeguard them from the systemic operational impediments in China. Unfortunately, the People's Republic does not bestow special treatment upon the Sino-foreign venture, or its foreign manager—

not on a business level or a cultural one. Like the Chinese factory director, the foreign manager must surmount the problems of task redundancy, worker laziness, and overlapping leadership while wrangling with a vast array of central and local bureaucratic entities. All fledgling China ventures inherit the problems characteristic of Chinese enterprise. FIEs do not, and cannot, exist in a vacuum in the People's Republic, free of the constraints and hardships experienced by the Chinese factory.

To grow and prosper in the People's Republic, an FIE must be constantly on the alert to avoid crisis. The manifold problems and dilemmas that impinge on FIEs can be best managed if a foreign company can consolidate leadership within its China venture, and gain the support of administrative entities affecting the venture externally. Effective joint management in the People's Republic requires team work and communication between partners as well as a system of planning and production geared to avoiding mishap. To this end, a hybrid management model meets the disparate needs of foreigners and Chinese alike. The foreign company must dovetail its objectives as a free enterprise with one in a state-controlled, bureaucratized socialist system—no small feat for foreign managerial personnel.

JOINT VENTURE MANAGEMENT: SYNTHESIZING OBJECTIVES

Appropriate management systems build on shared strengths. Joint venture management cannot be founded on Western management concepts or corporate strategy right at the outset. The Chinese factory will be unprepared to break with standard management methods and initiate foreign techniques, at least until well after the imported technology has been transferred. The Chinese also follow a different set of priorities. For example, the Chinese partner in a joint venture typically intends to create economies of scale rather than growth. The Chinese partner is prone to want a price reduction of joint venture products as profits accumulate, while the American side usually desires to expand the factory by reinvesting the profit. In trying to market products manufactured by a joint venture, the foreign partner may find it difficult to convince the Chinese partner that selling on export markets necessitates competitive pricing and superior quality.

Though the differing objectives of each partner are not always inherently in conflict, they can lead to contradictory expectations and operating procedures. The table on page 250 presents an overview of divergent priorities within a China venture that the foreign manager can expect to encounter. If these differences are not fully identified and contained by the foreign partner, and jointly by both parties, they may become the seeds of discontent within the factory and the administrative structure surrounding it, and might lead to a falling out in the future. Obviously, firms are well advised to begin discussions with their Chinese counterparts regarding all of these points early in contract negotiations.

The key to success seems to be in the creation of a management structure that promotes integration of operational systems as well as the cultural characteristics of Chinese and Western enterprise.[1] Hewlett-Packard has transferred Western-style management from the shop floor up. A tour of its joint venture in Beijing begins with a typically Western reception room, open-bay work areas, dust-free electronic testing rooms, and even a Western-style restroom. Every department has a deputy manager in charge of operations. Workers are managed by American expatriates and Chinese managers who work as a team, says venture manager John So. On the other hand, the factory maintains a low profile and fosters good relations with its adjacent Chinese neighborhood. The factory is considered as much Chinese as it is American.

Augmenting Venture Autonomy

Although the various authorities that assume approval control over joint ventures will vary, they typically include: the local partner factory, the larger corporation of which the factory is a part, the provincial bureau in the related industry, the municipal import/export office, MOFERT, and, depending on the size and type of project, certain top government authorities in Beijing. Consolidating leadership within the venture begins when the venture conceives its bylaws and initiates a mode of management organization.

The Management Charter.   Organizing the management structure of a joint venture begins with a power struggle over the venture's board of directors. Joint venture partners must write their own articles of association, which vary according to the complexity of the

Disparate Priorities in Joint Venture Management

U.S. side	Chinese side
desires clear-cut timetable	desires loose schedule
reduce work force	employ more workers
reduce number of middle managers	maintain number of middle managers
set up team/task force management	retain cadre management system/ managers are often replaced unexpectedly
initiate pay raises based on performance	pay raise for all workers and increased bonuses
plans to fulfill contract and expects Chinese to do same	wants to renegotiate agreement when project becomes constricting
keep technology hidden	share new technology
emphasis on constant interaction between managers and directors	desires single point of contact between foreign partner & China plant director
increase domestic sales in China	distribute production overseas to earn foreign exchange
quality control assurance	rapid utilization of local sources
pro forma profit and loss to indicate real costs to foreign partner	expects ongoing "favors" from foreign side in the form of training, technology, etc.

SOURCE: Based on interviews with U.S. corporate managers in China and a seminar conducted by Andrew Chu of Cummins Engine Company at I.B.E.A.R.'s China Program, University of Southern California; May, 1986.

venture and the nationality of the foreign partner. The board establishes the organizational structure of the venture, sets up its departments, appoints a general manager and deputy managers, selects a chief engineer, accountants and auditors, and stipulates their responsibilities and the extent of their authority. The board governs annual expenditure, distribution of profit, formulates production plans, and monitors all significant operational activities. Its members stay apprised of Chinese regulations affecting the venture, monitor labor and welfare contracts, as well as initiate financial and production strategies for the long term. Typically, boards consist of eight members, four foreigners and four Chinese. Operational decisions are usually carried out by two managers—one foreign and one Chinese—under the auspices of the board. In one survey in the Shenzhen SEZ, however, 70 percent of the thirty-four joint ventures tested (twenty-four from Hong Kong/Macao) were governed by boards consisting of four to seven members.[2] Joint venture boards do not necessarily convene often. Fujian-Hitachi's board, for instance, only meets once a year.[3]

Equity share governs each partner's degree of influence, although the chairman, as noted above, must be Chinese. Hewlett-Packard's joint venture board represents an unbiased leadership, consisting of four members from each side.[4] Where more than two partners are involved, the structure of the board grows more complex. Beatrice Foods' joint venture in Guangzhou is run by an eight-member board composed of one representative from CITIC, three from Guangzhou Foodstuffs, and four from Beatrice. The chairman is Chinese and the vice chairman is American. Beatrice chose the venture's general manager and the Chinese chose the deputy general manager.[5]

Compared to corporate boards of the West, joint venture boards in China appear sluggish in decision making and unresponsive to market mechanisms. Foreign firms can enhance their influence on the joint venture board by delineating in articles of the original contract exactly how the board will govern itself. Early on, joint venture partners must decide how board decisions are to be made, and how voting will be structured. Clear governing rules can help to prevent the Chinese board members from being influenced by organizations with which they are affiliated. External government agencies can wield direct influence over the joint venture by changing Chinese board members without notice. The Chinese board members, as John Henley has noted, "wear many 'hats' and . . . in many instances, they merely serve as figureheads. Some are retired senior cadres with no business experience. Their new 'jobs' are merely rewards for their past service to the state."[6] Second, board voting procedures can be varied according to the type and importance of the decision; that is, one decision may require a consensus, another a majority, while an extremely crucial one might require unanimity. As Chinese corporate law does not treat board voting precisely, U.S. venture managers should give careful consideration to this ongoing aspect of venture management.[7]

The figure on page 253 illustrates the confounding nature of government-enterprise alliances that can ensnarl a Sino-foreign joint venture. Both the party and the workers' union at the national level have a command relationship with the local trade union that supplies workers to the joint venture; thus, central-level functionaries can influence the joint venture from afar. The redundant linkages that exist between the local bureau/industrial corporation and the joint venture's board, general manager, and trade union greatly restrict joint venture autonomy. The position of general manager at a Sino-foreign joint venture is hardly enviable. The board of directors makes demands on the manager that often contradict requests made of him by the union (under the aegis of the party) as well as the local bureau (under the aegis of the state ministry).

ORGANIZING CHINESE WORKERS AND MANAGERS

The Chinese often view a new China venture as an opportunity to employ workers and managers from the production unit associated with the Chinese partner company. Because the Chinese will be responsible for hiring workers and managers at all but the highest levels of joint venture management, the country's archaic system of management tends to get transferred into joint ventures, much to the distress of the foreign partner. Too many middle-level administrators populate the joint venture, which results in productivity slowdowns. In theory, the middle managers can be fired, but that rarely happens. Otis Elevator's Tianjin joint venture started with a ratio of 70 percent administrative employees to only 30 percent workers. Smith-Kline succeeded in reducing the number of administrators in its joint venture to 30 percent by agreeing to export 30–35 percent of their production.[8] Such tradeoffs may be necessary in order to shave off redundant layers of middle management that can hamper efforts to fortify a managerial system even remotely resembling what the foreign manager may be conditioned to expect from his experience in other Asian settings. Once entrenched, the old system in which many unqualified managers get hired proves hard to dissolve. Foreign firms can push to get an expatriate placed in the position of personnel manager, but this issue should be agreed upon during negotiations. The benefit is that a foreign personnel manager, unlike a Chinese manager, hires objectively rather than out of loyalty to old friends, family members, and past co-workers.[9]

Furthermore, foreign managers have to contend with the fact that a Chinese worker's loyalty will continue to flow toward his, or her, danwei even after becoming a worker at an FIE. Under the auspices of various party, union, and welfare entities associated with the danwei

The Organizational Bureaucracy Surrounding a Sino-Foreign Joint Venture

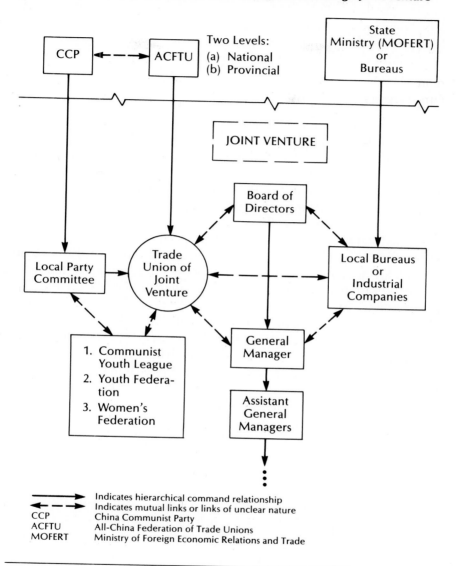

SOURCE: John S. Henley and Nyaw Mee-kau, "The System of Management and Performance of Joint Ventures in China: Some Evidence from Shenzhen Special Economic Zone" in *Joint Ventures and Industrial Change in China*, edited by Nigel Campbell and John S. Henley (London: JAI Press, 1988), by permission.

system, a worker's loyalty tends to flow out of the venture toward the danwei, driving a wedge between a joint venture's management and its labor force. As a foreign counterpart, attempts must be made to align the interests of the danwei with those of the venture in order to fortify the venture's authority over its human resources.

Hiring and Firing

Almost all joint ventures suffer from overstaffing. Many workers are holdovers from the previous Chinese enterprise. These residual workers create an obvious conflict because the foreign partner often brings substantial amounts of new technology into the venture that requires a smaller, more skilled work force. What the foreign partner finds, though, is a large staff of workers unfamiliar with modern technology-based manufacturing.

The foreign manager should not act on his first inclination, however, which is usually to slash the size of the work force. The Chinese do not readily accept the value of scaling down the number of laborers. Since the workers in a joint venture typically are members of the Chinese partner's unit, the Chinese partner will act as the labor contractor. Decisions regarding worker incentives, hiring and firing, and discipline will be handled by the relevant labor union and the local chapter of the CCP. Overstaffing can be ameliorated, but the task will require worker relocation to other units, rather than firing. Increasingly, U.S. joint venture partners have gained some control over labor contracting by successfully bringing the process inside the joint venture, and out of the hands of Chinese labor agencies.

Yet worker transfer problems that result from unit ownership are real. In Tianjin, an Australian joint venture partner offered twenty specialized jobs to 800 applicants over an eight-month period, but was able to hire only two workers who could secure transfers from their home units.[10] China's foreign enterprise labor organization, FESCO, is responsible for procuring workers for FIEs. Unfortunately, FESCO sets wages unrealistically high and skims off most of the worker's wages into the state treasury, an obvious form of disguised taxation according to many foreign representatives.[11] Foreign companies usually have to accept the workers offered and often in more numbers than they need.[12] This proves costly to foreign partners because it threatens the venture financially, while depressing productivity and quality. Ironically, FESCO cannot meet the demand for employees, which has created a long waiting list.[13] As a FESCO member, a Chinese employee can be transferred by FESCO from a foreign firm at any time.[14] This increases the risk of losing employees after paying for their training and sharing with them sensitive technology. It is also well known that FESCO politically screens workers and trains them to report on their foreign managers.[15]

A growing number of cases exist, however, where foreign firms have reduced overstaffing and have secured scarce competent workers. Foxboro, for instance, halved its original labor force by transferring workers to another enterprise under the jurisdiction of its Chinese partner.[16] Gillette reduced its joint venture work force to sixty from 240 employees, and now requires new workers to pass exams.[17] Hewlett-Packard broke new ground in China by completely sidestepping FESCO. Hewlett-Packard wields total control of its workers and has no labor deal with either FESCO or the government. The Hewlett-Packard joint venture maintains its own salary structure and has tied wages to performance, increasing worker incentives. Taking advantage of close relations with its official government partner, Hewlett-Packard has acquired the right to an allotment of Chinese graduates from various service schools, filling slots on a yearly basis. By conducting recruitment seminars at such schools, the firm attracts top-quality applicants. According to one of the firm's managers, the reasons for this success are "good management techniques that the Chinese want to assimilate and high-level interfacing with Chinese officials who can get the seemingly impossible approved."[18]

Many U.S. firms gain some control over hiring and firing in the initial phase of start-up through an examination selection process that includes intelligence, psychological, and manual dexterity testing. For example, instead of relocating welders, William A. Fischer found that Global Multinational (fictitious name) trained selected workers for four months and then conducted examinations of trainees for knowledge and skill levels. Those workers who passed the exams became welders in the construction of their new factory.[19]

The 3M Company found another solution. It has actually created its own danwei, which is managed by both the U.S. firm and local Chinese labor and welfare agencies. From this foreign production unit, new workers can be hired as needed, and relocated smoothly. This novel idea has created good relations and goodwill on both sides.

Training Workers.   Success in almost all manufacturing joint ventures hinges on the training of Chinese workers and engineers. The problems and inefficiencies many firms experience in training Chinese relate directly to improvident contracting. For example, some firms find that the Chinese transfer trainees to other enterprises, or substitute trainees halfway through the training program, in an attempt to maximize the number of trained workers. Yet the Chinese contradict this policy by often appointing trainees for political reasons, or because of their guanxi connections, rather than out of need to be trained for a certain job.[20] In addition, the Chinese lessen the return on their investment in training workers by not sending those with good English skills.[21] The author interviewed one U.S. oil company executive whose complaint was that they were obligated in contract to train Chinese oil-rig operators, but have no control over selecting candidates for training. Most of the trainees are unqualified and/or do not understand English well enough to absorb the training. Obviously, training through interpreters lengthens programs substantially and reduces their effectiveness. Fortunately, incisive contracting avoids these problems by stipulating exact prerequisites for trainees.[22] These stipulations demand that trainees agree to work for the joint venture for a specified period of time and fulfill a predetermined role. Many firms now leverage for worker contracts of five or more years to ensure the Chinese partner will keep workers at the joint venture after being trained.

It should come as no surprise that the training system itself encourages dissatisfaction in workers. For one thing, trainees are not informed completely about their joint venture agreements. In one case, a U.S. firm was able to get a five-year contract for trainees after they had trained them in the United States in factory management operations for one month. Interviews suggest that the trainees were not altogether satisfied with their employment situation. They were understandably upset because they had not themselves chosen to be trained overseas. They were also disgruntled and disillusioned that they had been not only committed to work for the joint venture for five years, but were to be relocated in China without any say on their part. These trained workers also thought it unfair that although the U.S. firm was paying $4,000 per year to the Chinese side for each of their salaries, they themselves were being paid by the Chinese side only 4,000 yuan as salary. With the difference in exchange rates, the workers concluded that 2.7 yuan on the dollar was being skimmed off and paid to local official agencies. (In this case, the agency was not FESCO because the joint venture was located in a SEZ where FESCO has less control.) If that were not enough, the joint venture could fire them at any time during the five-year contract.[23] It remains to be seen whether this exploitative contract, sanctioned by the Chinese side and demanded by the U.S. side, will dampen the morale of these workers to work hard for the China venture in the future.

Measuring and Rewarding Worker Performance.

As we have seen in the indigenous Chinese factory, the notion of measuring the individual production performance of workers is misleading because of the variation in the quality of raw materials used, the unpredictability of transportation, distribution, and power supply.[24] Nonetheless, the effective joint venture manager must find methods of enhancing the performance and dependability of his work force. Foreign firms in the People's Republic utilize various forms of Western motivational techniques in their China ventures, including systematic evaluation of worker performance, promotions, and wage increases tied to productivity. However, Chinese attitudes about foreigners tend to prevent the wholesale transfer of the foreign firm's managerial methods without considerable modification.[25] The extent to which foreign firms are able to guide incentive programs in their enterprises with the Chinese partner depends largely on government permission.

Setting Wages.

When a worker is moved into a joint venture, a firm must also transfer all of his or her previous benefits associated with the worker's past production unit. The expenses of offering Chinese-style worker benefits add up rapidly. The partners of a major hotel joint venture in Guangzhou pay the following in worker wages and benefits:

1. *Wages:* Including basic wages, living allowances, floating wages.
2. *Bonuses:* Based on worker performance; exact amount depends on seniority; distributed twice a year
3. *Diligence award:* 10 yuan per month
4. *Other allowances:* 5 yuan per month for an only child; 2.5 yuan a month for an infant.
5. *Social security fund:* Partner pays 25 percent of total payroll to the labor bureau to cover expenses arising from work-related injuries and deaths, unemployment, and retirement. People's Republic uses part of the fund to cover the administrative costs of the bureau.

6. *State subsidies:* The state requires enterprise to contribute 70 yuan per month to the finance department for every worker on its payroll which helps to defray state subsidies of rent, transportation, medical services, and food.
7. *Medical expenses:* The joint venture is responsible in full for the medical and hospitalization expenses of its workers.
8. *Retirement fund:* The retirement age is sixty for men, fifty for women. Retiring workers who have been with the company for at least fifteen years must be paid 75 percent of the wage they are collecting before retirement, plus food and rent subsidies.
9. *Accident compensation:* Partners pay the family of a worker who dies on the job thirty-six months of wages, and compensate workers who suffer work-related injuries as the law provides. Partners are also responsible for all medical expenses and must grant the injured worker paid leave and pay allowance to family members in difficulty.
10. *Food:* It is the venture's responsibility to provide meals or a meal allowance.[26]

Creating Worker Incentives Through Management

Taking a close look at the survey on page 259, one can surmise from the survey results that the Chinese worker: (a) is loyal to state directives; (b) values bonus increases (in general, rather than his alone); (c) identifies with Communism; and (d) is ambitious. Notice that being promoted rates well below raising bonuses and wages, as well as rating below bearing an honorable title. This implies that the Chinese worker, unlike his Western counterpart, differentiates between wage increase and promotion. Chinese workers pursue upward mobility, in the Western sense of getting to the top, less intensely than a Western worker. Notice also that ambition is not identified with being promoted or becoming famous.

In the Chinese worker's mind, ambition stands as an entity to be valued of itself. Less than a 2 percent pay differential exists between the highest and lowest paid workers in a factory. Individual incentives are not readily accepted by egalitarian workers. Chinese workers balk at the idea of nonconforming. But neither do they like getting paid poorly. A more effective approach might be to use pay raises in the initial

Chinese Worker Motivation and Dissatisfaction

What is important to a Chinese worker?
(in order of importance)

To Realize the Four Modernizations*

To Raise Bonuses and Wages

To Believe in Communism

To Have Ambition

To Have an Honorable Title

To Be a Famous Expert

To Be Promoted

To Have No Strong Beliefs

* National goals articulated in 1978 for "The Socialist Modernization of Agriculture, Industry, National Defense, and Science and Technology."

What "chills" Chinese workers' motivation?
(in order of importance)

Unhealthy Tendencies†

Low Wages

Housing Problems

Privileges of Cadres

Dull Life

Dissatisfaction with Job

Factional Strife

Problems with Children's Education

† Any thought or action by leaders (managers) deviating from or not supporting the current ruling ideology.

Source: Based on the 1980 study of 343 Chinese workers by Dr. Xu Liancang of the Chinese Academy of Sciences.[27]

stages of such an incentive program, then apply more novel techniques when appropriate.

Work groups should be encouraged to share responsibilities and divide labor among themselves. Fujian-Hitachi implemented a system of worker responsibility that starts at the top with the general manager and cascades down through every level of the company, to cadres and workers. The cadres were put in charge of defining worker duties, individual rights, and the penalties for making mistakes. (One such mistake resulted in the factory having to reconstruct 6,000 television sets.)[28]

Work groups should be rewarded for innovations and efficient productivity. Group tasks should be rotated so that each group begins to take on a more general knowledge of the workings of the joint venture. John Reeder writes that joint venture partners "should concentrate on the motivation of work groups and particularly on creating an organization that is highly respected by both employees and the community at large—in short, an organization capable of inspiring loyalty. . . . an organization which helps its employees to better their lives and the lives of those they love and which promises to do so on a continuing basis." Reeder suggests a number of approaches to this end, including setting up a lounge in the joint venture factory, constructing a recreation room, providing entertainment, sponsoring classes, providing a library, and installing shower and bath facilities on the premises. Safety, cleanliness, and good food should also be part of the joint venture regimen. [29]

Motivating Chinese Managers to Lead

Most Chinese managers simply lack the extensive managerial skills necessary to effect significant organizational changes in a joint venture. For years Chinese managers spent their time finding ways of satisfying politically motivated party officials and the local welfare interests of their enterprises, instead of concentrating their energies on implementing modern management techniques in their factories to upgrade production performance. One U.S. manager in Shanghai described Chinese managers as accepting of new ways of management in principle, but that they have difficulty putting them into practice. Chinese managers may be able to define a problem, yet the reasons for failure are neither accepted nor explored. They avoid organized meetings in

Incentive Guidelines

▶ Encourage workers not only to believe in the current enterprise reforms, but to apply them in the joint venture and celebrate their implementation.

▶ Motivate employees to work hard for raises in bonuses and wages, but be cautious not to single out individuals from the group for exceedingly high or low rewards. Moreover, do not isolate workers, but consolidate them in task groups.

▶ Link progress with political ideology. Chinese value the utilitarian, as well as personal, aspects of Chinese politics.

▶ Allow workers to be ambitious without monetary reward or promotion. Reward them with recognition for being ambitious workers. Offer upward mobility to workers by training them as versatile managers, teaching them skills that will further their career outside the joint venture.[30]

▶ Ensure worker satisfaction by helping with housing and welfare.

▶ Maintain a worker's titular role longer than for a worker in the West. Western workers value being promoted into new positions of authority; Chinese workers don't value changing their working role as much as possessing an honorable title.

▶ Give the factory interior and exterior a new look. Clean up working environments, add lighting, renovate workshops, showrooms, etc.

▶ Initiate a reward system to encourage workers to voice criticisms and make suggestions.

▶ Promote a factory philosophy based on the Western axiom: Time Is Money.

▶ Create training programs for young workers based on breaking old habits.

which management problems or operation failures are discussed, because of the repercussions from superiors should they be held responsible. The U.S. manager went on to say: "[The Chinese] don't like to get into a meeting where they have to talk about problems. No one will commit to anything until the problem has been solved. That's been the toughest thing to try to change."[31]

Garreth Chang, president of McDonnell-Douglas China, Inc., admitted that the firm had underestimated the difficulty of implementing management improvements. He said: "You cannot turn a guy in a factory into a manager in a year or two. It takes experience and it's that kind of hands-on experience that we have on the American side that the Chinese lack."[32] Countering management incompetence, Fujian-Hitachi initiated a system of manager and cadre "checking," in which the general manager of the joint venture has the power to promote or dismiss management cadres below him. Twice a year, the company carries out checks on cadres and workers, assessing diligence, ability, achievements, work style, and discipline. Similarly, mid-level cadres carry out checks on ordinary management personnel and encourage, promote, or dismiss them. Appraisals are then rechecked for accuracy to prevent favoritism. The close monitoring of workers and managers has resulted in tight management control, worker loyalty to the joint venture, and increased production efficiency.[33]

Controlling Politics in the Venture

Since the CCP is powerful within the governmental planning entities that wield control over joint ventures, its influence is always felt through the Chinese joint venture managers and members of the ventures' boards. Foreign partners have few complaints concerning the party, yet acknowledge that party presence must be recognized.[34] A foreign manager can be certain that having the backing of local and central CCP officials will be an asset to the venture. This support may not be present at start-up and could require informal networking among factory cadres. As a general rule, firms should attempt to convince party members of the benefits that Sino-foreign joint ventures represent to China's modernization. Urge them to perceive the venture as the foreign side perceives it, as a production and profit-making center in which Chinese and foreigners can work together as equals. Party members are skeptical of foreign management of Chinese workers, but do not be thwarted from initiating a creative incentive system. Enlist

Chinese managers to the cause of generating the groundswell of necessary enthusiasm for management changes. During negotiations, consider whether your Chinese partner and factory manager will be tough enough to carry out plans that may conflict with CCP ideologues.

In some cases, the attractiveness of working with foreigners draws a manager closer to foreign interests than to the local interests. And getting close to foreign managers can be dangerous. A case in point is Parker-Hannifin's joint venture in Hubei, where two Chinese factory directors were dismissed for not keeping greater distance from their Western counterparts. The Hubei provincial bureau of the machine building industry dismissed the director and deputy director of the factory in April 1986 without first consulting the factory's board of directors. The foreign investment administration bureau (under MOFERT) intervened at the insistence of the foreign partner and reversed the decision. The two returned to their posts as director and deputy director of the Hubei-Park Hermetic Parts Factory, only after much publicity and controversy.[35]

Labor Unions.   As with the Chinese enterprise, the Chinese compel foreign joint venture partners to set up labor unions at their ventures. The participation of workers in the management of a joint venture is organized and channeled through the trade union of the joint venture. Labor unions and FESCO also play key roles in managing Chinese workers in a China venture. Labor unions do not play much of an adversarial role in promoting wage increases or worker safety. Under the auspices of the CCP, the unions school workers in the current political stance. They play a cooperative role throughout the enterprise management structure, monitoring benefits and supervising employee relations.[36]

Labor unions readily accept the adoption of foreign managerial techniques in Chinese enterprises and have made reasonable efforts to help workers adjust to them. Sometimes, however, a labor union can be a nuisance to the foreign partner by meddling in the hiring and firing of workers and in the process of implementing incentive programs that it believes infringe on the inalienable rights of Chinese workers. In one case, an obtrusive labor union gladly stepped aside when the foreign partner—C. P. Pokphand—set up an office in the factory exclusively for the trade union representatives. Pokphand gave the union an office under the condition that they stay out of the management affairs of the joint venture.[37] This rather prosaic solution appears to have sufficed.

Bridging the Communication Gulf

Management depends on the effective flow of applied information. Besides the obvious language barrier, a foreign firm must overcome the Chinese resistance to the systematic exchange of information between venture partners. The Chinese side may not only resist the exchange, but see it as a threat to their political well-being. Although foreign partners can ignore Chinese sentiment on this subject, going so far as to install a telex system and hiring an appropriate individual to coordinate communications, they should anticipate that translating documentation will be a time-consuming and costly task. One U.S. company overlooked this aspect of technology transfer in its implementation plan and encountered a one-year delay of start-up as a result of the immense number of translations required.[38] McDonnell-Douglas employs about 300 translators working full-time on document translation, and another 100 interpreters facilitating communication in the factory. The factory also is conducting English language training schools.[39]

Cummins Engines' personnel believe that many of the inefficiencies which they experience in the technology transfer process result directly from limited communication between partners. They feel that the information from the Chongqing Engine Plant is insufficient for making a proper evaluation of the Chinese product and the progress of the technology transfer procedure. The communication gap is widened because the Chongqing factory limits access by Cummins personnel to Chinese facilities and engineers. Consultations concerning equipment, testing, etc., take place in reception rooms removed from the shop floor or in the offices of Chinese executives. In addition, the Chinese partner was unwilling to pay the per-diem expenses to have an American expatriate resident in Chongqing in order to facilitate the technology transfer process after start-up.[40]

In spite of the technological obstacles to effective communication in China, the way to bridge the gap is to position your firm within the flow of information. The problem is that inside the Chinese enterprise, communication between factory managers and workers, and between workers themselves in the presence of managers, is virtually nil. But an effort can, and should, be made to get workers and managers talking to each other, and to their foreign counterparts. The amenability of the Chinese to the meaningful participation of Western managers in the information exchange process is often a function of the compatibility of personalities and the level of preparation of those Western managers prior to their relocation to the People's Republic. In order to cross the cultural and communication abyss, several U.S. companies have discovered profound advantages in using ethnic Chinese expatriates as mediators when possible, making sure they are equally trained as factory managers. Most firms interviewed in China employ ethnic Chinese to run their China offices and joint ventures in China. With Chinese background and language training, these expatriates can be more effective in dealing with China's socialist bureaucracy. There are some interesting variations of effectiveness, however, among ethnic Chinese from Hong Kong, Taiwan, Singapore, the United States, and the People's Republic itself. American companies should consider carefully the pros and cons of hiring a person from one of these Chinese ethnic groups. The following represents an overview of the benefits and drawbacks of each general ethnic nationality, in order of desirability to U.S. corporations seeking to employ expatriates for China duty.

Chinese from the People's Republic.
The best possible prospects for hiring China-based expatriates are Chinese from the People's Republic. Of course, few such candidates will be available to foreign corporations. Native Chinese often attend American business schools, their intention being to work for U.S. firms in the future rather than to return to China. If these potential employees lived in China during the Cultural Revolution, they will have a unique knowledge of how the Chinese behave and can offer an American firm desirable connections in China. They will also be able to readily access Chinese bureaucrats and end-users, because of their intimate understanding of Chinese business culture.

Chinese from Hong Kong.
Hong Kong Chinese offer connections in China through family relations. They also have an intimate knowledge of China and offer U.S. firms a communication bridge between themselves and their Chinese partners.

Chinese Americans.
These expatriates offer language abilities only. They have the same lack of knowledge of China that Anglo-Americans have. However, they may find it easier to penetrate the Chinese social fabric and management organization than would an Anglo-American.

Singapore Chinese.   Ethnic Chinese from Singapore may lack an appreciation and solid understanding of China's socialist organization. They may not want to accept that a foreigner, even one that is an ethnic Chinese, has to entreat the interests of Chinese government officials in order to have one's future requests fulfilled. Conditioned by their efficient government in Singapore, they might not agree with the well-established fact that you cannot fight China's bureaucratized system, only adapt to it.

Taiwan Chinese.   In terms of penetrating the social fabric of the Chinese business world, hiring someone Chinese from Taiwan may not always be a prudent decision for a U.S. firm. There could be negative implications for a U.S. firm if the Chinese government discovered that the expatriate was originally from Taiwan. In light of the mainland Chinese distrust of this expatriate, Chinese security would also keep a close eye on his or her movements. If the expatriate had relocated in Taiwan after China's liberation in 1949, the Chinese might even suspect he or she is a spy.

PREVENTATIVE MANAGEMENT FOR MANUFACTURING OPERATIONS

Foreign managers in China must attempt to transform an indigenous system of crisis management into one of preventative management. They must cope with daily operational problems such as power shortages and insufficient supplies, which force them to assume a posture of fighting against the current. Many problems can be avoided by considering the past experiences of other firms in China and developing strategy agendas for supply sourcing, quality control, modes of distribution, and repatriation of profits prior to start-up of operations.

Foreign firms should present a schedule by which the joint venture board can handle problems before they crop up and resolve them as a unified team within the venture. By creating a situation in which the board, managers, and departments in charge all collaborate in preventing mishap, rather than waiting for a disaster to occur, the venture will not only survive but enjoy greater likelihood for prosperity. The following sections deal with solutions, strategies, and formulas that may assist executives in preventing and resolving operational problems.

Sourcing Raw Materials and Components

Both sides of a joint venture benefit when raw materials and components can be sourced inside China because it helps the venture balance foreign exchange. By sourcing raw materials within China, foreign partners can circumvent the cost of purchasing, shipping, and tariffs associated with importing supplies, as well as avoid exorbitant customs duties. For example, one of AMC's problems in its joint venture, Beijing Jeep Corporation, has been a 60 percent tariff on its imported kits and components that siphons off the venture's foreign exchange. The Chinese encourage local sourcing by joint ventures and solely foreign-owned foreign enterprises because it usually entails the technological upgrading of local suppliers by the foreign partner, thus enhancing the export potential of the relevant manufacturing sector in the People's Republic. Investment often flows into peripheral, often depressed Chinese enterprises, making joint venture sourcing in China especially attractive to provincial decision makers. In light of China's foreign exchange shortage, MOFERT has intensified pressure on foreign joint ventures to source raw materials and parts locally, while admitting China-made products rarely meet the needs of joint venture enterprises in variety, quality, price, or delivery schedule.

Local content requirements represent an important aspect of China's modernization program. Regulations that pertain to local sourcing grow out of China's broader objective, which is to attract foreign partners willing to make long-term, more participatory business commitments. Article IX of the Joint Venture Law requires that joint ventures use Chinese sources of raw materials where available. New regulations concerning wholly owned foreign ventures go so far as to require that ventures using raw materials must consider Chinese sources before foreign sources.[41]

Many firms depend on the localization part of the offshore manufacturing equation to accumulate profit. In many cases, this objective is a central part of a firm's success in other parts of the world. In the People's Republic, however, the strategy has not been altogether workable. Joint venture agreements usually include contributions of building materials by the Chinese side, or at least an understanding that materials such as cement, steel, glass, etc., will be sourced in China. However, construction materials are often difficult to procure because of their constant overallocation, which has been a fact of doing business in China since its construction program intensified in the late

1970s. One may be able to buy a prototype of a specific component, but few can expect to procure a large number of components made in China on a consistent schedule of delivery. Many localization programs misjudged Chinese capabilities, and have been too optimistic in conception. The foreign firm often must upgrade components to foreign standards by injecting additional investment and equipment into supplying factories. Some foreign firms have gained significant leverage in negotiations by agreeing to increase their use of locally manufactured inputs only later to find the whole process of retooling Chinese enterprises a huge investment of time, energy, and money. Because prices are controlled, local suppliers lack incentive to direct inventory away from Chinese buyers and sell to foreign ventures or upgrade quality to international standards. Many firms interviewed claim that importing raw materials and components costs less in the long run than sourcing in China, even when high tariffs are added to the base price.

The traditional form of resource allocation management inside the indigenous Chinese enterprise often pollutes the sourcing streams of the joint venture. Chinese managers at the McDonnell-Douglas plant in Shanghai find it difficult to accept the prescheduling of resource needs to accomplish tasks, as their American partner urges, since they have had little exposure to the notion of planning ahead for what will be needed to accomplish various production goals.[42] Often, a lack of foreign exchange at a Chinese plant discourages preplanning of resource needs. As a result, most Chinese counterparts in joint ventures cannot order parts or kits from the foreign partner until a customer orders a product. Thus, many joint venture factories are constrained from establishing an inventory. One U.S.-based engine manufacturing company had assumed its Chinese joint venture partner would at least be able to acquire the foreign exchange to fulfill its contract. However, it discovered that its Chinese partner had to obtain approval for every allocation involving foreign exchange, even when purchases are prescribed in the contractual agreement.

Local content requirements vary from sector to sector. In most sectors, content requirements are open to negotiation; however, the trend is toward stricter, more regularized content requirements. Unless sufficient research and trial sourcing indicate otherwise, it is prudent to avoid basing the short-term economic viability of a joint venture on the prospect of local sourcing of components. The experience of many large, high-profile firms demonstrates the improvidence of a strategy aimed at upgrading Chinese suppliers so that they may produce usable components. First, required investment in time and money is substantial because new machinery, quality-controlled equipment, and the training of workers are needed. Second, such projects may be difficult to coordinate because they may be under a different bureaucratic jurisdiction than the joint venture. Third, once upgraded, the source supplying the factory will be less willing to sell production for Rmb if it can begin exporting to earn foreign exchange. Also, the local FTC will often raise the price of upgraded goods to match international prices, nullifying the purpose of localizing in the first place—to source components at lower cost. Successful joint venture contracts stipulate a cost-ceiling clause with Chinese suppliers, making it clear that if domestic prices cannot compete with international prices, the joint venture can choose to buy overseas.

The Chinese have pushed extremely hard for localization in the automotive sector. As of July 1986, Volkswagen's Santana assembly plant in Shanghai had carried out only two of 100 planned supplier upgrading projects since its joint venture inception. By the end of 1987, over 170 Chinese factories were producing some of the Santana's 4,200 parts. However, as the *Beijing Review* reported, these factories "have yet to reach the quality standards Volkswagen AG has specified."[43] In some cases, materials that were supposed to be allocated for the Volkswagen plant were simply diverted by relevant departments for other uses.[44] At one point, Volkswagen's deputy managing director, Martin Posth, was forced to return to Germany and ask Volkswagen's German-based suppliers to set up joint ventures in the People's Republic in order to supply the Santana plant.[45] Similarly, AMC has had to contend with an ongoing debate over the rate of localization in their joint manufacturing factory with Beijing Jeep.[46] Retooling the factory has been costly and slow. Only slightly more than 9 percent of the parts are currently produced in China, even though the joint venture's general manager, Don St. Pierre, believes that the figure will reach 90 percent by 1990.[47] The problems foreign automakers have in sourcing auto parts in China simply reflect the highly fragmented and dispersed nature of China's automotive industry (as described in Chapter 4).

Most sourcing difficulties in China stem from the country's antiquated supply system, which consists of a complex grid of interlocked and overlapping bureaucratic systems. When needed goods are made in another province, sourcing problems prove close to insurmountable. For instance, FTCs in Shanghai will refuse to sell export quality components to Beijing for Rmb. Procuring materials outside the "system" directly attached to a Chinese partner is usually frustrated by scarcity of supplies, inflated price, and delays in delivery. A top executive from Squibb Pharmaceutical scoured the country looking for clean sugar to be used as filler in drugs produced in the firm's joint venture. He found some, but was asked to buy sugar in fifty-ton lots, three times what the joint venture needed. He bargained the supplier down to fifteen tons, but since officials at the Chinese National Railway refused to ship a load smaller than fifty tons, Squibb had to accept the supplier's terms.[48] Sometimes, Chinese negotiators make contractual commitments on behalf of a Chinese corporation in a totally separate system under an industrial ministry, without knowing whether the corporation can actually fill the order.[49]

Foreign negotiators should seek protection against discrimination of the foreign partner to the benefit of local Chinese enterprises or other joint ventures in terms of price, availability, and quality of the supplies. If price increases and delivery interruptions do occur, sourcing arrangements should place equal burden on all joint venture partners. One should remember that raw materials are made more available to FIEs whose products are part of mandatory plans; relevant Chinese departments will take responsibility for supplying required materials to these joint ventures for production and local construction. Firms that produce products outside such plans must rely on regularized buying methods that are affected by unpredictable forces of domestic supply and demand.[50]

Simply getting specific allocations and obligations into a contract may not solve the problem, however. Chinese partners may not know any more about China's crazy quilt supply system than the foreign partner, especially beyond their local system. Sourcing plans should be followed by test buying of needed materials to ensure access, delivery, and quality. Typical of the Chinese supply system, Foxboro has had little problem sourcing sophisticated circuit boards, yet has had great difficulty obtaining tiny screws, aluminum, and cement, which it has had to borrow from a Chinese enterprise.[51] In a system not based on price, the foreign firm has to be more concerned with sending buyers into the field to foster vendor relations rather than simply looking for suppliers offering a low price.[52]

Quality Control in Manufacturing

As much as one-third of all goods produced in China are defective or do not conform to China's national industrial standards.[53] As previously discussed, most Chinese factories feature minimal quality-control schemes, and many have none at all. Sourcing materials of substandard quality typically leads to a chain of dilemmas during production that foil attempts to export the end product into competitive world markets. Problems with quality control in joint ventures usually stem from the Chinese partner's unwillingness or inability to step up quality control. Sometimes, the Chinese factory manager (fearing loss of face) does not admit openly to the foreign buyer that a certain part of the manufacturing process of a set of equipment is beyond the capabilities of the factory, or that quality specifications cannot be achieved. This results in subsequent breakdowns in the field. Also, one or more components will be manufactured under the auspices of a separate ministry, making it impossible for the contracted supplier factory to ensure the quality of the entire set of equipment. Simple products generally do better in this respect, such as toys, crafts, razors, textiles, hair products, O-ring seals, and simple components. Complex production projects have been seriously impaired by quality problems, in some cases resulting in failure to export any production at all. AMC's component quality problems led to the decision to import semi-knocked down Cherokee Jeep kits.

Quality problems with locally sourced components present the foreigner with a formidable obstacle. In 1981, Eastman Kodak set up a joint venture slide projector factory known as Greenfield No. 1 in Shanghai, China's most advanced electronic area, with the intention of sourcing many of the components. Quality levels could not be met, however, and virtually all components for the projectors had to be imported. (Bear in mind, the product was a slide projector, not an advanced electronic component.)

Fujian-Hitachi Co. signed their joint venture contract in 1981, agreeing that the television factory would use 50 percent domestically sourced parts within three years. By 1982, a Chinese publication claimed the company's use of domestic parts had climbed to one-third of parts used. However, in 1986, *The Nineties* reported the factory had actually been unable to maintain the quality of its production using Chinese parts, and had been importing all needed parts since start-up, even for domestic sales.[54] The *People's Daily* reported that Fujian-Hitachi has contracted seventy-one domestic enterprises to produce various television parts, but has been unable to export a single television because of inconsistency in the quality of domestically supplied parts. Although the factory earned substantial profits for both partners between 1981 and 1985, the venture's quality and sourcing dilemmas eventually had a debilitating effect on output and profits. (See the chart on page 273.) In 1987, Fujian-Hitachi achieved a turnaround, which is described in the last chapter of this book.

In these cases, low quality is a tangible condition of the end product. Many firms have been forced to refrain from using their brand names on Chinese-made products. Moreover, many foreign companies have had difficulty convincing their Chinese partner that cosmetic defects in products are grounds to reject and destroy them.

To solve quality-control problems, U.S. firms have applied progressive systems of quality enhancement in their China ventures, including quality circles, cross-inspection plans, and multiple quality checkpoint schemes along assembly lines. To a great extent, foreign partners have been successful at raising quality levels in their joint ventures in China as these systems are integrated into production and fully accepted by Chinese workers and managers. Often, Chinese factory managers are given tours of similar U.S. factories to observe the equipment they will be using and/or building. Some firms have entered into contracts with Chinese suppliers that codify the exact specifications of components to be sourced, with clear stipulations regarding the rejection of goods on the basis of strict quality specifications. On-site quality-control inspection has become a required added expense for many joint ventures concerned with protecting their brand-name reputations. Others have pushed for reject-and-destroy clauses to prevent defective products from entering the Chinese domestic market or export markets with their trademark.[55]

To achieve quality-control standards, firms should pursue an incremental approach to localization, and obtain verifiable guarantees of quality and availability. Negotiations should push for the Chinese side to share the burden of retooling suppliers, monitoring quality, and hiring third-party inspectors such as the China Commodity Inspection Corporation (CCIC), if necessary. Most important, firms should conduct initial business plans under the assumption that all needed supplies and parts for the joint venture, excluding only the most basic materials such as water and electricity, will need to be imported indefinitely. Quality considerations also highlight the importance of fighting hard for preferential import tariff treatment for joint ventures manufacturing in China, as ongoing imported supplies may be required to maintain production schedules.

To encourage better quality control, familiarize the Chinese seller with the design and application of equipment by demonstrating how

Output and Profit of the Fujian-Hitachi Joint Venture

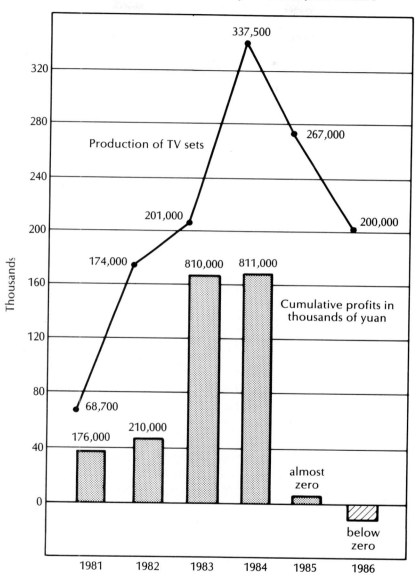

SOURCE: *South China Morning Post*, August 11, 1986, by permission.

the equipment is used in the field. In this way the Chinese engineers will better understand how the product is used, how it breaks down, and on what part of the merchandise their attention to quality should be concentrated. The Chinese should be encouraged to voice any fears they may have of not being able to fill the quality clauses of the contract. In general, foreign firms should steer clear of projects based on short-term localization of inputs, such as in the AMC and Hitachi joint ventures.

Selling Finished Goods in China

The decision regarding the percentage of production to be exported should be made by the board of the joint venture. Local and central bureaucratic entities, however, often push for the export percentage decision to be made before start-up. Rash decisions as to when and where to begin marketing FIE production can lead to disaster. In a joint venture between China and an EEC country, for example, the Chinese partner sold assembled trucks without paying attention to the rugged-ness of the terrain where they would be used. These trucks fell apart as soon as they were put into use, tainting the reputation of the EEC brand in China for several years.

Remember that the problem of perceived quality deficiency in Chinese-made products that exists among world market buyers also exists among Chinese end-users. Foreign partners of manufacturing joint ventures in China who intend to sell to China's domestic market discover that Chinese industrial customers and consumers have sim-ilar suspicions of Chinese-made goods, and do not regard products manufactured by Sino-foreign ventures as necessarily "foreign-made." Some firms with a manufacturing venture in China continue to sell sim-ilar products to China from outside. For example, direct sales consti-tute a major part of one engine manufacturing firm's business in China even though the company has set up a joint venture there producing the same model that it sells to China. These sales compete directly with the Chinese partner's plant. Since the joint venture factory has such a bad reputation in China, partly because of the low quality of engines pre-viously manufactured there, many Chinese customers prefer to buy en-gines directly from the American parent company in the United States. This embarrassing situation has forced the two companies to bid com-petitively against each other for sales in China.

Hewlett-Packard countered Chinese customer reluctance to "buy Chinese" by educating end-users and convincing local government officials to add its products to a list of preferred products. This helped to dispel negative perceptions of their Chinese-made computers and instruments among end-users. Fujian-Hitachi inadvertently elicited Chinese government promotion of its products, ironically, because of its inability to export. Faced with the possibility that Fujian-Hitachi might declare bankruptcy because of its failure to export production and slow domestic sales caused by the stiff competition from increasing supplies of imported color televisions, as well as the rapid appreciation of the yen in the mid-1980s, the Chinese government took an unprecedented action. As reported by the *People's Daily*, the Chinese government officially prohibited FTCs from purchasing color televisions from any supplier other than Fujian-Hitachi. Such an official-level solution is not available to most firms. Even in this case, it would not have been undertaken had not the failure of this high-profile joint venture likely meant the reduction, if not curtailment, of Japanese direct investment in China.

Marketing from a China Venture. Local bureaus and FTCs have influence over the Chinese end-user, making it difficult, though not impossible, to approach them directly. All parties—the end-user, FTC, and local ministry or bureau—must agree on import sales after lengthy negotiations. The process puts foreigners in a weak position because they must locate not only the end-user interested in purchasing their goods, but an FTC with the needed foreign exchange and the governmental authority to approve the sale. One good sign is that the end-user plays an increasingly important role in the acquisition of foreign goods.

An FIE should conduct China market research with the assistance of their Chinese partner, who may have to be convinced of the necessity of such analysis. However, the market knowledge possessed by the Chinese partner is invaluable in estimating the market potential of a product in specific areas of China.

One of the best marketing strategies, and certainly the most challenging to U.S. firms, is educating end-users. This strategy allows firms to enter the market through the end-user, placing the products directly into the workplace where quality and performance can be seen. Name recognition grows from here.

Marketing Feasibility Checklist

▶ Does the marketing study include an analysis of products made by the existing Chinese factory? How could these products be improved? Are similar products on the Chinese market? Is the price of the product controlled by the state or subject to supply and demand?

▶ Does the marketing study profile potential customers? What new products do Chinese customers need? How influential will the joint venture brand name be among them? Can customers afford to pay more for improved or newer products?

▶ Does the marketing plan include a profit-and-loss projection based on conservative estimates? Does it contain comparisons with other joint ventures, cooperative ventures, etc., in similar fields of endeavor?

▶ Does the marketing study profile domestic and foreign competition, taking into account the possible appearance of a competing joint venture? Does it calculate the time and resources required to break into new channels of distribution?

▶ Does the marketing plan outline methods for breaking into new markets in China, taking into account the difficulties and expenses involved? Will sales be regional only? How long will it take to expand market base?

Product Promotion

Labeled as a capitalist tool, advertising was totally banned for more than three decades prior to 1978. These restrictions were partially lifted under the government of Deng Xiaoping as a means of promoting product knowledge and economic growth. In 1978, China's only ad agency, the Shanghai Advertising Company, was reopened.[56] The Chinese government has permitted substantial increases of foreign advertising on Chinese television, despite the fact that Chinese television offers only one national channel.[57]

The Process of Selling to a Chinese Enterprise

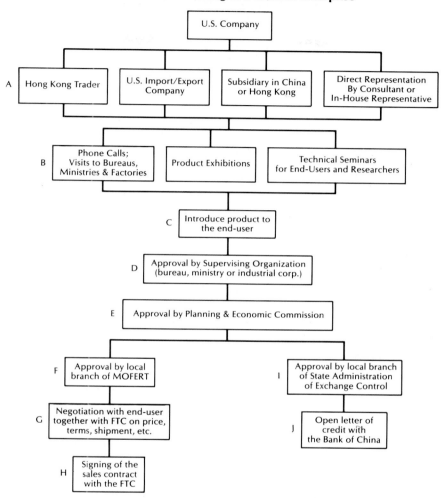

Successfully selling a product in China — whether produced in China or imported — depends on introducing the product directly to the end-user. Half of the respondents to one of the author's questionnaires discovered that the end-users they dealt with had the power to authorize or veto the purchase. Sixty-five percent of the respondents said they hold technical seminars (at an average cost of $20,450) to gain introduction to end-users. Once an end-user desires to buy, selling to China then becomes a task of gaining purchase approvals. If an FTC is the purchaser, MOFERT approval will be necessary (F, G, H); if a bureau, ministry, or industrial corporation is the purchaser, the sale can be made once the foreign exchange is released by the State Administration of Exchange Control (I, J).

SOURCE: Adapted from: *Intertrade*, February 1987. P. 35.

Only in selected sectors of the economy does competition warrant the use of promotional efforts. Chinese enterprises that have advertised find it highly effective in capturing new market shares. For example, the Tianjin Da Ren Tang pharmaceutical factory launched production of a new weight control pill with an advertising campaign budget of 45,000 yuan, which was more than the cost of developing the new pill. Although the approach was simple, the factory received an average of 300 letters per day from consumers asking about the new product. In 1982, another Chinese enterprise paid 3,000 yuan to advertise its measurement instruments, using two columns in the famous *Reference News,* which has a circulation of 10 million. These two-column advertisements generated 1,000 letters from technicians requesting more information. Since the average sale value per measurement instrument advertised was 200 yuan, the firm could break even on the advertising purchased if it sold only fifteen of these instruments per 1,000 potential customers.[58]

A handful of foreign firms have also discovered the benefits of advertising in China, especially manufacturing FIEs positioned close to the market. The West German Wella A. G. formed a joint venture in the Tianjin ETDZ—called Tianjin Liming Cosmetics Joint Industrial Company—and has enjoyed extraordinary success through an advertising campaign that emphasizes the importance of hair care. After production started in 1982, the venture created advertising films and posters, gave out free samples, and conducted classes in department stores for shoppers. Consumer demand for the advertised products surged. Producing at full capacity, the factory could not keep up with mounting orders. The products became hard to find even in Beijing. Wella's joint venture does not advertise on Central Chinese Television, where it costs 2,000 yuan for thirty seconds for the first commercial and 1,000 yuan for each subsequent commercial. Rather, the company chose to run three different commercials daily on local television in major cities, during two-thirds of the year, at a cost of 200–300 yuan per commercial.[59]

Gillette, Coca-Cola, and Pepsi are of some of the U.S. firms advertising consumer goods in China. Although Gillette's reputation is based on its *Rhino* blades which were sold to China years ago, its consumer advertising has been moderately effective. As described by a Gillette manager interviewed by the *New York Times,* the company has encountered a problem in China that it has elsewhere in Asia: the lack of facial hair on Chinese men. The Gillette manager said the solution was to educate Chinese men on shaving "as an integral part of good grooming. . . . as living standards rise the demand for razor blades and other grooming products will grow."[60] Coca-Cola has taken a different approach to promoting its product in China. To counter the limited access of Chinese television and the limited geographic availability of its soft drink, Coca-Cola has concentrated its advertising in point-of-purchase signs and billboards.[61]

In the industrial sector, product advertising is less effective. The Chinese are extremely loyal to their established suppliers; only a handful of American firms can claim customer loyalty in the industrial field. Mobil Oil introduced its logo in China forty years ago. Based on Mobil's experience in China, advertising is not helpful to oil firms without long-term recognition.[62] Mobil attributes its rising sales in China directly to the recognition of its Pegasus logo by Chinese users.

General Electric is another company well known in China because of its logo recognition. Decades ago, GE sold fans to China which displayed the common "GE" symbol. In 1986, GE decided to advertise using a billboard in Beijing. Despite the recognition it had built up over the years, only two calls were received in response. Hewlett-Packard has taken an even lower profile than GE in its advertising, catering to industrial end-users with technical advertisements on television and in magazines.

There is still a certain novelty value to advertising in China and the Chinese react to it with more enthusiasm than their more saturated Western counterparts.[63] Responses to the author's questionnaires indicate that advertising for industrial products leads to moderate sales about half the time. Foreign firms spend between $50,000 and $100,000 annually on advertising in China (usually through agencies based in Hong Kong). However, advertising as a firm located inside China will cost much less and potentially be more effective than promoting product lines from outside.

To ascertain the Chinese opinion of foreign sales efforts in China, John Frankenstein polled a sampling of twenty-seven mid-level executives from foreign trade organizations, including MOFERT and CITIC, "about the importance and effectiveness of various kinds of vendor promotional activities," which he ranked in order of effectiveness as follows:

1. Total Sales Promotions*

---

* "Total sales promotion" denotes a shotgun marketing effort, including personal contact, media advertising, trade show participation, product demonstration, etc.

2. Salespersons' Efforts
3. Supply of Technical Literature
4. Trade Shows
5. Advertising in Trade Journals

Frankenstein concluded that "the less personal the [promotional] effort, the less effective it is."[64] His findings underscore the importance of stationing marketing representatives in China who can attend trade fairs and introduce product lines, company history, and personnel to Chinese end-users and officials directly. Factory visits are effective as well. Telexing and mail communications should illustrate committed presence and be geared to the personalization of the business relationship.

Repatriation as a Management Challenge

Balancing foreign exchange and converting Rmb profits have emerged as the two most prevalent impasses for China ventures. China has remained firm in requiring that joint ventures avoid the convertibility quagmire by exporting sufficient production to balance their foreign exchange accounts. The model works reasonably well in ventures that attract foreign exchange directly (especially tourist ventures) and those that process Chinese raw materials or manufacture products using Chinese labor that can be sold to ready export markets.[65] On the other hand, the model fails in ventures producing products to be sold domestically for Rmb, or any venture starting production of export goods which may not be immediately competitive on world markets.

Profit distribution from joint venture revenue is both regulated and negotiable. The Joint Venture Law stipulates that net profit should be divided among the investors according to capital contribution. However, net profit represents three substantial deductions against the gross profit of a joint venture. After expenses and taxes, a venture must set aside a percentage (which is fully negotiable) that is divided among three funds: a reserve fund, an expansion fund, and a bonus and worker welfare fund. Total fund deduction typically runs around 15 percent of the gross.[66] The remaining profits, often substantial but in the form of Rmb, can then be divided among the investors or reinvested in the venture. Some U.S. firms have opted to increase their equity share in joint ventures by diverting Rmb profits back into their joint ventures rather than attempt to repatriate their dividends. AMC plans to increase

Effectiveness of Various Promotional Activities in the People's Republic

How has your firm advertised products or services in the People's Republic? (Respondents checked one or more of the following media.)

Chinese-language trade journals	80%
Sponsoring an event in China	35%
English-language journals in China	25%
Direct mail	25%
Chinese television	20%
Chinese newspapers	15%
Billboards in China	10%
Technical seminars	10%
Chinese radio	0%

What has been the response to your firm's advertising in China?

"Absolutely no response"	0%
"Some inquiries but no sales"	26%
"Moderate sales generated"	46%
"Significant increase in sales"	10.5%
"Too soon to judge"	17.5%

SOURCE: Author's survey (see appendix for complete form of this questionnaire).

Advertising Guidelines

▶ Rely on the precise presentation of a product's technical specifications to attract Chinese buyers rather than glossy graphics and alluring photographs.

▶ Advertise in the Chinese language translated from English by qualified professionals experienced in translating promotional literature.

▶ Avoid political and sexual innuendo and the use of cultural stereotypes.

▶ Highlight durability rather than innovation, performance rather than trendiness.

▶ Collect, collate, and follow-up on all direct consumer responses.[67]

▶ Promote brand and company loyalty by emphasizing quality and dependability.

its share of Beijing Jeep from an original 31.4 percent up to a possible 49 percent.[68] Other firms are stockpiling Rmb—a risky prospect in light of recent devaluations—while waiting for the repatriation problem to be solved, or to use the Chinese currency to initiate some other repatriating scheme.

The partners of the China-Schindler Elevator Company, Ltd., have decided to reinvest 75 percent of their dividends over the next two years to expand production of the venture. Schindler's elevator manufacturing joint venture has reaped 56.5 million yuan (about $15.2 million) in profit, which is 340 percent of the total investment capital the company started with. Schindler's joint venture is also maintaining a foreign exchange balance, and even a surplus, through exports.[69]

On January 15, 1986, the State Council ratified regulations concerning foreign exchange balancing in joint ventures. These regulations include nine methods of balancing foreign exchange, though most will not solve the long-term repatriation requirements of some 2,700 FIEs in China that either cannot export production for foreign exchange or lack direct access to sources of foreign exchange within

China, such as tourist hotels and the FIEs that indirectly serve them. Five of these repatriation methods warrant a closer look, however.

Pooling Foreign Exchange.   Article IX of the regulations legalizes the transfer of foreign exchange between joint ventures with a common foreign partner when one of the ventures incurs a foreign exchange imbalance. Government policymakers have indicated that import substituting ventures would receive payment for their goods in foreign exchange.[70] As one would expect, convincing the Chinese partner in the surplus producing venture to give up foreign exchange can be a tall order. A typical application of this foreign exchange transfer is to establish a hotel, which generates hard cash for struggling joint venture factories. Most U.S. manufacturing firms lack hotel management expertise and the prospect of hiring an outside managerial outfit could make such projects unprofitable. Even so, some U.S. firms are engaging in foreign-related construction projects. One such example is M. W. Kellogg's "expat village" near the Beijing airport.[71] Another example involves AMC's Beijing Jeep Corporation president, Don St. Pierre, who obtained $2.5 million from the Great Wall Hotel in his search for foreign exchange.[72]

Substituting Import Sales.   Article V allows joint ventures to sell their products to Chinese industrial ministries and corporations for foreign exchange, rather than Rmb. (These goods would substitute imports of similar goods, turning the joint venture into a local producer.) Certainly, U.S. firms selling capital equipment could see increased sales during the Seventh Five-Year Plan (1986–90) since technology acquisition in priority areas will be stepped up to lessen foreign exchange expenditures on imports.[73]

Import substitution pacts require MOFERT approval of foreign exchange usage. The MOFERT stamp of approval verifies that local buyers have access to foreign exchange, and identifies those customers willing to spend precious foreign exchange on products not readily available in China. Responsibility lies with local authorities to ensure the existence of foreign exchange to be used. Local bureaucratic reluctance to implement long-term import substitution deals often surfaces as these agreements are negotiated.

Nevertheless, as coordination between Chinese agencies and departments increases, import substituting agreements could become a more useful means of repatriation. With local government backing and solid partnership secured, the project could be viewed by Chinese officials as an experiment in saving foreign exchange that would be spent on more costly imports.[74] As of this writing, few import substitution arrangements exist. The greatest obstacle is that most joint ventures cannot yet produce import substitutes of foreign-made quality. Although the trend is toward import autonomy for local FTCs and enterprises in China, most Chinese customers possessing foreign exchange prefer to buy components made in Japan, the United States, or Europe.

Exporting Chinese Products. Article VI makes it possible for joint ventures to purchase Chinese-made goods using Rmb and then export them, thus earning foreign exchange. This may be an option for joint venture partners possessing marketing networks unavailable to Chinese FTCs, but it is doubtful that most joint ventures could conduct successful trading company practices in China. The difficulty centers on finding producers in China willing to sell their products for Rmb rather than foreign exchange. Moreover, products already exported by Chinese FTCs are not eligible for sale to joint ventures for the purpose of exporting. Products that local Chinese officials may be able to offer the foreign partner include soybeans, prawns, salt, tea, carpets, royal jelly, herbal medicines, ceramics, sporting goods, and plastic products.

Product supplies could be unpredictable, or even terminated, if the supplier or FTC usurps the export markets developed by the joint venture. If a firm does not manufacture the components or materials itself, it cannot expect to export the products from China without a long negotiation. Even then the firm may receive nothing more than a small percentage of export profit.

One of the leading innovators in new ventures, 3M, has established a joint venture buying company with Shamash Limited. The new company, called 3M-Shamash Ltd., is registered in Hong Kong but has a pilot operational office in Shanghai. The company will use the Rmb profits generated by 3M's solely owned factory in Shanghai to purchase various goods from factories in Shanghai and export them to earn foreign exchange. This company will also buy silk in China on behalf of S. Shamash & Sons, a company that has been doing business in China for a century, and will continue its import business through the newly established trading joint venture company in Shanghai. The trading joint venture can use foreign exchange to buy Chinese export goods to be resold overseas. The firm may become a ground-breaker for such triangular offset/countertrade arrangements.[75] In 1986, another trade-related repatriation solution was quietly introduced. By issuing internal trading certificates (ITCs), the hope was that the purchase of Chinese products for export would be standardized. Nothing of the sort has been officially implemented, however.[76]

Investing in Chinese Enterprises.

Regulations also allow joint ventures to make Rmb investments in Chinese export enterprises, thereby capturing a share of foreign exchange earned by the Chinese enterprise. The scheme could benefit from the recent cutback in commercial Rmb loans to Chinese enterprises, which, as a result, are seeking new forms of capital.[77]

Government-organized Foreign Exchange Balancing.

Another method outlined by the regulations permits the government to collect foreign exchange from joint ventures that have a surplus and place it in those ventures with a deficit. This method could be used by enterprises in which a government department oversees both joint ventures that can accumulate foreign exchange and those that cannot. Though the scheme may solve imbalances at some China ventures, it has ominous implications for ventures that earn foreign exchange but that have no intention of giving it up.

Hong Kong's "Gray Market" Exchange Strategy.

Hong Kong traders possess the most successful scheme for repatriating profits. Whether this process, which is of questionable legality, can, or should, be used by large foreign corporations is a matter of corporate choice. Nevertheless, a substantial amount of business is being conducted by U.S. corporations through Hong Kong traders all over China using the following method. First, one locates an enterprise in China that wants to purchase imported equipment, usually after a phone solicitation from a Hong Kong trader to the Chinese enterprise, or vice versa. Familial and personal connections almost always play a significant role in the solicitation. Prices are quoted and the supplier—most often American, Japanese, or European—is notified of a possible sale. Next, an FTC overseeing the Chinese enterprise is told of the plan. Together the parties attempt to locate the needed foreign exchange, since the actual Chinese buyer rarely will have sufficient reserves for a direct purchase. The two parties then attempt to convince an exporting Chinese enterprise that earns foreign exchange to sell its foreign exchange surplus for Rmb at roughly twice the official government exchange rate. The exchange is made to the benefit of all four parties: the buying enterprise receives imported foreign equipment it has paid for using Rmb; the FTC receives a cash percentage; the exporting enterprise receives a windfall of Rmb, which it can use to pay wages and buy domestic supplies; and the Hong Kong trader and foreign supplier earn their profits in foreign currency.[78]

Though not legal in China, this scheme is tolerated. Because much of Chinese business practice is not yet written into law, this strategy may eventually generate regulations. Some China trade consultants suggest that buying foreign exchange at unofficial rates is one way to supply small Chinese enterprises with foreign exchange with which to buy a firm's products.[79] Obviously, a company's success in the endeavor will depend on its network of guanxi connections.

Most firms agree that foreign exchange repatriation calls for creative approaches, a long-term view to finding solutions, and real financial flexibility. There are a few solutions worth mentioning that exemplify the varied approaches to this problem. One multinational corporation uses its Chinese partner as an agent to sell the parent firm's products in China for hard currency.[80] Some firms, such as Cummins Engines and Volkswagen, have arranged to source components in China as a way of offsetting imbalances. A firm transferring technology can meet its foreign exchange requirements by combining both commissions paid to its joint venture sales and service subsidiary (which sells the company's imported products for hard currency), and the initial foreign exchange capitalization contributed by both sides.[81] One U.S. automaker has agreed to take home 25 percent in foreign exchange and accept promissory notes for the rest, to be paid four to five years later. Profits come slowly, but that doesn't bother the firm.

Prospering in China

Resolving the problems of operating a venture in China requires skillful application of a firm's unique points of leverage. The Chinese partner must be induced to reciprocate with tangible concessions. Concessions such as increased market access, better supplies, more skilled labor, and timely repatriation of profits can lead a foreign firm to prosperity in the China market. The key element of leverage that U.S. firms possess is usually the firm's specific technology. To attain the freedom to expand and profit in the People's Republic, a firm must work in concert with its Chinese partner to solve operational problems, independent of the surrounding bureaucracy, and be willing to transfer its technology to the venture.

A young woman tends to cotton spinning machines in a textile mill. Chinese industrial enterprises offer workers wages as well as social services such as prepared meals, medical care, schooling for their children, and retirement pensions.

China Hewlett-Packard's joint venture computer electronics factory in Beijing emulates the "open-bay" floor layout of Hewlett-Packard's firms elsewhere.

A Chinese technician works in a dust-free testing room at China Hewlett-Packard's joint venture factory.

Portraits of model workers are posted outside a factory in Shehezi. In the past, labor wages in China were increased as a worker ascended a graded scale. A new bonus system has helped create more worker incentive by rewarding actual performance rather than seniority.

A video production team films a television commercial in a Chinese department store.

Computers and calculators for sale in Beijing, but clerks stick with the abacus for tallying purchases.

Inside a welfare carpet factory, a handicapped worker weaves intricate designs using traditional tools. A factory with 53 percent of its employees disabled qualifies for tax-free status. Each worker produces about half a square meter of carpet every month.

Inside a Chinese enterprise, the foreigner is often dismayed by the lack of worker discipline and shop-floor supervision by managers. Beset by breakdowns and power shortages, much of the machinery often stands idle.

Next door to the Great Wall Hotel (a U.S.-China joint venture) looms a new hotel being built by the Chinese. Foreign partners of joint ventures have found it difficult to prevent competing ventures from being established nearby.

A billboard in Beijing advertises Japanese electronic products. Japan has taken the lead in consumer product advertising in China.

This Coca-Cola billboard in Beijing illustrates a key dilemma for foreign firms attempting to attract consumers; namely, to get the Chinese to lower xenophobic barriers between themselves and Western lifestyles.

McDonald's hamburgers and Americana provide a day's relief for China-weary Americans living in Beijing, shown here attending the annual Fourth of July gala held on the grounds of the U.S. Embassy.

Foreign Technology in China

A new technological revolution is currently taking place in the new world. This presents both an opportunity and a challenge to the economic development of our country. We should seize this opportunity and make selective use of the new scientific and technological achievements so as to accelerate our modernization and narrow the economic and technological gap between China and the developed countries.
General Secretary Zhao Ziyang, 1984

The emerging Third Wave civilization does not provide a ready-made model for emulation. . . . The poor as well as the rich are crouched at the starting line of a new and startlingly different race into the future.
Alvin Toffler
The Third Wave

A couple of years ago the first Chinese translation of Alvin Toffler's book *The Third Wave* caused quite a stir. In response to the book a debate ensued among Chinese leaders over what China's response should be to the growing importance of the "third wave" technologies: biotechnology, microelectronics, information technology, and new materials. Several Chinese leaders have argued that unless China is able to make significant advances in these four key areas, the technological gap between China and the West will grow even wider. Since the present leadership has based much of its credibility on its ability to close the gap and position China as a major force in world economic and technological affairs, anything short of its goal would be politically unacceptable. At the same time, those party leaders still committed to the self-reliance principles often associated with the Maoist era argue that China has gone too far and too fast in importing foreign technologies.

Chinese leaders have long faced the same quandary: How can they increase the flow of foreign technology without making concessions that may threaten China's sovereignty or ability to fully control its economy? Moreover, foreign firms ask whether the current Dengist regime, and especially the next one, will be willing to forgo long-standing tenets of self-reliance and culturally ingrained (though hardly unfounded) fears of foreign domination in the interests of compelling foreign firms to trade technology for sustained access to the China market. As early as 1976, Deng Xiaoping was refuting his technologically conservative opponents with the argument that increased foreign technology acquisition would: (1) enable China to export; (2) promote technological transformation; and (3) put more Chinese to work. In rebuttal, his opponents charged, in the political journal *Red Flag*, that his policy meant "nothing less than opening the gate wide to foreign monopoly capitalists, who would use money and equipment to plunder China's natural resources and suck the blood of the Chinese people whom they regard as low cost manpower." They went so far as to claim that "Deng Xiaoping, who works as a comprador of imperialism, represents the interests of foreign big bourgeoisie."[1] In the years since these statements were made, most Chinese have come to realize that China will have to commit a larger share of its domestic market to foreign firms to attract the capital necessary to develop China's resources and consumer market, as proponents in China of the so-called northward strategy have advocated. Under this strategic imperative, China's inland markets would be opened to induce foreign capital to expand northward, easing shortages of domestic capital, introducing advanced technology, and promoting "technical advancement in the national economy."[2]

China's leaders also know that in the future of which Toffler speaks, a nation's independence of action will be inextricably linked to its technological diversity, the skill level of its labor force, and its ability to manufacture goods of superior quality. In seeming opposition to their quest for self-reliance, Chinese leaders in Beijing have charted a course for China's modernization that depends highly on the efficient assimilation of imported technology. They have paid increasing attention to the role of foreign technology in pursuit of their modernization goals because of the catalytic role that they anticipate it will play. China's leaders have reaffirmed their open-door commitment of maximum access to foreign technology and capital to support its economic objectives. Given the general state of China's industrial capabilities at the present time, the success or failure of China's technology acquisition policies may be the deciding factor in the outcome of the country's overall modernization goals. The recent relaxation of export controls on the U.S. side and the streamlining of the Coordinating Committee for Multinational Export Control's (COCOM) once dilatory process of export approval have put the Chinese in a more advantageous position to purchase advanced equipment and technology in a number of important industrial fields. Nonetheless, many questions remain about China's ability to seize this new and potentially critical opportunity.

An estimated 25 percent of the state-owned enterprises in the industrial sector actually require complete renovation, which entails revamping both plant and equipment. In Shanghai, more than $1 billion has been spent over the last several years in an effort to refurbish plants in the electronic, computer, construction materials, food processing, and metallurgy sectors. Even with more than 11,000 contracts signed with foreign companies since China opened its doors, the short-term results of China's foreign technology acquisition program, in the opinion of many Chinese leaders, have not been satisfactory. Though China's leaders have decided to pursue a more gradual approach for fear of the risks inherent in adopting a more ambitious course, the priorities contained in the Seventh Five-Year Plan, initiated in 1986, evidence no less of a high-level commitment to massive technological development. The program contains three fundamental objectives: (1) the renovation of outmoded and inefficient factories; (2) the improvement in process and product technologies; and (3) more efficient use and substitution of raw and processed materials.

Unfortunately, the task of updating production equipment, product designs, processing technologies, and quality-control capabilities is a major undertaking for which the Chinese are largely unprepared. The Chinese complicate this task by refusing to depend on one firm or country any more than necessary. This means, of course, that numerous foreigners are transferring technology into Chinese industry simultaneously, which creates serious equipment compatibility problems.

CHINA'S INDIGENOUS TECHNOLOGICAL CAPABILITIES

Technological innovation in China outstripped that in Europe until the 1600s. Maintained chiefly through the trading of luxury goods via the

Silk Road and missionaries residing in China, scientific contact between China and the European continent has been continuous since
the time of the ancient Greeks. The old Jesuit Observatory still stands in
Beijing, where Father Verbier was commissioned by the Chinese em-
peror in 1674 to build a set of astronomical instruments, including an
azimuth theodolite and an altazimuth. The arrangement was one of the
earliest official technology transfers to China. Before this, however,
innovation flowed in the opposite direction. The Chinese invented
gunpowder in the tenth century and the printing press in the eleventh
century. The magnetic compass was invented in the twelfth century,
when a Chinese mariner discovered that a chunk of the naturally magnetic lodestone, when floated on a stick in water, pointed to the pole-
star. These inventions had revolutionary impacts on the European continent, though their origin went largely unrecognized and unap-
preciated.[3]

Because early Chinese society distrusted merchants and in-
ventors, the development of new technology was confined to the country's bureaucratic organizations. This hampered the pursuit of the practical arts flourishing in Europe. Given China's Confucian/Buddhist
conception that an inner harmony pervaded the natural world, it was to
be expected that Europe's Galilean science, which is founded on math-
ematical explanations of dead matter, did not fall on open ears in
China, and thus was not accepted. China's isolation from outside innovation and scientific research was intensified by the events emanating
from the European occupation of the country in the mid-nineteenth
century, about the time Japan embraced Western technological progress wholeheartedly.[4]

Throughout the twentieth century technology has entered China
through a number of conduits, including high-technology trade, technology licensing, acquisition of turnkey plants, joint venture enterprise,
scholastic exchange, literature collection, and study abroad by Chinese students. Following the virtual technology blackout imposed on
the country during the fanatical years of the Cultural Revolution
(1967–76), the role of technology in the economic development of the
country—especially foreign technology—was completely redefined.

In 1975, at the Fourth National People's Congress, Zhou Enlai announced the modernization of China's organizations, industries, national defense, and science and technology. By the late 1970s, scientists and intellectuals who had been ravaged by the Red Guards were
being rehabilitated and conscripted to pursue research under the Out-

line Plan for the Development of Science and Technology, promulgated at the National Science Conference in 1978. In 1979, China purchased $2.5 billion worth of foreign technology and equipment; by 1986, the country signed over 744 technology and equipment import contracts worth $4.45 billion.

However, advanced technology developed in the First World is not automatically appropriate for the Third World, no matter how tantalizing it may be to those wagering their country's future on technological modernization. On the other hand, as Alvin Toffler suggests, developing nations will not be forced to wait for the technology to develop through the long stages that have occurred in the Western world. Some fortunate countries have been able to join the international technology race as late starters, and move quickly to the front of the pack. Chinese leaders are acutely aware of this phenomenon in Japan, Singapore, Taiwan, and South Korea, and they hope that China can be next. But the acquisition of technology does not necessarily foster modernity in a developing nation if it lacks the human and infrastructural requirements to fully actualize the potential of the acquired technology. Ironically, the Chinese once ridiculed Europeans as being cultural barbarians, but now they are facing the reality that they may become what Arthur Koestler has called "urban barbarians"—men who cannot comprehend the technology that they possess.

Chinese leaders have discovered that their stepped-up technology acquisition effort means very little unless it is accompanied by extensive domestic reforms designed to enhance indigenous technological capabilities. An attempt is now being made to strengthen domestic capabilities to assimilate foreign technology more effectively and to attain greater capabilities with respect to emerging technologies. A broad array of modifications in the Chinese research and development (R&D) and science and technology (S&T) sectors has been implemented. China's leaders realize that many of the problems in absorbing technology originate within the Chinese system itself. According to an article in *Intertrade*, "the [Chinese] management system for technology import lacks overall control and planned guidance. . . . There are nearly 100 departments that have the right of examination and approval. . . . And after the local autonomy was expanded, the various supervisory departments lost control of various trades."[5] More specifically, there is a deepening recognition among Chinese leaders that their modernization problems stem from not only China's own technological backwardness, but from a mix of interrelated problems that include a lack of incentives in Chinese management, an artificial price system, underemphasis on the role of scientific and technical personnel, and misdirection in their previous policies regarding the import of foreign technology. Ironically, China could actually be losing ground in its race to catch up to Western levels of technology, and possibly failing in its attempt to localize technology production. Recent developments in microelectronics and biotechnology in the West and in Japan have had a major impact on many influential Chinese, leading some to suggest that moderation of its technology goal would leave China permanently behind the West without much hope of ever catching up.[6] As the rest of the world pulls away in the field of advanced microelectronics, China's urgent renovation of existing industries such as aviation, textiles, machine tools, automobiles, and precision instruments becomes more critical.[7]

Chinese press reports continually cite the current regime's emphasis on the role of science and technology in China's modernization. If the country is to make a serious attempt to increase factory output and reduce energy consumption via its planned multisector programs, its S&T activities must be better planned and funded. The notion that China must somehow leapfrog stages of S&T development through imports of advanced technology and equipment and indigenous programs—a notion popular in 1978—is still popular within the leadership circle.[8]

A far-reaching and ongoing program of training and reorganization of the indigenous technological effort is already being carried out. A viable S&T network of management organizations, research units, and educational institutions has been put in place. Though many of these new organizations and institutions are still in embryonic form, their symbolic value is significant. The appearance of these organizations suggests that the authority for decision making in the S&T areas has devolved to lower levels. Local leaders are in a better position to avoid costly errors and maximize existing opportunities by relying more on a select group of experts to assist in making appropriate policy decisions and avoiding unwanted political and administrative intervention in their affairs.

The broad-based reforms being introduced in S&T enterprises lend credibility to China's new science and technology goals, and promise to alter the climate in which research and the application of technology takes place. The reorientation includes the introduction of the responsibility system in the research sector, implementation of a contract research system, improvement of the status and benefits of scientists and technicians, and a general shift away from reliance on whole plant importation as the primary vehicle for acquiring technology. The general reordering of S&T priorities in recent years has culminated in a move away from basic research to an increased focus on applied R&D. As part of this movement, granting greater autonomy to research units has decentralized economic authority within the S&T sector at the enterprise level. The reforms in this sector include bold initiatives for establishing new funding mechanisms for research and the formation of technology markets, in hopes of intensifying the commercialization of R&D results. New training programs and educational institutions aim to create a modernized labor force of technically qualified personnel. Shanghai now has 711 scientific research institutions staffed with over 55,000 S&T personnel; this city is also home to 400,000 technicians, 108 S&T associations and over 100 S&T consulting firms. Shanghai has also set up a development zone in the Caohejing district for joint ventures in microelectronics. Perhaps the most important development over the last several years in terms of the structure of the Chinese S&T system has been the establishment of special leading groups, or task forces, for managing national and provincial priority areas.

The creation of the Special Leading Group for Science and Technology under the State Council has been complemented by the creation of several high-level, highly focused groups in the areas of electronics and computers, equipment development and acquisition, and foreign investment. Headed by Vice-Premier Li Peng, the group's primary responsibility is to ensure that China makes sustained and substantial progress in such critical areas as large-scale integrated circuits. The group is also directly attached to the State Council, which helps to alleviate the bureaucratic boundary problems encountered by the Ministry of Electronics Industry in its efforts to coordinate electronics development among the relevant ministries. A growing number of special leading groups concerned with both S&T affairs and the import of technology have appeared at the provincial and municipal levels. For instance, Shanghai has organized a special task force for handling the import of critical technology. In Hubei Province, a high-level entity has been created above the provincial S&T commission for overseeing S&T activities.[9]

Over the last several years Chinese leaders have become increasingly sophisticated regarding the science and technology modernization drive. These new levels of awareness are most clearly reflected in their attempt to link the economic reforms at the enterprise level with the technology reforms within the research sector so as to promote greater communication and coordination of activities. The mesh between technological research and productive application of technological know-how has long been an unresolved dilemma for S&T planners. Traditionally, the majority of China's research endeavors have been relegated to the various institutes under the aegis of the Chinese Academy of Sciences (CAS), which conducted the bulk of its research in defense-related fields. Today the production enterprise and the research unit are being fused, however, as the CAS has begun to form new companies that conduct high-technology R&D under commercial contract. The new CAS has been called an incubator for new enterprises, such as Beijing Software Experimental Factory, Hope Computer Company, and the Stone Corporation, a *minban* conglomerate of ten businesses in computer production, service center operation, and office automation.[10] This increasing sophistication has had important implications for China's activities concerning acquisition and utilization of foreign technology since the new high-technology conglomerates are being encouraged to acquire foreign technological know-how. As the research system improves, and current education programs begin to produce larger numbers of qualified individuals, the Chinese modernization program and the accompanying technology acquisition effort are likely to become even more sophisticated. This could mean that in certain areas China may move much farther and faster toward its modernization goals than previously expected.

Emerging Pockets of Technological Excellence

Though it is doubtful China will become a major exporter of third wave manufactured goods in the near term, there are signs of real achievement within certain sectors of the country's industry. By knowing when and where Chinese technological capabilities will appear, a foreign firm can locate Chinese counterparts that can handle the assimilation of a specific technology. This foresight can help the partnership avoid a technology snafu. Transfer problems usually occur because the foreign technology vendor sold equipment that, if the proper assessment was done, would have been recognized as too complicated for the Chinese host factory. Foreign companies that succeed in Chinese technology projects usually bring to the project knowledge of current technologi-

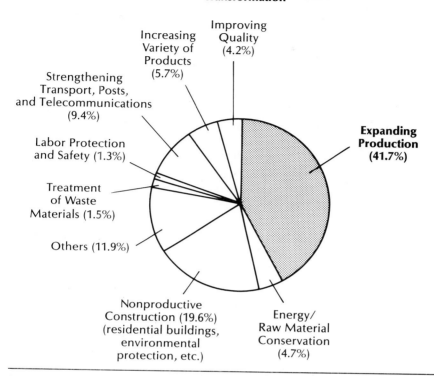

**How China
Invests in Technological
Transformation**

Increasing
Variety of
Products
(5.7%)

Improving
Quality
(4.2%)

Strengthening
Transport, Posts,
and Telecommunications
(9.4%)

Labor Protection
and Safety (1.3%)

Treatment
of Waste
Materials (1.5%)

Others (11.9%)

**Expanding
Production
(41.7%)**

Nonproductive
Construction (19.6%)
(residential buildings,
environmental
protection, etc.)

Energy/
Raw Material
Conservation
(4.7%)

SOURCE: *Statistical Yearbook of China, 1985*, State Statistical Bureau, People's Republic of China.

cal developments in China, an understanding of the evolution of China's technology policy, and some idea of where it seems to be going.

The Maoist policy of developing technologies locally in order to promote village self-sufficiency has given way to one promoting regional technological excellence in strategically selected high technologies (e.g., integrated circuit boards in Shanghai, aerospace technology in Xian, and computers in Beijing). By 1990, under China's new "Baliusan" program, S&T planners hope to establish new research centers in robotics, biotechnology, and new materials, as well as fifty new national laboratories utilizing larger budgets and more numerous research grants.[11] Scientific innovation and coordination of R&D efforts are present in chosen cities and industrial sectors that enjoy central government nurturing. This is particularly true of defense-related industries, such as military electronics. There have been outstanding examples of research achievement: the successful connection of telephone substations with optical fibers; the artificial synthesis of crystalline bovine insulin as early as 1965; the creation of 900 automated units on factory production lines; and the production of laser products for export, including sealed helium-neon lasers and electro-optical modulars.[12] The electronics industry was selected as the first to be modernized at a national industry conference held in Beijing in 1977, because of its importance in all four areas of Chinese modernization.[13]

Today the focal point of the Chinese electronics industry is Shanghai. China's ultimate intention is to create a version of Silicon Valley in the city. To attain this goal, China has promoted the rapid development of "the magnificent seven" technologies: microelectronics, fiber optics, lasers, bioengineering, marine engineering, new materials science, and robotics. So far the transformation has indeed produced important research results, most notably involving semiconductors and integrated circuits, and all seven of these emerging industries evidence a high degree of initiative and performance potential. As mentioned previously, the Ministry of Electronics Industry and the State Machine-Building Industry Commission were merged in March 1987 to form the Machine-Building and Electronics Industry. This move is part of the larger objective to increase indigenous capability in "mechatronics," the industrial hybrid so famous in Japan that results from the proper interfacing of mechanical and electronic engineering.[14]

China aims to develop its domestic manufacturing capabilities for the purpose of substituting imports of technology from countries like Japan and South Korea, and exporting high-technology products made in China. In fact, China licensed $20 million worth of technology overseas in 1986 and $60 million in 1987. The Chinese have earned well over $1 billion annually since 1984 by supplying engineering construction services to foreign countries.[15] To play a role as a producer in the age of "informatics," and to reduce imports of components necessary to build computers, a major effort is being focused on upgrading semiconductor and integrated circuit (IC) production. China can produce 53 million ICs annually, but because only 4 percent of total production are medium-and large-scale ICs, China will have to import advanced ICs for some time.

Computer Technology.
Major accomplishments have been achieved in the field of computer development. As a national priority, official directives state that the application of computers has been emphasized in every industry where their presence will help achieve economic goals. Although China's domestic computer production lags behind end-user needs, a concerted push is under way to increase computer research, manufacturing, and educational programs designed to offer computer-related training. As early as 1983, over 90,000 Chinese were involved in computer research, production, application, and education in over 130 institutions.[16] In Shanghai alone, 4,000 S&T personnel are currently engaged in computer R&D production, while 12,000 workers in the city are employed in seventeen computer manufacturing plants. An estimated 3,000 students take computer courses or major in computer science at any of the city's twenty college-level institutions.[17]

In contrast to the previous emphasis on scientific calculation, over 75 percent of the computer equipment in China is used in the industrial/transportation and science/education sectors. Computer applications in China are widespread and varied, including the use of computer systems in flood warning, thermal power, safety analysis, oil prospecting, scientific data storage, earthquake-proof architecture, and even computer dating! While domestic machines have a long way to go before they will be competitive with foreign imports, the appearance of Chinese-built machines such as the "Great Wall 0520" microcomputer offer hope that progress is just around the corner. In fact, the Great Wall 0520 series, an IBM clone, is currently being manufactured in three factories in China in three specialized models for use in engineering design, scientific research, and factory management, respectively.[18]

Unfortunately for foreign firms that export computers, China's computer market has been saturated with units beyond its ability to absorb them. Although only 4,500 microcomputers were imported in 1983, an avalanche of 75,000 microcomputers were imported in 1984, coinciding with the decentralization of FTCs under MOFERT. Presently, the country possesses between 250,000–300,000 microcomputers and 7,000 mainframes and minicomputers. As a result, imports of microcomputers have been cut and one can expect increased reliance on domestic producers, along with intensified protectionism. However, China will improve its budding computer expertise in numerous computer-related fields by drawing on substantial foreign technology

Major Achievements of China's Computer Industry, 1977–88

1977   Development of China's first microcomputer (DJS-050)

1979   Development of HDS-9 (5 MIPS) by CAS Institute of Computer Technology

1980   Development of DJS-052 microprocessor (8-bit, one chip) by Anhui Institute for Electronics Technology

1983   Development of China's first supercomputer ("Yinhe" ["Galaxy"], 100 MIPS) by the Changsha S&T University for National Defense

1983   Development of the 0520 microcomputer (IBM PC compatible) by the MEI Institute No. 6

1983   Development of the "757" 10 MIPS parallel computer by CAS Institute of Computer Technology

1983   Development of a 16-bit desktop computer (77-II) by the Lishan Microcomputer Corporation

1984   Development of a 16-bit TQ-0671 microcomputer system by the Tianjin Computer Institute (CPU: MC 68000)

1985   Development of NCI-AP 2780 superminicomputer (32 bit) by North China Institute of Computer Technology

1985   Development of 8030 computer by East China Institute of Computer Technology (compatible with IBM 370/138)

1985   Development of YH-X1 superminicomputer by the Changsha S&T University for National Defense

1985   Development of YH-F1 emulator by the Changsha S&T University for National Defense

1985   Development of the TJ-82 image computer by Qinghua University

1987   Production of new generation of microcomputers, including the 286 (0530) series and the 386 model

1988   Deployment of SMELTER ONE, the first industrial robot completely made in China, by the Beijing Institute of Steel

SOURCE: Office of Technology Assessment, 1987, and recent discussions with Denis Fred Simon, Tufts University.

and assistance. For example, as part of the ongoing effort to establish the country's first full-fledged manufacturing line of peripheral computer products, the Jiannan Machinery Plant in Changsha, Hunan, imported a magnetic disk production line from France, which has the capacity to produce 500 Type A and 3,000 Type B disks annually.[19]

Aerospace Industry.   When the U.S. space program became bogged down after the *Challenger* disaster, and European space programs were beleaguered by high satellite insurance rates, China entered the race to commercialize space with a vengeance. Using their Long March III rocket, they have put two communication and broadcasting satellites into geosynchronous orbit since 1984, and have launched ten satellites of various types since 1975 with a 100 percent success rate. Two Chinese-developed recoverable satellites, the FSW-I and the FSW-II, are being marketed. French, American, and Swedish concerns have rented space on other Chinese satellites to conduct microgravity experiments and geological surveys.[20] In March 1986, a letter of intent to jointly launch a telecommunications satellite was signed between the Chinese and the government-owned Swedish Space Corporation.[21] The Chinese have also signed contracts with two U.S. companies—Tersat, Inc., of Houston and Pan Am Pacific Satellite Corporation—to launch Westar 6 satellites.[22] Hughes Aircraft is also considering Chinese rockets and launching technology for use in launching U.S. satellites from Hawaii.[23]

Reported rental rates for Chinese payload space run 15 percent below Western competitors, with preferential insurance available.[24] Domestic applications of space technology are important as well; such areas include broadcasting, national communication networks, and the operation of permanent space stations where space technology can be developed that will be applied in the creation of new products for commercial industry.[25]

Superconductivity.   Thirty years ago, Chinese researchers began working in the area of superconductivity, defined by *Superconductor News* as a physical state, dependent on a critical temperature, that facilitates the flow of electricity without any resistance. The development of superconductors could, in the near future, miniaturize the modern computer by permitting calculations at a rate of a trillion per second, provide clean energy from nuclear fusion, allow deep-space communication transmissions, make it possible to build frictionless mechanical devices, and reduce electricity loss over power lines to zero.[26] Quite remarkably, thirteen researchers at the Institute of Physics under CAS discovered a new superconductor (containing bismuth instead of yttrium) that can achieve zero electrical resistance at a higher temperature ($84.1°K$) than before possible. This breakthrough could lead to more cost-effective applications of superconductive materials in numerous industries. The discovery is especially important to China, which suffers chronic energy shortages and electricity loss of up to 60 percent in transmission over power lines.

CHINA'S EXPERIENCE ASSIMILATING FOREIGN TECHNOLOGY

Chinese leaders have been successful in increasing the flow of technology into China because of their solid understanding of international markets, shrewd negotiating ability, sending delegations to trade fairs and foreign plant tours, and promoting the training of Chinese workers and technicians by foreign firms. They have also witnessed large production increases in plants using foreign technology. One such case is the joint venture with Otis Elevators in Tianjin, where productivity soared 51 percent in the first year following the inclusion of the foreign firm in the enterprise.[27] The Chinese have cited their progress in assimilating many of the 3,000 items imported between 1983 and 1985 as evidence of their greatly enhanced technology assimilation capabilities.

A primary factor contributing to this improvement has been the new economic reforms introduced into the industrial sector since 1981. These reforms have forced factory and research managers to pay more attention to an expanded application of imported technologies and equipment. As a result, the needs of the Chinese end-user have become better matched with the available technology over the last several years.[28] Without such reforms to complement stepped-up technology imports, it is likely that the present level of progress would have been unattainable.

Between 1950 and 1980, over 90 percent of China's foreign exchange expenditures on technology imports went for whole plant imports rather than the licensing and acquisition of know-how. This policy was followed by a decisive move away from whole turnkey plant imports, to a sharper focus on the import of key technologies employing alternative forms of acquisition. The three most popular modes of technology acquisition include countertrade, compensation trade, and the so-called one purchase—three cooperations,[29] in which the foreign vendor participates in a joint venture, accepts produced products as partial compensation, and is willing to trade off a percentage of the production process to a Chinese manufacturer in return for purchase commitments.

This policy is nowhere more prevalent than in China's civil aviation market. With most of the world's largest aircraft manufacturers targeting China for increased export sales, civil aviation has become the most competitive market in the People's Republic. Because the Chinese have long-term needs for civilian aircraft, they desire to serve their own market. Currently producing a variety of aircraft from microlights to heavy bombers, China also intends to expand its aircraft exports, which presently include two jets—the Yun-11 and Yun-12. By demanding that foreign suppliers offset production in exchange for market share, the Chinese foresee in the not-so-distant future the production of complete 747s, A310s, and other highly exportable aircraft taking place in the People's Republic.[30]

A willingness to offset production gives the foreign firm an edge, but given that Boeing, McDonnell-Douglas, Short Brothers, and Messerschmitt-Boelkon-Blohn (MBB) of West Germany have all entered coproduction ventures in exchange for sales of airplanes, foreign aerospace firms are having to offer more, like exclusive training centers, auxiliary high-technology projects, and commitments to participate in future joint ventures on newer-model airliners. Moreover, the China National Aeronautic-Technology Import and Export Corporation (CATIC) is now required to disapprove aviation contracts with foreign firms if they do not agree to offset part of the purchase price with purchases of components made in China.[31] McDonnell-Douglas has undertaken a "two-pronged offset program" with their Chinese partner. The first point of this program is a coproduction agreement. The second is that the U.S. firm and its Chinese partner have developed a countertrade agreement in which McDonnell-Douglas offers the Chinese partner the option to recoup foreign exchange they spend on coproduction.[32] "We agreed that for every dollar China spends on coproduction of aircraft, we will offset 25 to 30 percent with Chinese product," says Garreth Chang, president of McDonnell-Douglas China, Inc.[33] Both McDonnell-Douglas and Boeing purchase parts in China, the former buying landing gear doors from Shanghai and the latter fabricating tail fins in Xian.[34] MBB has formed a joint venture with the CATIC involving the design, manufacturing, and marketing of the MPC75, the project amounting to upwards of $1.2 billion, of which $100 million will be spent during the development phase of the venture, somewhat like the

McDonnell-Douglas venture in Shanghai. On this project (located in Xian) the Chinese will build the fuselage and the tail while MBB handles the cockpit, wing, and final assembly.[35] As more firms in manufacturing industries compete with one another for the China market, China hopes to localize whole manufacturing processes in scores of high-technology industries. As other developing countries are following in kind, many U.S. firms worry that they may end up trading away the manufacturing of their most competitive products to future rivals.

With China's general shift away from plain-and-simple technology acquisition has come a movement away from the simple expansion of plants and factories to the intensification of the country's existing capabilities. Often, older and cheaper technology is utilized rather than state-of-the-art equipment. To encourage the transfer of technical expertise there has also been a turn away from the acquisition of semi-knockdown (SKD) technology; foreign firms are now encouraged to import complete knockdown (CKD) packages that allow the Chinese to achieve a deeper understanding of the internal functioning of the technologies that they purchase. Overall, while China's technology acquisition program has not necessarily had an impressive beginning, results in certain areas have been appreciable.

We should be careful about underestimating the difficulty that any society, advanced or less developed, would have in handling some of the complex technical efforts China is attempting. One must distinguish between the problems of specific cases and those that derive from more generic causes. At a symposium in Guangdong in 1984, three main problems concerning technology import activities were cited: (1) lack of an overall plan, resulting in excessive duplication, (2) excessive emphasis on hardware while neglecting imports of software, and (3) poor preparation, leading to inadequate results and unfulfilled expectations.[36]

Computer imports have been singled out again as representative of these larger problems. For example, there is a tendency to buy machines based on their advanced state rather than on actual needs. Purchases are often made without considering software availability. The underuse of computers is attributed to a lack of trained personnel; only 468 out of 2,000 applicants passed a programmer's qualifying examination in May 1985.[37] Lack of maintenance on China's several thousand imported computers may have cost the country as much as $100 million between the years of 1985 to 1988.[38]

A serious bottleneck in China's development and utilization of computer software has impeded efforts to reap the benefits of fully actualized computerization of industrial management. The impasse involves a shortage of software and a lack of access for industrial users to China's scarce advanced computer systems, most of which are located at universities and research units. This fact, combined with a managerial aversion to incorporating computerized information systems in the enterprise, has downgraded the need for and thus the development of software in China. And that which is developed—usually under the auspices of the China Computer Systems Corporation—is spearheaded by research institutes rather than computer manufacturers, which creates a poor mesh between hardware production and software application.[39]

In response to the need to bring hard and soft technology into balance, China has increased its imports of technology software from 1.3 percent of total technology imports in 1978 to 35 percent in 1988. The Japanese have been among the most active in working with the Chinese in the area. A high priority has been the development of Chinese character information processing systems. Several Japanese firms including Fujitsu, as well as IBM and Wang Labs of the United States, have been working with the Chinese toward this end.

These shortcomings in planning and approach are compounded by a series of broader limitations that fall into three categories: financial, managerial, and technical. First, in many cases where foreign exchange is available for technology imports, the lack of domestic investment capital prevents Chinese enterprises from providing the auxiliary inputs on the domestic end to support the introduction of foreign technology. This is most certainly the case regarding investment in infrastructure to support new projects.[40] In light of this, most Chinese importers of technology or equipment are looking for projects that can bring them a quick return; hence China's emphasis on consumer projects in industrial activities.

Second, a dearth of qualified managers continues to plague Chinese industry. While efforts to rectify the situation through testing and additional training are under way, it will take time before a cadre of qualified managers exists that can handle the complex task of putting foreign technology and equipment to work within Chinese industry.

Finally, because of the financial constraints noted above, as well as China's own technical backwardness, much of the machinery, testing equipment, and special instrumentation needed to employ imported technology efficiently is still absent. There is also insufficient attention paid to the problems of maintenance and spare parts. Even in advanced industrial areas such as Shanghai, plants and equipment are old. The machinery tends to be from a variety of sources and of widely varying vintages, especially in light industry where investment has been severely lacking. The key exceptions appear to be in the electronics and computer industries, where it is clear that large quantities of technical resources are being made available to enhance China's capabilities.

In 1986, partly in response to the above constraints, Chinese technology decision makers began to rethink their strategy of acquiring turnkey plants. Intermediate technology was viewed anew as an essential ingredient in supporting higher technological development. Since used factories were becoming available in developed countries that were phasing out (or retooling) lower-technology industries, the Chinese saw new advantages in whole plant purchases, especially in energy-related sectors, mining, steel, and petrochemicals. By acquiring used whole plants, the Chinese can both fill a persistent gap between low- and high-technology industry in China and put scores of unemployed back to work, most of whom receive a monthly stipend even though work has been postponed. New and used turnkey plant sales continue to be a thriving market. In fact, during 1986–87 the Japanese completed $315.2 million worth of plant projects in China.[41] Incidentally, whole (used) plant deals can provide lucrative countertrade opportunities to U.S. firms currently replacing old production machinery.

Ultimately, Beijing wants neither to depend entirely on outside sources for technology—foreign suppliers are unlikely to make available their latest technology—nor to concentrate its technology purchases on one or two partners.[42] Chinese end-users and trade officials have disparate opinions on the technology transfer approaches of the European, Japanese, and U.S. firms. Discussions with Chinese trade officials and foreign business people in China suggest that, in general, the Chinese find the European firms more flexible and more willing to transfer technology than U.S. firms. Both European and U.S. firms are respected for their direct, no-nonsense approach in negotiating technology transfer contracts. Though U.S. firms are thought to possess the best technology in the world, they have the reputation of being frustratingly slow in transferring it. During an interview with the author in Beijing in 1986, a CITIC business officer spoke about millions of dollars of sales that ended up going to European firms because U.S. firms were slow in approving deals and they failed to communicate effectively with their Chinese counterparts. In contrast to both European and U.S. firms, the Japanese firms tend to keep their technology hidden from the Chinese. Some of these firms are known to transfer technological equipment only to keep it "black boxed" within the Chinese enterprise, out-of-sight from Chinese engineers. However, as one anonymous observer has written in a U.S. Consulate circular, the Japanese "offer a level of technology which is more easily assimilated . . . because the Japanese have, according to the Chinese, done their homework better and understand the [Chinese] factory's situation."[43]

Transferring Appropriate Technology

A central dilemma foreign firms encounter when transferring technology to China is one of trying to satisfy China's desire for state-of-the-art technology while supplying technology that is appropriate to specific Chinese environments. Chinese factory managers request the most advanced technology from foreign firms as a matter of protocol during initial negotiations, whether or not sufficient foreign exchange, trained personnel, or adequate infrastructure are present to support such technology. American firms are often pressured into offering their most advanced technology—often displaying blueprints and conducting technical seminars—only to see the contract go to a European or Japanese firm offering technology a decade old and at half the price. With some notable exceptions, the reality is that the Chinese may talk quality and sophistication but they tend to base their buying decisions on price.

Japanese, European, and U.S. firms pursue different approaches to this problem. The Japanese have taken advantage of their proximity and historical links with China to penetrate interior provinces and offer technology closely tied to existing Chinese capabilities at the factory level. However, the Japanese suffer a reputation among many Chinese of not being forthcoming with even basic technological know-how, often described as "more talk, less do." Yet Japanese firms offer consistently lower prices and seem to be better prepared to interface their newer technology with older equipment inside Chinese enterprises. In contrast, European firms are said to be more willing to transfer their highest technology, and do so rapidly and straightforwardly. They also enjoy the concessionary government financing typical in Europe. Chinese leaders have courted European firms throughout the mid-1980s, stepping up competition with the United States for technology transfer projects. Lastly, the U.S. firms have pursued a direct approach to technology transfer, though they have been neither as flexible in sharing high technology as some of the Europeans nor as able to offer the low prices of the Japanese firms.

A foreign firm's competitive edge in renovation projects depends on a combination of factors. Chinese trade officials in a position to approve contracts often consider price and credit terms more important than appropriateness, quality, and service backup. Also, technology acquisition decisions made by enterprise directors and official decision makers are often influenced by the place of origin of existing equipment in the importing Chinese enterprise. For instance, Shanghai steel factories were installed with German equipment in the 1930s, so when it came time to renovate, new German equipment was installed.[44]

Service backup and management training are considered important in terms of China's larger objectives to achieve self-reliance in key industries. The Chinese insist that foreign firms not only sell technology but also provide for its successful assimilation within a reasonable period of time, including the transfer of necessary expertise for the Chinese to manufacture it independently under license or freely.[45] Although it is common for factory managers to want only the latest technology, representatives of foreign firms must remember that selling what the Chinese end-users desire may not be as prudent as it sounds.

If the technology proves to be too advanced for the Chinese factory, or the equipment is inadvertently damaged or ruined by workers whose training level is not commensurate with the level of technology, the reputation of the foreign firm may be seriously damaged.

Although the president of Otis Elevators Company, Francois Jaulin, told a Chinese reporter at a press conference heralding Otis's joint venture in Tianjin that the company's Chinese partner would have the same access to Otis technology as other Otis subsidiaries, the company soon discovered that the notion was out of line with Chinese workmanship. Colin McDonall, then president of the joint venture, realized this when he found Chinese workers in the factory drilling holes in steel while other workers held the material in place, rather than using clamps. And instead of using mechanical measuring devices, workers were bending sheet metal and measuring by hand. Half-assembled pieces were being dragged from station to station, causing damage along the way and fatiguing the workers. Otis began by reorienting the shop floor so that raw materials enter at one side of the factory and undergo assembly in steps as they move through the factory. Before, a steel cutting saw used during the first steps of assembly stood in the center of the factory.[46] The Chinese have come to recognize problems associated with the assimilation of foreign technologies and have begun to request technology more closely geared to the local environment.

Unfortunately, foreign firms must negotiate licensing contracts with people and organizations other than the factory managers and technicians who operate the destination factory, such as a local FTC or ministerial bureaucrats. The unfortunate aspect is that the decisions concerning the organization of construction and the implementing of technology in the Chinese factory are made on the Chinese side without ample consideration of the compatibility of the transfer technology to the Chinese setting. For example, in a case study by William A. Fischer, negotiators from Global Multinational (fictitious name) found that during their negotiations to sell a turnkey chemical plant to China, the firm dealt mainly with a Chinese technology import agency. Personnel from the ministry, bureau, and the recipient chemical factory merely sat in on the negotiations. Officials from the factory were consulted on construction and production matters only. Because the import agency operates under the incentive to keep foreign exchange expenditure to a minimum by importing as little foreign equipment as needed, the decision was made to exclude the purchase of water treatment equipment for the project. The import agency accepted assurances by its technicians that local river water was clean; however, it was not. The corrosion caused by the high turbidity of the water led to long production delays associated with resolving the problem and thirty-three production shut-downs over a fourteen-month period during the start-up of the project.[47] There are also many cases in which Chinese technicians fail to insist that technical specifications be met by workers under their authority. The foreign partner should plan on maintaining a presence on-site for at least a year. For example, in one venture between China and Japan that is called a model for emulation, the Japanese partner stayed ten months after start-up for the purpose of implementing a managerial and technical system and training the Chinese how to utilize it.[48]

Both parties must ensure that compatibility exists among the foreign technology, the product line, and the conditions at the Chinese recipient factory, even to the point of providing backup systems to guarantee that production continues when breakdowns occur. Further provisions, such as installing supplementary generators, may be necessary to deal with all-too-frequent power outages and surges. Local water problems may require installation of water purification equipment. In general, serious consideration must be given to the modification of production equipment according to the local Chinese environment to avoid unnecessary delays and costly mishaps associated with technical incompatibility.

Leverage Your Technology for Market Access

Chinese policymakers have announced their willingness to offer access to China's domestic market to foreign firms ready to transfer crucially needed technology. In June 1985, Wei Yuming, deputy minister of Foreign Economic Relations and Trade, wrote in the *Beijing Review* that "the extent to which the [Chinese] market can be open to Chinese-foreign joint venture and foreign enterprises in China is closely linked with our demand for the technology [foreign firms] supply and the products they manufacture." The China market is being opened progressively to firms that offer technology to produce products that China (1) cannot produce at a sufficient level of quality in order to capture world export markets and (2) cannot produce in sufficient quantity to meet domestic market demand. A good example is Parker-Hannifin's joint venture in Hubei that produces synthetic O-rings and other polymer products to be both used and exported by China. The Chinese sought U.S. manufacturing technology and quality-control techniques to improve their own noncompetitive sealing devices. In the agreement Parker-Hannifin won the right to sell 40 percent of the venture's production to China's domestic market.[49] In another example, Molins, a manufacturer of cigarette machines, was able to gain market access on an escalating scale in return for transferring increasing levels of technology to its China venture. Molins transfers additional technology as the Chinese meet guarantees to buy cigarettes produced by Molins machinery licensed in China. The contract has worked extremely well; in 1983 Chinese orders were 15 percent above the figure guaranteed; in 1984 they were 30 percent above the guarantee.[50] (Molins' contract recalls the concept of the organic contract presented in Chapter 3.)

Also, by choosing to leverage their technology, foreign companies have indirectly speeded up the process of advancing from a stage of direct sales to coproduction and joint venture. Successful China ventures are usually the product of a long-term evolution of stages: direct export, nonequity coproduction, equity coproduction, and finally, joint venture. Offering technology that is attractive to the Chinese end-user can speed the evolution. One or more of the approval steps can be bypassed if a firm offers technology that will assist China in reaching its specific economic objectives in a particular sector. Knowing these objectives is crucial in attempting to tailor your firm's technology to China's needs.

Foreign firms that not only understand broad Chinese objectives and specific needs but are willing to work closely with the Chinese end-users gain considerable advantage and possess additional leverage into the market. As Chinese end-users relax their insistence on obtaining only state-of-the-art technology and become convinced of the need to procure appropriate technology, the quality and scope of communication and collaboration between the end-user and the foreign firm become crucial.

A list of thirty-nine priority categories to receive foreign investment was released in August 1985 by Chinese government authorities and summarized in the *South China Morning Post* in Hong Kong. Written in light of financial constraints that developed in early 1985, the list also included twelve categories which would be curbed. It was disseminated among government officials in various provinces who were requested to comply with it in approving projects. The author has combined the 1985 list with a newer list disseminated by top-ranking officials of the China Enterprise Management Association in May 1988 at the China Trade Talks sponsored by the City of Los Angeles. One of the key trends indicated by the two lists was the increased interest in purchasing used plant apparatus.

Priority Areas for Foreign Investment

Microcomputer and compatibles (coproduction)
Digital telecommunications equipment production
Laser typesetting and printing equipment (coproduction)
Polyethylene cable materials manufacturing technology
Coal mine exploration, liquefaction and gasification of coal, and pipelines to transport coal gas
Metal deposit exploration including iron and copper, and the production of iron, lead, aluminum, and other metals
Compound fertilizer and pesticide production, especially those less toxic and more effective

Power generator design and production
Construction and building materials production including glass, cement,
  asbestos, marble, and ceramics
Used electric cable manufacturing equipment, especially copper/alumi-
  num conducting wires and cables
Offshore oil platform and equipment production
Automaking and heavy truck design; tractor parts manufacturing (espe-
  cially bearings)
Antibiotics and ultrasonic medical equipment production
Technology for extracting plant proteins and freezing techniques for ex-
  porting foods
Agricultural processing equipment, especially for sugar and fruits
Deep-sea fishing techniques
Passenger airplane parts (coproduction)
Diesel engines (coproduction)
Artificial leather production line
Carpet-making equipment
Peripheral equipment for jet looms
Used equipment for manufacturing dyes
Used water glass manufacturing line (6,500 tons annually)
Used petrochemical manufacturing equipment
Used baking soda manufacturing line (17 tons annually)
Optical fiber production line (10,000 tons annually)

Activities to Be Curbed

Radio, television, and videotape recorder production
Van and taxi rental, and vehicle repair
Photographic film processing techniques
Shopping arcade operation
Household appliance repair
Liquor, cigarette, and soft drink production
Camera, vehicle, bicycle, elevator, wristwatch, refrigerator, sewing ma-
  chine, and electronic calculator production

Plugging into Chinese R&D: The Role of Trade Fairs

In planning China ventures, foreign companies should acquaint themselves with the most technologically dynamic sectors of Chinese industry. They should make an effort to pinpoint those areas (with Chinese

assistance) where pockets of excellence are likely to emerge. One proven method has been through cooperation and interaction in China's R&D sector. This may involve participation in one or more of China's numerous trade fairs, collaboration with a Chinese research institute, or sponsoring technical seminars. All three of these activities should be considered essential in a firm's long-term strategy in China.

The biannual Canton Trade Fair is the most famous of the trade fairs, once estimated to foster half of China's annual export trade. Its main goal, however, has been to sell and buy commodities and manufactured goods. Since 1979, the fair has become much less important as an entrepôt for foreign technology. Out of the S&T reform effort, however, has come a new and increasingly important institution, namely, the local science and technology fair. Today, a multitude of annual technology fairs are being held around the country, each focused on a different industrial sector. Successful market penetration could begin with participation in an applicable technology fair. This low-cost project ($9,000–25,000 total expenses) may be part of a firm's initial market investigation of business opportunities. The trade fair offers a firm the chance to ascertain the broad goals of the Chinese participants. If the visiting firm is well-prepared (with company brochures, portfolios, etc.), the Chinese will have an opportunity to understand the objectives and business philosophy of the foreign firm as well. It should be mentioned that in one of the questionnaires used to research this book, U.S. corporations which believe they have achieved brand-name recognition for their products in China indicated that technical seminars and trade fair participation were the most important factors in doing so.

As a next step, companies are advised to visit and initiate interaction with the Chinese research institutes working in related fields. A firm's active participation in this way will help to determine the level of technical sophistication already present in the industry. The interfacing of the foreign firm and the Chinese R&D institute could reveal specific and mutually beneficial forms of cooperation. In addition, the nature and extent of foreign competition in the sector can be investigated. To be sure, knowledge of past projects in the sector involving foreign firms, the types of foreign technology already acquired, and the business approach used by other firms is essential in formulating venture options.

An effective third step in the process might be to sponsor a technical seminar. At this event, foreign firms describe and display technolog-

Has your firm succeeded in establishing brand-name recognition for its product(s) in China? If yes, how has this been accomplished?

Technical seminars, trade exhibitions	47%
Chinese references	35%
Direct promotion by sales reps	35%
Media advertising	30%

NOTE: Percentages do not add up to 100 percent since many firms claimed to have achieved brand-name recognition by more than one method. Also, 24 percent of the respondents indicated their firm had not achieved brand-name recognition in China.

SOURCE: Author's survey (see appendix for complete form of this questionnaire).

ical ideas and engage in discussions and negotiations with participating Chinese ministry officials. Relationships are fostered between foreign and Chinese engineers in an informal atmosphere. Particular technical problems can be discussed directly with researchers or the R&D managers. With the right partner and workable licensing agreement, a relatively uncomplicated and low-risk form of cooperation can get a start and serve as the base from which a full-fledged relationship can blossom. The Chinese partner will feel comfortable in soliciting the foreign company for bigger projects, and the foreign company will feel at ease in developing additional ventures with its Chinese counterpart.

COULD CHINA BECOME THE NEXT "ASIAN TIGER"?

Aside from the bureaucratic hassles and the processing delays, one reason for the reluctance of some foreign firms to transfer their more advanced technological expertise is the fear that China is planning a modernization program similar to that of Japan. That is, one that involves the acquisition and subsequent improvement of foreign technological products, only later to reintroduce them on the international market as competing export commodities. China has chosen a path similar to other countries of the Pacific Rim, attempting to integrate foreign technological know-how with indigenous processes in order to capture a selected market niche in the world economy. Whether they can remold foreign technology with the same success as Japan, Taiwan, Singapore, and South Korea is difficult to predict. Certainly, many more obstacles block China's path to modernization than other Asian nations experienced.

The world economic community has changed markedly since Japan began its drive to increase high technology exports in the mid-1960s. The export of foreign technological expertise into Third World nations, especially in the East Asian region, is an increasingly risky prospect for foreign firms that depend on exports for their survival. Western firms are not as enthusiastic about transferring their innovations and production methods as they were in the 1960s and 1970s when the largest firms rushed to set up factories in Asian countries to take advantage of cheap labor, favorable tax laws, and highly attractive investment climates.

Essentially, China would like to emulate the modernization programs of both Japan and Taiwan as it seeks to reach a point of near technological equality with the West. Internally, however, Chinese leaders have found it virtually impossible to encourage exports without drastically restructuring the Chinese economy. When certain government controls were lifted in 1979 in an effort to promote exports, local governments used the opportunity to accumulate precious foreign exchange by undercutting the export prices offered by MOFERT, earnings they spent acquiring mainly foreign consumer electronic goods, automobiles, etc. These activities forced down the price of China's exports, while the trade deficit soared.[51] Government control of the local economy had to be reasserted, but only after a thriving black market in foreign commodities had taken hold. Hence, the vulnerability of the Chinese socialist economy will be a negative factor in China's attempt to create export revenue on a large scale.

Another internal aspect of China's development that will slow down the development of competitive technology exports is the absence of both a marketplace for high-technology products and a competitive private sector. In Japan, the government encouraged preselected, private sector firms with incentives to speed the development of production in a controlled, yet highly competitive, environment. For example, Japan's program promoting the production of very large scale integrated (VLSI) circuits generated 600 patents.[52] This dynamic relationship between the public sector and commercial interests is hard to find in China's S&T sector.

Though China may have to postpone its challenge to Western economic prosperity, it is likely that China will soon be creating products that will compete with foreign products in the markets of developing nations. China may be able to sell its low- or medium-level technological commodities for a lower price because of its cheap labor costs.

Externally, China's objective to catch up to the West meets additional obstacles. China's most important export goods are textiles and oil, which are sold in great quantities to the United States and Japan, respectively. However, protectionist measures in the United States that inhibit the import of textiles from China, the massive drop in oil prices, and the appreciation of the yen, have all combined to constrain China's ability to generate the revenue to support its technology modernization plans. Nevertheless, China is preparing to enter the world economy. In a broader sense, however, it is conceivable that much of the world is simply unprepared to accept the arrival of a new exporting nation possibly greater in magnitude than South Korea, Taiwan, or even Japan.

The Security of Foreign Technology: China's Patent Law

In light of Japan's success in the effective application of technological innovations developed in the United States, it has become a central concern of U.S. executives to seek assurances from China regarding the use of the technology that U.S. firms intend to license there. The stealing of proprietary know-how has cost U.S. companies billions of dollars in lost sales. Counterfeiting has been rampant in Asia and especially costly to firms producing consumer goods that can be easily cloned and peddled in familiar places like Nathan Road in Hong Kong and Itaewon in South Korea, where fake Louis Vuitton handbags sell for $12 and Reebok athletic shoes for $10. Traditionally, Asia has perceived intellectual discoveries as part of the public domain. Most countries, in fact, initiate patent law only when they need to protect domestically developed technology. Resistance to playing fair also stems from the fact that textbooks, food, pharmaceuticals, and other goods purchased from the West are both extremely expensive relative to individual income in these countries and yet are desperately needed.[53] Hopefully, China will come to see that playing the game of proprietary protection fairly—much as South Korea has—will result in an increased technology flow into China than if the Chinese attempt a program of copying and reverse engineering.

The Chinese have been reluctant to meet the demands of foreign firms concerning the ownership of intellectual property, enforcement of the existing patent law, and impartial dispute arbitration. Traditionally, the Chinese apply a different definition to what constitutes intellectual property. Throughout recent history, innovation and invention in China have been the product of communal effort; therefore, inventions are believed to be public property. The Chinese also grossly undervalue the cost of R&D spent by foreign firms in developing their products. It is difficult for the Chinese to conceive of the vast sums a Western firm will spend, for example, on the development of one piece of software. Hence, the development of a comprehensive and enforceable body of patent law in China has been frustratingly slow.

China's patent law went into effect on April 1, 1985, and resembles the standardized patent legislation recommendations embodied in the United Nations Fourteen Group Laws. During the first three months after ratification of the patent law, over 7,000 applications flooded in, 2,100 of them from foreign companies. This was indicative both of rising Chinese technical capabilities as well as foreign interest in obtaining early protection for their products.* The adoption of the law is a major breakthrough—an indication that China's attitude toward the economic value of mental labor and proprietary rights has undergone a highly progressive change. This is surprising in view of the fact that some argued against the patent law on the grounds that it would be used by foreign firms to constrain Chinese access to technology. However, the scope of the law was seen by many foreign firms and their lawyers as relatively incomplete, inexact, and vulnerable to interpretation on the part of the Chinese. For instance, only new inventions— those possessing the quality of novelty—can be protected. Left uncovered by the law are scientific discoveries, software developments, chemical substances, pharmaceuticals, health treatments, and diagnostic methods.

Much to the dismay of foreign firms, the body of law enacted in 1985 contains no definition of infringement, either on the part of the Chinese importing entity or on the part of an outside importer of pirated

---

*To register trademarks in China, foreign firms must contact: Trademark Registration Agency, China Council for the Protection of International Trade (CCPIT), Beijing, People's Republic of China.

products. The omission raises serious questions among foreign firms as to whether China will entertain claims of infringement, such as contributory infringement and inducement to infringe.[54] In essence, this initial body of patent law will be greatly influenced by Chinese legal interpretation and subsequent amendment. A set of provisions adopted during 1985, covering the import of foreign technology, may help to clarify the legal framework for technology transfer. These provisions constitute an attempt to protect the Chinese importing enterprise from restrictions on the use of licensed foreign technology. In addition, they require foreign firms to make specific guarantees concerning the eventual output and quality level of products produced by the foreign technology.

In light of these provisions, most lawyers feel obliged to advise firms they should license technology in China with utmost caution. They see the regulations as a disincentive for firms to transfer technology because the law requires foreign firms to guarantee specific production targets and product quality while allowing the Chinese to maintain and operate the technology without foreign control over inputs. First of all, the provisions limit technology import contracts and royalty payments to ten years. After this time the Chinese licensee enjoys unrestricted use of the foreign technology. Second, the Chinese importing enterprise cannot be required in the contract to use raw materials, spare parts, or equipment deemed by the foreign firm as appropriate for its technology. Ultimately, these regulations downgrade China's patent protection laws, turning licensing agreements into direct sales of technology after ten years. Technology import agreements under these conditions could easily result in the violation of a contract by a foreign firm if the Chinese enterprise fails to use appropriate spare parts or raw materials with the foreign equipment or simply uses the technology in an unproductive way. It should be noted that the Chinese intend to treat these provisions not as fixed law, but as starting points for negotiation.[55] Obviously, foreign firms should write technology import contracts with these considerations in mind.

Also disturbing about the security of foreign technology in China is that it appears that most serious contract disputes will continue to be settled via third-party arbitration, which inhibits the formation of a body of legal precedent. Relatedly, interviews in China suggest that U.S. firms would choose against taking legal action in the event of a patent infringement because they believe such action would seriously damage their reputation in China. As one representative of a large U.S. computer firm said about pursuing compensation against infringement of proprietary rights in China: "There is no recourse unless you want to leave China with no plans of returning."

While China has been assembling and ratifying its patent law, the outside world has been growing increasingly sensitized about transferring expensive technological equipment and know-how to foreign countries, especially East Asian countries. In home factories as well as those overseas, Western firms have begun to take serious action in protecting their expertise. A prime example is IBM's policy of preventing key designers from participating in the "hands on" aspects of computer component manufacturing. The control of advanced technology has also become an important security issue for the West because of its use in defense industries. The coupling of these integral concerns with Chinese uneasiness about ratifying patent laws that could constrict Chinese importing enterprise in the future has impeded the development of China's patent law and the entities to enforce it.

In summary, what the Chinese gain by maintaining flexibility in their technology import and patent laws is increased freedom to utilize acquired technology. The disadvantage, however, remarked an American lawyer in Beijing, "is that fewer foreign firms will readily transfer their advanced technology to China." American firms selling easy-to-copy products should consider registering them in China whether they plan to market the product there or not. The case of Parker Brothers' Monopoly game should be incentive enough. Recently, a Shanghai factory started cloning the board game under the name Strong Hand. Thousands of the games have sold, to the chagrin of Parker Brothers, which did not register a copyright for the game in China. One businessman called it the veritable image of increasingly capitalist China— a huddle of Chinese children hunkered over the familiar property deeds and plastic hotels of a Monopoly game board manufactured in Shanghai in blatant violation of international copyright.

NATIONAL SECURITY ISSUES: EXPORT CONTROLS AND COCOM

The liberalization of U.S. export control policy has greatly encouraged the movement of U.S. high-technology products into China. Fearing the use of such high technology in defense-related industries, U.S. policymakers have had to weigh national security risks with the commercial benefits associated with the increase of U.S. exports of high-technology manufactured goods.

Foreign firms are concerned about the long-term implications of licensing advanced technology in a country where political currents can shift quickly. With such uncertainty in the background, many observers are concerned about the military aspects of technology transfer. To be sure, since the late U.S. secretary of commerce, Malcolm Baldrige, announced a substantial relaxation in U.S. restrictions toward China in 1983, the Chinese have asked for increasingly higher and more advanced technologies: 75 percent of their requests are for microelectronic circuits, computers, various electronics instruments, and equipment for producing semiconductors. As dual-use technologies, these can be used in military as well as civilian areas—particularly for strategic weapons such as the intercontinental ballistic missiles (ICBMs), which the Chinese have already deployed.

One of the ironies of Chinese technological modernization is that the country has developed a nuclear weapons industry, put 18 satellites into space, and has launched a ballistic missile from a submarine despite their problems in implementing civilian technology. They have been able to do this largely because their centralized system can concentrate its best-educated scientists and most advanced resources on high-priority projects. In many fields of technology, the gap between China and the industrialized nations is being closed, and this disturbs many U.S. policymakers. Indeed, China developed its first computer in 1958, only twelve years after the United States, and only one year after Japan. It developed its first integrated circuit in 1969, eleven years after the United States and only one year after England. Finally, China possessed its own hydrogen bomb by 1967, fifteen years after the United States, and one year *before* France.[56] Even in light of these achievements, the Chinese would have to engage in considerable research and development in order to build modern strategic weapons systems using these technologies. Despite the overlap between military and civilian sectors in China, as well as its refusal to accept restrictions on the internal use of imported technologies, it is widely assumed that the Chinese will try to incorporate civilian technologies into their military sector, particularly because of the profitability of selling arms abroad. China earns roughly $2 billion annually selling arms, the fifth largest exporter of military hardware in the world.

Prior to 1983 the United States was cautious about selling technology to the Chinese military. American export policy toward China had originated as a child of the Cold War, when the Soviet Union and China were thought of collectively as Communists. In 1979 new laws were enacted that restricted, among other things, the re-export of American-made products. As flexibility toward individual countries increased, China opened its doors to U.S. high-technology exports. China's status was once again modified, this time as a result of an effort by the United States to distinguish the People's Republic from the U.S.S.R. According to a so-called China differential, established when the Soviets invaded Afghanistan, it was decided China could be sold technology at twice the level of sophistication of that sold to the Soviet Union prior to the invasion. This policy was somewhat vague yet politically expedient. It created a flood of applications for technology exports to China.

During both the Carter and Reagan administrations, China pressed the United States to move forward in lifting restrictions on the sale of advanced technology. China was eventually placed in the less sensitive "Group V," with technology transfers being denied only if they would demonstrably contribute to nuclear weapons and their delivery systems, antisubmarine warfare, electronic warfare, intelligence gathering, and power projection capabilities such as long-range bombers. In short, advanced military technologies were not to be exported, although many of the building-block technologies that the Chinese need for military purposes, such as advanced materials and electronics, could be exported.

Serious concerns remain about the possible diversion of ostensibly civilian technologies into the military sector. When China has been unable legally to obtain technologies that it desires, it has been willing to turn to clandestine means. Lieutenant General James A. Williams, director of the Defense Intelligence Agency, said at a congressional hearing in the summer of 1982 that China had begun to set up dummy firms to bypass export controls. Such firms operate in the United States but employ Chinese nationals who learn about new technologies and return home with their knowledge. Some U.S. firms have regretted sharing blueprints and selling single prototypes expecting large orders that never materialize.

Although the U.S. government acknowledges that the technology acquisition problems encountered by the People's Republic suggest that the potential for significant dual-use violations is slim, the Office of Technology Assessment (OTA) predicts that the risk of China using advanced technology to produce sophisticated weapon systems will grow over the years as Chinese technological capability improves. Using antisubmarine warfare as an example, the OTA makes the point that defense technologies are integrated from a broad spectrum of critical technologies, some easily controlled, some difficult to control but available commercially, and others that are impossible to control. Judging an individual technology export license takes time, because the combination of past purchases of technology may enable China to assemble a complete technological set that can match U.S. strategic defense capability in a certain area. At present, the average processing time for export licensing cases referred to the Department of Defense and other agencies (not including COCOM) is about six months. However, over 130 cases had been in the system for more than a year as of January 1987.[57] Large numbers of applications submitted to COCOM forced the Department of Commerce, in late 1986, to once again liberalize export controls concerning China. Twenty-seven categories of technological items were formed, all to be approved for export to China with the stipulation that the Chinese end-user guarantee the proposed usage of the items by submitting written certification. Subsequently, a bottleneck formed on the Chinese side. As financial constraints on end-users mounted, it became more difficult for them to obtain certification from Chinese trade authorities to import high technology.

In 1988, U.S. Customs Service officers expressed alarm at the number of Chinese agents working in the U.S. for the purpose of gathering technological information for the People's Republic. The majority of this information is readily available to visiting scholars in the U.S. and involves relatively insensitive technology such as non-current microprocessors for computers. Even so, nearly half of the technology transfer cases being investigated by the U.S. Customs Service concern the Chinese.

Complaints in China persist over what the Chinese believe to be a lethargic approval process for the transfer of technology in the United States. Some observers suggest the Chinese may be creating a subterfuge to cloud over financial problems on their side. On the U.S. side, most firms interviewed expressed positive opinions regarding the speed of recent COCOM decisions, though firms that sell sophisticated or defense-related technology tend to discredit the COCOM approval process for a number of reasons. First, they question the integrity of COCOM, claiming that delays can be made by member countries in an effort to tip off their national firms about competing bids being pre-

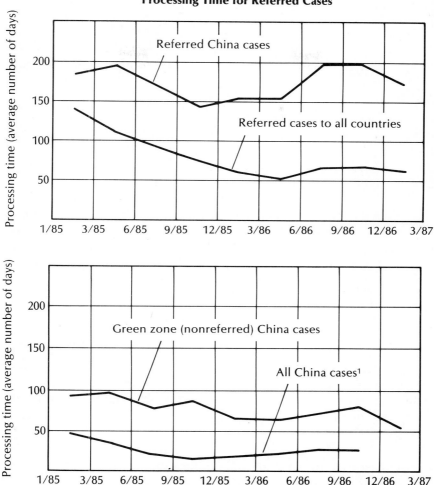

Processing Time for Referred Cases

NOTE: 1. Average for (referred and nonreferred) all China cases.

About one month is the average time necessary to obtain a license to export goods to China. For low-sensitivity cases within the "green zone," the Department of Commerce can process the license in about two months, down from three months in 1985. When the case is referred to the Department of Defense, the Department of State, and/or COCOM, expect to wait about six months, more than twice the average time necessary to obtain a similar license to export to other countries.

SOURCE: Office of Technology Assessment, 1987.

sented to the Chinese. Second, the egalitarian premise of the organization is considered suspect by some since the overwhelming majority of
COCOM applications are submitted by U.S. firms. There is also deep
concern among U.S. officials about the extent to which the approval
process is circumvented by certain COCOM member countries and
their firms, known as "COCOM distractors," who sell sensitive technology disguised as benign.

   Many U.S. firms are frustrated by the mystique of COCOM—its aura
of secrecy, hearsay, and rumor—because it is difficult for companies to
influence the approval process. How does a firm lobby for COCOM
approval? "They really can't," said a U.S. military attaché in Hong Kong.
The only advice one can offer firms is to package their technology in the
most benign way possible and answer all export control and COCOM
questions thoroughly. Those U.S. firms unable to get approval should
investigate whether China has already obtained similar technology
from non-COCOM countries. If so, the firm can submit a claim to the
Office of Foreign Availability within the Department of Commerce,
which will try to determine if foreign availability exists. If so, restriction
may be lifted on an otherwise security controlled item.[58]

Governmental Coordination Efforts.

As the expe-
rience of U.S. firms in other parts of the world indicates, in the process
of transferring technology to developing nations, the relationship between the supplying firm and its home government is as vital as that
between the recipient firm and its government. Technology transfers
are being increasingly viewed by Beijing and Washington as part of
emerging economic relations and not as part of a strategic alignment.
This does not mean that issues such as China's purported sale of Silk-
worm missiles to Iran in 1987 will not have an impact on the commercial aspects of the relationship. (In this case, the U.S. deliberately
slowed down the review process associated with further relaxation of
technology transfers to China.) Without improved government-to-government coordination, the prospects for successful technology transfer
between the United States and China may be hampered.

   The U.S. government can offer a number of incentives for American firms to transfer technology to the People's Republic. These might
include:

   1. a tax credit on technology transfer investments in China;

2. ratification of a bilateral investment treaty in which tax exemptions and/or deferral could be offered to U.S. firms involved in China;
3. beneficial tax treatment of China expatriate income;
4. a concerted effort to spearhead the technology transfer activities of small- and medium-size firms throughout the Pacific Rim with an emphasis on China;
5. subsidies for industrial exchange programs which might increase the American technological foothold in China; and
6. incentives for firms in specific technological sectors to enter China once the best mode of technology transfer for the Chinese situation is defined by government-funded researchers.

Ultimately, the government could play a stronger role in coordinating the technology transfer process and put the whole policy of technological exchange between the United States and China within the prevailing framework of our stated political interests by incorporating business promotion into the policy formulation process. The following chapter includes a discussion of some of the issues related to this broad objective.

Formulas for China Business Success

It is surprising how much foreign expectations have been out of synchronization with the realities of the Chinese economy. . . . There have been times when [ ] foreign traders were cautious and [ ] China expansive, but more often the traders were exuberant while the Chinese were beset with problems they understandably preferred not to publicize. In retrospect it is amazing that euphoria about long run prospects of China trade has survived . . . short-run contradictory desires.

Lucian Pye

We cannot formulate business expectations in China because there are no ground rules here. We are living a case study.

Representative of General Electric in Beijing

The drama of the U.S.-China corporate encounter has revolved around the divergent expectations held by each country. False expectations have led to misguided prioritizing and ill-laden planning on both sides. On the U.S. side, executives have had to reassess their perception of the China market as one of vast, untapped potential where American goods can be easily peddled by subsidiaries with an office in Beijing. On the Chinese side, decision makers have been taken aback that foreign companies have not lined up on China's doorstep eager to transfer their technology in exchange for a piece of the China market. Having opened their market to an unprecedented degree, the Chinese are surprised that more of the world's corporations have not rushed into China to make huge investments.

The types of firms entering China and the intentions of those firms have been somewhat of a letdown as well.

The majority of firms committing to joint ventures in China are willing to transfer one element of their technology to China, but few have been willing to conduct R&D in China, thus nullifying the short-term hopes of the Chinese to indigenize foreign technological processes in their country. Few Chinese expected at the outset that many of the world's largest firms would enter the China market simply in search of market share to combat their traditional rivals. So, too, few U.S. firms venturing in China as pioneers foresaw the intransigent problems of doing business in China and the high cost of sustaining a presence there.

As the U.S.-China corporate encounter unfolded in the mid-1980s, however, expectations on both sides began to come into alignment with the realities of China's business atmosphere and the market-seeking imperatives of foreign firms investing in China. After an investment slowdown in 1987, foreign firms are investing again in China at a brisk pace, though in smaller projects more in line with the limitations of China's investment landscape. On the Chinese side, investment policy has been geared increasingly to attract foreign firms willing to transfer technology to China and export from China in exchange for market share. Firms that simply want to sell to the Chinese or source cheaper raw materials are being weeded out. At the same time, the new impetus to invest in China has been driven by China's growing skilled labor force and better supply lines to foreign-invested enterprises. Rather than enter China expecting to repatriate profits as if this were the divine right of a China venture, foreign managers are learning to structure deals based on compensation trade, exportation of a percentage of production to earn needed foreign exchange, and other stratagems to circumvent the repatriation dilemma. As expectations become less contradictory and more complementary, higher profits are being seen by Sino-U.S. ventures.

In fact, contrary to recent press reports auguring that the China bubble has burst, a growing number of foreign firms have found success in the People's Republic. In its first three years of operation, Remy Martin recovered nearly half of its initial investment and has earned a profit of over 500,000 yuan. At this rate the venture will recover its total investment in nine years.[1] The Tianjin Liming Cosmetics Corporation, a joint venture involving Wella of West Germany, has increased its sales to 3.7 million yuan per year in China, Hong Kong, and Japan.[2] Indicative of the vast size of the market, Wella has captured only a 1 to 2 percent share of the China market, yet half of its production is going to satisfy domestic demand, while the other half is being exported.[3] As another example, in 1986, the China-Schindler Elevator Company earned $5.5

million in foreign exchange and expected to earn $7 million in 1987.[4] Even AMC (now owned by Chrysler), which initially struggled during its start-up, is said to have balanced its foreign exchange account and is on the way to a profitable future, manufacturing China-assembled Jeeps and selling American-made spare parts. In terms of their collective objective to penetrate a new market, it is now fair to say that U.S. firms in China have been at least moderately successful. In a growing number of cases—Foxboro, Coca-Cola, PepsiCo, Hewlett-Packard, Gillette, and Kodak, to name only a few—U.S. market positioning has paid off. By establishing China ventures, firms such as these have seen significant marketing success, given the complexities of the market.

A growing number of firms have begun expansion of operations in the People's Republic, in part to circumvent the inherent problems of repatriation and sourcing in China, but also as part of a concerted effort to widen their China business presence and enhance profit making. Through expansion, firms are laying the foundation necessary for them to prosper in China for years to come. Beatrice Foods has begun to deal with repatriation problems by setting up a "trading house" collaboration with CITIC. ES-Pacific Development Corporation now offers financial services via the Great Wall Hotel to help solve the currency conversion problems of other foreign ventures in China. 3M has made inroads in labor recruitment and marketing from its solid position in its wholly owned factory.

In some cases, the commitment to expand portends a truly long-term potential for present and future success in China. Nowhere is this success better exemplified than by China Hewlett-Packard (CHP). In addition to its joint venture in Beijing, CHP now has a branch in Shanghai to promote sales, maintenance, and training. The company also has a liaison office in Chengdu to augment its production venture in Beijing. The company expects China sales to triple during the next few years. CHP is producing more computers, electrical testing equipment, and chemical analysis apparatus for export from China.[5] Similarly, according to a knowledgeable source, Foxboro has been so successful at exporting production from China that its China venture may soon replace its home factory as the manufacturer of one of the company's electrical products.

For the Japanese, the corporate future in the People's Republic is looking brighter as well. The reader might recall from Chapter 6 the disastrous drop in profits experienced by Fujian Hitachi Television Company, Ltd., in 1985–86. Miraculously, and with the help of the Chinese government, the joint venture engineered a total turnaround in

1987, hauling in a year-end profit of 1.2 million yen. After being exempted from taxes, collateral requirements, and assisted by the Chinese government in upgrading component suppliers, the venture exported 60,733 televisions in 1987, while bringing the percentage of domestically produced parts and components for its 19-inch sets to 56 percent, up from 34 percent in 1986. The venture's total net profit in 1987, after two grim years in the red, came to a formidable $5.8 million.[6]

Moreover, many of the China-Hong Kong ventures in the SEZs are thriving well beyond original expectations. One example is the Jingbao Light Fixtures Company, Ltd., involving three partners, two Chinese and one from Hong Kong. Only fourteen months after production was started in 1984 the owners had recouped their initial start-up investment of 1.02 million yen. Then profits began rolling in—1.26 million yen in 1985, 1.46 million yen in 1986, and 1.92 million yen in 1987.[7]

How have these firms achieved success in China's unforgiving investment climate? Can a surefire formula for business success in China be drawn from the experiences of these pioneering firms? In conducting interviews in China, the author heard repeatedly that no black- and-white rules existed for success in China business. Many executives acknowledged that the whole China undertaking had the quality of a living case study, with no preconceived outcome. Over time, however, some of the gray area has given way and a few clear lessons have been learned.

PROSPERING IN CHINA: DO FORMULAS EXIST?

Looking at the methods employed by foreign firms that have achieved China business success, one can delineate three areas of corporate capability that can be termed "formulaic." These three tactical imperatives should remain in focus during the planning, implementation, and evaluation of China business activities: (1) building up in-house China expertise; (2) plugging into Chinese bureaucracy; and (3) starting small while pursuing a bifurcated corporate strategy in China.

Building In-house Expertise:
The Role of the China Subsidiary

Multinational firms usually form wholly owned subsidiary companies to conduct their international business. When China opened its door to trade in 1978, U.S. firms saw that China could become a huge market for their products, and in response they formed China subsidiaries. These companies were given the mandate to act as the marketing arm of the parent firm in the People's Republic. They were put in charge of identifying the need for the firm's product lines and services, generating sales, organizing service backup, and coordinating deliveries to Chinese buyers. China subsidiaries are usually small, sometimes employing as few as a dozen people, reflecting the reality that China business is still only a very small part of the overall business conducted by U.S. firms in China.

Ironically, the modest level of importance attached to the China market by most parent companies can be a big advantage for the China subsidiary. It may enjoy an exceptional amount of operating flexibility, since it will not necessarily be tied into other parts of the company in the same way as other larger subsidiary units. In this sense, it may be free to set up its own operating model in China for what it deems most appropriate. This independence and flexibility could become its key to success in China. Hopefully, through that success, the parent company will come to accept the subsidiary's *modus operandi* as a model for other transcultural ventures. However, until the China unit can prove the success of its approach, it remains vulnerable to the control imposed on it by the parent company.

Infatuated with the short-term benefits of overseas subsidiaries, parent firms may be too little concerned with long-range goals to offer the nurturing a fledgling China venture requires. Indirect damage has been caused when managerial turnover in the parent firm jars the stability of its subsidiary in China. One firm suffered a succession of CEOs, the first highly enthusiastic about the firm's venture in China, the next highly pessimistic, and the third lukewarm. The firm's China venture experienced directly the ebb and flow of the parent's changing leadership, and it barely survived the ordeal.

Strong commitment from the parent in the decision to undertake China activities must be secured and constantly enhanced. China-related decisions should emanate from the top in quick response to the needs of the China subsidiary. In fact, the CEO should be personally committed to China endeavors. The less separation between the parent and the China subsidiary, the better. China operations need to be connected directly to the parent firm and managed closely by those at the core of the company. From the earliest stages, key officers from the parent company should be included on the board of the China subsidiary, so as to build a bridge between parent and subsidiary. Officers from the China subsidiary must make a concerted and continuing effort to enlighten the parent's board of directors about the unorthodox and long-term nature of the China market, the necessity of making a long-term commitment to the market, and the associated costs of doing so.

A firm must determine whether typical measures of performance should be used to gauge the success of a business in the China market. For example, the firm must reduce any preoccupation with return on investment (ROI) on the part of the parent's board of directors and the company's major stockholders. China is not a place to reclaim market share lost to Asian competitors. Setting priorities in China based on ROI leads to improvidence and false expectations of both the China market and the China subsidiary. When profits do not emerge, frustration and disillusionment invariably set in and the China subsidiary is faulted and thus weakened.

Firms have to rethink return on investment as it applies to China. Competitive bidding on China projects works to depress profit margins. As one Japanese executive in China said, "There is good growth in volume but the situation is that of poor profit."[8] Government attempts to diversify sources and partners often make it impossible for a firm to obtain successive contracts after the first has been won. Sharply rising office and overhead costs (described in Chapter 2) also take their toll on the profit potential of the China subsidiary. Consequently, the performance of the subsidiary should be evaluated using criteria appropriate to the realities of China's commercial setting. Rather than measure performance in terms of bottom-line profit, which has been low for all parties involved, a firm should judge the China unit in areas such as growth in China-based equity, new venture start-ups, broadening of the marketing network, new sourcing opportunities, and increasing business clout due to widening guanxi. A manufacturing venture should be evaluated in terms of market share rather than foreign exchange earnings.

An M.I.T. survey of five telecommunications companies that have entered the China market was especially revealing about the trouble U.S. firms have encountered by misjudging the potential of the China market and its dissimilarity with other overseas markets. One of the companies behaved with little concern about any future *strategic advantage* to be gained from its presence in China. That is, management viewed the entry into China only in terms of immediate revenue. This company expected to see revenues of $400 million a year by the third year of operation in China. The other four companies saw their firms' progress in the market in terms of long-term potential for profits, developing business contacts, and winning contracts in the future. Interestingly, of the five firms studied in the survey, the firm expecting $400 million annually from China is currently withdrawing from the market. In most successful ventures in China, top management does not perceive ROI as especially relevant in the initial stages; they take a five- to ten-year view on profit making.[9]

A long-term commitment combines patience, perseverance, and persistence on the part of both the parent and the subsidiary. A commitment to the market is manifested in the number of activities the firm is willing to support, such as co-ventures, office presence, service centers, and promotional sales staff dedicated to China sales. The replies on the author's questionnaires indicated that many of the "high commitment" firms perceive their role in China less in terms of mere marketing objectives, and more as a collaboration with the Chinese. These (mostly large) firms see themselves becoming insiders through a process of learning and expanding their involvement. A few responses about their role in China were as follows:

- "To raise the level of health care in China by introducing higher-quality products produced at a higher technological level."
- "To play a significant role in the development of China's air transportation system."
- "To provide a conduit for information and know-how exchange through publications between China and the West."

On the other hand, most of the small and medium-size companies (usually of 250 to 12,000 employees) have concentrated their China activities solely on their efforts to sell products in the market. They tend to perceive their role in China's future strictly in terms of that effort rather than as a broader, more collaborative commitment. Respondents from these firms described their roles in China's future in the following ways:

- "A persistent and conservative sales effort."
- "To sell used technology and old technology."
- "To see modest improvement in sales, subject to fluctuations."

Though these firms probably have modest intentions because they are smaller and specifically sales-oriented, their shorter-term, less collaborative corporate approach in China may be in part the cause of their limited success so far, and thus their lower expectations of China's market in the future.

The questionnaire also revealed that those firms which regard the potential of the market with what one executive termed "guarded optimism" have invested significant amounts of capital, technology, and human resources into their endeavors, setting up China ventures as well as marketing products. These executives perceive the market along a spectrum ranging from "modest" and "worthwhile" to "unlimited" and "very promising." Firms attempting merely to sell products in China, with little intention of participating in any sort of co-venture with the Chinese, stood out as most "dissatisfied" with the China market. These respondents felt that the market was "sluggish," subject to "fits and starts," and "dependent on China's political situation and ability to improve its physical and regulatory infrastructure." They also felt the pressure of Japanese competition more intensely than those firms that have positioned themselves in joint ventures.

Assembling the China Unit

Many firms organize special China task groups. A task group consists of individuals who have a thorough understanding of the relevant business, who have technical as well as operational knowledge of the parent company, and who can work effectively at all levels of the company. Technical consultants are hired on an as-needed basis.

Given that the China market puts a premium on cultural affiliation and personalized sales promotion, firms have to commit significant resources to train personnel for the China post. Foreign firms often send expatriates into China on a rotation system, with each staying in the country roughly four months a year. Lessening the hardship of living in China is clearly the advantage of this system, but the one drawback is that the Chinese may find it difficult to reacquaint themselves with the expatriates again and again. Long-term personal relationships tend to become valuable to the foreign firm after start-up. The firm should strive for continuity of personnel from the negotiation stage through venture start-up and beyond, and it should select expatriates first on the basis of their ability to live comfortably in China for long periods. Chinese language training appears to be the second most important prerequisite for China duty.

Unfortunately, average salaries for China expatriates are not altogether high. A survey published in the by *China Business Review* in 1985 indicated that "the typical U.S. business person in China is a 37-year-old marketing manager earning a base salary of $52,700 per year on a two or three-year stint."[10] A survey undertaken by Runzheimer International found that the hardship premium paid to U.S. expatriates working in China averaged 26 percent of base salary.[11] In addition to increasing salaries, foreign firms must place added emphasis on R&R for expatriates. Typical arrangements involve three paid, one-week trips to Hong Kong and one four-week trip to the United States per year, with paid air fare. Rosalie L. Tung has recognized a need for longer-term overseas assignments for U.S. expatriates, but understands that the rapid turnover stems from "the concern among expatriates (particularly those from U.S. multinationals) that a prolonged absence from corporate headquarters may negatively affect their chances of promotion within the corporate hierarchy."[12] These and other factors make it difficult for foreign firms to persuade good managers to relocate in China.

One cannot blame them, given the drawbacks of living and working in China as an expatriate. As a group, the Americans stationed in China are highly educated, materially prosperous, independent achievers. Upon arrival in the People's Republic, they find themselves living in cramped quarters, often feeling a sense of isolation, both geographically and socially. As managers they must cope with seeming swarms of workers whose collectivist training and traditions contradict the Western concepts of "best personal performance." These and other factors combine to make the China post highly unattractive to the American manager. As one U.S. consulate circular describing the China post warned:

> Foreign business people have to agree to live in hotel rooms (usually without cooking facilities) for several years, to eat all their meals in restaurants, and to forgo accustomed sports activities, recreation, and cultural entertainment. The normal friendships and circle of acquaintances among host nationals that an expatriate in almost any other assignment would develop as compensation are largely barred to the foreigner in China. So he leads a

somewhat isolated existence, artificially isolated from local culture and society.[13]

Although great courtesy is shown during the negotiation and start-up phases, according to Americans now working in China, the courtesy wears off as the mundane routine of working shoulder to shoulder takes hold. Chinese bureaucracy tends to force the expatriate into a position of dependency on a so-called sponsoring unit, which like the Chinese production unit, takes responsibility for the expatriate while in China.[14] Some expatriates find it difficult to accept and adjust to the arbitrary nature of the country's supply and service system when they discover how many of the necessities of living are sought and obtained through the "back door." Frustrations flare when expatriates witness special advantages being given to ethnic Chinese expatriates. In addition, foreign managers have discovered how hard it is to earn the respect of their counterparts; the perception of the foreigner in the Chinese factory is often viewed with insensitivity and even skepticism. Referring to Chinese managers, one foreign manager warned:

> You have to earn their respect. That takes time. They check everything you do. . . . it probably takes you six months to gain their respect, if you can. [Only then will you] find that your decisions [get] implemented without cross-checking and cross-referencing.[15]

Inefficiencies, lack of scheduling, and all-too-frequent disregard for safety in Chinese factories conflict with the professional standards and personal values held by U.S. managers in China, causing personal discontent and creating animosity between them and their Chinese counterparts.

Customs treatment of foreigners working in China receives similar reviews. Treatment is unpredictable and seemingly depends on the ethnic background of the foreigner. Customs rates may turn out to be higher than those published. Rates often depend on the guanxi of the Chinese partner. Some U.S. companies pay no duty on office equipment, while another finds rates exceedingly high.[16] One businessman had to pay a customs charge of 145 percent of the value of a copying machine.[17] Once again, customs rates cannot be specified in enforceable contracts because of bureaucratic sectionism. This lends itself to more resentment and frustration for the expatriates because, as representatives of a company, they feel responsible for keeping expenses under control.

Because the Chinese attempt to isolate foreigners physically and socially, cultural disorientation occurs as well. The Chinese frown on foreigners dating Chinese, and any sort of social mixing is discouraged. In most parts of the country, foreigners seeking social interaction are relegated to foreign clubs, which are off limits to native Chinese. Conversely, a foreigner's privacy remains unrespected. There is a disregard for confidentiality in business dealings and telex messages seem to be considered public domain.[18] Added to this sense of infringement of personal privacy, expatriates living in China face feelings of isolation and even fear, in that they are far from home, Chinese medical facilities are lacking, and there are few foreigners in most areas of China outside the major cities. Moreover, Western-type consumer goods are largely unavailable and entertainment is virtually nonexistent.

China's civil law and system of justice are especially disconcerting as they pertain to the foreigner living in China. The most notable case of an American businessman caught up in the Chinese criminal justice system was that of Richard S. Ondrik, whom the *China Business Review* identified as "an American businessman who was detained, interrogated, arrested, tried, and sentenced to eighteen months in a Chinese jail on charges of causing a fire in a Harbin hotel that resulted in the deaths of ten persons [in 1985]." This was the first public trial of a Westerner since China opened its doors in 1978. Ondrik underwent long interrogations and a two-month detention in which he had no access to a Chinese lawyer, although he was permitted to move around the city of Harbin and meet with friends and foreigners. Ondrik was found guilty of accidentally starting the hotel fire through careless smoking. In the United States, it is highly unlikely that he would have been prosecuted since the hotel had failed to install smoke detectors, its fire extinguishers were inoperative, and the local fire brigade was delayed a half hour from arriving at the fire.[19]

All these feelings of acute "foreignness" are accentuated by the crowding in residential areas and office spaces. Foreigners given managerial responsibility for the Chinese joint venture find themselves going from spacious stateside offices to claustrophobic cubicles. Some Shanghai-based U.S. firms have specified in contracts, with mixed results, that the Chinese partner take responsibility for locating housing for foreign expatriates. The Chinese interpret minimum housing standards to be Chinese-style "shared living space and togetherness," which the U.S. expatriates find unacceptable.[20] Often there are restrictions on expatriates' free travel in China. The single-entry visa, which one obtains by getting an invitation from a sponsoring unit, requires expatriates to reapply each time they enter China—a bothersome formality.[21] The problem with visa status stems from the fact it is decided upon by a system outside the one which governs the sponsoring unit. Gaining influence over the outside unit is difficult. Often the status of foreign expatriates is negotiated, leaving them altogether uncertain about their position.[22]

Plugging into Chinese Bureaucracy: Public Relations for the "Corporate Guest"

The second key formula for China business success entails gaining the support of influential members of local government, rallying officials, managers, and local people into a team of allies who actively support the China venture. Back-room politics should not be underestimated as key to the survival and prosperity of China investments. Consequently, "learning the power games common in local politics" should read at the top of the "must-do" list for foreign businessmen.[23] Why? Because with increasing frequency joint ventures solve their problems with the help of government officials.

In one case, Otsuka Pharmaceutical Company of Japan, which has a joint venture in Tianjin, could not find a market for its intravenous bottles, and inventory stocks were piling up. Otsuka's Chinese manager, Nie Yuhe, remained desperate until Li Ruihuan, Tianjin's mayor, summoned the city's hospital staff to a conference at which his aides convinced the hospital personnel to buy Otsuka's bottles. Suddenly, the joint venture was making plans to double its output. What motivated Tianjin's mayor to resolve the problem? Cleverly, Nie Yuhe, the Chinese manager, had broached the subject of the inventory problem in a conversation with Gu Mu, a state counselor, while in the presence of Tianjin's Mayor Li. In order to save face with his bureaucratic superior, Li had issued the remedy. Gu Mu was a good choice for a Chinese official to speak with about the problem, since he is an outspoken advocate of foreign investment in China. In an article in the *Wall Street Journal* covering the incident, Nie Yuhe underscored the pertinence of forming relationships with Chinese officials by emphasizing the importance of conducting factory tours for Chinese officials, saying, "The more visits senior cadres pay, the better."[24]

A firm should expand its network of contacts in order to generate new business ties and potential opportunities—just as in any business environment. This is accomplished by reading the Chinese press and committing time and money to efforts that Western businesses broadly define as public relations. Firms should constantly scan the business scene, conducting intelligence-gathering on what is occurring month to month in local and central politics, especially regarding specifics of reform implementation. Public relations by a foreign company should not be limited to contacting people in the local FTC or the bureau in which the enterprise exists. A firm operating in Shanghai must make the requisite trips to Beijing to ascertain how far and how fast the government is pushing implementation of reform programs that may either benefit the venture or threaten it.

In extraordinary instances, public relations cases taken to the world press can serve as a *de facto* appellate court to bring about resolution of problems unsolved through the normal channels. Consider the case of AMC and its use of public relations to resolve the auto manufacturer's foreign exchange dilemma. AMC felt it could afford a public relations gamble because its was a high-profile joint venture, visited by then Vice President Bush and leading Chinese officials. Unleashing the press broke the foreign exchange bottleneck, but AMC could have a price to pay later in the form of lost concessions.

AMC had been "stewing in its own juices," said an AMC official, over its factory's financial problems. The firm had solicited help from all of the firm's contacts in China to obtain foreign exchange, but to no avail. AMC halted training and technology transfer, cut its staff, and discontinued importation of components. As a last resort, the company sought the intervention of a higher authority: It invited the world press to run stories about the problems at the joint venture, encouraging the press to run a photograph of a Chinese factory worker sleeping at his post, which was published in the *New York Times* in a major business feature article.

The strategy set the Chinese into motion. Protracted negotiations with government officials started and ultimately led to a new contract. One interpretation of AMC's position was that China cannot be permitted to set the stage for foreign investment while refusing to take responsibility for possible joint venture failures. Whether AMC was merely voicing real dissatisfaction or positioning for later bargaining leverage remains unanswered. One must doubt that AMC was ever serious about its stated threat of "deregistering." Some critics believe that the company halted production simply to maneuver for the future. The U.S. firm has only 31.5 percent equity in the venture, and the campaign could have been part of an effort by the company's executives to push hard for additional influence in the decision-making control of the enterprise.

In comparison, Volkswagen resolved its problems, which have been as serious as AMC's, in a less bellicose manner. For whatever reason, the funding for Volkswagen's venture, which had been expected to come from Shanghai, did not come through. Foreign exchange was diverted away from the importation of parts, automobile sales were slow, and China's infrastructural problems caused delays. Chinese banks refused to honor credit lines and loans. Skilled construction labor for the renovation of the project turned out to be more scarce than expected. Component plants are not yet on line. Shanghai has obviously stalled in ameliorating Volkswagen's problems, yet the Germans have not attempted to embarrass their Chinese partners. Volkswagen does have more experience bargaining in developing countries than AMC, and it has chosen to wait out its problems.

Another case to study is the American blunder of omission, which can be as harmful as AMC's error of commission. The Hyatt hotel built in Shanghai by Americans is a case in point. The U.S. side forgot to invite the local FTC to the opening ceremony, so the FTC—which handles tourism—did not send delegations to that hotel. The Americans tried to make amends with the FTC by holding a special dinner for them, but the Chinese did not show up.[25] Companies must strive to be realistic and responsible, and should attempt to understand the cultural differences that could hinder their ability to do business in China.

Other activities could include grass-roots endeavors which will further the image of the firm at the local level. As the "new kid on the block," foreign enterprises could get an antagonistic reaction if they make products similar to those made by the Chinese, but of higher quality. As a foreigner, one must always be cognizant not to appear threatening to local workers and managers who have significantly more clout with local supplying FTCs than a new Sino-foreign venture. The firm must work to get the venture accepted into the social and economic landscape, and the company profile should be kept low. In short, a firm should invest in expatriate staff rather than Madison

Avenue corporate image making. The local business environment will respond to a time-honored business relationship based on trust and responsibility.

According to the author's follow-up survey of U.S. corporations, corporate image was found to play a significant role in their decision to invest in China. Some firms value the positive image associated with breaking into the China market. In the words of John Wong, managing director of Remy Nicolas, the Far East subsidiary of Remy Martin: "Profit is not our main concern. What we want out of the joint venture winery is a successful product which will enhance our image."[26] As a Sheraton manager said about a new hotel in China that the company was to manage, "Five years from now there will certainly be four or five more Sheratons. . . . It's a high-profile industry . . . image is a big thing. A hotel in Guilin or Xian is not a big thing to ITT headquarters. It makes less money, but there's an image payoff."[27] Pacific Telesis went so far as to purchase a full-page advertisement in the *Wall Street Journal* in 1986, associating the company with China and Deng's modernization policies. The advertising campaign was an attempt to exploit the fact that Pacific Telesis was a pioneer in China and therefore could be identified with the innovation and ground-breaking aspects of China's reforms. In actuality, Pacific Telesis has only a minimal presence in China, a small office whose staff (as of 1986) was involved in no China ventures or significant sales.[28] Such exploitation of the Chinese through identification with the country's reforms, it seems, could only damage a firm's reputation among the Chinese.

In the minds of Chinese policymakers and decision makers, there seems to be a model foreign company, which demonstrates commitment to the following: (1) improving the situation for the Chinese; (2) making them money; (3) increasing Chinese wages; (4) enhancing the reputation of the Chinese partner; and (5) taking on the "grass-roots concept." The grass-roots vision entails building a broad base of support before consolidating power. Something should be done to improve life at the local level: employing local people, helping local-level officials and cadres gain favorable attention. Once the local base is built, then the company should deal with Beijing. Dhanin Chearavanont, president of the very successful C. P. Pokphand company in China, follows a "three benefits" program—benefit the state, the people, and the investor.[29]

Enterprises seeking to build grass-roots support should take care to include all local centers of influence that may be affected by or have an effect on the venture. When Wella received approval from Tianjin's mayor to build a factory in a residential area, the company didn't realize that local officials who resisted the project would put up hurdles. Getting electricity and plumbing involved the coordination of seven or eight bureaus. Wella's managing executives found that bringing various bureaucrats together in a general meeting did not solve the problem: "If one bureau sends the bureau head to the meeting, and another sends cadres several rungs below, no solutions can be taken," says Stanley Kwong, Wella's executive in Tianjin. A year later, Wella decided to relocate in a suburban zone outside the control of the urban bureau.[30]

To defend against administrative interference, the company should establish adequate communication and work for concurrence by all parties involved. Conversely, the surest way to destroy an enterprise is by directly challenging the jurisdiction or power of government officials at any or all levels. Problems should be identified and addressed with traditional Western directness. But differences should be resolved in a style compatible with the Chinese concepts of group consensus and saving face.

Starting Small and Bifurcating China Strategy

In essence, market-seeking corporate strategy in China aims to gain access to the domestic market by manufacturing a product line that China otherwise has to import, or that is produced domestically but is in short supply. With all the hoopla about large projects in China, one finds that small ventures set up to serve local needs in China (and adjacent Asian markets) have proven, in a growing number of cases, extremely successful profit makers. Interestingly, some of the most successful China ventures respond to the rather arcane needs of the China market on its most fundamental level. The success of these ventures portends that it may be better, and possibly more lucrative, to begin China operations on a very small scale and build from there. For example, the Thai agro-industrial conglomerate Charoen Pokphand Group has initiated a number of successful ventures in China through its subsidiary, C. P. Pokphand, including a seed mill, a chicken breeding farm, a carpet factory, and a highly successful motorcycle plant in Shanghai that produces an older-model Honda under license. The joint venture generated 13.5 million Rmb in 1987 alone![31]

A firm should begin by investigating China's newly emerging niche markets. What products does China have to buy in order to maintain the momentum of its industrial goals? What would the Chinese save producing them on their own? The firm should transfer technology through licensing the manufacture of low-technology products in order to secure an export platform in China serving Asian markets. Once this is accomplished, the domestic market often opens up to the venture. The huge risk of starting large projects is reduced by starting small and putting many eggs in many baskets. A firm can build on this base while keeping costs down. In some cases, a matrix of symbiotic, low-profile activities in the People's Republic have put firms like C. P. Pokphand in an enviable position in the China market.

Bifurcating a Firm's China Strategy.   Once a firm is entrenched at the ground level in China, the next phase could be to move on to a more complex venture. Much has been written about the "staged," or gradual, approach to the China market, whereby a foreign firm upgrades involvement progressively from, say, a compensation trade deal to a technology license and then to a joint venture or a wholly owned venture. Foreign firms that begin selling directly to China and later license technology or engage in cooperative production and joint ventures tend to gain the marketing experience, knowledge of China business environment, and the necessary guanxi connections to keep financial risk within reason. These firms keep their experience commensurate with financial participation. This approach is conducive to developing Chinese management, ascertaining the capabilities of the Chinese partner to assimilate technology, and testing the existing infrastructure surrounding the joint venture. Coproduction schemes are less risky for foreign firms, and they also give the Chinese side a chance to assimilate technology step by step and to come to understand the process of manufacturing for export.

Mercury Marine, a division of the Brunswick Corporation, started its China involvement with direct sales through Hong Kong. The motors that the Chinese bought soon fell into disrepair because Chinese end-users had no knowledge of maintenance and nowhere to send motors for repair. Mercury Marine signed a three-year technology transfer contract in which the Weimin Machinery Factory in Leping, Jiangxi, would produce older-model outboard motors (7.5 and/or 9.8 horsepower) to be sold in China. The venture also served a vital local need: it provided outboard motors for small coastal fishing vessels. In this case, licensing an older-model outboard engine was appropriate since parts and service were not available in China.[32]

Hewlett-Packard also followed this approach by setting up a service center first, from which it sent workers to service products that the company had sold to Chinese customers. Later, the firm found a suitable Chinese partner and set up a manufacturing joint venture after gaining two to three years of experience working with that partner—selling, servicing, developing trust, etc.[33]

As part of a staged approach, larger projects can be phased in as modular programs, perhaps as a condition of the original contract. The most prominent example of such a strategy is the joint venture manufacturing arrangement between Shanghai Bell Telephone and Belgium's ITT. The contract for this venture stipulates a phased-in transfer of technology starting with 100,000 "System 12" lines, to be followed by the transfer of assembling equipment to manufacture switching systems in China. During the second phase, all manufacturing technology and some assembling will be transferred to the joint venture. The plan provides that all parts for "System 12" lines eventually be manufactured in China by the joint venture.[34]

The notion of starting small and increasing participation sequentially through a staged approach is valid and prudent. In the long term, however, a more expansive approach has been followed by the highly successful foreign firms in China. Their strategic approach is less one of moving from project to project than it is diversifying into new areas of opportunity simultaneously. In this sense the China market—in all its component elements—has been approached by a handful of firms through different branches of an integrated China strategy. Firms that enter the market with a one-dimensional, vertical strategy in which the firm intends to excel in only one aspect of the China market (for example, selling to the domestic market) tend to find their expectations unfulfilled. As one China consultant in an interview observed: "Firms that have entered the [China] market under a one-dimensional strategy, and subsequently have branched into additional dimensions of the market, while integrating those China activities into one multifaceted corporate presence, are now in a strong position to see the inevitable benefits that China opportunities have to offer." This is called a "bifurcated" approach: a firm secures its operations in promising emerging business niches; expands its relationships with appropriate Chinese business partners and influential associates; anticipates that what may have begun as a one-dimensional business approach should eventually branch into multiple endeavors; and works toward the goal that in time these varied business activities will coalesce into a permanent corporate presence at many levels of the Chinese economy.

One cannot ignore the success that Japan's Hitachi has generated by bifurcating its China activities. As mentioned earlier, the Fujian Hitachi joint venture has become an important penetration point into China's domestic market, winning the privilege to sell to Chinese buyers for foreign exchange currency (i.e., the Chinese government permits the venture to register its domestically sold televisions as import substitutes). Second, the venture has become an export platform of televisions into the Asian markets of Hong Kong, Nepal, and Indonesia. Third, the company is quickly securing hold of a vast network of Chinese supplying factories that will bring down overhead and increase the competitiveness of the venture. Amazingly, Fujian Hitachi has brought fifty-eight domestic component manufacturing factories under the umbrella of the venture's new Joint Enterprise Group, formed in 1987. A committee has been established to help ensure quality and compliance to technical standards set by Hitachi among all of the suppliers. Hitachi is affiliated with the manufacture of picture tubes in China for domestic television manufacturers as well. This sort of bifurcation of corporate strategy promises to produce corporate prosperity for Hitachi in the People's Republic well into the twenty-first century.[35]

To reap the benefits offered—now and more importantly in the future—Western firms must know where they are going with their China strategy. At the same time, companies must remain flexible in order to diversify according to the changing opportunities. One problem is that Western (particularly American) business activities seem to aim, for the most part, at bigger, more ambitious projects. Many failures in the People's Republic reflect the foolhardy trend of starting in the treetops instead of building from the ground up on solid business foundations. Firms should start with small, workable projects, realize success, then set up other low-profile projects that can be tied in to the original venture. They should continue the process, keeping costs down and risks low, until their corporate presence in the economy is secured. At the risk of overgeneralizing, U.S. firms seem less prepared to do business in countries such as China because their activities are coupled with a corporate reluctance to understand or appreciate fully the nuances of doing business in Pacific Basin countries. The weakness of their positions results from a lack of a detailed understanding of

Options in a "Bifurcated" Strategy

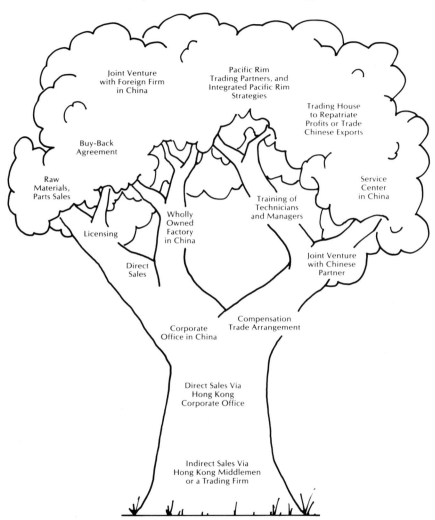

the organizational interrelationships between local and central government entities as well as among the key industrial ministries. The problems are further compounded by an apparent corporate aversion to making an attempt to bridge the cultural and language barriers.

Hopefully, more firms will pursue the strategic modes that are not yet followed in China but are followed in other Asian nations. From

Chapter 1, recall that firms enter Asia to share the burden of R&D and acquire new technology. Increasingly, firms willing to conduct some of their R&D in China could gain significant long-term leverage in the market.

UNFULFILLED EXPECTATIONS: WHO IS TO BLAME?

Throughout this book, numerous examples of China venture successes and failures have been cited. The successes have been the result of various combinations of the formulas just discussed. The failures, however, are not as easy to explain. Whether the cause of the venture's failure is derived from the foreign firm's approach or from the Chinese response, both contribute to the overall weakness of the business environment. The nature of the business encounter of course has its own generic failings, such as poor infrastructure support, hidden agendas, and a lack of human and capital resources. In fact, many firms cite these things as the causes of most venture failures. In this study of the China market, however, specific reasons for the success or failure of a China venture became clear.

From the foreign firm's perspective, a China venture fails because of an inadequacy at the approach planning stage, the operational level, or a combination of both. In general, approaching the China market without both a clear understanding of how things get done there and the preparation necessary to manifest that understanding, certainly is a prescription for failure. The specific ramifications of an inadequate approach strategy have been explained throughout this book. The following list is a helpful recall of the general approach problems:

- picking the wrong partner
- unrealistic initial market assessment
- lack of clarified objectives
- unprepared expatriates
- insufficient investment
- poor management-expatriate relations
- insensitivity to the Chinese
- sluggish and inflexible response to opportunities
- poor price setting
- overconfidence about product quality

The problems at the operational level, such as profit repatriation and product quality, are direct results of poor negotiating and insufficient research. There is a tendency to accept the Chinese estimation of the foreign exchange issues and their assurances of product quality without verification. This naivete has led to many disappointments once production has begun. The only way to insure one's venture—especially if it is a large project—is to obtain written contract approval on all aspects of the venture directly from Beijing.

China-derived Problems

Though it may seem that the ultimate responsibility for a venture's success rests with the foreign firm, certain aspects of a venture are beyond the foreigner's control. Chinese bureaucrats have contributed to some of the equity venture problems, and even failures, by not treating Sino-foreign joint undertakings as truly unique opportunities for modernization. Often, the Chinese bureaucracy fails to protect joint ventures from being, as an American lawyer in Beijing put it, "lynched by red tape."

As shown by the author's questionnaire on page 355, U.S. corporations are most frustrated by China's bureaucratic red tape and dilatory decision-making. The majority of respondents also indicated that differences in business style was indeed discouraging, but only slightly so. Interestingly, 60 percent of the respondents consider U.S., Japanese, and European competition in China as having no effect on their China activities. Twenty percent, however, feel that Japanese competition is strongly discouraging.

The ongoing complaints of foreign firms that have attempted to set up and operate an equity-based venture in China can be loosely divided into three areas: (1) labor issues, (2) management issues, and (3) problems associated with China's foreign investment policy.

Labor Issues.   There are three broad areas of labor problems: (1) recruitment, (2) training, and (3) on-the-job incentives.

1. Difficulty of recruiting skilled workers
    As modernization outpaces the availability of trained manufacturing and assembly workers, the pressure grows for China to assign many of its precious few skilled workers to joint venture activities. To the contrary, however, FESCO seems primarily interested in obtaining additional foreign exchange by overstaffing joint venture projects with far

What factors are discouraging your firm in terms of trading with China?

	No Effect	Slightly Discouraging	Strongly Discouraging
"Bureaucratic red tape/Chinese delays in decision making"	10%	45%	45%
"Lack of communication/ infrastructure"	14%	54%	32%
"Conflicting business styles between U.S. and Chinese negotiators"	26%	65%	9%
"Japanese competition"	60%	20%	20%
"European competition"	60%	27%	13%
"U.S. competition"	60%	40%	0%

SOURCE: Author's survey (see appendix for complete form of this questionnaire).

too many Chinese workers, many of whom are not qualified to handle complex production tasks. Employment imperatives overshadow even partial satisfaction on the part of the foreign firm.

2. Problems with training

Western firms have been quick to undertake training programs to give their joint venture operations a cadre of workers with the skills and hands-on orientation to compensate for their lack of direct experience. Many of these same firms have been shocked to discover that the Chinese government can and often does reassign the trained workers to other projects. Such practices strip the Western partner of the advantages that should have resulted from its investment in intensive worker training.

3. Resistance to Western-type incentives

Most Western firms recognize that attitudes toward productivity and work in China are the products of Chinese culture, a legacy of state-controlled quotas, three generations of contradictory five-year plans, and a social disdain for Western individualism. Western-type incentives are based on the traditions of melting-pot, heterogeneous groups achieving material success and personal gain through individual hard work and thrift, in an environment free of extensive government intervention. When Western-type incentives are thrust upon Chinese workers, the results can be mixed or even counterproductive. Moreover, if individual output were to increase, the resulting inequalities in pay combined with the thrust away from collective interests might be seen by various leaders as problematic.

Management Issues.   There are two areas of management problems: (1) resistance to Western management style and (2) middle management bloat.

1. Resistance to Western management style

The Chinese are currently faced with competing and conflicting models for increasing employee productivity and satisfaction in the workplace. Guidelines for choosing the right worker incentive models seem to be missing. On the other hand, because there is no distinct Chinese style of management, the present management structure represents a loose amalgam of indigenous and foreign techniques. Because the economic signals in the society remain mixed, there is little opportunity for the creation of programs that custom-fit the needs of particular joint ventures.

2. Solving the problem of middle-management bloat

The Chinese have a tendency to assign large numbers of unneeded middle managers to every project, especially those involving a foreign partner. In many cases, a large percentage of these managers have limited skills and capabilities, and therefore are a hindrance to the implementation of the project. The Chinese must come to the understanding that aside from the economic burden associated with middle management bloat, the inclusion of a throng of supervisors can stifle the managerial effectiveness of other more competent managers. One solution appears to be contractual limitations on management assignments at the time the Sino-Western arrangement is negotiated.

Foreign Investment Policymaking

As discussed at length in Chapter 2, many aspects of China's investment climate could be made to better accommodate the multinational firm, and help "maiden ventures" avoid running aground. Five areas of foreign investment regulatory policy are of immediate concern.

Economic Discrimination.

Because foreigners have little choice of subcontractors, or the setting of prices, a situation has emerged wherein the foreigner must pay inflated prices for labor, goods, services, and rent. Moreover, in times of short supply, it is the foreign firm that is likely to be shut off from access to needed resources or components.

Unfair Restrictions.

The Chinese understandably maintain restrictions on duplicate purchases of equipment and technologies by different local firms. The Chinese remain adamant in many cases that all or most of a joint venture's output, as well as that of a wholly foreign-owned plant, must be exported overseas.

Repatriation Restriction.

The Chinese have not fully relaxed regulations requiring that Beijing review and approve the spending of foreign exchange for virtually all but the most rudimentary imports of equipment and technology. Even taking into account the October 1986 changes in the investment regulations, the existing foreign exchange laws do not go far enough to ensure smooth repatriation of dividends.

Technology Assimilation.

There are numerous technological problems created by the fact that a large number of Chinese enterprises and local officials continue to insist on obtaining only advanced or state-of-the-art technologies. At the same time the Chinese are still limited in their capability to assimilate or maintain advanced equipment and technologies. A lack of openness by the Chinese in the transfer process hinders assimilation, as does their general reluctance to pay for the software aspects of technology transfer. The Chinese could improve the situation by requesting and compensating ongoing technological assistance and service on most projects.

Ultimately, the problems facing China are twofold. On one hand, China has encountered a number of internal bottlenecks as a result of

its modernization drive that limit the creation of an attractive investment climate. On the other hand, there has been a conspicuous over-
expectation by Western businesses and a failure to appreciate fully the
domestic political obstacles China has had to overcome to move in the
current direction. Much of the success of the Four Tigers* has derived
from their commitments to participate fully in the world economy during the 1960s and 1970s as well as having the right set of governmental
policies in place at the right time. The Asian quartet also benefited from
their undervalued currencies relative to the dollar and their privileged
status under the Generalized System of Preferences (GSP), insuring the
duty-free entrance of their products into the U.S. market. Some say that
China has come out of its self-garnered cocoon too late to reap the
benefits enjoyed by the Four Tigers. In the broader view of the history of
open-door policies in other Asian countries, one finds many of the
same internal difficulties that China is now encountering. The Chinese
are not unique in their transformation from being an insulated, planned
economy toward the dynamic vitalization afforded by greater interaction with the outside world. The unique aspect of this transformation,
however, is that China's jurisdictional and bureaucratic complexities
are profoundly more enormous because it is much larger than all of the
emerging Pacific Basin countries.

Admittedly, China's business climate is hardly ideal. Yet as one
looks back to the "openings" of the Four Tigers in the early 1960s, one
can easily recall the same complaints from the foreign business
community—meddlesome bureaucracy, limited market access, currency conversion difficulty, and lack of proprietary protection that are
now being voiced in China. In comparison with the investment climates of other countries in the Pacific Basin, China offers many of the
same concessions and pitfalls. For instance, many investors have been
deterred by the inadequate proprietary protection in Taiwan, which has
drawn innumerable complaints of commercial counterfeiting. South
Korea also provides only spotty protection: patents are nonrenewable
after twelve years. In the field of pharmaceuticals in South Korea, as in
China, only the process to manufacture is patentable, not the product,
which encourages cloning. Similarly, many of the other complaints
heard about China's investment climate can be said about other business climates in the region. In Japan, workers are unconvinced of the

---

* Taiwan, South Korea, Hong Kong, and Singapore.

reputation of foreign companies and thus are not interested in working for a foreign joint venture. Foreign businesses also have to contend with customer loyalty to Japanese firms and a distribution system that is tough to penetrate. Although South Korea is gradually opening its domestic market and lifting investment restrictions, it levies many imports with high tariffs. Taiwan imports oil, machinery, metals, grains, and chemicals under attractive duty exemptions, but consumer goods incur taxes of 50–100 percent. This all suggests that while there may be unique aspects to doing business in China, the problems are not always particular to the Chinese situation.

The Potential High Cost of a "Wait-and-See" Approach

Most large Western firms have come to accept that the China market has turned out to be a contrarian market. Most have lowered their profile, cut costs, and positioned themselves in the market for possible opportunities in the future. Although the U.S. corporate retrenchment has the aura of corporate failure, many American firms realize their role in China, while not as grandiose as once expected, still promises to be steady and deliberate. Given the problems enumerated throughout this book, it would be easy for companies to walk away from the China market in favor of other sites that are far less problematic. One strategy that some firms have taken is to wait until China's investment climate is more developed before making major, if any, business commitments. The 1986–87 downturn of foreign investment in China seemed to indicate that the wait-and-see strategy was gaining. Yet, while these U.S. firms wait for China to learn the business ways of the West, Japanese firms are moving ahead in China, raising a serious question for corporate America: What are the costs of *not* entering the China market?

In all likelihood, China will modernize with or without outside participation. Competitive pressures will only intensify as the market becomes crowded with domestic and foreign firms that have gained substantial footholds. Hence, to wait and see may be to wait and not see the benefits enjoyed by other, bolder firms. Trends in China's economic growth and technological progress suggest this prognosis.

Reasons for Optimism.   The broader question is whether the momentum of China's progress is going in a direction conducive to international business opportunity in the future. Most China-watchers

tend to think it is, but qualify their affirmation by saying that the whole process will be much more tedious and time-consuming than previously believed. Most sinologists are cautiously optimistic, recognizing the difficulties as well as the potential.

A series of indications portend that the China market is indeed destined to blossom; it may never become the "market of one billion," but it will certainly be a major force in the world economy. First, growth rates in the Chinese economy promise to remain substantial. One can reasonably expect China's economic and technological expansion to continue on an upward cycle through the end of the century. It seems certain that China will achieve its goal of quadrupling the gross value of its agricultural and industrial output by the year 2000. Although the Chinese have strengthened the diversity and quality of their exports, China's success as an exporter will depend on the extent of protectionism in places such as the United States. Nonetheless, the push to expand exports will be a concerted one. China undoubtedly will have its greatest impact in the export markets as the world's largest coal producer. For example, exports of coal increased 54 percent in the first six months of 1986, combined with the same period in 1985. These increases are largely the result of the approximately 50,000 small mines that peasants have reopened to supply local need, with output sold at decontrolled prices.[36] In the long run, increased Chinese exports will finance increased imports, particularly greater quantities of equipment, machinery, and technology that will further support improvements in the production system. The emphasis on export expansion has given Chinese industry a new impetus to become more efficient and productive. There seems little doubt that eventually China's exports of consumer electronic goods will break into world markets. The question is whether they will do so unilaterally or in concert with foreign firms.

Second, the growing demand within China's domestic market for higher-quality products has prompted the manufacture of consumer goods at a new level of excellence. China increased its production and sale of wristwatches by 43 percent between 1984 and 1985, its camera production by 42 percent, and refrigerator production by 164 percent.[37] The country produced over 4.3 million color television sets in 1985, more than double the number in 1984. And this quantity is still far short of demand.[38]

A sophisticated view of China in the 1990s focuses less on the difficulties of doing business there and more on just how far the Chi-

China's Industrial Output Growth, 1978-85
(1978 = 100%)

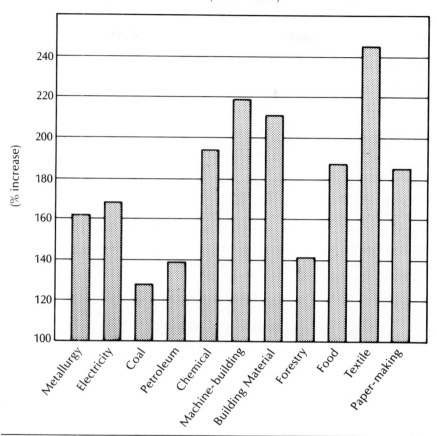

SOURCE: *Statistical Yearbook of China, 1986,* State Statistical Bureau, People's Republic of China.

nese have come since 1978. Today a foreign company can do things in China that in 1978 would have been impossible. The Chinese are addressing the foreign exchange repatriation problem and have legitimized internal foreign exchange trade transactions. Foreigners can now wholly own facilities and enterprises, a status that few thought China would accommodate before the reforms of the 1980s. Foreign managers also have greater control over their Chinese labor force. Moreover, the Chinese seem more willing to be flexible on negotiating and implementing projects. While still far from ideal, the momentum is shifting in the right direction.

The political picture is optimistic as well. The problems of political succession are gradually disappearing. Many Western analysts and Sino-Western business managers anticipate minimal policy reversals or business disruption in the post-Deng era. The midrange projections are that the political framework in China will be conducive to modernization well into the late 1990s. This is not to suggest that there will not be a few unanswered questions along the way, but only that a radical reversal seems more unlikely each day.

Moreover, the longevity of China's open-door policy increases the likelihood that these policies will become a permanent element of the country's approach to interacting with the international economy. Some of the policies are designed to place market-oriented business practices on a firmer foundation. China's new bankruptcy law begins to address the problem of contradiction in granting enterprises responsibility while protecting them from many forms of risk. The law may lack some of the force necessary to fully achieve its objectives, but it is a move in the right direction.

LEARNING FROM AMERICA'S RIVALS IN CHINA

American firms are not the only ones scrambling into China in search of a vast export market. With the help of their respective governments, firms from Japan and the EEC have been able to greatly expand their involvement throughout the Chinese economy. More important, many of these firms have demonstrated a flexibility and perspective on the China market that has helped them achieve an increasingly larger market share—often to the detriment of U.S. industry.

The Japanese dominate the China market for reasons other than their obvious geographic proximity to China. Their domination has been cultivated over a long history of dialogue between Japanese executives and the trade officials of the People's Republic. The continuous, albeit uneven, contact of Japanese firms with the People's Republic since 1949 has afforded them a considerable head start over U.S. firms.[39] Another advantage Japan enjoys over the United States is that the industrial needs of Japan and China are naturally well suited to each other. Japan's dependence on foreign oil and coal can be relieved through development of China's resources. And China's desire for modern technology and manufacturing equipment is easily satisfied through Japan's robust economy.

Japanese firms, in concert with the Japanese government, have been keen to lay the foundation for a long-term relationship with China through the Long-Term Trade Agreement and the 1978 Treaty of Peace and Friendship. The Japanese approach to China places great value on creating continuity and mutual trust in political and commercial dealings. Long-term commercial relationships based on mutual benefit may be valued relatively more by Japan than by Western countries.[40] One of the ramifications of this approach is that Japanese executives are able to negotiate more effectively within the Chinese environment because they possess the patience and understanding to influence Chinese group decision making. Japanese representatives are also well prepared to deal with China's bureaucracy and management style. To put the United States at a further disadvantage, China is also very interested in emulating, in part, the Japanese style of economic organization.

This evolving relationship between Japan and China may be more symbiotic than the relationship between the United States and China. After all, Japan and China have been involved in continuous social and cultural intercourse for over 2,000 years.[41] In spite of the relatively recent amicable relations Japan has pursued with the People's Republic, many observers of Sino-Japanese trade relations often wonder why China is so receptive to Japanese businessmen, when one considers that Japanese troops were clearly unwelcome intruders in China during World War II. The Japanese have turned this apparent cultural animosity to their advantage. They have learned to defer a cultural heritage of exploitation of the Chinese by playing the role of apologetic sympathizers of the China predicament. This tactic seemingly empowers Chinese negotiators to deal effectively with the Japanese. The Chinese often play upon Japanese guilt by mentioning investment concessions in terms of war reparations. These reparations, or concessions, are made willingly by Japanese businessmen. Other agreements are made that favor Chinese entities, giving them the satisfaction of negotiating an attractive deal with a one-time oppressor, an ultimate form of "giving face" in the Chinese business atmosphere.

Japan's political intentions also play a role in its approach to the China market. Since the Soviet Union is seen by many to pose an ongoing threat to Japan's security, it is in Japan's best interest to assist China in modernizing in order to resist Soviet influence. It follows that if

Western nations help China to achieve its modernization objectives, well-established political relationships between China and the West will be strengthened. This restructuring of the political alliances between China and the West will further counter Soviet influence in Asia.

In general, Japanese firms concede short-term profits in exchange for the long-term benefit of a presence in the China market. Many Japanese firms have been investing heavily in the development of the China market while expecting higher profits in the future. The Japanese assist the Chinese in collecting the minerals and other resources which Japanese industries need, and at the same time help them develop the roads, rail lines, ports, and communication facilities to expedite the movement of those materials to the ports for delivery to Japan. Realizing their China endeavors are an integral part of their Asia-Pacific regional strategies, Japanese firms focus their capabilities carefully on the China market. Many firms have a specialized department to formulate China market strategies. Japanese business people in China are said to outnumber American corporate representatives by at least five to one.[42] (Japan maintains close to 400 offices in China, which far exceeds the U.S. presence of 150 offices.) Japanese firms also station more people for a longer period of time in order to wait out dilatory negotiations and build personal friendships and trust among counterparts. One often hears the Chinese complain that while American business people stay a few months and then leave, the Japanese remain in the country indefinitely.

Where Japan's corporate strategy differs from others, however, is its presence not only in the coastal areas but in the interior provinces as well. In Tianjin, as of 1985, Japanese firms have set up more than twenty offices; American companies operate fewer than five.[43] Similarly, in Dalian, Japan operates twenty offices; one U.S. firm has an office there. Between 1979 and 1983 the province of Liaoning acquired technology and equipment valued at $256 million, 32 percent of which was acquired from Japan and only 2 percent from the United States.

The Japanese have not jumped into the market in the sense of taking great risks, however. Much of their success is attributable to low price, ready availability, large quantity, and a unique marketing strategy. The Japanese marketing strategy consists of first capturing a large market share, then developing a dependency among Chinese end-users for Japanese in components and maintenance. Although Chinese leaders and economic officials may claim a preference for dealing with Americans, the reality is that the Chinese penchant for basing their buying decisions on price makes the sourcing of Japanese consumer products and industrial equipment most attractive.

The best example of Japan's ability to adapt its corporate strategy to China's reliance on price considerations is in the textile industry. Japan dominates all facets of the textile industry in China by offering high quality and low price for their machinery and products. Closer inspection, however, reveals that Japan may offer low prices for an initial main-operating unit, but later demands inflated prices on parts. Nevertheless, the Japanese have made a serious commitment to promoting their goods in China. They have taken advantage of the Chinese importing convention of "following the precedents," getting their machines on-line early, and promoting the emulation in other Chinese enterprises.[44]

The Japanese have also been quick to recognize which raw materials associated with the textile industry—chemical fibers, wool, ramie, and cotton—that China must import. To get around import controls, Japanese textiles are being produced with more value added, which forces Chinese textile manufacturers to produce higher-quality goods and clothes of higher fashion. This development has placed Japan in a fortuitous negotiating position. Japan has obtained several textile agreements that have proved lucrative for both sides. For example, the Japanese Itaman Company started a men's shirt business with Chinese Qingdao No. 1 Knitting Mill under a compensation trade agreement in 1980. In that same year Itaman Company imported 2 million shirts from the Chinese side; by 1985 imports reached 10 million. Japan's largest underwear manufacturer Gunze signed an agreement with Jinan Knitting Mill in which the Japanese company claimed exclusive marketing rights. In 1981 Gunze imported 1.5 million pairs of underwear; by 1987 the number had grown to 5 million.[45]

In terms of direct sales, the Japanese have begun to dominate the telecommunications sector as well, though they face stiff competition from Western Europe. As of 1987, Japan held a 77 percent share of China's telecommunications market; Hong Kong claims 13.8 percent; and the United States, 2.5 percent. As in other large investment sectors, the Europeans will make future inroads into this sector via concessionary government financing.

The issue of balanced trade between Japan and China is bound to play a key role in determining which nations the Chinese will do business with in the coming years. Eventually, the Chinese hope that they will sell goods produced with foreign technology into the Japanese market. One has to wonder how the Chinese will gain significant access to the Japanese market when one considers the difficulty that American and European firms have had in penetrating Japan's protectionist tariff and nontariff barriers, tightly knit distribution system, and Japanese taste for only the highest quality goods.[46]

As part of an effort to encourage Japanese firms to pursue China trade, the Japan-China Association for Economy and Trade (JCAET) was formed in 1972 to supply Japanese firms with market surveys and introductions for Chinese business ventures. In Japan, organizations such as the Ministry of International Trade and Industry (MITI), the Japan External Trade Association (JETRO), and the Japan Federation of Economic Organization (JFEO) are well coordinated and unified in their efforts to give Japanese firms data about China's specific modernization needs. Japan's institutional coordination of Japanese firms serves to expedite technology transfer approvals to China, though the occurrence of such transfers has been limited.

China encourages competition among foreign firms on most projects. However, U.S. firms are often made to compete against one another as well as other multinational firms. American firms are at a decided disadvantage, because they lack the governmental assistance to coordinate the shared interests of American companies doing business in China. Japanese firms tend to deal with the problem of encouraged competition by generally refusing to bid against each other on investment projects. They operate, in a sense, under the auspices of government influence, and therefore can create an approach based on the shared interests of Japanese firms in China. But the possibility of U.S. firms forming a coalition seems highly improbable.

How long will Japan's domination of the China market last? To answer that question one needs to examine the current Chinese sentiment toward the Japanese. There is growing concern in China about the number and influence of Japanese executives in the country, which has caused a decline in Japan's business reputation. Similar to the view other countries hold, China sees Japan as a seller rather than a buyer; a country unwilling to alter its economic course to alleviate trade friction between China and Japan. In addition, Japanese firms are viewed as unwilling to transfer technology or engage in scientific cooperation. The Chinese perceive the Japanese as being interested only in commercial intercourse.

The 1985 student demonstrations in China were a clear sign of a high degree of animosity toward the Japanese. Further damage to Japan's image was brought about by the issuance of revisionist textbooks by Japan's Ministry of Education, which suggested that the violent occupations of Nanking in 1937 were devoid of the horrors that remain deeply embedded in the minds of the Chinese people.

Yet, between 1980 and 1984, China moved from twenty-sixth on the list of recipient countries of Japanese technical aid to the top five. If the United States is not careful, Japanese successes in China could make it difficult for American firms to significantly expand their activities in the future. While there are strong misgivings on the part of the Chinese in having an ever-expanding relationship with the Japanese, there is also a deep-seated respect for the Japanese ability to modernize and achieve technological parity with the West. Should U.S. firms remain lethargic in their response to the China market, the Chinese will have no choice but to deal with Japan, and to a lesser extent, their European trading partners.

The Potential of EEC Nations. Among the many reasons that the Chinese are drawn to Europe is the fact that they are interested in limiting their dependence on supplies and technology from the United States and Japan. European nations are in a beneficial position because they are generally anti-Soviet, technologically rich, and removed from Asian rivalries. The Sino-EEC trade surge began in the mid-1980s when Party Secretary (then Prime Minister) Zhao Ziyang, former Party Secretary Hu Yaobang, and foreign trade minister Zheng Tuobin conducted diplomatic/trade missions to Western Europe during which they urged European leaders to accept Chinese exports and make larger investments in China.[47] Similarly, the Europeans, who have had historical links to China dating back to before the nineteenth century, have wanted to renew economic ties and address market opportunities in the midst of Chinese frustration with Japan and America's procrastination to transfer significant amounts of technology to China. The highest levels of the French government have pushed hard in a number of areas to widen the door for their electronics, oil exploration, and other industries. The Germans, British, and Italians are all becoming more active in terms of government-business efforts to gain a share of the China market.

China and the EEC signed a most-favored-nation agreement in 1978. As a group, the EEC is China's third largest trading partner, trading $8.32 billion worth of goods with China in 1986. Between 1970 and 1985, the value of trade between China and Italy rose from $100 million to $1.15 billion, an increase of 1,100 percent. Conversely, Chinese penetration of the European market promises to be slow and prone to political shifts in Europe. For instance, China's principal exports, which include carpets, cereals, and animal by-products, are severely limited by tariff barriers in the EEC. In addition, a bilateral textile agreement signed in 1983 was designed to minimize imports of Chinese textiles.[48] China's trade deficit with the EEC peaked at $2.5 billion in 1985,[49] which led to a 4.3 percent reduction of total trade between China and the EEC by 1987.

As suggested, European participation in the market is noteworthy because of the role that their respective home governments play in helping their firms do business in China, especially through the use of concessionary financing and technical assistance programs. Italian government and aid organizations have provided mixed loans and donations.[50] The Swedish government has also indicated that it will continue to provide soft loans for the development of telecommunications systems in Liaoning and Jiangsu using equipment supplied by L.M. Ericsson.[51] The Canadian government has offered China $300 million in soft loans to be used in purchasing Canadian telecommunications supplies.[52]

THE NEED FOR THE U.S. GOVERNMENT TO PLAY AN ACTIVE ROLE

The pervasive role of government in investment policymaking in China suggests that government-to-government collaboration on large projects is often vital in winning contracts. The critical role of government participation was exemplified in the Dayawan Bay nuclear power plant project proposed in 1980 to be constructed outside of Shenzhen SEZ in Guangdong Province. Although this joint venture was between China and Hong Kong, other countries provided nuclear reactor facilities, power generation equipment, and design and consultancy services for the overall construction. Total investment required was $3.5 billion, which was billed as "one of the largest joint investment projects ever undertaken in cooperation with foreign countries under China's open-door economic policy."[53] The foreign governments of the countries which were providing equipment and services for the project play a crucial role in financing the project. Specifics regarding this financing are largely unknown, but several British banks reportedly have helped to indemnify loans, thereby making sales of power equipment from Britain's General Electric possible.[54]

American companies, however, were intentionally left out of the project for two reasons, both related to U.S. government policies. First, the official U.S. position on selling nuclear technology to China hardened over the unresolved issue of nuclear waste disposal, and because of China's alleged sale of nuclear equipment to Pakistan in the mid-1980s. Second, had they been invited, it is unlikely that U.S. companies could have been competitive on the project since "soft" government loans to China were impossible to arrange in light of the official U.S. position at the time.

The United States may also be closed out of the Three Gorges hydroelectric dam project because the Chinese have pinned their hopes of financing the project on the World Bank and the export-credit agencies of the countries being considered.[55] Although the United States has been providing technical assistance in this effort since 1944, when the Bureau of Reclamation first recommended that a dam be constructed at the Three Gorges site, the design and construction of the dam likely will be done by the firm(s) offering the most attractive financing.

In addition to a lack of U.S. government participation on large projects, corporate America's failure to capture a larger share of the China market in general reflects a number of critical deficiencies within the U.S. commercial system as well as within private U.S. industry. Just how much information the U.S. government can provide private business without upsetting the traditional separation between government and business is a major issue concerning not only U.S. participation in China, but U.S. positioning in the overall international market. It may be time to consider seriously whether the United States should have some kind of direct government support to assist those U.S. firms that will help to realize U.S. industrial policy. In a world of "neomercantilist" trade and industrial policies, the current U.S. approach to managing external and internal economic relations may be obsolete. This is certainly the case in regards to U.S. business in the People's Republic.

The U.S. government is intentionally restricted from disseminating information to companies in a way that will provide particular firms a distinct competitive edge. American firms have equal access to government information. However, the U.S. government lacks a method by which business information—commercial intelligence—can be kept within the confines of U.S. industry and government. For example, assume the U.S. government learned that the Civil Aviation Administration of China (CAAC) was seeking to buy a number of commercial airliners. In theory, that information must be made public. Once in the public domain, the information becomes available to Japanese and European companies as well. In other countries, such information would not necessarily be made public. The information might be disseminated through a meeting of the relevant industrial associations.

In order for corporate America to pursue a productive economic and technological relationship with China, one that involves reciprocal trade, foreign investment, and the transfer of know-how, the U.S. government must offer increased guidance and orchestration of the U.S.-China business relationship. This is especially important if smaller firms are to participate in the multiple aspects of China's modernization program. In some cases, assistance has come from the U.S. Foreign Commercial Service, which is staffed by American diplomatic personnel stationed in Chinese cities and in the Department of Commerce in Washington. (A list of U.S. consulate telex and telephone numbers appears in the appendix.) Although limited in their capacity to assist corporations, these diplomats can introduce Chinese trade officials and end-users in China, and can provide consultation on current Chinese trade policy. Additional government help comes directly from the Department of Commerce in the form of literature and basic market analysis information. Interviews with American executives in China and Hong Kong suggest that American corporations find U.S. government support helpful but not an integral part of their business activities. Trade development programs pursued by the U.S. government are the target of the majority of its China trade-related budget. Most of this money is spent on feasibility studies in China, including some very useful market analyses. (The *Trade Opportunities Bulletin*, a newsletter published jointly by the Department of Commerce and the U.S. Department of State is highly recommended. Although its China listings are scarce, it does include current notice of government tenders and can be instrumental in successfully bidding on new projects.)

In some sectors of U.S.-China trade, U.S. government assistance has been more helpful than in others. For example, in the field of aviation, the Foreign Commercial Service coordinated the Presidential Aerospace Trade Mission to China in July 1984. This mission produced the U.S.-China Work Program on Aviation and Aerospace. Throughout this program, top executives of American firms producing aviation products participated in exchanges with top-level Chinese officials.

The event led to the successful sales of American aviation products to China in the ensuing two years.[56]

In the telecommunications field, support has been creative, though less effective. The Department of Commerce has signed an umbrella agreement with the Chinese consisting of twenty-seven protocols. This agreement, made public in 1986, calls for American telecommunications experts to go to China, study the Chinese telecommunications system, and formulate a plan of recommendation to China's Ministry of Posts and Telecommunications. No purchase obligation is placed on the Chinese and the project is funded by the U.S. government. In this case, the goal is to convince the Chinese that American companies could supply the best and most appropriate telecommunications technology available.[57]

In one extraordinary case, a major U.S. telecommunications company asked the U.S. government to offer the Chinese a concessionary loan package so that it could close a lucrative deal in China in face of Japanese competition. Though a company representative was asked not to be identified, the U.S. government made a no-strings-attached loan to the Chinese to show good faith. Since the loan was unconditional, the Chinese used the money to buy Japanese telecommunications products because they were cheaper!

Diversified Government Efforts Growing

The U.S. government also supports the National Council for U.S.-China Trade (NCUSCT), a private organization that promotes trade by acting as a liaison between American corporations and Chinese entities, as well as publishing first-rate articles and information in the bimonthly *China Business Review.* Although its outlook on the China market is believed by some to be overly optimistic, the staff of the NCUSCT provides sound advice to its several-hundred member firms through its offices in Beijing and Washington.[58]

Unfortunately, the individualistic nature of American companies tends to limit the effectiveness of organizations such as the NCUSCT, which attempts to spearhead U.S. corporate efforts in the People's Republic. For instance, the American Electronics Association (AEA) tried and failed to open the China market to its member firms. From the perspective of the member companies, the AEA could not offer them anything that they themselves could not obtain on their own. One would hope that this outcome was more a reflection of the limited capabilities of the AEA than a disbelief in the potential resourcefulness of industrial associations.

The Prospect of a Model Joint Venture.

The most conspicuous response that U.S. government officials have mustered to help American businesses in China came in 1986. American commercial officers working in Beijing responded to a litany of complaints by American executives concerning China's investment policy and corporate climate with a widely publicized proposal that the Chinese form a single "model" joint venture in China based on a series of government-assured freedoms. These operating freedoms would include (1) the ability to hire Chinese workers from anywhere in China, (2) to fire them if need be, (3) to establish incentive systems within the joint venture, and (4) to have freedom from interference by the CCP. The model joint venture would have access to China's domestic market and the capability to repatriate all profits within thirty days. It would enjoy direct communication by telephone with Hong Kong, the United States, Europe, and suppliers in China. It would have access to transportation between end-users and raw materials. The venture's energy supplies would be reliable and adequate. Investment regulations concerning the joint venture would be fast and final. Its contract could not be renegotiated, and official approvals would be completed within three months. The joint venture would be taxed only after its fifth year of operation, and financed by cash investment from both sides, with each partner owning 50 percent equity in the venture. The joint venture partners would have ready access to Chinese decision makers, and specific penalties would be enforced if contracts were breached. If disputes arose, mandatory international arbitration would take place if unsettled within three months. The model joint venture would be assessed by an independent reputable U.S. company after a formative period.

The model venture proposal proved controversial to journalists and business specialists both in China and the United States. As one consultant pointed out, by granting such freedom of action to an FIE, the Chinese would be in effect relinquishing control over the activities of the foreign firm in the local economy. Should a model joint venture prove successful—it is hard to imagine it failing given its extremely beneficial privileges—the Chinese would be placed in a position of having to offer a similar set of concessions to all foreign firms, robbing the Chinese of much of the leverage that they possess in collaborating with multinational corporations. Should the model joint venture fail, it is questionable whether the Chinese could continue to attract significant amounts of foreign investment in the future.

In the end, the idea seemed unsympathetic to the Chinese predicament and to the real constraints on the country's economy. Most important, a hypothetical joint venture could only encourage misconceptions between foreigners and Chinese, which is already a prime source of business difficulty. The assumption underlying a model joint venture is that somehow everything the Chinese do is wrong, and everything the Americans do is right. In many cases, the opposite is true. As one of China's industrial ministers indicated on a trip to the United States in 1986, "U.S. firms spend an inordinate amount of time telling the Chinese how they should change to accommodate American industry, while the Japanese take the Chinese as they are, warts and all, and seem to do just fine!"

Local Linkages. One reason that the governments of the People's Republic and the United States have not fully developed economic linkages is that private organizations generate most of the commercial activity between the two countries. Local efforts such as sister-city relationships and the promotion of local and state product lines in China have begun to proliferate, however, resulting in some potentially lucrative, long-term relationships.[59] Squibb Pharmaceutical is one of a growing number of firms that has been introduced to the China market through a sister-city relationship. (See Appendix B for list of sister cities.) The decreasing role of the federal government is also a reflection of the strategy among provincial and municipal Chinese organizations to by-pass as much bureaucracy on both sides as possible. While there are some mutual benefits for pursuing such linkages, they tend to diminish the pressures on the federal government to provide the appropriate financial and related support to allow U.S. industry to enhance its overall position in the Chinese marketplace.

Doing Business with China Is Still Too Political

While Japan and the EEC concentrate on nonpolitical issues in high-level government meetings (e.g., concessionary financing, bilateral trade agreements, and trade balancing), meetings between Washington and Beijing—even when they are ostensibly aimed at economic and trade issues—are usually preoccupied by political/security issues (e.g., the United States selling arms to Taiwan and the Chinese acquiring dual-use technologies). This type of topical agenda has tended to preempt government-to-government coordination on large projects, aid packages, and other business issues.

There are many influential people in the United States who believe that the present levels of technology supplied to China are not commensurate with the development of the U.S. political and diplomatic relationship with the People's Republic. The three main areas of contention between China and the United States are: (1) the issue of arms sales to Taiwan and status of the "one China" principle; (2) the issue of so-called discriminatory barriers set up by the United States against China in areas such as technology transfer and trade; and (3) the issue of arms sales made by China to the Middle East, especially Silkworms to Iran and an airbase to Saudi Arabia.

An unsettling feature of the Asia-Pacific region has been the tendency over the last few years for it to become a focal point for U.S.-Soviet rivalry. Moscow's position has been buttressed by its close relationship with Communist Vietnam and the instability within some of the Southeast Asian nations. The shared concern about the Soviet Union's desire for expansion in the region has provided the basis for the growing commonality of interests between the United States and China. In general, the American perspective on Asian-Pacific affairs seems to be in accord with Chinese views. The United States believes an economically modern and politically stable China is in its own best interest. Accordingly, the U.S. government and private institutions are prepared to render assistance to the People's Republic, particularly in the areas of training, science and technology exchanges, and interactions in the social sciences. Within the context of Sino-American relations, however, the Chinese cannot expect to reap the benefits of being an ally without accepting any of the concomitant responsibilities. Unfortunately for corporate America, the Sino-U.S. business relationship is both political and strategic.

THE U.S.-CHINA BUSINESS ENCOUNTER: IMPLICATIONS FOR AMERICAN COMPETITIVENESS

While corporate America's problems in China have much to do with the limited role played by the U.S. government, the majority of them are managerial rather than governmental. The U.S.-China business encounter brings to light many of the difficulties and shortcomings that American firms have in doing business in non-Western markets. There is a predilection in American corporate culture that one can depend on the standard rules and theories of international business practices developed in the West. However, as original expectations of the China market are diffused by reality, it has become clear that U.S. firms must dedicate more time and energy to training company people to work within a culturally foreign environment.

But recognizing the need for better training is only a diagnosis. The treatment for American corporate unpreparedness must be carried out in fundamental training methods. American management training programs need to instruct managers from a much more international perspective, yet relative to the particular country's language, negotiating style, people, and culture. There has been considerable talk about the advantages of this course of action for U.S. businesses, but little in the way of implementing it. In contrast, management training in the EEC countries addresses international business from the point of view of an interaction of different economic systems, governments, and cultures, rather than a technical program isolated on technical issues. In a world where operating environments resembling that of the United States are the exception rather than the rule, Americans must rethink their approach to management training in all the major functional areas of business.

In addition to altering internal functions, U.S. firms must turn their attention to realigning their external corporate strategy. Instead of approaching China as a single, demographic element, firms should view the country as one facet of a broader Asia-Pacific regional strategy. American industry can now become involved in various aspects of China through their other Asia-based subsidiaries. Several large U.S. firms are pursuing such strategies. Allied-Signal Corporation, which operates electronics and auto parts plants in Japan, India, Hong Kong, and elsewhere across Asia, is negotiating a "tie-in" joint venture in China to manufacture and assemble auto components and electronics systems.[60]

As the Chinese further develop their competitiveness in the Asia-Pacific region, they will begin to export to the United States and penetrate third-country markets. In the face of this growing competitor, it is wise for U.S. firms to pursue the industries in China that offer the most competitive benefits, establishing closer working links with China's S&T programs in areas such as electronics, telecommunications, aeronautics, computer hardware, and medicine. Plugging into Chinese R&D

is really at the cutting edge of corporate strategy in China. Through an integrated strategy of international training and regional perspective, American firms can build a long-term competitive position in a region that includes the most competitive of nations—Japan. These forward-looking firms cannot ignore China's potential not as a source of cheap labor but as the next great battleground in the economic and techno-logical wars with Japan and the European trading nations. More impor-tant, U.S. firms should not ignore the fact that all the know-how, equip-ment, and training flowing into China will create a partner worth aligning with in the effort to sustain American competitiveness in the world.

Rather than view China as an economic or political threat, one should perceive it as a marketing challenge that will be there for a long time to come. It could be argued, therefore, that U.S. companies have a long time to respond to opportunities in China. What we have wit-nessed in the past few years, however, is that the Chinese economy and society are changing very rapidly. While China may not become the next Japan by the year 2000, eventually it will be among the world's important centers of industrial production. The sooner U.S. industry realizes the mid-term and long-term opportunities associated with the People's Republic, the greater the opportunities will be for rectifying American trade imbalances and revitalizing America as the economic leader of the world.

It is not a question of whether China will develop, but only when. The companies that become part of this process will be in a better position to take advantage of that involvement. The longer U.S. com-panies wait before including a "China component" in their Pacific Rim strategic plans, the greater the obstacles will be to implementing ad-vantageous manufacturing and trading activities.

Although China's investment climate has turned out to be far more complex, beguiling, and problematic than it first appeared, the Chinese are addressing these flaws. New entrants to the China market should follow the better-informed recommendations of their corporate prede-cessors, who know the best avenues to penetrate the China market and how to obtain the information about the Chinese way of doing business.

As the 1980s come to an end, so to does the "beginning" of the reformist opportunities. Those companies that wait another few years to begin their involvement in the People's Republic will probably find that being late-comers carries additional risks and costs in terms of opportunities lost forever. The Chinese will have either accomplished their objectives by themselves or become economic captives of the Japanese. Neither of these outcomes would be in the interest of the U.S. economy or U.S. firms.

Will the China euphoria return? As an American business person involved in the early stages of setting up a joint publishing venture in Chongqing remarked: "The window of false sunshine has closed but the light of China's investment realities will continue to lure the foreign company committed to the long haul."

Foreign Exchange Guarantors

The following financial institutions in the People's Republic of China have been approved by the State Administration of Exchange Control to provide foreign exchange guarantee services:

Banks

1. The Bank of China and its branches
2. The Hongkong and Shanghai Banking Corp., Shanghai Branch
3. Standard Chartered Bank, Shanghai Branch
4. Overseas Chinese Banking Corp., Ltd., Shanghai Branch
5. The Bank of East Asia, Shanghai Branch
6. Nanyang Commercial Bank, Ltd., Shenzhen Branch
7. Nanyang Commercial Bank, Ltd., Shekou Branch
8. Nantong Bank, Ltd., Zhuhai Branch
9. The Kwangtung Provincial Bank, Shenzhen Branch
10. The China Investment Bank
11. Xiamen Intl Bank
12. The Hongkong and Shanghai Banking Corp., Shenzhen Branch
13. Bank of Credit and Commerce Intl Overseas, Ltd., Shenzhen Branch
14. United Overseas Bank, Ltd., Xiamen Branch
15. Banque Indosuez, Shenzhen Branch
16. Standard Chartered Bank, Shenzhen Branch
17. Chiyu Banking Corp., Ltd., Xiamen Branch
18. Societe Generale, Shenzhen Branch
19. The Hongkong and Shanghai Banking Corp., Xiamen Branch

20. Banque Nationale De Paris, Shenzhen Branch
21. Bank of Tokyo, Ltd., Shenzhen Branch
22. The Hokkaido Takushoku Bank, Ltd., Shenzhen Branch
23. The Sanwa Bank Ltd., Shenzhen Branch
24-32. The Industrial and Commercial Bank of China (The ICBC), branches in Guangdong, Fujian, Shanghai, Shenzhen, Xiamen, Foshan, Shantao, Fuzhou, and Guangzhou.
33. Bank of the Orient, Xiamen Branch
34. The Agricultural Bank of China, Guangzhou Branch
35. The Agricultural Bank of China, Foshan Branch
36. Standard Chartered Bank, Xiamen Branch
37. Fuji Bank, Shenzhen Branch
38. The Industrial and Commercial Bank of China, Sichuan Branch
39. CITIC Industrial Bank
40. Bank of China Merchants

Investment Corporations

1. China Intl Trust and Investment Corp.
2. Shanghai Investment and Trust Corp.
3. Guangdong Intl Trust and Investment Corp.
4. Fujian Provincial Investment and Enterprise Corp.
5. Hubei Provincial Intl Trust and Investment Corp.
6. Tianjin Intl Trust and Investment Corp.
7. Zhejiang Intl Trust and Investment Corp.
8. Bank of China Trust and Consultancy Company
9. Liaoning Intl Trust and Investment Corp.
10. Hebei Intl Trust and Investment Corp.
11. Guangzhou Intl Trust and Investment Corp.
12. Jiangsu International Trust and Investment Corp.
13. Beijing Intl Trust and Investment Corp.
14. Jiangxi Provincial Intl Trust and Investment Corp.
15. Shenzhen Intl Trust and Investment Corp.
16. Shenyang Intl Trust and Investment Corp.
17. China Chongqing Intl Trust and Investment Corp.
18. Shaanxi Provincial Finance and Joint Investment Corp.
19. Guangdong Intl Trust and Investment Corp. Shenzhen Branch
20. The Trust and Investment Co. of The ICBC
21. Zhongyuan Development, Trust, and Investment Corp. (Henan)
22. Changjiang Intl Trust and Investment Corp. of Sichuan Province
23. Anhui Intl Trust and Investment Service Corp.
24. China Jilin Province Intl Trust and Investment Corp.
25. China Ningxia Islamic Intl Trust and Investment Corp.

26. Shantou Intl Trust and Investment Corp.
27. Henan Provincial Intl Trust and Investment Corp.
28. Shanxi Economic Development and Investment Corp.
29. Guangxi Intl Trust and Investment Corp.
30. Hunan Intl Trust and Investment Corp.
31. China Venturetech Investment Corp.
32. Dalian Intl Trust and Investment Corp.
33. Nanjing Intl Trust and Investment Corp.
34. Lianyungang Intl Trust and Investment Corp.
35. Xiamen Intl Trust and Investment Corp.
36. Shanghai Aijian Banking, Trust, and Investment Corp.
37. Ningbo Intl Trust and Investment Corp.
38. Wuhan Intl Trust and Investment Corp.
39. Guangzhou Intl Trust and Investment Corp., Economic and Technology Development Zone Branch
40. Foshan Trust and Investment Corp.
41. Xinjiang Intl Trust and Investment Corp.
42. Tianjin Trust and Investment Corp. of The ICBC
43. Chongqing Trust and Investment Corp. of The ICBC
44. Fujian Overseas Chinese Investment Company
45. Wenzhou Intl Trust and Investment Corp.
46. Beijing Travel, Trust, and Investment Company
47. Trust, Investment, and Consultancy Company of Bank of China, Chongqing Branch.

Financial Companies

1. Shenzhen SEZ Development and Finance Company
2. Everbright Finance Company

Leasing Companies

1. China Electronics Leasing Company
2. China Foreign Trade Leasing Company
3. China Leasing Company, Ltd.
4. Guangdong Intl Leasing Company

SOURCE: State Administration of Exchange Control
List released April 30, 1987.

U.S.-China Sister Cities and States

U.S. City	Chinese City	Date Established
Anchorage, AK	Harbin, Heilongjiang	8/85
Baltimore, MD	Xiamen, Fujian	11/85
Birmingham, AL	Changsha, Hunan	pending
Boston, MA	Hangzhou, Zhejiang	5/82
Boulder, CO	Lhasa, Tibet	4/87
Charlotte, NC	Baoding, Hebei	pending
Chattanooga, TN	Wuxi, Jiangsu	10/82
Chicago, IL	Shenyang, Liaoning	9/85
Denver, CO	Kunming, Yunnan	5/86
Des Moines, IA	Shijiazhuang, Hebei	8/85
Detroit, MI	Chongqing, Sichuan	7/85
Erie, PA	Zibo, Shandong	5/85
Flint, MI	Changchun, Jilin	6/85
Harrisburg, PA	Luoyang, Henan	11/84
Honolulu County, HI	Hainan Island, Guangdong	8/85
Houston, TX	Shenzhen, Guangdong	4/86
Jersey City, NJ	Wenzhou, Zhejiang	pending
Joliet, IL	Liaoyang, Liaoning	12/85
Kansas City, MO	Xi'an, Shaanxi	pending
Long Beach, CA	Qingdao, Shandong	4/85
Lorain County, OH	Taiyuan, Shanxi	pending
Los Angeles, CA	Guangzhou, Guangdong	12/81
Midland, TX	Dongying, Shandong	6/86
New York, NY	Beijing	2/80
Norfolk, VA	Lianyungang, Jiangsu	pending
Oakland, CA	Dalian, Liaoning	3/82

Orlando, FL	Guilin, Guangxi	5/86
Paramus, NJ	Huainan, Anhui	pending
Philadelphia, PA	Tianjin	12/79
Phoenix, AZ	Chengdu, Sichuan	5/87
Pittsburgh, PA	Wuhan, Hubei	9/82
Portland, OR	Suzhou, Jiangsu	pending
Sacramento, CA	Jinan, Shandong	6/85
San Diego, CA	Yantai, Shandong	7/85
San Francisco, CA	Shanghai	1/80
Seattle, WA	Chongqing, Sichuan	6/83
Spokane, WA	Jilin City, Jilin	5/87
St. Louis, MO	Nanjing, Jiangsu	11/79
Syracuse, NY	Fuzhou, Fujian	pending
Toledo, OH	Qinhuangdao, Hebei	10/85
Tulsa, OK	Beihai, Guangxi	pending
Washington, DC	Beijing	5/84
Wichita, KS	Kaifeng, Henan	12/85
Wilmington, NC	Dandong, Liaoning	10/85

U.S. State	Chinese Province	Date Established
Alabama	Hubei	10/85
Alaska	Heilongjiang	2/85
California	Jiangsu	possible
Colorado	Hunan	9/83
Connecticut	Shandong	5/86
Georgia	Fujian	pending
Hawaii	Guangdong	6/85
Idaho	Shanxi	10/85
Illinois	Liaoning	9/82
Indiana	Zhejiang	pending
Iowa	Hebei	10/82
Kansas	Henan	6/81
Kentucky	Jiangzi	10/85
Maryland	Anhui	6/80
Massachusetts	Guangdong	11/83
Michigan	Sichuan	11/82
Minnesota	Shaanxi	10/82
New Jersey	Zhejiang	6/81
New York	Jiangsu	6/84
Ohio	Hubei	10/79
Oklahoma	Gansu	6/85
Oregon	Fujian	12/84

Texas	Shandong	pending
Utah	Jiangxi	9/85
Washington	Sichuan	10/82
Wisconsin	Heilongjiang	10/82

This article first appeared in the July/August 1987 issue of the *China Business Review*, and has been reprinted with permission of the U.S.-China Business Council.

Current as of June 1987

Compiled by Sarah R. Peaslee

SOURCE: National Council files; Sister Cities International; National Committee on United States-China Relations

Questionnaire

1. Name of firm: _____ (optional)

2. How many people are employed by your firm worldwide? (approx.) ____ .

3. Brief description of your firm's product lines: _____
   _____

4. To how many countries does your firm export? _____
   Developed countries _____ (percent)
   Less developed countries _____ (percent)

5. Brief description of China activities or plans (products marketed, type of operations, start-up date, etc.)
   _____

6. Why did your firm become interested in China? (Check principal reason only.)
   To export from China?   _____
   To sell products to China?   _____
   To buy raw materials?   _____
   To utilize lower-cost labor?   _____
   Other _____

7. By what method did your firm establish initial contact with the organization in China with whom you are engaged in business?
   _____ Trade exhibition or tech fair
   _____ Hired consultant

_____ Introduction through U.S. embassy or other trade liaison organization

_____ Direct Chinese solicitation of your firm

_____ Chinese trade delegation in the U.S.

_____ Other: _____

8. What group(s) in China does your firm view as potential purchasers of its product lines?

_____ Consumers

_____ Industrial end-user (specify field: _____)

_____ R&D or S&T organizations/agencies

_____ Agricultural sector

_____ Other: _____

9. How does your firm monitor and analyze the China market?

_____ Consultants in U.S.

_____ Consultants in Hong Kong

_____ Consultants in China

_____ English-language business publications

_____ Chinese-language business publications

_____ Representative office in China

_____ Trips to China to meet officials/end-users

_____ Other: _____

10. What developments in China affected your firm's decision to pursue China trade?

Rapidly rising income of China's one billion-plus population	_____
China's modernization plans suggest need for your firm's products	_____
Increasing size of China's open-market sector (as part of economic reforms)	_____
Other competing firms entering the China market	_____

11. What does your firm consider crucial in order to succeed at selling products in China?

	Not Important	Important	Crucial
Old-friend status among Chinese in a position to influence decision to purchase	_____	_____	_____
Low bid price	_____	_____	_____
State-of-the-art technology and superior quality	_____	_____	_____
Knowledge of specific needs of the end-user	_____	_____	_____
Firm/brand-name recognition among Chinese industrial managers and officials	_____	_____	_____
Flexibility in payment terms/financing	_____	_____	_____

12. What factors are discouraging to your firm in terms of trading with China?

	No effect	Slightly discouraging	Strongly discouraging
Bureaucratic red tape/ Chinese delays in decision making	_____	_____	_____
Lack of communication infrastructure	_____	_____	_____
Conflicting business styles between U.S. and Chinese negotiators	_____	_____	_____
Japanese competition	_____	_____	_____
European competition	_____	_____	_____
U.S. competition	_____	_____	_____

13. Has your firm advertised products or services in China?

_____No _____Yes If yes, in what media?

_____ Chinese-language trade journals (name:_____)

_____ English-language journals in China (name:_____)

_____ Chinese newspapers (name:_____)

_____ Billboards in China

_____ Chinese radio

_____ Chinese television

_____ Direct mail

_____ Sponsoring an event in China

_____ Other: _____

14. What has been the response to your firm's China advertising?

_____ Absolutely no response

_____ Some inquiries, but no sales

_____ Moderate sales generated

_____ Significant increase in sales

_____ Too soon to judge

15. If your firm does not currently advertise in China, is such advertising planned for the future?

_____ Yes

_____ Maybe, if other firms find China advertising effective

_____ Maybe, if our China sales increase

_____ Undecided

_____ No

16. Has your firm succeeded in establishing "brand name" recognition for its product(s) in China? _____No _____Yes

If yes, how was this accomplished?

_____ Direct promotion by sales reps

_____ Media advertising

_____ Technical seminars, trade exhibition

_____ Chinese references

_____ Other: _____

17. How long do you think it takes to establish brand name recognition in the PRC?

_____ 1 year	_____ 5–7 years
_____ 2 years	_____ 7–9 years
_____ 3–5 years	_____ A decade or more

18. How has your firm created its China advertising campaign?

_____ In-house advertising designers

_____ Outside advertising agency (Location: _____)

19. How much is your annual advertising budget (approx.) for the China market?

$_____

20. What factors does your firm perceive as crucial to its competitive advantage in the China market, as opposed to other markets of other Asian countries to which your firm exports?

CHINA				OTHER ASIAN NATIONS		
No advantage	Some advantage	Crucial advantage		No advantage	Some advantage	Crucial advantage
_____	_____	_____	Low base price	_____	_____	_____
_____	_____	_____	High quality	_____	_____	_____
_____	_____	_____	Service back-up	_____	_____	_____
_____	_____	_____	Warranty	_____	_____	_____
_____	_____	_____	Mass advertising	_____	_____	_____
_____	_____	_____	Technology sharing	_____	_____	_____
_____	_____	_____	Low installation costs	_____	_____	_____
_____	_____	_____	Attractive payment terms	_____	_____	_____
_____	_____	_____	Top product design	_____	_____	_____
_____	_____	_____	Quantity discount	_____	_____	_____
_____	_____	_____	Maintenance-free use	_____	_____	_____

21. Did your firm meet with Chinese end-users of your products (as differentiated from distributors) before the sale of equipment? _____No _____Yes

What influence do you believe the end-user had in the decision to buy?

_____ No influence

_____ Consultative role only

_____ Power to authorize or veto

_____ Final decision maker

22. Has your firm licensed technology in China? _____No _____Yes

If yes, has licensing increased direct sales of your firm's product line in China? No_____ Yes_____

Was licensing a condition for doing business in China?

No_____ Yes_____

23. Has your firm attended technical fairs or exhibitions in China?
    _____No   _____Yes

    If yes,

    What is the average total cost for your firm to attend a tech fair or exhibition in China? $_____

24. Does your firm hold technical seminars on applications of your products for potential Chinese customers? _____No   _____Yes

25. Does your firm have offices (how many _____) and personnel (how many _____) based in China? _____No   _____Yes

26. What would you consider your firm's general expectations of China trade and investment from Now until 2000?

    _____

27. What do you consider your firm's role in China's future?

    _____

Respondents to Questionnaires

Northrop Corporation
The Gillette Company
Florasynth, Inc.
Johnson & Johnson
American Motors Corporation
R. J. Reynolds Tobacco International, Inc.
Lummus-Hubei Machinery Company, Ltd.
3M
AT&T
Merck & Company, Inc.
Xerox Corporation
Mobil Oil Hong Kong, Ltd.
D-M-E Company
Brockway, Inc.
American Specialty Machinery
PCB Piezotronics, Inc.
AAA Machinery & Equipment Company
Occidental Petroleum Corporation
Molytek, Inc.
French Oil Mill Machinery Company
Gould, Inc.
McDonnell-Douglas China, Inc.
Navistar International Corporation
The Coca-Cola Company
Drever Company
Varian Associates
International Light, Inc.

---

*In addition, twelve questionnaires were returned without company names included, bringing the total number of returned questionnaires to thirty-nine.

Periodicals

Asia Today	East Asia News and Features (Aust) Pty Ltd Box N7, Grosvenor Street Post Office Sydney, NSW 2000
Business China	Business International Asia/Pacific Ltd 1111-1119 Mount Parker House Cityplaza Taikoo Shing, Hong Kong
Business P.R.C.	Enterprise International 1064 Eastern Commercial Centre 393-407 Hennessy Road, Hong Kong
China Business Review	National Council for U.S.-China Trade 1050 17th Street, Suite 350 Washington, D.C. 20036 U.S.A.
China Economic News	Economic Information and Consultancy Co 342 Hennessy Road, Hong Kong
The China Letter	The China Letter GPO Box 33477, Sheungwan Post Office Hong Kong
China Market	Economic Information and Agency 342 Hennessy Road Hong Kong
China Reconstructs *Beijing Review* *China's Foreign Trade* *China Pictorial*	Guoji Shudian PO Box 399 Beijing, People's Republic of China

Far Eastern Economic Review	GPO Box 160 Hong Kong
Jetro China Newsletter	Publications Department Japan External Trade Organization 2-5 Toranomon 2-chome Minato-ku Tokyo 105, Japan
Sino British Trade	Sino-British Trade Council 5th Floor, Abford House 15 Wilton Rd London, SW1V 1LT, UK
Xinhua Weekly *(English Edition)*	Xinhua News Agency 387 Queens Road East Hong Kong
China Law and Practice	China Law and Practice, Ltd., G.P.O. Box 11886 Hong Kong
Intertrade	Intertrade P.O. Box 23063 Wanchai, Hong Kong
China Oil	Wen Wei Enterprises, Ltd. Wanchai Road Hong Kong
China Offshore Oil	Panasice Book Distributors Ltd. 6th Floor, Morning Post Building Tong Chong Street Hong Kong
Maritime China	Maritime China Ltd. 4306 China Resources Building 26 Harbor Road Hong Kong
China Daily	China Daily Distribution Corp. 15 Mercer Street New York, N.Y. 10013
United Nations *Development Forum* *Business Edition*	United Nations, Subscriptions Department Room 559-DC1 New York, N.Y. 10017
Asian Wall Street Journal	Dow Jones Co., Inc. 22 Cortland Street New York, N.Y. 10007

FBIS Reports (Foreign Broadcast Information Service)	National Technical Information Service U.S. Department of Commerce 5285 Port Royal Road Springfield, Virginia 22161
China Report Series (Political, Sociological and Military Affairs, Economic Affairs, Agriculture, Science and Technology), irregular.	Joint Publications Research Service National Technical Information Service 5285 Port Royal Road Springfield, Virginia 22161
China Trade Report	SINO Information Resources 130 East Second Street Davenport, Iowa 52801
China Trade Weekly Bulletin	Sino Communication Ltd. Block B, 5th Floor, Vita Tower, 29 Wong Chuk Hang Road Hong Kong
East Asian Executive Reports, Ltd.	1101 Vermont Avenue N.W. Suite 400 Washington, D.C. 20005

SOURCE: Adapted from Nigel Campbell, *China Strategies: The Inside Story*, University of Manchester/ University of Hong Kong, 1986, by permission.

U.S. CONSULATES IN CHINA

Beijing: Telephone: 532-3831
           Telex: 22701

Shenyang: Telephone: 290035

Shanghai: Telephone: 332492
            Telex: 33383

Chengdu: Telephone: 24481
            Telex: 60128

Guangzhou: Telephone: 677842
              Telex: 44888

Notes

Introduction

1. U.S. Congress. House. Committee on Small Business. "Trade and Competitivness Issues." 100th Cong., 1st sess., 1987. H. Rept. 100-4, p. 2.

Chapter One: The China Market: Myth or Reality

1. Ernest R. May and John K. Fairbank, eds., *America's China Trade in Historical Perspective: The Chinese and American Performance* (Boston: The Committee of American-East Asian Relations of the Department of History and the Council on East Asian Studies/Harvard University, 1986), p. 12.
2. Ibid., p. 10; and Philip Chadwick Foster Smith, *The Empress of China* (Philadelphia: Philadelphia Maritime Museum, 1984), p. 10.
3. May and Fairbank, *America's China Trade*, pp. 151–154.
4. All of these trade figure are from Karen Green, "Anniversary Musings," *China Business Review*, May/June 1988, pp. 12–16.
5. Mark Van Fleet and William C. Jackson, " 'It's Your Business]; Briefing Book on Asia: Far East Trade Up for Grabs." Report by U.S. Consulate, International Division Staff, Taiping, 21 November 1984, unpaginated.
6. Green, "Anniversary Musings," pp. 12–16.
7. David L. Denny, "U.S. Market Share in a Growing China Trade," *China Business Review*, May/June 1988, pp. 24–26.
8. For a detailed analysis of the China market see: Bohdan O. Szuprowicz and Maria R. Szuprowicz, *Doing Business with the People's Republic of China* (New York: John Wiley and Sons, 1978).
9. The concept of the China market consisting of five market segments was contributed by Denis Fred Simon of Tufts University. The three types of international market scenarios is from: Warren J. Keegan, *International Marketing and Management*, 3rd ed. (New Jersey: Prentice Hall, 1984), p. 228.
10. M.V. Searls, "CMP Industry Sector Analysis; Industry: Power," U.S. Consulate, Beijing Circular, August 1985, unpaginated.
11. *Financial Times*, 26 April 1988, p. 9.
12. Ned Quistorff, "CMP Industry Sector Analysis; Industry: Telecommunications," U.S. Consulate, Beijing Circular, September 1985, unpaginated.

13. Ibid.
14. Joel Haggard, "Making Room in the Rice Bowl," *China Business Review*, November/December 1988, pp. 20–25.
15. Ibid.
16. Pam Baldinger, "Leading the Fast Food Flock," *China Business Review*, November/December 1988, p. 30.
17. *Los Angeles Times*, 1 February 1988, Part IV.
18. *Business Week*, 22 July 1985, p. 88.
19. Interview at the U.S. Consulate in Hong Kong and with U.S.endlaywers in Beijing, July 1986.
20. James P. Sterba, "Great Wall—Firms Doing Business in China Are Stymied by Costs and Hassles," *Wall Street Journal*, 17 July 1986.
21. Bruce Horovitz, "Beijing Beckoning Madison Avenue," *Los Angeles Times*, 14 April 1987, Part IV.
22. Tom Gorman, Jeffrey S. Muir and Thomas Potzman, *Advertising and Selling to the People's Republic of China*, 3rd ed. (Hong Kong: China Consultants International, 1987) p. 9.
23. Benny Rigaux-Bricmont and Chen Zhe, "Marketing in the Chinese Enterprises: A Field Study in Tianjin (PRC)." Paper delivered at The Chinese Enterprise Conference, Manchester Business School, U.K., 1–2 June 1987, p. 20. [Authors cite Orvell Schell, *To Get Rich Is Glorious* (Maine: Mentor Books, 1985, p. 16.]
24. Ibid., p. 13. [Authors cite *Time*, 3 November 1986.]
25. Richard E. Gillespie, "Foreign Engineering Opportunities in China," *China Business Review*, September/October 1988, pp. 14–20.
26. *China Trade Report*, September 1988, p. 8.
27. Carol Goldsmith, "Teeing Up for Tourists," *China Business Review*, November/December 1988, pp. 6–7.
28. Charles K. Moser, "Where China Buys and Sells," in *The Commercial, Industrial, and Economic Situation in China: 1926, 1927, 1928, 1930.* (Great Britain: Garland, 1980), p. 3.
29. *Intertrade*, February 1987, pp. 35–36.
30. Carol S. Goldsmith, "China's U.S. Sales Strategy: The First Steps," *China Business Review*, November/December 1980, pp. 25–26.
31. "German MNCs Outline the Key Ingredients for Successful Deals in China," *Business International*, 9 August 1985, p. 250.
32. "The Road To China: Opportunities and Pitfalls Along the Licensing Route," *Business International*, 30 June 1986, p. 201.
33. Kenneth Lieberthal and Michel Oksenberg, "Understanding China's Bureaucracy," *China Business Review*, November/December 1986, p. 30.
34. Tom Engle, "Making Money In China," *China Business Review*, November/December 1985, p. 32.
35. *Financial Times*, 12 April 1988, p. 9.
36. Interview with managers at China Hewlett-Packard in Beijing, July 1986.
37. Engle, "Making Money In China," pp. 32–35.
38. Ibid.
39. The concept of linking up a firm's Asia strategy with its China strategy is the product of discussions with Denis Fred Simon of Tufts University between October 1987 and June 1988.
40. Kathryn Rudie Harrigan, "Strategic Alliances: Their Role in Global Competition," *Columbia Journal of World Business*, vol. XXII, no. 2 (Summer 1987), p. 68.
41. Thomas W. Roehl and J. Frederick Truitt, "Stormy, Open Marriages Are Better: Evidence from U.S., Japanese, and French Cooperative Ventures in Commercial

Aircraft," *Columbia Journal of World Business*, vol. XXII, no. 2 (Summer 1987), pp. 88–89.

42. Richard N. Osborn and C. Christopher Baughn, "New Patterns in the Formation of U.S./Japanese Cooperative Ventures: The Role of Technology," *Columbia Journal of World Business*, vol. XXII, no. 2 (Summer 1987), p. 59.
43. Ibid., p. 64.
44. Stephen E. Weiss, "Creating the GM-Toyota Joint Venture: A Case in Complex Negotiation," *Columbia Journal of World Business*, vol. XXII, no. 2 (Summer 1987), pp. 23–38.
45. John D. Daniels, Jeffrey Krug, and Douglas Nigh, "U.S. Joint Ventures in China: Motivation and Management of Political Risk," *California Management Review*, vol. 27 no. 4 (Summer 1985), p. 48.
46. Jin Yanshi, "How, Why Foreigners Invest Capital in China," *Shijie Jingji Wenhui* [*World Economy Forum*], June 1985, pp. 21–22 [JPRS-CEA-86-037 (8 April 1986)]. This article outlines the Chinese perspective on the investment strategies followed by multinational corporations in China. The author divides MNC investments into five basic types: (1) exploratory investments, (2) investments of a strategic nature, (3) investments of a competitive nature, (4) defensive investments, and (5) transfer investments in which the foreign company invests to get closer to China's market, cheaper labor, and lower taxes.
47. *Business International*, 24 February 1986 [page unrecorded].
48. Interviews in Hong Kong at the U.S. Consulate and at Mobil Oil Hong Kong, May 1986.
49. Cheng, "Single Ministry Plan," pp. 71–72 and China Investment Economic Consultants, *The China Investment Guide*, 3rd ed. (Hong Kong: Longman, 1986), p. 419.
50. Yanshi, "How, Why Foreigners Invest," pp. 21–22.
51. In this section, the statistics regarding the size of U.S. companies and the number of their overseas ventures are from Lawrence G. Franco, "New Forms of Investment in Developing Countries by U.S. Companies: A Five Industry Comparison," *Columbia Journal of World Business*, vol. XXII, no. 2 (Summer 1987), pp. 39–55.
52. Engle, "Making Money In China," pp. 32–35.
53. Interview with Unison Pacific Corporation employee in Beijing, July 1986.
54. Nissho Iwai Corporation, Annual Report, 1987, p. 14.
55. "Torrential Rush To Tap Teeming China Market," *Oriental Economist*, March 1985, pp. 4–10.
56. Shibasaka Yukio, "Current Status of the Future Prospects for Japanese-Chinese Economic Cooperation: The Fourth in a Series of Papers Delivered at the Academic Exchange Between the Foreign Trade Institute and the Nomura Research Institute," *Intertrade*, no. 10 (October 1984), pp. 46–48.
57. Li Jianguo, "Open New Prospects for Sino-Japanese Economic Cooperation," *Intertrade*, no. 11 (27 November 1984), pp. 16–19.

Chapter Two: Foreign Investment in China: A Stocktaking

1. For insight into China's reaction to the West in the nineteenth century see: Frederick Wakeman, Jr., *The Fall of Imperial China* (New York: Free Press, 1975).
2. Nai-Ruenn Chen, "Foreign Investment in China: Current Trends" (February 1986) Washington, D.C.: Office of the PRC and Hong Kong, p. 3.
3. *Intertrade*, September 1984, p. 19.
4. Ibid., p. 15.

5. Ibid.
6. Ibid.
7. This concept was suggested to the author during an interview with Peter Kwok, vice president of Bankers Trust Company, in Hong Kong, July 1986.
8. Peter J. Buckley and E. Jehle, "Forms of Entrepreneurial Co-operation Between Chinese and Foreign Enterprises in the People's Republic of China: Legal and Taxation Implications." Paper delivered at The Chinese Enterprise Conference, Manchester Business School, U.K., 1–2 June 1987, p. 16.
9. *Joint Ventures in the People's Republic of China: A Corporate Guide, Business International*, 1985 p. 11.
10. "Scrambling for Oil," *Business Week*, 31 May 1982, pp. 94–95.
11. James P. Sterba, "Firms Doing Business in China Are Stymied by Costs and Hassles," *Wall Street Journal*, 17 July 1986.
12. See Buckley, "Forms of Entrepreneurial Co-operation."
13. Buckley, "Forms of Entrepreneurial Co-operation," p. 11.
14. Yaun Liu, "The Hidden Burdens of Doing Business in China" *The Nineties*, no. 12 (1 December 1985), pp. 64–65.
15. Buckley, "Forms of Entrepreneurial Co-operation," p. 11.
16. "Tax Burden on Foreign Firms," *South China Morning Post*, 22 November 1980.
17. Perry Keller, "Liberating the Land," *China Business Review*, March/April 1988, pp. 40–44.
18. Frank Ching, "Foreign Partners Face Frustrations in China Factory," *Asian Wall Street Journal*, 12 December 1980.
19. Colina Macdougall, "China Compensation Deal with Foreigners Runs into Trouble," *Financial Times*, 10 October 1980, p. 8.
20. Ching, "Foreign Partners Face Frustrations," p. 1.
21. Ibid.
22. "China To Boost Joint Ventures this Year," *Hong Kong Standard*, 15 December 1980.
23. Ching, "Foreign Partners Face Frustrations," p. 1.
24. James B. Stepanek, "Direct Investment in China," *China Business Review*, September/October 1982, p. 20.
25. "Peking Pullout Is a Big Blow, Says Okita," *South China Morning Post*, 12 February 1981.
26. Ibid.
27. "Tax Burden on Foreign Firms" *South China Morning Post*, 22 November 1980.
28. "Questions Concerning Use of Foreign Capital," *Caizheng [Finance]*, no. 2 (February 1980), pp. 23–25.
29. *Beijing Review*, 21 December 1981, p. 24.
30. Friedrich W. Wu, "External Borrowing and Foreign Aid in Post- Mao China's International Economic Policy: Data and Observations," *Columbia Journal of World Business* (Fall 1984), p. 55.
31. "Questions Concerning Use of Foreign Capital," pp. 23–25.
32. Patrick L. Smith, "Western Investment Sought In China's Modernization Effort," *New York Times*, 21 June 1980, Business section.
33. Fox Butterfield, "Peking Promises Profits on Foreign Investments," *New York Times*, 1 October 1979, Part IV.
34. Macdougall, "China Compensation Deal," p. 8.
35. "Beijing Will Not Expand Foreign Ventures in '81," *Hong Kong Standard*, 12 February 1981.
36. Ivan Tung, "Beijing Cannot Guarantee Pacts with Firms Yet," *Hong Kong Standard*, (date unrecorded).

37. "Beijing Will Not Expand Foreign Ventures in '81," *Hong Kong Standard*, 12 February 1981.
38. *Asian Wall Street Journal*, 25 January 1987.
39. "Beijing Will Not Expand Foreign Ventures in '81," *Hong Kong Standard*, 12 February 1981.
40. Christopher Wren, "China Lists 130 Projects for Foreign Investment," *New York Times*, 24 March 1982, Part IV.
41. Wang Jiyuan, "Some Problems in the Use of Foreign Capital To Bring in Advanced Technology," *Jingji Ribao*, 21 September 1983, p. 2+.
42. Wren, "China Lists 130 Projects."
43. Stepanek, "Direct Investment in China," pp. 24–26.
44. Jiyuan, "Some Problems in the Use of Foreign Capital," p. 2+.
45. John S. Henley and Nyaw Mee-kau, "The System of Management and Performance of Joint Ventures in China: Some Evidence from Shenzhen Special Economic Zone." Paper delivered at The Chinese Enterprise Conference, Manchester Business School, U.K., June 1–2, 1987, p. 9. [Paper also appears in *Joint Ventures and Industrial Change in China*, edited by Nigel Campbell and John S. Henley (London: JAI Press, 1988).]
46. Frank Ching, "Chinese Official Says Foreign Investment Soared in 1981," *Asian Wall Street Journal*, 25 January 1982.
47. Nai-Ruenn Chen, "Foreign Investment in China," p. 4.
48. Frank Ching, "Chinese Attracted More Than $1 Billion In Investment from Foreigners," *Wall Street Journal*, 12 March 1981.
49. Takashi Uehara, "Changes in China's Policy Regarding the Introduction of Foreign Capital," *Jetro China Newsletter*, no. 66 (January/February 1987), p. 17.
50. Robert Delfs, Thomas D. Gorman, and Owen D. Nee, Jr., *China* (London: Euromoney Publications and Bank of East Asia, 1986), p. 150.
51. Ibid.
52. See Hironao Kobayashi, "Special Economic Zones and China's Open Economic Policy," *Jetro China Newsletter*, no. 57 (July/August 1985); and Vigor Keung Fung, "Foreigners Boost Industry in South China," *Asian Wall Street Journal*, 27 January 1983.
53. Louis Kraar, "A Little Touch of Capitalism," *Fortune*, 18 April 1983, p. 121.
54. Hironao Kobayashi, "Special Economic Zones and China's Open Economic Policy," *Jetro China Newsletter*, no. 57 (July/August 1985), p. 16.
55. For a full description of SEZ incentives see *China Daily*, 27 May 1986.
56. Delfs et al., *China*, pp. 130-138.
57. Kraar, "A Little Touch of Capitalism," p. 121.
58. "China Tries to Instill Business Confidence," *Hong Kong Standard*, 2 August 1983.
59. Ibid.
60. Lin Chen and Lu Zhongyun, "Allow Them to Stride Through the Wide-open Door: Jing Shuping Discusses Introduction of Foreign Capital," *Liaowang* [*Outlook*], no 31 (30 July 1984), pp. 22–24.
61. Stepanek, "Direct Investment in China," p. 20.
62. Lin Chen and Lu Zhongyun, "Allow Them to Stride Through," pp. 22–24.
63. Ibid.
64. Ibid.
65. Stepanek, "Direct Investment in China," p. 20.
66. See Zhang Peiji, "Stick To Open Policy and Expand Foreign Trade," *Economic Reporter*, May 1982, p. 2; *Jingja Ribao*, 27 September 1983; and "Profit Can Only Lure Investors," *Hong Kong Standard*, 5 May 1983.
67. "Full Use of Investment Funds Urged," *China Daily*, 17 July 1984.

68. Rick Gladstone, "China Tells Investors We Guarantee Profits," *Hong Kong Standard*, 30 March 1984.
69. "Try Again, Foreign Investors Told," *Hong Kong Standard*, 3 January 1984.
70. Chen Guanfeng, "China Sets To Woo More Investment," *China Daily*, 20 October 1984.
71. *Beijing Xinhua*, 19 October 1984.
72. Wei Yuming, "Wei Yuming On Utilizing Foreign Capital," Beijing Radio, 15 August 1983).
73. Vigor Fung, "China Laying Ground Rules For Opening of 15 Coastal Cities to Foreign Investors," *Asian Wall Street Journal*, 21 July 1984.
74. Ibid.
75. Zhang Quan, [interview] "Foreign Capital Speeds Modernization," *China Reconstructs*, June 1985, pp. 18–21.
76. "Open Cities Offer New Projects to Investors," *China Daily*, 8 November 1984.
77. See Madelyn C. Ross, "China's New and Old Investment Zones," *China Business Review*, November/December 1984, pp. 14–17.
78. "Bid To Lure Foreign Funds Intensifies," *China Daily*, 19 October 1984.
79. Madelyn C. Ross, "China's New and Old Investment Zones," *China Business Review*, November/December 1984, pp. 14–17.
80. Zhang Quan, [interview] "Foreign Capital Speeds Modernization," *China Reconstructs*, June 1985, pp. 18–21.
81. Lui Shulong, "China's Absorption of Direct Foreign Investment Last Year Exceeded Foreign Loans," *Gouji Shangbao*, 4 April 1985, p. 1.
82. Quan interview, "Foreign Capital Speeds Modernization," pp. 18–21.
83. Yao Guoguang, "This Year Our Province Will Use Foreign Funds To Introduce More than 100 Projects—Combining the Reform of Enterprise Technology with the Importation of Advanced Foreign Technology," *Xinhua Ribao*, 15 January 1983.
84. Zhu Rongying, "Fujian Gets $109M in Investment," *China Daily*, 23 October 1984.
85. "Foreign Investment Soars," *China Daily*, 25 August 1984.
86. Fan Zhilong, "Dr. Armand Hammer and China," *China Reconstructs*, October 1985, pp. 36–37.
87. David L. Denny, "The Quest for Control," *China Business Review*, May/June 1983, p. 28.
88. "Try Again, Foreign Investors Told," *Hong Kong Standard*, 3 January 1984.
89. Lin Shenmu and Xu Li, "The Influence of Policies and Institutions on the Introduction of Foreign Capital," *Jingji Yanjui*, no. 12 (20 December 1986), pp. 14–21.
90. Catherine Houghton, "Investment Environment in China," U.S. Consulate, Beijing Circular, 24 April 1986.
91. Lin Shenmu and Xu Li, "The Influence of Policies and Institutions," pp. 14–21.
92. Xu Xinli, "Management Should Be Strengthened in Foreign Trade Under Open-Door Policy," *Caijing Yanjing*, no. 6 (18 December 1985), pp. 12–16.
93. Olivia Sin, "Official Reports Foreign Ventures Exchange Deficit," *South China Morning Post*, 16 July 1986, Business Post.
94. Ibid.
95. The Peugeot case is reported in: "Squabble Over Pricing Brings Peugeot's China Venture To a Standstill," *Asian Wall Street Journal*, 2 February 1987.
96. Vigor Fung, "China Devalues Currency 13.6% Against the Dollar," *Wall Street Journal*, 7 July 1986, Part II.
97. Ibid.

98. "MOFERT Loosens its Grip," *China Trade Report,* April 1988, pp. 1, 3.
99. This description of recent investor complaints was supplied to the author by Denis Fred Simon of Tufts University.
100. "Xiamen Curbs Exaction of Charges From Joint Ventures," *Zhongguo Xinwen She,* 16 July 1986.
101. Lin Shenmu and Xu Li, "The Influence of Policies and Institutions," pp. 14–21.
102. "Xiamen Curbs Charges," 16 July 1986.
103. Yuan Lui, "The Hidden Burdens of Doing Business in China," *The Nineties,* 1 December 1985, pp. 64–65.
104. Catherine Houghton, "Investment Environment in China," U.S. Consulate, Beijing Circular, 24 April 1986.
105. See "The Remanufacturing of America: U.S. Firms Gain A Competitive Egde" *Los Angeles Times,* 2 August 1987.
106. "Jeep Helped Broaden Investment Focus," *Journal of Commerce,* 1 October 1986, p. 16C.
107. "Foreign Businesses Represented in China," *Beijing Review,* 22 December 1986, p. 31.
108. Buckley, "Forms of Entrepreneurial Co-operation," p. 14. [Author cites 14 Article III Law, 12 April 1986.]
109. Catherine Houghton, "Investment Environment in China," U.S. Consulate, Beijing Circular, 24 April 1986.
110. *People's Daily,* 15 September 1986.
111. Material regarding these regulations was supplied, in part, by Denis Fred Simon of Tufts University.
112. Lucille A. Barale, "China's Investment Implementing Regulations," *China Business Review,* March/April 1988, pp. 19–24.
113. "China Improves Climate for Investment," *Beijing Review,* 29 October 1987, pp. 5–6.
114. "Better Term for Foreigners," *Intertrade,* (November 1986), pp. 57–58.
115. Zhou Dongfa, "Joint Ventures Get Privilege Documents," *China Daily,* 21 November 1986.
116. "Provisions on the Right of Autonomy of Enterprises with Foreign Investment in the Hiring of Personnel and on Wages, Insurance and Welfare Expenses of Staff and Workers," *Beijing Review,* 19 January 1987, p. 26.
117. Lin Shenmu and Xu Li, "The Influence of Policies and Institutions," pp. 14–21.
118. Ibid.
119. *South China Morning Post,* 11 August 1986, Business section.
120. "Four Special Zones Draw 20% of Foreign Financing," *China Daily,* 14 May 1986.
121. Thomas Chan, "Economic Zones Lose Their Special Status," *South China Morning Post,* 26 June 1986.
122. Olivia Sin, "One-third Fujian Joint Ventures Short of Foreign Exchange," *South China Morning Post,* 25 June 1986, Business Post.
123. Lin Shenmu and Xu Li, "The Influence of Policies and Institutions," pp. 14–21.
124. Louis Kraar, "The China Bubble Bursts," *Fortune,* 6 July 1987, p. 86.
125. *People's Daily,* 29 August 1986.
126. Zhu Qingwei, "Investment Climate Must Be Improved to Further Attract Foreign Investments," *Intertrade,* no. 6 (27 June 1985), pp. 50–52.
127. *Tianjin Ribao,* 13 October 1986.
128. Ji Chongwei, "Make Efforts To Properly Run Sino-Foreign Joint Ventures," *Renmin Ribao,* 29 August 1986, p. 5.

129. Ibid.
130. James R. Schiffman, "China's Policy Shift on Joint Ventures Heartens Investors," *Asian Wall Street Journal,* 29 December 1986, p. 1+.
131. Ibid.

Chapter Three: Negotiating and Organizing China Ventures

1. "3M Enters the People's Republic of China: Environment and Conditions in Negotiating Within the PRC, 1980-5." Case study prepared by Dilbert C. Hastings with assistance from Ezra Gencturk: Case Development Center, University of Minnesota, School of Management, p.18.
2. Carla Sydney Stone and S. Alexander Billon, "Anticipating 1997," *China Business Review,* May/June 1988, p. 47.
3. Ned Quistorff, "CMP Industry Sector Analysis; Industry: Aerospace," U.S. Consulate, Beijing Circular, July 1985, unpaginated.
4. Ibid.
5. Otto Schnepp, Arrind Bhambri, and Mary Ann Von Glinow, "Cummins Engine Company's China Licensing Agreement." Case study presented by Andrew Chu at the I.B.E.A.R. China Program at University of Southern California, May 1986, p. 28.
6. Thomas N. Thompson, "The Wrong Way To Do Business," *China Business Review,* January/February 1985, p. 6.
7. Roy F. Grow, "Japanese and American Firms in China: Lessons of a New Market," *Columbia Journal of World Business,* (Spring 1986), p. 50.
8. "China's Push for Exports Is Turning Into a Long March," *Business Week,* 15 September 1986, p. 68.
9. Yao Jianguo, "The Collapse of a Joint Venture," *Beijing Review,* 29 February–6 March, 1988, pp. 24–25.
10. Tom Engle, "Making Money In China," *China Business Review,* November/December 1985, pp. 31–34.
11. Interview with managers of China Hewlett-Packard in Beijing, July 1986.
12. "Treaty Official on Foriegn Investment Law," *Bejing Review,* 21 January 1985, p. 16.
13. "A Legal Opinion," *China Trade Report,* vol. XXIV (August 1986), pp. 4–5.
14. Nancy Yoshihara, "Doing Business in China Is Profitable and Frustrating," *Los Angeles Times,* 11 April 1988, Part IV.
15. Pitman B. Potter, "Seeking Special Status," *China Business Review,* March/April 1988, pp. 36–39.
16. "3M Enters the People's Republic of China," p. 20.
17. Ibid., p. 24.
18. For a description of concessions that foreign firms have been willing to offer Chinese partners, the reader should review the corporate cases in: Nigel Campbell, *China Strategies: The Inside Story* (Hong Kong: University of Manchester, 1986).
19. F. L. Edwards and A. H. Ringleb, "A Managerial Economics Analysis of Technology Transfers To China." Paper delivered at The Chinese Enterprise Conference, Manchester Business School, U.K., 1–2 June 1987, p. 10.
20. Campbell, *China Strategies,* p. 57.
21. See "The Road To China: Opportunities and Pitfalls Along the Licensing Route," *Business International,* vol. XXXIII, no. 26 (30 June 1986), pp. 201–2.
22. "The Road To China: Opportunities and Pitfalls Along the Licensing Route," *Business International,* vol. XXXIII, no. 26 (30 June 1986), pp. 201–2.

23. Jerome Alan Cohen, "Equity Joint Ventures: 20 Potential Pitfalls the Every Company Should Know About," *China Business Review*, November/December 1982, pp. 23–30.

24. For a case of this see: A. N. Hakam "Negotiations Between Singaporeans and Firms in China: The Case of a Singaporean Electronic Firm Contemplating Investment in China." Paper delivered at The Chinese Enterprise Conference, Manchester Business School, U.K., 1–2 June 1987, p. 6.

25. Cohen, "Equity Joint Ventures," pp. 23–30.

26. "Beatrice Foods J.V. In Production," *China Trade News*, 23 August 1985.

27. See Campbell, *China Strategies*, pp. 94–102.

28. See Hakam, "Negotiations in China," p. 5.

29. Ibid., pp. 8–9.

30. Ibid., pp. 8–10.

31. Richard H. Holton, "The Myth of the Chinese Enterprise." Paper delivered at The Chinese Enterprise Conference, Manchester Business School, U.K., 1–2 June 1987, p. 6.

32. Lucien Pye, *Chinese Commercial Negotiating Styles* (Boston: Oelgeschlager, Gunn, and Hain, 1982), pp. xi–xii.

33. Ibid., p. x.

34. Interview with a U.S. company executive in Shanghai, May 1986.

35. John L. Graham and Roy A. Herberger, Jr., "Negotiators Abroad Don't Shoot from the Hip" *Harvard Business Review*, July/August 1983, pp. 162–63.

36. Schnepp et al., "Cummins' China Licensing Agreement," pp. 46–48.

37. "The Minhang Solution," *China Trade Report*, June 1988, p. 10.

38. Timothy A. Gelatt, "Negotiating a Joint Venture," *Asian Wall Street Journal*, 18 June 1985, Advertising Supplement.

39. "Domestic Investment Financing," *China Trade*, vol. 1; no. 7 (19 July 1986), p. 5.

40. Interviews with American bankers in Beijing, Hong Kong, and Los Angeles, 1985–88.

Chapter Four: Understanding China's Business Culture

1. The source of some of the themes in this chapter regarding the history of China's industrial organization and bureaucratic decision making are contained in a case study that the author highly recommends to China-bound executives: Kenneth Lieberthal and Michel Oksenberg, "Bureaucratic Politics and Chinese Energy Development," U.S. Department of Commerce: Washington, D.C., 1986.

2. Kenneth Lieberthal and Michel Oksenberg, "Understanding China's Bureaucracy," *China Business Review*, November/December 1986, p. 25.

3. Wang Zheng-xian, "Feudalism and the Chinese Enterprise." Paper delivered at The Chinese Enterprise Conference, Manchester Business School, U.K., 1–2 June 1987, p. 3.

4. Denis Fred Simon and Detlef Rehn, *Innovation in China's Electronics Industry: the Case of Shanghai* (forthcoming: Ballinger), pp. 63–64. [Page numbers refer to an unpublished manuscript supplied by Denis Fred Simon.]

5. Interview with an economic analyst working for the United Nations in August 1988.

6. Barbara Krug, "Changing Economic Behavior Under Changing Constraints: The Chinese Manager and the Economic Reforms in the Industrial Sector." Paper de-

livered at The Chinese Enterprise Conference, Manchester Business School, U.K., 1–2 June 1987, pp. 17–18.

7. Based on Susan L. Shirk and James B. Stepanek, "The Problem of Partial Reform," *China Business Review*, November/December 1983, p. 8.

8. Wang Zheng-xian, "Feudalism and the Chinese Enterprise," p. 8.

9. Albert Keidel, "China's 1985 Industrial Record," *China Business Review*, March/April 1986, p. 44.

10. Audrey Heung-heung Chan "Managerial Reforms in Chinese Enterprises: The Roadblocks that Remain." Paper delivered at The Chinese Enterprise Conference, Manchester Business School, U.K., 1–2 June 1987, p. 10.

11. Robin Porter, "Centralization, De-centralization, & Development in China: The Case of One Industry." Paper delivered at The Chinese Enterprise Conference, Manchester Business School, U.K., 1–2 June 1987 p. 13.

12. Ibid., p. 11.

13. Simon and Rehn, *Innovation in China's Electronics Industry*, p. 221. [Page number refers to an unpublished manuscript supplied by Denis Fred Simon.]

14. David L. Denny, "The Quest for Control," *China Business Review*, May/June 1983, pp. 28–29.

15. Xu Xinli, "Management Should Be Strengthened in Foreign Trade Under Open-Door Policy," *Caijing Yanjing*, no. 6 (18 December 1985), pp. 12–16.

16. "Economy Aided by Transport Link-ups," *China Daily*, 26 March 1987.

17. Si Jiuyue, "Two Ministries Bury Bureacratic Hatchet," *China Daily*, 11 June 1986.

18. Ibid.

19. "Hebei Auto Company Sets the Standard In China Drive to Form Conglomerates," *Asian Wall Street Journal Weekly*, 27 April 1987.

20. Han Baocheng, "Wuhan: Enterprises Compete and Thrive," *Beijing Review*, 18–24 January 1988, p. 25.

21. "Superiority of Enterprises Combining Foreign Trade Noted," *Guoji Maoyi Wenti* (International Trade Journal) no. 3 (March–April 1985), p. 114.

22. Ibid., p. 117.

23. Lin Shenmu, "The Influence of Policies and Institutions on the Introduction of Foreign Capital," *Jingji Yanjui*, no. 12 (20 December 1986), pp. 14–21.

24. Catherine Houghton, "Investment Environment in China," U.S. Consulate, Beijing Circular, 24 April 1986.

25. See R. Johnston and Paul Thiel, "Developments in China's Business Legislation, Part I," U.S. Consulate Circular; Beijing, 1984.

26. Interview with a U.S. lawyer in Beijing in July 1986.

27. Interviews with U.S. company representatives in Beijing in July 1986.

28. Xu Xinli, "Management Should Be Strengthened in Foreign Trade Under Open-Door Policy," *Caijing Yanjing*, no. 6 (18 December 1985), pp. 12–16.

29. Based on J.M. Livingstone, "Chinese Management in Flux," *Euro-Asia Business Review*, vol. 6, no. 2 (April 1987), p. 18.

30. Kenneth Lieberthal and Michel Oksenberg, "Understanding China's Bureaucracy," *China Business Review*, November/December 1986, pp. 24–31.

31. Ibid.

32. Based on Livingstone, "Chinese Management in Flux," pp. 17–18.

33. Wang Zheng-xian "Feudalism and the Chinese Enterprise," p. 4.

34. These conclusions are adapted from: Kenneth Lieberthal and Michel Oksenberg, "Understanding China's Bureaucracy," China Business Review November/December 1986, p. 29.

35. Louis Kraar, "The China Bubble Bursts," *Fortune*, 6 July 1987, p. 86.

36. Marco Lobo, [letter to the editor] *Far Eastern Economic Review,* 9 October 1986, p. 2.
37. "3M Enters the People's Republic of China: Environment and Conditions in Negotiating Within the PRC, 1980-5." Case study prepared by Dilbert C. Hastings with assistance from Ezra Gencturk: Case Development Center, University of Minnesota, School of Management, p. 23.
38. Simon and Rehn, Innovation in China's Electronics Industry, p. 182. [Page number refers to an unpublished manuscript supplied by Denis Fred Simon.]
39. Ibid., pp. 183–184.
40. Ibid.
41. Sally Stewart and Yeung Yun Choi, "Chinese Decision-making: A Case Study of How the Hexian Paper Pulp Project Was Accepted For Possible Inclusion in China's Seventh Five-year Plan." Paper delivered at The Chinese Enterprise Conference, Manchester Business School, U.K. 1–2 June 1987, pp. 11–12.
42. Stuart Schram, *The Political Thought of Mao Tse-Tung* (New York: Praeger, 1969), p. 308.
43. *Intertrade,* May 1986, p. 21.
44. "Guang Dong Warning On Foreign Exchange Certificates," Guangzhou, Guangdong Provincial Service in Mandarin, 2350 GMT (23 June 1983).
45. Barbara Krug, "Changing Economic Behavior Under Changing Constraints: The Chinese Manager and the Economic Reforms in the Industrial Sector," p. 21.
46. "State Workers Warned Against Engaging In Trade," Ren Min Ribao 20 November 1984, p. 1.
47. "China's Conservatives Act to Mold Education, Culture," Los Angeles Times 29 May 1987, p. 1.
48. Ibid.
49. "Prospects for Profits—China Through 1989," Business International 17 May 1985, p. 158.
50. *Financial Times,* 4 May 1988, p. 4.
51. John D. Daniels, Jeffrey Krug, and Douglas Nigh, "U.S. Joint Ventures in China: Motivation and Management of Political Risk," *California Management Review,* vol. XXVII, no. 4 (Summer 1985), p. 54.
52. "China's Conservatives Act to Mold Education, Culture," *Los Angeles Times,* 1 February 1987, Part I.
53. From questionnaires distributed by the author.
54. Daniels et al., "U.S. Joint Ventures in China," pp. 47–57.
55. Jerome Alan Cohen, "Equity Joint Ventures: 20 Potential Pitfalls that Every Company Should Know About," *China Business Review,* November/December 1982, pp. 23–30.

Chapter Five: Chinese Management Style

1. *Statistical Yearbook of China, 1986* (Beijing: State Statistical Bureau, 1986).
2. Ibid.
3. Edward E. Williams, "The Emergence of Entrepreneurship in China." Paper delivered at The Chinese Enterprise Conference, Manchester Business School, U.K., 1–2 June 1987, p. 18.
4. *Los Angeles Times,* 26 September 1988.
5. Ibid.
6. Audrey Heung-heung Chan, "Managerial Reforms in Chinese Enterprises: The Roadblocks That Remain." Paper delivered at The Chinese Enterprise Conference, Manchester Business School, U.K., 1–2 June 1987, p. 8.

7. "Zhao Outlines key Tasks for Country," *China Daily*, 26 March 1987.
8. Rosalie L. Tung, *China's Industrial Society After Mao* (Lexington, Mass.: Lexington Books, 1982) p. 158.
9. Audrey Heung-heung Chan, "Managerial Reforms," p. 9 [Author cites Tian, 1982, pp. 93–95.]
10. This comment was made by William A. Fischer in a lecture given at the I.B.E.A.R. China Program at the University of California, May 1986. The history of Chinese industrial management since 1949 is covered in many volumes; the author made use of three in particular: *China's Socialist Economic Development: Country Study* (World Bank) vol. II, annex D, 1983, p. 107+; Willy Kraus, *Economic Development and Social Change in the People's Republic of China* (New York: Springer-Verlag, 1982); and Rosalie L. Tung, *China's Industrial Society After Mao* (Lexington, Mass.: Lexington Books, 1982).
11. "Wide Range of Economic Reforms Set in Liaoning," *China Daily*, 28 March 1987.
12. Huan-ming Ling, "Enterprise Management in the PRC: Problems, Recommedations, and Likely Scenarios for the Future." Paper delivered at The Chinese Enterprise Conference, Manchester Business School, U.K., 1–2 June 1987, p. 5.
13. "Capitalism in China," *Business Week*, 14 January 1985, p. 53.
14. "Yu Shows How To Succeed In Business," *China Daily*, 2 April 1986.
15. Max Boisot, "Management Training in the PRC: The Task Ahead," *Euro-Asian Business Review*, vol. 6, no. 2 (April 1987), p. 12.
16. Zhou Xiaochuan, "Contract System in China's Enterprises," *Beijing Review*, 4–10 April 1988, pp. 22–23.
17. Han Baocheng, "Wuhan: Enterprises Compete and Thrive," *Beijing Review*, 18–24 January 1988, pp. 24–27.
18. See William A. Fischer, "Chinese Industrial Management: Outlook for the Eighties." Paper delivered at the I.B.E.A.R. China Program at University of Southern California, May 1986, p. 29.
19. Huan-ming Ling, "Enterprise Management in the PRC," p. 5.
20. Zhou Liang-yi and Yang Jie-Qeng, "Chinese Enterprises and Technology Transfer." Paper delivered at The Chinese Enterprise Conference, Manchester Business School, U.K., 1–2 June 1987, p. 2.
21. Stephen R. Hendryx, "The China Trade: Making the Deal Work," *Harvard Business Review*, July/August 1986, pp. 75, 81–84.
22. Martin Lockett, "Culture and the Problems of Chinese Management." Paper delivered at The Chinese Enterprise Conference, Manchester Business School, U.K., 1–2 June 1987, p. 2. [Article also appears in Organization Studies, 4 September 1988.]
23. Huan-ming Ling, "Enterprise Management in the PRC," p. 7.
24. Tung, *China's Industrial Society*, p. 152.
25. From a lecture by William A. Fischer given at the I.B.E.A.R. China Program at University of Southern California, May 1986.
26. Ray G. Hunt and Gao Yang, "Decision-making and Power Relations in the Chinese Enterprise: Managers and Party Secretaries." Paper delivered at The Chinese Enterprise Conference, Manchester Business School, U.K., 1–2 June 1987, p. 9.
27. Ibid.
28. Huang Zhengqi, "Several Questions Related to the Expansion of State Enterprises' Decision-making Power in Operations and Management," *Jingji Yanjiu*, no. 3 (20 March 1981), p. 39.
29. Alex J. Easson, "The Role of Taxation in the Reform of China's Enterprise System." Paper delivered at The Chinese Enterprise Conference, Manchester Business School, U.K., 1–2 June 1987, p. 5.

30. Based on a lecture by William A. Fischer given at the I.B.E.A.R. China Program at University of Southern California, May 1986.
31. *Business Week*, 1 January 1985, p. 58.
32. Tung, *China's Industrial Society*, p. 150.
33. Based on interviews with numerous Chinese workers in Guangzhou, Beijing, and Chongqing, 1986–88.
34. Zhang Xinxin and Sang Ye, *China Profiles* (Beijing: Panda Books, 1986), pp. 68–69.
35. Huan-ming Ling, "Enterprise Management in the PRC," p. 3.
36. Based on a lecture by William A. Fischer given at the I.B.E.A.R. China Program at University of Southern California, May 1986.
37. Arne J. De Keijzer, "Doing Business in Post-Mao China Is Both a Cultural and an Economic Transaction," *Asian Wall Street Journal*, 18 June 1985, Advertising Supplement.
38. Tung, *Chinese Industrial Society After Mao*, pp. 140–43.
39. Hironao Kobayashi, "Reforms in the Chinese Wage System," *China Newsletter*, no. 67 (March/April 1987), pp. 12–13.
40. Ibid.
41. Gao Shangquan, "1987: Year of Enterprise Autonomy" *Beijing Review*, 9 March 1987, p. 18.
42. Huan-ming Ling, "Enterprise Management in the PRC," p. 3. [Author cites Beijing Shi Renmin Zhengfu Wenjin, no. 158 (1985), p. 16.]
43. Tung, *Chinese Industrial Society After Mao*, pp. 140–43.
44. John Child, "The Structure of Earnings in Chinese Enterprises and Some Correlates of Their Variation." Paper delivered at The Chinese Enterprise Conference, Manchester Business School, U.K., 1–2 June 1987, p. 7.
45. Ibid., p. 12.
46. Based on Barbara Krug, "Changing Economic Behavior Under Changing Constraints: The Chinese Manager and the Economic Reforms in the Industrial Sector," p. 5 [Author cites Cheung 1952; Shirk 1984.]
47. Huan-ming Ling, "Enterprise Management in the PRC," p. 7.
48. Krug, "Changing Economic Behavior," p. 2.
49. Lockett, "Culture and the Problems of Chinese Management," p. 4.
50. Krug, "Changing Economic Behavior," p. 6.
51. Xiao Liang, "Changing the Leadership System in State Enterprises," in *China's Economic Reforms*, eds. Lin Wei and Arnold Chao (University of Pennsylvania Press, 1982), p. 151.
52. See Tung, *Chinese Industrial Society After Mao*, pp. 220–224.
53. For a seminal study on the democratic aspects of Chinese management see: William Brugger, *Democracy and Organization in the Chinese Industrial Enterprise: 1948–53* (Cambridge, England: Cambridge University Press, 1976).
54. William A. Fischer, "The Transfer of Western Managerial Knowledge To China." Report prepared for the Office of Technology Assessment, May 1986, p. 32.
55. "China's Embrionic Stock Market Expands," *Wall Street Journal*, 12 November 1986.
56. Mun Kin-chok, "Shareholders in Chinese Enterprises: An Examination of Li Ying-ling's Ownership Reform Model." Paper delivered at The Chinese Enterprise Conference, Manchester Business School, U.K., 1–2 June 1987, p. 1.
57. Ibid., pp. 1–2.
58. Easson, "The Role of Taxation in the Reform of China's Enterprise System," p. 7.
59. Mark Sidel, "Some Preliminary Notes on the Chinese Bankruptcy System for Enterprises and the Development of the Chinese Bankruptcy Law." Paper delivered

at The Chinese Enterprise Conference, Manchester Business School, U.K., 1–2 June 1987, p. 21.

60. Ibid., pp. 2–20.
61. "Specialist Management Demands 'Three Chiefs,' " *China Daily*, 30 April 1985.
62. Lockett, "Culture and the Problems of Chinese Management," p. 3.
63. Audrey Heung-heung Chan, "Managerial Reforms," p. 14.
64. Ibid.
65. "Specialist Management Demands 'Three Chiefs,' " *China Daily*, 30 April 1985.
66. See Willian A. Fischer, "The Transfer of Western Managerial Knowledge To China." Report prepared for the Office of Technology Assessment, May 1986, p. 1.
67. For a concise historical recounting of how Western management techniques have entered China, see: Joseph Battat, *Management in Post-Mao China: An Insider's View* (Ann Arbor, Michigan: UMI Research Press, 1986).
68. Beth Keck, "China Looks West for Programs Offering Management Training," *Asian Wall Street Journal*, 18 June 1985, Advertising Supplement.
69. Max Boisot, "Management Training in the PRC: The Task Ahead," *Euro-Asian Business Review*, vol. 6, no. 2 (April 1987), p. 14.
70. Dennis B. Kelly, "A Project Manager's Notebook" *China Business Review*, September/October 1984, pp. 10–12.

Chapter Six: Operating a Venture in China

1. Martin Lockett, "Culture and the Problems of Chinese Management." Paper delivered at The Chinese Enterprise Conference, Manchester Business School, U.K., 1–2 June 1987. [Article also appears in *Organization Studies*, 4 September 1988, p. 6.]
2. John S. Henley and Nyaw Mee-kau, "The System of Management and Performance of Joint Ventures in China: Some Evidence from Shenzhen Special Economic Zone." Paper delivered at The Chinese Enterprise Conference, Manchester Business School, U.K., June 1–2, 1987. [Paper also appeared in *Joint Ventures and Industrial Change in China*, edited by Nigel Campbell and John S. Henley (London: JAI Press, 1988).]
3. Sun Guanhua and Wang Yuan, "We Must Attach Importance To the Summing Up of Experience Acquired From Joint Ventures—An Investigation of the Fujian-Hitachi Television Company, Ltd.," *Jingji Guanli*, no. 3 (5 March 1984), pp. 38–41, 45.
4. Interview at Hewlett-Packard's joint venture in Beijing, July 1986.
5. "Beatrice Foods J.V. In Production" *China Trade News*, 23 August 1985.
6. John S. Henley and Nyaw Mee-kau, "The System of Management and Performance," p. 3.
7. Jerome Alan Cohen, "Equity Joint Ventures: 20 Potential Pitfalls that Every Company Should Know About," *China Business Review*, November/December 1982, pp. 23–30.
8. Charles S. Mayer, Jing Lun Han and Hui Fang Lim, "An Evaluation of the Performance of the Joint Venture Companies in the People's Republic of China." Paper delivered at The Chinese Enterprise Conference, Manchester Business School, U.K., 1–2 June 1987, p. 7.
9. Stephen R. Hendryx, "The China Trade: Making the Deal Work," *Harvard Business Review*, July/August 1986, pp. 75, 81–84.
10. Charles S. Mayer, Jing Lun Han, and Hui Fang Lim, "An Evaluation of the Performance," p. 7.

11. Jeane Chiang, "What Works and What Doesn't," *China Business Review,* September/October 1983, pp. 26–29.
12. R. Johnston and George Lee, "Background Paper—Business Facilitation," U.S. Embassy Circular, Beijing, 13 March 1986, p. 10 [report paginated by hand].
13. James Sterba, "Foreign Firms in China Tire of Meager Payoffs Beyond the Open Door," *Asian Wall Street Journal,* 21 July 1986.
14. Nigel Campbell, *China Strategies: The Inside Story* (Hong Kong: University of Manchester, 1986), p. 43.
15. Sterba, "Foreign Firms in China," p. 1.
16. Interviews with a U.S. company manager in Beijing, July 1986.
17. Micheal Parks, "Gillette Pursues a Pot of Gold Marketing in Mainland China," *New York Times,* 2 September 1984.
18. Interview with managers of China Hewlett-Packard in Beijing, July 1986.
19. William A. Fischer, "The Tanggu Chemical Factory." A case study presented at the I.B.E.A.R. China Program at the University of Southern California, May 1986, p. 6.
20. Interviews with commercial officers at the U.S. Consulate in Beijing, May 1985.
21. Interview with a company representative of a U.S. oil company in Beijing, July 1986.
22. Ibid.
23. Interview with a Chinese trainee at a U.S. firm in California, August 1987.
24. Dennis B. Kelly, "A Project Manager's Notebook," *China Business Review,* September/October 1984, pp. 10–12.
25. John A. Reeder, "Motivating Chinese Employees in Joint Ventures in the PCR." Paper delivered at The Chinese Enterprise Conference, Manchester Business School, U.K., 1–2 June 1987, pp. 3–4.
26. Adapted from Yuan Liu, "The Hidden Burdens of Doing Business in China," *The Nineties,* no. 12 (1 December 1985), pp. 65–65.
27. Edwin C. Nevis, "Cultural Assumptions and Productivity: The United States and China," *Sloan School of Management Review* Spring 1983, pp. 17–29.
28. Guanhua and Yuan, "We Must Attach Importance To the Summing Up of Experience," pp. 38–41, 45.
29. Reeder, "Motivating Chinese Employees," p. 8.
30. Ibid., p. 10.
31. "After the Contract Is Signed: The Experience of U.S. Companies in Shanghai," Foreign Consulate Service Circular; U.S. Embassy in Shanghai. [Author: Dean: Circular undated and unpaginated.]
32. Charles Barton, "McDonnell-Douglas Project Still Rolling in Shanghai," *Journal of Commerce,* 1 October 1986, p. 12C.
33. Guanhua and Yuan, "We Must Attach Importance To the Summing Up of Experience," pp. 38–41, 45.
34. Interviews with U.S. joint venture managers in Beijing, July 1986.
35. "Joint Venture Officials Reinstated," *China Daily,* 28 September 1986.
36. J. M. Livingstone, "Chinese Management in Flux," *Euro-Asia Business Review,* vol. 6, no. 2 (April 1987), p. 18.
37. "Rare Case of Success," *China Trade Report,* June 1988, p.3.
38. Kelly, "A Project Manager's Notebook," pp. 10–12.
39. Barton, "McDonnell-Douglas Project," p. 12C.
40. Otto Schnepp, Arrind Bhambri, and Mary Ann Von Glinow, "Cummins Engine Company's China Licensing Agreement." Case study presented by Andrew Chu at the I.B.E.A.R. China Program at University of Southern California, May 1986, pp. 56–58.

41. "A Legal Opinion," *China Trade Report,* vol. XXIV (August 1986), pp. 4–5.
42. Barton, "McDonnell-Douglas Project," p. 12C.
43. Dai Gang, "Booming Foreign Ventures in Shanghai," *Beijing Review,* 21–27 December 1987, p. 27.
44. Sterba, "Foreign Firms in China," p. 1.
45. Gail Bronson, ed., "The Long March," *Forbes,* 15 December 1986, p. 185.
46. "Sino-U.S. Car Assembly Venture Begins Production," Hong Kong AFP in English 1336 GMT, 26 September 1985; JPRS-CEA-85-095 930, October 1985, p. 59.
47. *People's Daily,* 18 August 1986. See also "Problems at Two Joint Ventures," *China Business Review,* July/August 1986, pp. 34–35.
48. Bronson, ed., "The Long March," p. 185.
49. "After the Contract Is Signed: The Experience of U.S. Companies in Shanghai," Foreign Consulate Service Circular, U.S. Embassy in Shanghai. [Author: Dean, Circular undated.]
50. Wu Chao, "China's Policy for Absorbing Direct Investment," *Wen Wei Po,* 18 April 1986, p. 10+.
51. *Asian Wall Street Journal,* 28 April 1981.
52. Holton, "The Myth of the Chinese Enterprise," p. 8.
53. Benny Rigaux-Bricmont and Chen Zhe, "Marketing in the Chinese Enterprises: A Field Study in Tianjin (PRC)." Paper delivered at The Chinese Enterprise Conference, Manchester Business School, U.K., 1–2 June 1987, p. 19. [Authors cite *China Daily,* 1 July 1986.]
54. *The Nineties,* no. 195 (April 1986), p. 25; see also "Hitachi TV Project Misses Key Targets," *South China Morning Post,* 13 August 1986.
55. Chiang, "What Works and Doesn't," p. 27.
56. Tom Gorman, Jeffrey S. Muir and Thomas Potzman, *Advertising and Selling to the People's Republic of China* (Hong Kong: China Consultants International, 1987) p. 9.
57. Horovitz, "Beijing Beckoning Madison Avenue," p. 9.
58. Both examples from Rigaux-Bricmont and Chen Zhe, "Marketing in the Chinese Enterprises," pp. 10–11.
59. Ibid., p. 12.
60. Parks, "Gillette Pursues a Pot of Gold," p. 40.
61. Bruce Horovitz, "Beijing Beckoning Madison Avenue," *Los Angeles Times,* 14 April 1987, Part IV.
62. Interview with executives at Mobil Asia in Hong Kong, July 1986.
63. Gorman et al., *Advertising and Selling to China,* p. 17.
64. John Frankenstein, "Business in China: Western and Chinese Perspectives," *Euro-Asia Business Review,* vol. 6, no. 1 (January 1987), p. 26.
65. Interviews with U.S. commercial officers in Hong Kong, May 1986.
66. Jerome Alan Cohen, "Equity Joint Ventures: 20 Potential Pitfalls that Every Company Should Know About," *China Business Review,* November/December 1982, pp. 23–30.
67. This list is based in large part on Gorman et al., *Advertising and Selling to China,* pp. 14–22.
68. Chiang, "What Works and What Doesn't," p. 28.
69. "Elevator Venture Rises to New Height," *China Daily,* (date unrecorded).
70. James R. Schiffman, "China's Policy Shift on Joint Ventures Heartens Investors," *Asian Wall Street Journal,* 29 December 1986.
71. Interview with an official for M. W. Kellogg at the company's Beijing office in July 1986.
72. Schiffman, "China's Poilcy Shift."

73. See: "US Investors, Part 2: Sober Thoughts on China's Current Business Climate," *Business China*, 28 July 1986, p. 108.
74. Informal interview with Sydney Rittenberg at the I.B.E.A.R China Program at the University of Southern California, May 1986.
75. Andrew Heyden, "How U.S. Firms Took the Silk Road To Repatriate Joint Venture's Profits," *Asian Wall Street Journal*, 18 June 1985, Advertising Supplement.
76. *China Daily*, 1 April 1986.
77. Catherine Houghton, "Investment Environment in China," U.S. Embassy Circular, Beijing, 24 May 1986, p. 15.
78. Interview with a Hong Kong trader in Shenzhen, July 1986.
79. Interviews with U.S. consultants in Beijing, December 1987.
80. "How Firms Can Keep Business Viable While China Retrenches," *Business International*, 4 October 1985, p. 315.
81. "US Investors, Part 1: Survey Shows Glitter of China Wearing Off," *Business China*, 30 June 1986, p. 90.

Chapter Seven: Foreign Technology in China

The author would like to acknowledge the assistance of Denis Fred Simon in the writing of this chapter, which borrows concepts and factual information from a number of Dr. Simon's published, and unpublished, papers on technology transfer to China. Taken as a whole, these articles represent a significant contribution to the work in the field.

—"The Evolving Role of Foreign Investment and Technology Transfer in China's Modernization Program," in *China Briefing 1987* (Boulder, Col.: Westview Press, 1987).
—"Science and Technology Reforms," *China Business Review*, March/April 1985, pp. 31-35.
—"Technology for China: Too Much Too Fast?" *Technology Review*, October 1984, pp. 39–49.
—"Rethinking R&D," *China Business Review*, July/August 1983, pp. 25–29.
—"China Trade: An Open Door Still Must Be Entered," *Mass High Tech*, 28 October–10 November, 1985, p. 1+.
—"China's Entry into the World Information Revolution: The Development and Application of Computers." Paper delivered at The Chinese Enterprise Conference, Manchester Business School, U.K., 1–2 June 1987.
—"The Evolving Role of Technology Transfer in China's Modernization: A Look at the Critical Issues." Paper prepared for U.S. Congress: Joint Economic Committee, 1986.
1. Jon Sigurdson, "Technology and Science: Some Issues in China's Modernization," in *Chinese Economy Post-Mao*, U.S. Congress: Joint Economic Committee, 9 November 1978, p. 487.
2. "Renewed Study of Foreign Investment Strategy," *China Daily*, 12 December 1985.
3. *Encyclopaedia Brittanica*, 15th ed., s.v. "Science," "Gunpowder," "Compass," "Printing," and "China."
4. Ibid.
5. *Intertrade*, March 1987, p. 31.
6. Huan Xiang, "Try Hard To Catch Up Rather than Trailing Behind," *Jingji Ribao*: FBIS-PRC, 29 February 1984, pp. K9–14.
7. See "The Magnificent Seven—High Tech-tonics To Restore Shanghai's Economic Vitality," American Consulate General, Shanghai, 25 July 1985, p. 1.
8. See "Upsurge in Worldwide Technological Revolution," *Beijing Review*, 23 April 1984, pp. 27–29.

9. "S&T Leading Group Formally Established," *Hubei Ribao* [*Hubei Daily*], 17 July 1984 (translated in JPRS-CST-84-034, 29 October 1984), p. 2.
10. Richard P. Suttmeier "Laying Corporate Foundations for China's High Tech Future," *China Business Review*, July/August 1988, p. 22.
11. Ibid.
12. "The Magnificent Seven," p. 5.
13. Jon Sigurdson, "Technology and Science," p. 519.
14. Denis Fred Simon, "Integrating the Electronics Industry," *China Business Review*, July/August 1988, p. 27.
15. Keisuke Odagawa, "A Japanese View of China's Plant and Technology Market," *China Newsletter*, no. 69, p. 9.
16. Detlef Rehn, "China's Computer Industry at the Turning Point," in *China's Economy Looks Toward the Year 2000*, U.S. Congress: Joint Economic Committee, 21 May 1986, p. 216.
17. "The Magnificent Seven," p. 5.
18. Denis Fred Simon, "Managing Technology in China: Is the Development and Application of Computers the Answer?" in *Management Reforms in China*, edited by Malcolm Warner (London: Frances Pinter, 1987), pp. 212–213.
19. "Zhao Ziyang Visits Machinery Plant in Hunan," *Xinhua*, 13 May 1984.
20. Yao Jianguo, "China at the Frontier of Space Technology," *Beijing Review*, 14–20 March 1988, pp. 18–23.
21. *Wall Street Journal*, 25 March 1986.
22. "Joint Ventures and Joint Opportunities," Aviation and Aerospace '88 (special section) *Far Eastern Economic Review*, 4 February 1988, pp. 50–56.
23. *China Trade*, vol. 1, no. 7 (July 1986), p. 1.
24. "Joint Ventures and Joint Opportunities," Aviation and Aerospace '88 (special section) *Far Eastern Economic Review*, 4 February 1988, pp. 50–56.
25. Yao Jianguo, "China at the Frontier of Space Technology," *Beijing Review*, 14–20 March 1988, pp. 18–23.
26. *Superconductor News*, August/September 1987, p. 4.
27. *China Daily*, 1 November 1986.
28. Song Jiwen, "Digestion and Absorption of Imported Technology Is a Shortcut to Technological Progress," *Jingji Guanli* [*Economic Management*], 3 September 1985, pp. 4–8 (translated in FBIS-PRC, 4 November 1985), pp. 20-27.
29. Odagawa, "A Japanese View," p. 9.
30. "Joint Ventures and Joint Opportunities," Aviation and Aerospace '88 (special section) *Far Eastern Economic Review*, 4 February 1988, pp. 50–56.
31. Ned Quistorff, "CPM Industry Sector Analysis; Industry: Aerospace," U.S. Consulate, Beijing Circular, July 1985.
32. *South China Morning Post*, 28 January 1986, Business News Supplement.
33. "McDonnell-Douglas Flies High in China," *China Daily*, 1 January 1985.
34. Quistorff, "CPM Industry Sector: Aerospace," [unpaginated].
35. "Joint Ventures and Joint Opportunities," Aviation and Aerospace '88 (special section) *Far Eastern Economic Review*, 4 February 1988, pp. 50–56.
36. "Technology Import Symposium Held in Guangdong," FBIS-PRC, 2 August 1984, p. P2.
37. Interview at the U.S. Consulate in Beijing, July 1986.
38. Sam Howe, "China's High-Tech Troubles," *New York Times*, 5 May 1985.
39. Erik Baark, "An Area of Top Priority," *China Trade News*, November 1987, pp. 13–14.

40. See "Transportation Development Strategy and Aviation," *Ziran Bianzhengfa* [*Dialectics of Nature*] (translated in JPRS-CEA-85-005, 18 January 1985), pp. 100–113.
41. Odagawa, "A Japanese View," p. 9.
42. Zhang Aiping, "Strengthen Leadership and Do a Good Job in Importing Technology," *Hongqi* [*Red Flag*], 16 December 1985, pp. 4–9.
43. "East China's Business Suitors—Japanese, German, American." Anonymous circular distributed by the U.S. Consulate in Beijing, 1986 (unpaginated).
44. Ibid.
45. Campbell, *China Strategies*, p. 89.
46. Amanda Bennett, "While Chinese Seek New Technology, Otis Elevator Profers Return to Basics," *Wall Street Journal*, 9 August 1984.
47. William A. Fischer, "The Tanggu Chemical Factory." A case study presented at the I.B.E.A.R. China Program at the University of Southern California, May 1986, p. 3.
48. Ibid., p. 10.
49. "Parker-Hannifin Hubei Plant Operational," *China Trade News*, August 1985.
50. Campbell, *China Strategies*, p. 54.
51. *Wall Street Journal*, 19 May 1985.
52. Roy Hofheinz, Jr., and Kent Calder, *The East Asian Edge* (New York: Basic Books, 1982), p. 156.
53. Elliott Hurwitz, "Copyrights Are as Vital as Merchandise," *New York Times*, 5 October 1986.
54. See Ellen R. Eliasoph "China's Patent System Emerges," *China Business Review*, January/February 1985, pp. 52-53.
55. R. Johnston and Paul Thiel, "Developments in China's Business Legislation, Part I," U.S. Consulate Circular, Beijing, 1984, pp. 16–23 [report paginated by hand].
56. From Manfredo Macioti, "Scientists Go Barfoot," *Successo* (January 1971) as reprinted in: Jon Sigurdson, "Technology and Science: Some Issues in China's Modernization," in *Chinese Economy Post-Mao*, U.S. Congress: Joint Economic Committee, 9 November 1978, p. 486.
57. "Technology Transfer to China—Congressional Summary," Office of Technology Assessment, Washington, D.C., June 1987, pp. 16–17.
58. Teresa J. Taylor, "Commerce Provides Opportunity for Business Input to Export Controls," *Business America*, 20 January 1986, pp. 15–16.

Chapter Eight: Formulas for China Business Success

1. Charles S. Mayer, Jing Lun Han, and Hui Fang Lim, "An Evaluation of the Performance of the Joint Venture Companies in the People's Republic of China." Paper delivered at The Chinese Enterprise Conference, Manchester Business School, U.K., 1–2 June 1987, p. 6.
2. Ibid.
3. Ibid., p. 7.
4. "Elevator Venture Rises to New Height," *China Daily*, (date unrecorded).
5. Da Chansong, "Computer Firm Woos Buyers with Renminbi Price Tags," *China Daily*, 6 May 1987.
6. Satoshi Imai, "Case Studies of Joint Ventures in China II," *China Newsletter*, no. 75 (July/August 1988), pp. 16–18.
7. Ibid., p. 21.

8. "Torrential Rush To Tap Teeming China Market," *Oriental Economist*, March 1985, p. 10.

9. Neil Francis Foster, "The Entry of Foreign Telecommunications Corporations Into the People's Republic of China," Unpublished dissertation submitted to Alfred P. Sloan School of Management at M.I.T., May 1987, p. 114.

10. "The Rewards of China Duty," *China Business Review*, November/December 1985, p. 18. Report based on a survey conducted by Runzheimer International.

11. Rosalie Tung, "Corporate Executives and Their Families in China: The Need for Cross-cultural Understanding in Business," *Columbia Journal of World Business* (Spring 1986), p. 22. [Author cites *Wall Street Journal*, 3 September 1985.]

12. Ibid., pp. 21–25.

13. "After the Contract Is Signed: The Experience of U.S. Companies in Shanghai," Foreign Consulate Service Circular; U.S. Embassy in Shanghai. [Author: Dean; Circular undated, unpaginated.]

14. See: Anita Li, "Foreign Investors Are Encouraged Despite Labor Problems," *China Business Review*, September/October 1981, pp. 42–44.

15. J. M. Zamet and M. E. Bovarnick, "Employee Relations for Multinational Companies in China," *Columbia Journal of World Business* (Spring 1986) [as quoted in John A. Reeder, "Motivating Chinese Employees in Joint Ventures in the PRC." Paper delivered at The Chinese Enterprise Conference, Manchester Business School, U.K., 1–2 June 1987, p 14.]

16. "After the Contract Is Signed," unpaginated.

17. R. Johnston and George Lee, "Background Paper—Business Facilitation," U.S. Embassy Circular, Beijing, 13 March 1986, p. 6 [report paginated by hand].

18. "After the Contract Is Signed," unpaginated.

19. Stanley B. Lubman and Gregory C. Wajnowski, "Criminal Justice and the Foreigner," *China Business Review*, November/December 1985, p. 27.

20. "After the Contract Is Signed," unpaginated.

21. Johnston and Lee "Background Paper," p. 8.

22. "After the Contract Is Signed," unpaginated.

23. Julia Leung, "Foreign Ventures in China Learn to Play Local Politics," *Asian Wall Street Journal*, 23 June 1986.

24. Ibid.

25. Anecdote supplied by Denis Fred Simon of Tufts University.

26. *South China Morning Post*, 13 August 1986.

27. Tom Engle, "Making Money in China," *China Business Review*, November/December 1985, p. 34.

28. Anecdote supplied by a U.S. commercial officer in Beijing, July 1986.

29. "Rare Case of Success," *China Trade Report*, June 1988, p. 3.

30. Leung, "Foreign Ventures in China Learn to Play," p. 1.

31. "Rare Care of Success," *China Trade Report*, June 1988, p. 3.

32. Interview with Mercury Marine Company official, May 1985; and *China Trade*, vol. 1, no. 7 (July 1986), p. 2.

33. Interview with China-Hewlett-Packard managers, July 1986.

34. Chris Brown, "The ITT Story," *China Business Review*, September/October 1983, pp. 40–42.

35. Imai, "Case Studies of Joint Ventures," pp. 16–18.

36. Jasper Becker, "China Takes Lead in Coal Output," *Jounal of Commerce*, 1 October 1986, p. 15C.

37. *Statistical Yearbook of China, 1986* (Beijing: State Statistical Bureau, 1986).

38. "Color Television Set Production," *Xinhua* (translated in JPRS-CEA, 5 March 1985).
39. David C. Buxbaum, Cassondra E. Joseph, and Paul D. Reynolds, *China Trade* (New York: Praeger Publishers, 1982), p. 247.
40. Ibid., p. 272.
41. Ibid.
42. See "East China's Business Suitors—Japanese, German, American" (anonymous circular distributed by the U.S. Consulate in Beijing, 1986.)
43. Preston Torbert, "Dalian: Gateway to the Northeast," *China Business Review,* November/December 1984.
44. Jing Shen and Duo Qin, "Aspects and Prospects of Joint Ventures and Foreign Trade in Chinese Textile Industry." Paper delivered at The Chinese Enterprise Conference, Manchester Business School, U.K., 1–2 June 1987, p. 10.
45. Ibid.
46. For an overview of the problems of selling to the Japanese, see Vernon R. Alden, "Who Says You Can't Crack Japanese Markets?," *Harvard Business Review,* January/February 1987, p. 52.
47. Becker, "China Markets Lure Europeans," p. 1.
48. "Diversified Trade Methods Forge China-Italy Ties," *Journal of Commerce,* 1 October 1986.
49. "EEC-China Talks Mean Business," *China Daily,* 3 March 1987.
50. "Diversified Trade Methods Forge China-Italy Ties," p. 37.
51. Foster, "The Entry of Foreign Telecommunications Corporations in China," p. 95.
52. Ibid.
53. "China's Dayawan Nuclear Power Plant Project," *China Newsletter,* no. 57 (July/August 1986), p. 13.
54. Ibid.
55. Catherine Caufield, "The Yangtze Beckons the Yankee Dollar," *New Scientist,* December 1985, pp. 26–27.
56. Ned Quistorff, "CMP Industry Sector Analysis; Industry: Aerospace," U.S. Consulate, Beijing Circular, July 1985, unpaginated.
57. From interviews conducted at the U.S. Consulate, Beijing, July 1986.
58. Interview with an intern at the National Council for U.S.- China Trade in 1986.
59. See Gene Linn, "Illinois Gives Major Push To Penetrate China Mart," *Journal of Commerce,* 1 October 1986, p. 14C.
60. Gail Bronson, ed., "The Long March," *Forbes,* 15 December 1986, p. 185.

Selected Bibliography

Baotai, Chu. *Foreign Investment in China.* Beijing: Foreign Languages Press, 1986.

Berstein, Richard. *From the Center of the Earth: The Search for the Truth About China.* Boston: Little, Brown, 1982.

Bloodworth, Denis. *Through the Chinese Looking Glass.* New York: Farrar, Straus & Giroux, 1981.

Brown, David G. *Partnership with China: Sino-Foreign Joint Ventures in Historical Perspective.* Boulder, Col.: Westview, 1986.

Butterfield, Fox. *China: Alive in the Bitter Sea.* New York: Times Books, 1982.

Campbell, Nigel. *China Strategies: The Inside Story.* Manchester: University of Hong Kong, 1986.

Engholm, Christopher. *The Pacific Rim Venture: Asia Strategies for Corporate America.* (forthcoming) Glenview, Ill.: Scott, Foresman, 1990.

Engholm, Christopher. *The Pacific Rim Venture: Strategies for Asia-Pacific Business Success.* (forthcoming) Glenview, Ill.: Scott, Foresman, 1989.

Gelatt, Timothy, and Ta-Kuang Chang. *Corporate and Individual Taxation in the People's Republic of China: A Specially Commissioned Report.* Hong Kong: Longman Group, 1985.

Goodman, David S. G., Martin Lockett and Gerald Segal. *The China Challenge.* London/New York: The Royal Institute of International Affairs, 1986.

Goosen, Richard J. *Business Law and Practice in the PRC.* Hong Kong: Longman Group, 1987.

Jao, Y.C., and C.K. Leung, eds. *China's Special Economic Zones: Policies, Problems, and Prospects.* Hong Kong: Oxford University Press, 1986.

Lieberthal, Kenneth and Oksenberg, Michel. *Bureaucratic Politics and Chinese Energy Development.* Washington, D.C: United States Department of Commerce, 1986.

Major, John S., and Anthony J. Kane, eds. *China Briefing, 1987.* Boulder, Col.: Westview, 1987.

Pye, Lucien. *Chinese Commercial Negotiating Styles.* Boston: Oelgeschlager, Gunn & Hain, 1982.

Solinger, Dorothy J. *Chinese Business Under socialism: The Politics of Domestic Commerce 1949-80.* Berkeley: University of California Press, 1984.

Solomon, Richard H. (editor). *The China Factor.* Englewood Cliffs, N.J.: Prentice-Hall, 1981.

Statistical Yearbook of China, 1987. Hong Kong/Beijing: Economic Information & Agency/China Statistical Information & Consultancy Service Centre, 1987.

Wik, Philip. *How To Do Business with the People's Republic of China.* Reston, Virg.: Reston Publishing Co., 1984.

Index